# The Economics of Public Health Care Reform in Advanced and Emerging Economies

EDITORS
Benedict Clements, David Coady,
and Sanjeev Gupta

INTERNATIONAL MONETARY FUND

© 2012 International Monetary Fund

Cover design: IMF Multimedia Services Division
Cover illustration: Design Army
Typesetting: Maryland Composition, Inc.

**Cataloging-in-Publication Data**

The economics of public health care reform in advanced and emerging economies / editors,
Benedict Clements, David Coady, and Sanjeev Gupta. – Washington, D.C. :
International Monetary Fund, 2012.
p. ; cm.

Includes bibliographical references.
ISBN 978-1-61635-244-8

1. Health care reform. 2. Health care reform—Developed countries. 3. Health care
reform—Developing countries. 4. Health care reform—Case studies. I. Clements,
Benedict J. II. Coady, David. III. Gupta, Sanjeev. IV. International Monetary Fund.

RA384 .E26 2012

Please send orders to:
International Monetary Fund, Publication Services
P.O. Box 92780, Washington, DC 20090, U.S.A.
Tel. (202) 623-7430     Fax: (202) 623-7201
E-mail: Publications@imf.org
Internet: www.imfbookstore.org

MIX
Paper from
responsible sources
FSC
www.fsc.org    FSC® C010236

# Contents

PART IV | COUNTRY CASE STUDIES: ADVANCED ECONOMIES

PART V | COUNTRY CASE STUDIES: EMERGING ECONOMIES

# Foreword

The mandate of the International Monetary Fund is primarily focused on macro-economic stability. While recognizing that the issue of health care reform has much broader implications, in this volume we look at health care reform through the lens of our mandate, focusing primarily on macroeconomic stability and—of special importance to us in the IMF's Fiscal Affairs Department—on fiscal stability.

Health care reform has key implications for fiscal stability. Public spending on health care has been a key driver of aggregate increases in public spending over the past 40 years. As discussed in this book, spending is projected to continue rising as a share of GDP unless reforms are undertaken to help break these trends. The projected increases in public health spending will take place at a time when most countries need to undertake large fiscal adjustments to help bring public debt ratios down to more prudent levels. In this light, public health care spending is indeed an important macro-fiscal issue. Moderating the growth of age-related spending, including on health, will have to be a major element of the fiscal con-solidation strategy in the advanced economies over the coming years. For many emerging economies, the outlook for health spending is better, and immediate pressures are expected to be more benign. But it will by no means be easy for emerging economies to expand access to and improve the quality of health care services in light of the limited fiscal space to increase public health spending.

Despite the fiscal importance of health care reform, there has been relatively little systematic work on the macro-fiscal implications of reforms in advanced economies and emerging markets. Recent work by the Fiscal Affairs Department has tried to fill that void, both by projecting future health care spending if current policies were to be maintained and by estimating the potential fiscal impact of various reform options to contain health spending growth. This book draws on a recent study on the macro-fiscal implications of health care reforms presented to the IMF Executive Board in January 2011 and on papers prepared by outside experts for conferences at the IMF Regional Offices for Europe and Asia and the Pacific in June 2011 and October 2011, respectively.

An important objective of the IMF's analytical work in this area—and of our continued dialogue with health experts—is to improve our understanding of how feasible it would be to slow down the projected growth of health spending. This, in turn, has an important bearing on the composition of fiscal consolidation strategies going forward, since insufficient scope for containing health spending increases would shift the burden of expenditure cuts to other areas or require revenues to increase.

Health care reform is a difficult policy issue. It involves complex trade-offs between policy goals, such as ensuring access to high-quality health care and keeping public spending at fiscally affordable levels. Preferences regarding the role of the state in the provision and financing of health care services also vary significantly across countries. Many of these issues go beyond the scope of our work in this area. However, with a combination of cross-country analyses and case studies—and not least based on the stimulating debate within and outside the IMF on these issues—this book identifies potential policy responses to contain public health spending pressures in an efficient and equitable manner. Of course, much remains for us to learn, and the IMF will continue to stay abreast of new developments and insights in this complex area of policy.

Carlo Cottarelli
Director
Fiscal Affairs Department
International Monetary Fund

# Acknowledgments

We first would like to thank the contributing authors. Without their hard work and dedication, this book would not have been possible. The book has also benefited from the comments of staff in the IMF's Fiscal Affairs Department, staff in other IMF departments, and seminar participants from the European Commission, the World Bank, and the Organization for Economic Cooperation and Development. Many of the chapters in this volume were presented as papers at IMF health conferences in Paris in June 2011 and Tokyo in October 2011. We would like to thank conference participants for their valuable comments.

We are grateful to Joanne Blake and Michael Harrup of the IMF's External Relations Department for managing the production of the book. We are thankful to Pierre Jean Albert, Jeffrey Pichocki, and Mileva Radisavljevic, staff in the Fiscal Affairs Department's Expenditure Policy Division, for their support throughout the entire process. We are also grateful to Baoping Shang—who worked with us from the beginning when the book project was conceived—for his written contributions and efforts to ensure that all steps in the production process were followed in a timely manner.

Benedict Clements
David Coady
Sanjeev Gupta

# Abbreviations

| | |
|---|---|
| AMNOG | *Arzneimittelmarktneuordnungsgesetz* (law regulating reimbursement for drugs) (Germany) |
| ASEAN | Association of Southeast Asian Nations |
| BNHI | Bureau of National Health Insurance (Taiwan Province of China) |
| CAGR | compound annual growth rate |
| CAPB | cyclically adjusted primary balance |
| CDHC | consumer-directed health care |
| CHIP | Children's Health Insurance Program (United States) |
| CSMBS | Civil Servant Medical Benefit Scheme (Thailand) |
| DALY | disability-adjusted life-year |
| DEA | data envelopment analysis |
| DMP | disease management program |
| DRG | diagnosis-related group |
| EAP | East Asia and the Pacific |
| ECG | excess cost growth |
| FDH | free disposable hull |
| G2 NHI | Second-Generation National Health Insurance (Taiwan Province of China) |
| G-BA | *Gemeinsamer Bundesausschuss* (Federal Joint Committee) (Germany) |
| GP | general practitioner |
| GSDP | gross state domestic product (India) |
| HIF | Health Insurance Fund (Hungary) |
| HISRO | Health Insurance System Research Office (Thailand) |
| HITAP | Health Intervention and Technology Assessment Program (Thailand) |
| HMO | health maintenance organization |
| HSA | health savings account |
| HSRI | Health Systems Research Institute (Thailand) |
| IHPP | International Health Policy Program (Thailand) |
| IQWiG | *Institut für Qualität und Wirtschaftlichkeit im Gesundheitswesen* (Institute for Quality and Efficiency in Health Care) (Germany) |
| LTC | long-term care |
| NCD | noncommunicable disease |
| NHA | National Health Account (Thailand) |
| NHI | national health insurance |
| NHI | National Health Insurance (Japan, Taiwan Province of China) |
| NHIC | National Health Insurance Corporation (Republic of Korea) |
| NHS | National Health Service (U.K.) |
| NRHM | National Rural Health Mission (India) |
| OECD | Organization for Economic Cooperation and Development |

| | |
|---|---|
| OLS | ordinary least squares |
| OOP | out of pocket |
| PHI | Popular Health Insurance (Mexico) |
| PPP | purchasing power parity |
| QALY | quality-adjusted life-year |
| RSBY | Rashtriya Swastya Bima Yojana (health insurance scheme for those below the poverty line) (India) |
| SHI | statutory health insurance |
| SHI | social health insurance (Thailand) |
| UHC | universal health coverage |
| WHO | World Health Organization |

# Trends and Outlook for Public Health Spending

# CHAPTER 1

# The Challenge of Health Care Reform in Advanced and Emerging Economies

SANJEEV GUPTA, BENEDICT CLEMENTS, AND DAVID COADY

According to the World Health Organization (WHO), the three fundamental objectives of a health care system are

- improving the health of the population it serves;
- providing financial protection against the costs of ill-health; and
- responding to people's expectations.

Improving the health of the population is the primary objective of a health care system. But because health care can be catastrophically costly and the need for it unpredictable, mechanisms for sharing risk and providing financial protection are also important. A third goal—responsiveness to people's expectations—reflects the importance of respecting people's dignity and autonomy and the confidentiality of information (WHO, 2000). In addition, there is implicitly a fourth objective: equity. Improving health means not only maximizing the average health of the population, but also minimizing the differences among individuals and groups. Thus, the need for health systems to provide financial protection is also driven by equity concerns.

Significant improvements in health have been achieved around the world in the past several decades, as evidenced by sizable improvements in life expectancy and access to health care (WHO, 2010a, 2010b). The welfare gains from these improvements have been tremendous (Murphy and Topel, 2006). In addition, the microeconomic findings of the impact of health on worker productivity, education, and savings imply that improved health leads to improved economic growth (Bloom and Canning, 2008; Basta, Soekirman, and Scrimshaw, 1979; Kalemli-Ozcan, Ryder, and Weil, 2000; Bloom, Canning, and Graham, 2003; Hurd, McFadden, and Gan, 1998; and Alsan, Bloom, and Canning, 2006). However, the macroeconomic evidence is mixed, with evidence of a large and significant effect in some studies (Bloom and Canning, 2008; Bloom, Canning, and Sevilla, 2004; Sala-i-Martin, Doppelhofer, and Miller, 2004; and Baldacci and others, 2008) but a small and insignificant

This chapter has benefited from contributions from Eva Jenkner and Baoping Shang.

effect in others (Acemoglu, Johnson, and Robinson, 2003; Acemoglu and Johnson, 2007). Nevertheless, the incomplete access to health care in many countries, high and rising health care costs, and inefficiencies in spending have made health reform an urgent priority in both advanced and emerging market countries.

# HEALTH REFORM CHALLENGES: AN OVERVIEW

## Incomplete Coverage

Universal insurance coverage is essential to achieve the objectives of a health care system. Health insurance, by design, pools risk and provides financial protection from the cost of illness. It improves health by providing access to services that would otherwise be unaffordable for a significant share of the population (WHO, 2010b; Card, Dobkin, and Maestas, 2009). Most advanced economies have achieved universal insurance coverage, with the exception of the United States, which passed landmark legislation to achieve near-universal coverage in 2010.

The picture is uneven for emerging market economies. Most of emerging Europe and some emerging countries in Asia and Latin America have achieved universal coverage. In the other emerging economies, however, universal coverage is still in progress. A key issue facing these countries is how to provide this at an affordable cost. Universal coverage can be achieved through a tax-financed system, a social insurance system, private insurance, or a mixed system. Each system has its advantages and disadvantages (Gottret and Schieber, 2006). The most important barrier to universal coverage in many countries is the insufficient availability of resources (WHO, 2010b). Political stability, a strong institutional and policy environment, and a well-educated population can facilitate achievement of universal coverage. However, also important is a political commitment to allocate health spending to the provision of basic services for the entire population, rather than concentrating resources on curative services benefiting middle- or upper-income groups.

## Health Inequalities

Despite progress in improving health indicators in many countries, inequalities in health status—both between and within countries—remain large (CSDH, 2008; European Commission, 2010). Inequalities are largely driven by socioeconomic factors, such as income, education, and occupation, and thus are determined outside the health care sector (Joumard, Andre, and Nicq, 2010). There is no evidence of a trade-off between raising the average health status of the population and improving equity, suggesting it is possible to simultaneously achieve both equity and efficiency goals. Some features of health care systems, however, contribute to inequalities in health outcomes. For example, informal payments for health care services, which are prevalent in many emerging economies, disproportionately burden the poor (Jakab, 2007).

## Escalating Cost

Health care costs have been growing rapidly in the past several decades. Since 1970, total real per capita health spending has increased fourfold, while spending as a share of GDP has increased from 6 percent to 12 percent in advanced economies. In emerging economies, total health spending has increased from below 3 percent of GDP to 5 percent. These increases have put great fiscal pressure on governments and financial pressure on households and businesses.

The primary drivers of growth in health spending include rising income, population aging, and technological advancements. Additional factors include the Baumol effect,[1] health insurance coverage, and health policies (Newhouse, 1992; European Commission, 2010; CBO, 2010; Smith, Newhouse, and Freeland, 2009; Finkelstein, 2007). These factors often interact with each other (Weisbrod, 1991; Smith, Newhouse, and Freeland, 2009), and the separate effects of each are difficult to identify. Looking forward, these factors are expected to continue being important catalysts for health spending increases.

An additional factor that will drive spending is the change in disease profiles and associated risk factors. Most advanced economies and some emerging economies have finished the transition from primarily having to address communicable diseases (CDs) to primarily addressing noncommunicable diseases (NCDs). Other emerging economies are still making this transition. NCDs are the leading causes of death globally, killing more people each year than all other causes combined and nearly 80 percent of NCD deaths occur in low- and middle-income countries (WHO, 2010c). The economic impact of NCDs is also large, as national health care budgets are being increasingly allocated to treatment of NCDs (WHO, 2010c). NCDs are caused, to a large extent, by lifestyle risk factors—tobacco use, unhealthy diets, insufficient physical activity, and the harmful use of alcohol—and are often preventable. For example, tobacco and alcohol tax increases, tobacco control measures, and salt reduction have proven to be effective in improving health (WHO, 2010c).

## Inefficiencies

It has been well established in the literature that inefficiencies in health spending are large (Gupta and Verhoeven, 2001; Hauner, 2007; Mattina and Gunnarsson, 2007; Verhoeven, Gunnarsson, and Carcillo, 2007; Gupta and others, 2008; and Joumard, Andre, and Nicq, 2010). This includes both

---

[1]The Baumol effect refers to the rising unit labor costs in sectors where it is difficult to achieve productivity gains, usually in services. Because salaries rise in these sectors in line with economy-wide averages, while productivity does not, unit labor costs rise in relative terms. For evidence of the Baumol effect in health spending, see Pomp and Vujic (2008).

allocative inefficiencies and productive inefficiencies (Garber and Skinner, 2008). Because of inefficiencies, many countries could achieve the same level of health outcomes with a lower level of spending. A study by the Organization for Economic Cooperation and Development (OECD) suggests that reducing inefficiencies in health systems by half in the OECD would raise life expectancy at birth, on average, by more than one year (Joumard, Andre, and Nicq, 2010). By comparison, a 10 percent increase in health care spending per capita would increase life expectancy by only three to four months. The WHO estimates that 20 to 40 percent of resources spent on health are wasted. The most common causes of inefficiency include inappropriate and ineffective use of medicines, medical errors, suboptimal quality of care, waste, corruption, and fraud (WHO, 2010b).

## THE COMPLEXITY OF HEALTH REFORMS

Because of the potential trade-offs between health care reform objectives—such as preserving continued progress in improving health outcomes and controlling costs—health care reform is intrinsically complex.

An important question confronting all countries is the appropriate level of health care spending (Savedoff, 2007). This is further complicated by the fact that in addition to health spending, other factors, including lifestyle factors (see above), as well as education, pollution, and income, also play important roles (Joumard, Andre, and Nicq, 2010). Although health care spending is one of the most important determinants of health status, health spending may be too high in high-spending countries (Weisbrod, 1991; Docteur and Oxley, 2003). Given the large inefficiencies of health care systems, attacking these inefficiencies—as discussed above—may be the best route to improve health outcomes, rather than raising spending.

The imperfections in the health care market imply that governments must play an important role. However, there is no single model that delivers the best results across all countries. The pervasiveness of market failures and a desire to ensure that access to basic health care reflects need and not ability to pay have motivated extensive government involvement in this sector in advanced and emerging economies (Musgrove, 1996). The nature of government intervention (e.g., mandates, regulations, provision, and financing) has varied substantially across countries and over time, as has the level of public health spending. These differing approaches to providing and financing health care, and the resulting differences in the level of public health spending across countries, reflect differences in country preferences and constraints. Therefore, there is no unique "optimal" level of public health spending that can provide a benchmark for comparing countries. Countries may place different weights on equality of access, face differing fiscal constraints, or attach different weights to health spending as opposed to other uses of public funds. Yet there is a need to ensure that whatever "model" for health care is adopted, public health care services are provided in an efficient way.

# HEALTH REFORM AS A KEY FISCAL CHALLENGE

Health care reform will be a key fiscal challenge in coming years. In the advanced economies, public health spending has risen by about 4 percentage points of GDP since 1970, about half the overall increase in noninterest public spending. These spending pressures are expected to intensify over the next two decades, particularly if technological advances and other nondemographic factors continue to drive up costs. Over the longer term, the challenge is even more severe. Based on the projections presented in this book, the net present value of these spending increases over 2011–50 is close to 100 percent of today's GDP. In the emerging economies, health care reform is also important, given their substantially lower health indicators, relative to the advanced economies, and their limited fiscal resources.

The increases in health costs will occur at a time when countries need to undertake large fiscal adjustments to reduce public debt ratios in the wake of the global financial crisis. One common gauge of how much fiscal adjustment would be needed is the change in the primary balance (that is, fiscal balance net of interest payments) needed to bring the public-debt-to-GDP ratio back to the precrisis median of about 60 percent of GDP. Based on the estimates published in the IMF's *Fiscal Monitor* (IMF, 2011), this needed change in the primary balance would average about 8 percentage points of GDP.

Fiscal consolidation will require both revenue increases and expenditure reductions in the advanced economies. On the expenditure side, stabilizing age-related-spending-to-GDP ratios, including by containing the growth of health spending, could constitute an important pillar of fiscal adjustment strategies in the advanced economies. In some emerging economies, there is fiscal space to increase health spending. For emerging economies with room to expand, such as many of those in Asia and Latin America, the challenge is to expand basic coverage to a larger share of the population in a fiscally sustainable manner while avoiding the inefficiencies and resulting high costs of the health systems of advanced economies. In others, where coverage is already extensive—as is the case in much of emerging Europe—the challenge is to enhance the efficiency of public spending and limit its increase as a share of GDP.

Country experiences in containing public health spending vary widely, as does the quality and efficiency of public health services across countries. Several important questions remain for policymakers seeking guidance on health care reform, including the following:

- What are the trends in spending in different time periods and country groups? What has influenced these trends? How much does population aging account for the increase in spending?
- What is the outlook for public health spending over the next 20 years? Given differing degrees of success in controlling the growth of public health spending, which countries face the largest public health spending pressures?
- What reforms could advanced economies consider to control the growth of public health spending in an efficient and equitable manner? What are the potential savings that could be realized with different reforms? What needs

to be done to ensure that health reforms do not conflict with goals for ensuring equitable access to health care?

- How can emerging markets expand health coverage and improve health outcomes without incurring high fiscal costs?

This book addresses these questions and makes several contributions to the literature. It provides an analysis of the developments in public health spending over the past 40 years, as well as projections of public health spending for 50 advanced economies and emerging markets over the years 2011 to 2050. The projections for advanced economies improve upon existing studies by using country-specific estimates. The book presents an analysis that quantifies the effects of specific health reforms on the growth of public health spending by drawing on a range of analytical approaches, including country case studies. This analysis highlights the reforms advanced economies could consider to control the growth of public health spending in an efficient and equitable manner. The book likewise explains how selected emerging economies have successfully expanded health coverage and improved health outcomes without incurring high fiscal costs, and analyzes in detail the reform experiences and outstanding challenges for some of the largest emerging economies in Asia and Latin America. It includes specific case studies prepared by experts on Japan, the Republic of Korea, Germany, India, Taiwan Province of China, Thailand, and the Asian region as a whole. Finally, the book discusses the issue of public and private insurance, the appropriate role of the private sector in health care, and the effects on health indicators of health care reforms.

# ORGANIZATION OF THIS BOOK

This book is organized into five parts. The chapters in Part I provide an analysis of trends in public health spending and projections for these expenditures for advanced and emerging economies. Part II focuses specifically on the role of the private sector in the financing and provision of health care. Part III comprises cross-country studies of health care reforms and discusses the potential lessons for future reforms. Parts IV and V consist of country case studies of health reforms in advanced and emerging economies, respectively.

## Part I: Trends and Outlook for Public Health Spending

Understanding past trends in public health spending and the projected increases under unchanged policies is critical for assessing the magnitude of the health reform challenge across countries. Two important methodological issues for research in this area have been the following:

- to what extent past trends will continue into the future, and whether spending growth—which has been rapid in the past—will at some point slow down and converge to a rate closer to the growth of GDP; and
- whether or not country-specific trends should be used in projections for individual countries.

Obtaining reliable econometric estimates for the country-specific drivers of health care spending has been particularly vexing for the health care literature. The effect of population aging per se on spending is well understood, given the availability of reliable data on how spending differs across different cohorts of the population and projections for the aging of the population. What is less well understood is how nondemographic drivers of health spending, such as technological improvements in medical care, will evolve in the future. The growth of spending attributed to these nondemographics has been coined "excess cost growth (ECG)." Assumptions regarding ECG are the most important factor behind health care projections, given that the effect of aging on spending increases is believed to be moderate (European Commission, 2009; Smith, Newhouse, and Freeland, 2009).

The conservative estimates for ECG in some cross-country studies imply that health care spending will grow at a slower pace in the future than in the past. The reference scenario for health care spending projections in the European Commission's *2009 Ageing Report* (EC and EPC, 2009), for example, assumes that the growth in health care spending, beyond that caused by an aging population, would be no more than 0.2 percent per year. This is a much lower rate than observed in the past and risks understating the fiscal challenge posed by health spending.

Some research has tried to blend assumptions regarding the high spending growth of the past with assumptions regarding a future slowdown in health spending (OECD, 2006; CBO, 2010). This has been motivated by the view that health spending cannot continue increasing at the rate observed in the past, lest it rise to a ratio of output that is fiscally unsustainable or, over the long run, to a ratio exceeding 100 percent of GDP. However, the assumptions made about convergence can be arbitrary and implicitly suppose a change in policies that would help achieve such a slowdown in spending. Thus, it appears preferable to avoid imposing such assumptions, especially when projecting spending pressures over the next 20 to 40 years.

In Chapter 2, Coady and Kashiwase analyze health care spending trends for 27 advanced and 23 emerging economies over the past four decades. Total health expenditures have risen sharply during this period, and two-thirds of this increase is due to greater spending by the public sector (see above). On average, approximately one-fourth of the increase in public-spending-to-GDP ratios is explained by aging, and the rest by ECG. In the emerging economies, the increase in total health spending has been more moderate over the same period (see above), and public spending on health has increased from around 1½ to 2½ percent of GDP, about the same as the increase in private spending. This reflects the low priority given to health spending relative to other spending needs. In advanced economies there has been some convergence in public health spending ratios over the past several decades, while in emerging markets the spending shares do not indicate such a pattern. Looking across countries, higher health spending has not always been associated with better health outcomes. While raising public outlays can help improve health outcomes—which vary widely in both advanced and emerging economies—improving the efficiency of public health spending could be even more powerful for achieving this important objective.

In Chapter 3, Soto, Shang, and Coady provide updated projections of public health spending in advanced and emerging economies, using a methodology that improves upon earlier studies. Their specific improvement is the use of realistic and country-specific estimates of ECG to project future spending. The results indicate that large increases in public health spending are projected in the advanced economies, rising on average by 3 percentage points of GDP over the next 20 years and by 6½ percentage points of GDP over the next 40 years. Around one-third of that increase would be due to the effects of population aging, and the remaining two-thirds would be due to ECG. The projections suggest that the outlook is grim not only in the United States but also in Europe. Recent health care reforms in most countries are unlikely to alter long-term public health spending trends. In the emerging economies, public health spending is projected to rise by 1 percentage point of GDP over the next 20 years, one-third of the increase in the advanced economies. This reflects, in part, the low initial spending levels in emerging economies. Aging would account for about half of the increase in expenditure. On average, spending pressures in emerging Europe and Latin America are expected to be higher than in emerging Asia. The modest projected increases suggest that rising health spending is unlikely to pose a heavy fiscal burden in emerging economies over the next 20 years, which is consistent with the view that the primary challenge for these countries is to improve the efficiency of this spending.

## Part II: The Role of the Private Sector in Health Care Financing and Delivery

Despite the market failures associated with health care, the private sector can still play an important role in achieving the objectives of a health care system. However, there is no optimal level of private involvement, and the role of the private sector in each country should depend on its preferences and constraints.

Kanzler and Ng, in Chapter 4, analyze the potential roles of private insurance in addressing the challenges facing Asian countries. In Asia, governments often take the primary responsibility for health care provision and private insurance only plays a minor role. However, since many Asian countries are facing the challenges of containing the growth of health care costs or expanding health insurance coverage in a fiscally sustainable manner, it may be necessary for them to rethink the role of private insurance. Should private insurance replace public insurance or work in coordination with public insurance? How would a larger role for private insurance affect health care costs and quality of care? What regulations are needed to ensure the functioning of the private insurance market? Could private insurance be involved in other aspects of health care, in addition to the traditional role of provider reimbursement? The chapter concludes that the role of private insurance in Asia is not expected to change dramatically, largely because of social beliefs. If private insurance only served as a supplement to public coverage, the growth of private insurance could potentially improve quality of care, although for this to materialize would require a strong regulatory system. Furthermore, there may be scope for private insurance to play a larger role in care coordination, for example, as disease management facilitators or provider network managers, which could potentially improve the functioning of the health care system.

The empirical evidence regarding the appropriate role of the private sector in the financing and provision of health care has been largely inconclusive, and the debate has proceeded mainly on the basis of ideology. Cheng and Reinhardt, in Chapter 5, instead focus on the potential role of the private sector in achieving the economic functions and goals of a health system. These roles include those related to financing and delivering health care, protecting individuals and families from catastrophic risks, and maintaining and enhancing the health of the population. However, the appropriate role of the private sector depends heavily on the "distributive social ethic" of the system. The role of the private sector is also constrained by market imperfections, such as asymmetric information, lack of transparency in pricing, and monopoly power. If a country is willing to let health care be rationed among its citizens by price and ability to pay, then it can delegate most of the functions to be performed by the health system to market forces, and use regulation to make private markets function honestly and efficiently. If a country aspires to a roughly egalitarian health system, in which the quality of health care is to be roughly the same for everyone regardless of socioeconomic status, then government inevitably needs to step in, as well as strictly monitor and regulate the private sector. It is feasible to combine a distributive social ethic of social solidarity, implemented through government-run health insurance, with a mixed public-private health care system. If social solidarity is important, private health insurers cannot properly perform the function of collecting premium contributions and risk pooling. Nevertheless, they can be incorporated into the system to perform purchasing, claims processing, and quality control, as well as cost control under competitive contracting.

## Part III: Cross-Country Studies

A good understanding of which reforms worked and which did not work is essential to design effective health care reform. Cross-country studies are an important way to assess the impacts of the common elements of reforms that were adopted by many countries. Country case studies, on the other hand, identify the unique elements and circumstances of reforms from the experience of individual countries (Parts IV and V). The impact of health reforms needs to be evaluated in a comprehensive manner, including the effects on costs, health outcomes, equity, and financial protection.

In Chapter 6, Tyson, Kashiwase, Soto, and Clements find that the most promising strategies to contain spending in advanced economies appear to involve a mix of macro-level instruments to contain costs and micro-level reforms to improve spending efficiency. Their results are based on econometric analysis, event studies, and the results of case studies. Among the macro-level instruments, budget caps and central oversight are powerful tools for reducing spending growth. Among micro-level reforms, strengthening market mechanisms—increasing patient choice of insurers, allowing greater competition between insurers, relying on a greater degree of private provision, and allowing more competition between providers—are particularly effective in containing costs. Management and contracting reforms, such as extending the use of managed care or shifting toward case-based payments, are central to improving the efficiency of spending. Although used less extensively, demand-side reforms—such as expanding private insurance and increasing the level of cost sharing—have also been successful in containing the growth of spending. Price controls appear to be among the less successful approaches for containing health care costs.

The simulation analysis in Chapter 6 indicates that reforms could significantly reduce the fiscal burden of health care over the next 20 years. The results suggest that the introduction of market mechanisms can be powerful, yielding savings of about ½ percentage point of GDP. Improving public management and coordination can also reduce spending by only a slightly lower amount. The analysis also underscores the importance of tighter budget controls and greater central oversight, which can reduce spending by ¼ percentage point of GDP. Finally, the simulated impacts of demand-side reforms, such as the use of cost sharing, are small but not negligible. The relative importance and desirability of each of these reforms, however, will vary across countries, depending on their current health care system. While the impact of the simulated reforms is substantial, it may still fall short of what would be needed in some countries to stabilize age-related-spending-to-GDP ratios at current levels. Therefore, achieving fiscal adjustment may require even greater revenue and expenditure measures than previously envisaged.

In Chapter 7, Jenkner, Shang, and Clements conclude that the challenges facing emerging economies are different from those in advanced economies and also vary substantially across this heterogeneous group. In emerging Europe, spending is relatively high by emerging economy standards, since coverage of the population is nearly universal and disease patterns mirror those of advanced economies. However, overall health outcomes remain relatively poor, so the challenge is to enhance the efficiency of spending to improve lagging health outcomes and the quality of service delivery. In most emerging economies of Asia and Latin America, on the other hand, the main challenge remains to expand basic coverage to a larger share of the population without generating undue fiscal pressures over the medium term as incomes rise and these systems expand. In emerging Asia, increased public spending on health could also catalyze growth as precautionary savings are reduced. The fiscal space across emerging economies to increase public health spending varies greatly. For some countries, little fiscal adjustment is needed, thus making it easier to accommodate a projected rise in health spending (Brazil, Estonia). However, adjustment needs are high in a number of emerging European economies (Bulgaria, Latvia, Lithuania, Romania, and Poland), which are projected to have above-average increases in health spending.

While all emerging economies should be targeting improvements in efficiency, this is especially important for these countries with limited fiscal space. Countries with high projected economic growth will be in a better position to expand health spending, owing to its favorable effects on fiscal sustainability, while countries with more moderate growth prospects will need to take a more gradual approach. Most of emerging Europe will need to rely on additional micro-level reforms to improve health outcomes, rather than increasing spending, while emerging economies in Latin America and Asia will have more scope to expand spending. In order for emerging economies to maintain fiscal sustainability, it is critical to restrict the benefit package to the most essential health services, until the capacity to finance higher public health spending increases.

Lagenbrunner and Tandon, in Chapter 8, assess the successes and challenges of health financing reforms in East Asia and the Pacific (EAP). Countries in the EAP region have achieved relatively good health indicators with relatively modest health expenditures. Despite this significant progress, many EAP countries are still characterized by large and persistent inequalities in health outcomes and access to care, reflecting deficiencies in the breadth and depth in health insurance coverage. Another cause of these inequalities is that public health spending in low- and middle-income countries is typically not pro-poor, with the exception of some higher-income economies and regions such as China–Hong Kong Special Administrative Region, Malaysia, and Thailand. The financing of health care from general government revenues and social insurance contributions varies across countries, as does the level of out-of-pocket (OOP) payments. There is growing concern that the current level of resources available for health is inadequate for meeting emerging health needs and achieving universal coverage. Other concerns include the high reliance on donor funding in low-income countries, high OOP financing in low- and middle-income countries, and a perceived lack of sustainability of current sources of public financing. Many countries also suffer from an excessive number of small insurance funds and inadequate pooling. This fragmentation limits the potential for cross-subsidies, increases administrative costs, and leads to inequities. In terms of health benefits, instead of financing a small package of essential services for universal coverage and targeting the poor, health resources are often allocated to tertiary care and urban health facilities. There are also variations in packages across insurance schemes within a country, leading to unequal access to health care.

Public health systems in EAP countries often involve significant external contracting with private sector providers. However, there is a need to ensure that contractors are chosen on the basis of quality, cost control, and performance. Some countries have also adopted elements of gatekeeping in contracts with primary care providers. Looking forward, many countries are looking to move beyond fee for service (FFS) to other types of payment systems such as geographic caps, hospital global budgets, and case mix adjustments. A perennial issue for the region is how much it should rely on insurance-based systems—which are assumed to expand as labor market informality declines—or on general government revenue financing to help achieve universal coverage. Several countries have begun to use general government revenues to bring in the newly covered. In several cases, spending has been well targeted to prioritize coverage for low-income groups and the poorest. Over the longer term, changes in the demographic and epidemiological profile of EAP countries are likely to be key determinants of health care costs and needs.

In addition to health spending, health outcomes should also be taken into account in designing health reforms; outcomes are discussed in Chapter 9 by Skinner and Suarez. All countries are struggling with rising health care spending. It is therefore not surprising that many countries have turned to health care reforms designed to create sustainable patterns of future growth in health care costs. This chapter first establishes what is the most challenging aspect of medical care—the remarkable range in efficiency of different specific treatments—ranging from the use of aspirin for patients after a heart attack and insecticide-treated bed nets (very high) to stents for stable angina (poor) and noninvasive surgery for arthritis of the knee (no known benefit). For this reason, there is often only a small (and sometimes even a negative) association between spending and quality of care, whether across hospitals or across countries. In practical terms, this means that health care reforms need to be evaluated on the basis of not only their effects on expenditure, but also their effects on the efficiency of care. Public savings achieved by cutting back on ineffective treatments are more desirable, for example, than those involving the scaling back of highly effective insecticide-coated bed nets. Countries need to make better use of existing data to monitor treatment and outcome data to ensure that health care reforms that seek to reduce public outlays do not undermine high-value care.

## Part IV: Country Case Studies: Advanced Economies

In Chapter 10, Tyson and Karpowicz assess the reform experiences of seven advanced economies to highlight specific episodes of success in containing public health spending over the past 30 years and the reforms that were behind these success stories. In each of these episodes, the countries achieved a reduction in the ratio of public health spending to GDP that was sustained for a period of time, as well as a moderation in real spending growth rates. The *Canadian* experience in the late 1970s and during the 1990s suggests that budget caps and supply constraints can be effective tools to limit increases in health care spending. Cost containment in *Finland* in the 1990s was achieved through a comprehensive set of reforms that acted at the macro- and micro-levels and included supply constraints, budget caps, price controls, and public management and coordination reforms. The *Italian* experience of the 1990s demonstrates that control of prices and cost sharing can be effective tools for cost containment in the short run. Whether or not these measures yield durable savings, however, is questionable. What appears to have been crucial to the success of Italy's cost containment was the shared recognition that, in contrast with past experience, the central government would not bail out regional health systems burdened with large deficits. In the *Netherlands*, the budgetary reform in the hospital sector in the 1980s seemed to have slowed the growth of public health expenditures. Greater use of budget caps and pharmaceutical reform in the mid-1990s reduced public health expenditures substantially. However, the history of reform in the Netherlands indicates that implementing radical reform of the system is difficult and takes time. The reforms of the 1980s and the early 1990s in *Sweden* show that budget caps and public management and coordination reforms, in particular those related to strengthening accountability under decentralization, were successful in reining in spending. However, market mechanisms were needed to counter some negative consequences for supply and to improve efficiency. The *United Kingdom* experienced slower or negative spending growth in the late 1970s and in the 1980s. Consolidating the health system by eliminating area health authorities and introducing new management practices appears to have contributed to the containment of expenditure growth. The major slowdown in health spending in the *United States* in the 1990s was attributable to the widespread adoption of managed care, which introduced gatekeeping and utilization reviews into the system. Negotiated prices for health services between the managed care plans and providers also contributed to slower growth in health care costs.

Chapter 11, by Ii, focuses on the Japanese health care system. Japan is often considered to be an efficient system in light of having the world's highest life expectancies and relatively low health care expenditures (Murray, 2011; Hashimoto and others, 2011). However, health care expenditures in Japan are underestimated, because expenditures not covered by public insurance are excluded from total health expenditures. This underestimation could be as large as one-third of the total expenditures. One of the challenges Japan is facing is to contain escalating expenditures for the elderly. These outlays receive substantial subsidies from both central and local governments and transfers from other insurers, but a sustainable financing mechanism for the elderly is still lacking. Another concern is the high number of hospital beds per capita and long hospital stays. One of the reasons for this situation is the lack of an efficient primary care system, as there is no clear distinction between primary care physicians and specialists. Low cost sharing and the fee-for-service system may have contributed to the problem as well. Japan's health insurance system also needs reforms. The responsibility of municipalities as insurers, for example, remains ambiguous. Furthermore, insurers should act as more than just payers, but also be involved in improving the efficiency of health care delivery. This could be done by excluding inefficient providers from their list of service providers to promote competition, developing clinical standards, and guiding investment decisions for expensive medical equipment.

In Chapter 12, Kwon assesses several important health care reforms in the Republic of Korea over the past decade designed to expand coverage, contain costs, and improve efficiency. These reforms include the merger of health insurance societies to a single-payer system, which reduced the inequity and inefficiency associated with fragmented insurance systems, increased risk pooling, and lowered administrative costs. Other reforms in Korea include the separation of drug prescribing from drug dispensing, which reduced the financial incentives for over-prescribing. Some elements of this reform, however, were diluted in light of physician opposition. Physician opposition also stopped the nationwide implementation of diagnosis-related groups (DRG)–based payments. This pushed the government to increase physician fees to compensate for loss of their incomes resulting from pharmaceutical reform. Another important reform has been the establishment of long-term care (LTC) insurance for the elderly, which was a response to population aging. LTC insurance is financed by a combination of premium contribution, government subsidies, and copayments. Eligibility for LTC is based on the age and functional status[2] of the patient. LTC insurance provides mostly in-kind benefits; cash benefits are provided only in exceptional cases where necessary to provide choice and promote competition among formal and informal caregivers. The challenges facing LTC include financial sustainability and coordination of care between health care insurance and LTC insurance. The chapter also indicates that the share of private health expenditures in total expenditures has decreased as a result of the expansion of health insurance. However, the impact of these reforms was tempered by the rapid increase in the prices of health services not covered by insurance, which are not regulated by the government. To contain rapidly growing pharmaceutical spending, the National Health Insurance Corporation negotiates prices with manufacturers instead of using formula-based pricing. However, generic prices in Korea are still among the highest in the OECD. In addition to prices, it is also important to control the volume and mix of brand name and generic drugs through regulations. In particular, these regulations should target the prescribing behavior of physicians or provide financial incentives for them to prescribe in a cost-effective way.

Chapter 13, by Stolpe, provides an overview of health care reforms in Germany since the 1980s. It argues that the increase in health care spending, as a share of GDP, is attributable to the country's unification in 1990. A wide variety of policy approaches and complementary reform elements have been discussed and introduced in Germany, including budget caps, market mechanisms, and pecuniary incentives. Many useful lessons can be drawn from the reform experiences of Germany. Budget caps can reduce spending for a short period of time, but are less effective in keeping spending low in the long run if the underlying causes of spending growth are not addressed. Market mechanisms, on the other hand, require the correct alignment of incentives and behaviors.

Germany's experience with different reforms has been mixed. The risk adjustment scheme, which was mainly based on age and sex, did not work well because of cream skimming by sickness funds. The morbidity-based risk adjustment scheme, known as Morbi-RSA, has fared better; it has substantially reduced sickness funds' incentives for risk selection, and even made some chronic diseases financially attractive for the risk pool. It remains to be seen whether Morbi-RSA

---

[2]Functional status refers to an individual's ability to perform normal daily activities required to meet basic needs, fulfill usual roles, and maintain health and well-being.

will provide sufficient flexibility to adjust its payment schedule in response to new medical technologies that could change the relative costs and benefits of treating specific diseases. Sickness funds' collective monopsony power vis-à-vis Germany's regional physicians' associations has long been effective in containing the cost of physician services in statutory health insurance (SHI). More recently, DRGs have helped to contain the cost of hospital care and triggered important changes in hospitals' competitive behaviors and management strategies. In the pharmaceutical sector, reference prices for generics alone have had ambiguous effects. Average prices of pharmaceuticals used in SHI began to decline substantially only after sickness funds were given the freedom to negotiate volume rebates. In sum, despite some setbacks, reforms in Germany have been successful in containing spending growth while maintaining high quality health care.

In Chapter 14, Cheng describes the health reform experience of Taiwan Province of China and discusses the lessons learned. Taiwan Province of China introduced a single-payer, government-run health insurance system in 1995 and achieved near universal coverage in less than a year. The delivery system, however, is largely private. The system is financed through a combination of government revenues, payroll taxes, household premium contributions, and cost sharing. The premium contributions vary by population groups, with government subsidies for the disadvantaged. Cost sharing varies by type of service and facility and constitutes around 37 percent of total health care spending. The extensive use of health information technology helps keep administrative costs low, at 1.3 percent of the National Health Insurance (NHI) budget. Private insurance plays a minor role, often in the form of a cash indemnity policy which provides cash benefits when insured contingency events occur. The system has so far received a high satisfaction rate from the population, with evidence pointing to improvements in health outcomes. One challenge for the health system in Taiwan Province of China thus far has been the financial stability of the NHI fund, as it has often been difficult to raise contribution rates to finance spending increases.

Several important lessons can be learned from the reform experience of Taiwan Province of China. First, total health care spending can effectively be controlled through global budgets and the government's ability to set and control prices in a single-payer system. Second, a single-payer system provides an excellent platform for achieving equity and adopting a uniform health information system. Third, a single-payer system can also perform well in terms of promoting choice when it is combined with private provision. In such a system, high productivity can be achieved through competing for patients on quality, not on prices. Fourth, the reform experience of Taiwan Province of China suggests that solid economic growth before, during, and after implementation of a universal health insurance scheme is important for the establishment and subsequent funding of the scheme.

Despite the successes of this system, there is scope for further improvement. The reform agenda should focus on building the capacity for comparative effectiveness analysis and health technology assessments, moving from fee-for-service payment to capitation payments, and addressing the challenges arising from non-communicable diseases and long-term care.

## Part V: Country Case Studies: Emerging Economies

In Chapter 15, Rao and Choudhury analyze the Indian health care system, which has been facing numerous challenges. These include low levels of public spending on health and poor-quality services, the low health status of the population, an inadequate focus on preventive care, high out-of-pocket spending, and large disparities across states. Several recent reform initiatives were introduced to address these challenges. The National Rural Health Mission, a comprehensive program to improve access to effective health care for the poor in rural areas, would increase health care spending by 1 to 2 percent of GDP between 2005 and 2012. However, there are a number of problems with its design and implementation: (1) the method for allocating spending did not adequately take into account the needs of states; (2) the requirement for states to match funds to help finance higher spending was not clear; and (3) there was a failure to execute the planned increase in spending, which was hampered by states' inability to make matching contributions. As a result, the impact of the program on health spending and outcomes has been negligible. An insurance scheme, Rashtriya Swasthya Bima Yojana, was introduced by the Union Labor Ministry to provide financial protection against high out-of-pocket expenditures. Rashtriya Swasthya Bima Yojana, jointly funded by the central government and the states, covers selected hospitalization and daycare expenses for the population below poverty line. However, program participation has been low at less than 50 percent. The limited success of these programs has largely reflected the fiscal constraints that both the central government and the states have been facing. In fact, econometric analysis suggests that states significantly reduced their own health expenditures when they received transfers from the central government, with an elasticity close to one.

In Chapter 16, Jongudomsuk and colleagues review how institutional capacity in health policy and health system research was gradually strengthened in Thailand. They also explain how evidence was translated into policy decisions and practice and guided health financing reforms, using two policy reforms as illustrations: the provider payment reform of the Civil Servant Medical Benefit Scheme and the inclusion of new health interventions in the benefit package for universal coverage. Factors that were central to Thailand's success in capacity building included strong national ownership, local initiative, and reliance on local resources for conducting policy-driven research. One indication of this success is the growth in the number of qualified researchers, as a result of collaboration and resource sharing within Thailand, international collaboration, and consistent support for capacity building by strategic partners such as the London School of Hygiene and Tropical Medicine. Also important were a number of infrastructure developments, including the creation of national health accounts, studies on the burden of diseases, and the strengthening of hospital administrative data and national household survey data sets for monitoring progress. These developments provided platforms for regular monitoring and informed decision making. Translating evidence into policy decisions required a systematic, transparent, and participatory process. An official subcommittee was established to examine the benefit package and has been an effective forum where evidence has informed policy decisions in a transparent and deliberate manner.

Shang and Jenkner, in Chapter 17, provide case studies for Estonia, Hungary, China, Chile, and Mexico. Health care systems and reform experiences vary substantially across these economies, and the case studies illuminate both successes and remaining weaknesses in these systems. Each case study provides an overview of the health care system and comparative data on key health indicators relative to the appropriate comparator group, a description of the experience with health reforms, remaining challenges, and lessons. After independence, *Estonia* introduced a compulsory social health insurance system, reformed primary care, and reduced the size of the hospital sector. Provision is now both public and private, while funding is predominantly public through mandatory contributions. Challenges remain, including shortages of health professionals, cost pressures, and high lifestyle-related risks. However, the Estonian experience illustrates the advantages of global budgets and a single health insurance fund as effective tools in containing public health spending and exploiting risk pooling. *Hungary* underwent similar reforms after its transition to a market economy, and its health system today relies largely on public financing and provision. It also faces cost pressures, high lifestyle-related risks, and an inefficient use of health care resources, reflected in an excessive use of tertiary and specialty care. This demonstrates the key importance of setting the right incentives for provider payment systems to ensure efficiency.

*China* has achieved good health outcomes with relatively low health care spending during the last 60 years, and it has recently taken major steps to expand coverage. However, many challenges remain, including high out-of-pocket spending, wide inequalities, and inefficient use of resources. China's reform experience indicates that an incremental approach can be an effective way to expand coverage and access to care. It also demonstrates the importance of preventive care and public health services and the need for payment reforms to improve system efficiency. *Chile* has achieved almost universal health care coverage through a mandatory social security system and explicit health care guarantees, but financing and provision are both mixed, and the health system is de facto segmented. One major challenge of the Chilean health care model is the inequity in the quality of care between the public and private system. Chile's success in extending coverage and sharply improving health outcomes is the product of strong fiscal and economic performance, efficient institutions, and a political consensus to provide care to all. By contrast, in *Mexico*, universal health care coverage has yet to be achieved. The health care system was segmented between many public and private insurers and providers. As a result, high fragmentation, inequality of access, and high administrative costs are crucial challenges for Mexico. Also of concern is the high level of OOP spending, which accounts for half of total health outlays. Going forward, the system of social protection in health has aimed at reducing the fragmentation of the system and achieving universal coverage based on affordable family insurance, or Seguro Popular.

# REFERENCES

Acemoglu, D., and S. Johnson, 2007, "Disease and Development: The Effect of Life Expectancy on Economic Growth," *Journal of Political Economy,* No. 115, pp. 925–85.

Acemoglu, D., S. Johnson, and J. Robinson, 2003, "Disease and Development in Historical Perspective," *Journal of the European Economic Association, Papers and Proceedings,* Vol. 1, pp. 397–405.

Alsan, M., D.E. Bloom, and D. Canning, 2006, "The Effect of Population Health on Foreign Direct Investment Inflows to Low- and Middle-Income Countries," *World Development,* Vol. 34, No. 4, pp. 613–30.

Baldacci, E., B. Clements, S. Gupta, and Q. Cui, 2008, "Social Spending, Human Capital, and Growth in Developing Countries," *World Development,* Vol. 36, No. 8, pp. 1317–41.

Basta, S., K. Soekirman, and N. Scrimshaw, 1979, "Iron Deficiency Anemia and Productivity of Adult Males in Indonesia," *American Journal of Clinical Nutrition,* No. 32, pp. 916–25.

Bloom, D., and D. Canning, 2008, "Population Health and Economic Growth," Working Paper No. 24 (Washington: World Bank, on behalf of the Commission on Growth and Development).

Bloom, D.E., D. Canning, and B. Graham, 2003, "Longevity and Life-Cycle Savings," *Scandinavian Journal of Economics,* No. 105, pp. 319–38.

Bloom, D.E., D. Canning, and J. Sevilla, 2004, "The Effect of Health on Economic Growth: A Production Function Approach," *World Development,* Vol. 32, No. 1, pp. 1–13.

Card, D., C. Dobkin, and N. Maestas, 2009, "Does Medicare Save Lives?" *Quarterly Journal of Economics*, May, pp. 597–636.

Commission on Social Determinants of Health (CSDH), 2008, "Closing the Gap in a Generation: Health Equity through Action on the Social Determinants of Health—Final Report by the Commission on Social Determinants of Health" (Geneva: World Health Organization).

Congressional Budget Office, 2010, "The Long-Term Budget Outlook" (Washington: June, revised August).

Docteur, E., and H. Oxley, 2003, "Health-Care Systems: Lessons from the Reform Experience," OECD Health Working Paper No. 9 (Paris: Organization for Economic Cooperation and Development).

European Commission, 2010, "Contributing to Universal Coverage of Health Services Through Development Policy," Staff Working Document to accompany COM(2010)128, *The EU Role in Global Health* (Brussels).

European Commission (EC) and Economic Policy Committee (EPC), 2009, *The 2009 Ageing Report: Economic and Budgetary Projections for the EU-27 Member States, 2008–2060,* European Economy Paper No. 2 (Brussels).

Finkelstein, A., 2007, "The Aggregate Effects of Health Insurance: Evidence from the Introduction of Medicare," *Quarterly Journal of Economics*, Vol. 122, No. 1, pp. 1–37.

Garber, A., and J. Skinner, 2008, "Is American Health Care Uniquely Inefficient?" NBER Working Paper No. 14257 (Cambridge, MA: National Bureau of Economic Research).

Gottret, P., and G. Schieber, 2006, *Health Financing Revisited: A Practitioner's Guide* (Washington: World Bank).

Gupta, S., G. Schwartz, S. Tareq, R. Allen, I. Adenauer, K. Fletcher, and D. Last, 2008, *Fiscal Management of Scaled-Up Aid* (Washington: International Monetary Fund).

Gupta, S., and M. Verhoeven, 2001, "The Efficiency of Government Expenditures: Experiences from Africa," *Journal of Policy Modeling*, Vol. 23, pp. 433–67.

Hashimoto, H., N. Ikegami, K. Shibuya, N. Izumida, H. Noguchi, H. Yasunaga, H. Miyata, J. Acuin, and M. Reich, 2011, "Cost Containment and Quality of Care in Japan: Is There a Tradeoff?" *Lancet*, Vol. 378, No. 9797, pp. 1174–82.

Hauner, D., 2007, "Benchmarking the Efficiency of Public Expenditure in the Russian Federation," IMF Working Paper No. 07/246 (Washington: International Monetary Fund).

Hurd, M., D. McFadden, and L. Gan, 1998, "Subjective Survival Curves and Life-Cycle Behavior," in *Inquiries in the Economics of Aging*, ed. D. Wise (Chicago: University of Chicago Press).

International Monetary Fund, 2010, *From Stimulus to Consolidation: Revenue and Expenditure Policies in Advanced and Emerging Economies*, IMF Departmental Paper (Washington).

———, 2011, "Addressing Fiscal Challenges to Reduce Economic Risks," *Fiscal Monitor*, September (Washington).

Jakab, M., 2007, "An Empirical Evaluation of the Kyrgyz Health Reform: Does It Work for the Poor?" (Cambridge, MA: Harvard University, Harvard School of Public Health, Department of Health Policy and Management).

Joumard, I., C. Andre, and C. Nicq, 2010, "Health Care Systems: Efficiency and Institutions," Economics Department Working Paper No. 769 (Paris: Organization for Economic Cooperation and Development).

Kalemli-Ozcan, S., H.E. Ryder, and D.N. Weil, 2000, "Mortality Decline, Human Capital Investment, and Economic Growth," *Journal of Development Economics,* Vol. 62, No. 1, pp. 1–23.

Mattina, T., and V. Gunnarsson, 2007, "Budget Rigidity and Expenditure Efficiency in Slovenia," IMF Working Paper No. 07/131 (Washington: International Monetary Fund).

Murphy, K., and R. Topel, 2006, "The Value of Health and Longevity," *Journal of Political Economy*, Vol. 114, pp. 871–904.

Murray, C., 2011, "Why Is Japanese Life Expectancy So High?" *Lancet*, Vol. 378, No. 9797, pp. 1124–25.

Musgrove, P., 1996, "Public and Private Roles in Health: Theory and Financing Patterns," Health, Nutrition, and Population Discussion Paper No. 29290 (Washington: World Bank).

Newhouse, J.P., 1992, "Medical Care Costs: How Much Welfare Loss?" *Journal of Economic Perspectives*, Vol. 6, No. 3, pp. 3–21.

Organization for Economic Cooperation and Development (OECD), 2006, "Projecting OECD Health and Long-Term Care Expenditures: What Are the Main Drivers?" Economics Department Working Paper No. 447 (Paris).

Pomp, M., and S. Vujic, 2008, "Rising Health Spending, New Medical Technology, and the Baumol Effect," Discussion Paper No. 115 (The Hague: CPB [Netherlands Bureau for Economic Policy Analysis]).

Sala-i-Martin, X., G. Doppelhofer, and R.I. Miller, 2004, "Determinants of Long-Term Growth: A Bayesian Averaging of Classical Estimates (BACE) Approach," *American Economic Review,* Vol. 94, No. 4, pp. 813–35.

Savedoff, W., 2007, "What Should a Country Spend on Health Care?" *Health Affairs*, Vol. 26, No. 4, pp. 962–70.

Smith, S., J. Newhouse, and M. Freeland, 2009, "Income, Insurance, and Technology: Why Does Health Spending Outpace Economic Growth?" *Health Affairs*, Vol. 28, No. 5, pp. 1276–84.

Verhoeven, M., V. Gunnarsson, and S. Carcillo, 2007, "Education and Health in G-7 Countries: Achieving Better Outcomes with Less Spending," IMF Working Paper No. 07/263 (Washington: International Monetary Fund).

Weisbrod, B., 1991, "The Health Care Quadrilemma: An Essay on Technological Change, Quality of Care and Cost Containment," *Journal of Economic Literature*, Vol. 29, No. 2, pp. 523–52. ·

World Health Organization (WHO), 2000, *The World Health Report 2000—Health Systems: Improving Performance* (Geneva).

———, 2010a, *World Health Statistics 2010* (Geneva).

———, 2010b, *The World Health Report 2010—Health Systems: Improving Performance* (Geneva).

———, 2010c, *Global Status Report on Noncommunicable Diseases* (Geneva).

# CHAPTER 2

# Public Health Care Spending: Past Trends

## David Coady and Kenichiro Kashiwase

This chapter analyzes the health care spending trends of 27 advanced economies and 23 emerging economies over the past four decades. Total health expenditures have risen sharply during this period, particularly in advanced economies (Figure 2.1).[1] Since 1970, real per capita total health spending has increased four-fold in advanced economies, while spending as a share of GDP has increased from 6 percent to almost 12 percent.[2] Two-thirds of this increase has been due to greater public health spending, whose share of total health spending rose from 55 percent to 60 percent. In the emerging economies, the increase in total health spending has been more moderate over the same period—from below 3 percent of GDP to about 5 percent—and public spending on health has increased from around 1½ to 2½ percent of GDP, about the same as the increase in private spending.

The remainder of this chapter is structured as follows. First, it offers an overview of trends in public health spending in advanced economies. This is followed by a similar assessment of the drivers of public health outlays in emerging economies, and a discussion of the relationship between health outcomes and health system efficiency. Finally, appendices are provided that describe, respectively, data sources and differing approaches to measuring the efficiency of health spending.

## TRENDS IN ADVANCED ECONOMIES

Public health spending in advanced economies has been characterized by short periods of accelerated growth followed by periods of cost containment (Figure 2.1). The rapid increase in spending during 1971–75 (rising by 1 percentage point

---

[1]The advanced economies in this study comprise 27 countries: Australia, Austria, Belgium, Canada, Czech Republic, Denmark, Finland, France, Germany, Greece, Iceland, Ireland, Italy, Japan, the Republic of Korea, Luxembourg, the Netherlands, New Zealand, Norway, Portugal, the Slovak Republic, Slovenia, Spain, Sweden, Switzerland, the United Kingdom, and the United States. The 23 emerging economies are Argentina, Brazil, Bulgaria, Chile, China, Estonia, Hungary, India, Indonesia, Latvia, Lithuania, Malaysia, Mexico, Pakistan, the Philippines, Poland, Romania, Russia, Saudi Arabia, South Africa, Thailand, Turkey, and Ukraine.

[2]All country group averages are weighted on the basis of GDP at purchasing power parity, unless otherwise noted. The public health spending data have been adjusted for structural breaks to ensure comparability over time (see Appendix 2.1).

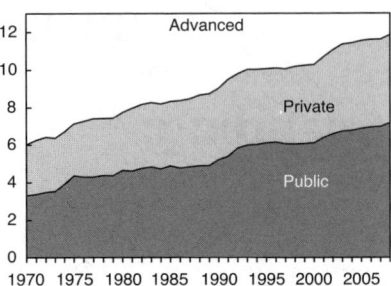
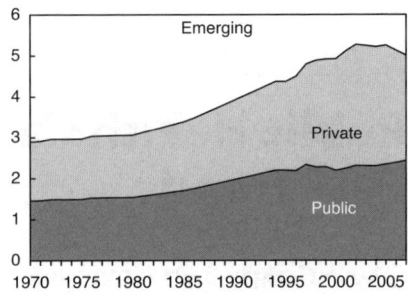

**Figure 2.1** Total, Private, and Public Health Expenditures, 1970–2008 (Percent of GDP)
Sources: Organization for Economic Cooperation and Development, OECD Health Data; World Health Organization; Sivard (1974–96); and IMF staff estimates.
Note: Average spending is weighted on the basis of GDP at purchasing power parity. For advanced economies without 2008 data (five countries), 2006 or 2007 data were used. The final year for spending data for the emerging economies is 2007.

of GDP) reflected the expansion of health insurance coverage in most countries. This was followed by a longer period of relative cost control when many countries introduced health reforms as part of broader fiscal consolidation efforts. Public health spending increased by less than 1 percentage point of GDP over the 15-year period from 1975 to 1990. Expenditures again began to accelerate in the early 1990s, before another period of containment in the second half of that decade. The slowdown in spending growth reflected reforms in both the United States and Europe as part of a broader restraint in total government spending. The growth of public health spending picked up after 2000, with outlays rising by 1 percentage point (to 7 percent of GDP) by 2008. This reflected a more widespread increase in total government spending over the 2000–08 period of 2 percentage points of GDP, following a period of spending containment in the 1990s (IMF, 2010).

The literature has identified income, aging, technology, and health policies as the key factors behind rising public-spending-to-GDP ratios. On the demand side, health care spending tends to rise as a share of GDP as countries develop. In addition, elderly people consume on average more health services than their younger counterparts. On the supply side, technological change has expanded the scope of what is medically possible by improving treatments and diagnostics. This expanding scope has increased the cost of medical services, reflecting improvements in quality (e.g., the diffusion of angioplasty and the use of MRIs instead of X-rays). Additionally, health costs have been driven upward by the relatively low productivity growth of services relative to other sectors of the economy (the so-called Baumol effect).[3] Among these drivers, nondemographic factors dominate. On average, approximately one-fourth of the increase in public-spending-to-GDP

---

[3]The Baumol effect refers to the rising unit labor costs in sectors where it is difficult to achieve productivity gains, usually in services. Because salaries rise in these sectors in line with economy-wide averages, while productivity does not, unit labor costs rise in relative terms. For evidence of the Baumol effect in health spending, see Pomp and Vujic (2008).

ratios is explained by changes in the age distribution of the population ("aging"). The rest—known as excess cost growth—is attributable to the combined effect of nondemographic factors, including rising incomes, technological advances, the Baumol effect, and health policies and institutions.[4] Of course, positive excess cost growth should not be interpreted to mean that the costs of public spending have exceeded its benefits, because technological advancements—the main driver of higher health care costs—have yielded enormous improvements in health status and well-being (Cutler and McClellan, 2001). In any case, the benefits of higher health spending would also need to be weighed against their costs, which is a task that is beyond the scope of this chapter.

The magnitude of increases in the ratio of public health spending to GDP has varied substantially across countries over the last three decades, and this has led to some convergence in this ratio. The ratio increased in virtually all advanced economies during this period (Figure 2.2). In 1980, the gap between the lowest-spending country (Greece) and the highest-spending country (Sweden) was 5 percentage points of GDP. By 2008, spending ranged from 5½ percent of GDP (Australia) to 8.7 percent (France)—a markedly lower spread than in 1980. On average, spending increased more rapidly in countries with low initial spending ratios (the correlation coefficient between increases in the spending ratio and the initial ratio is −0.8; Figure 2.2, right panel). The biggest increases occurred in the United States (3.8 percentage points), Portugal (3.4 percentage points), and New Zealand (2.7 percentage points), while the smallest increases were in Sweden (−0.7 percentage points), Ireland (0.0 percentage points), and Denmark (0.1 percentage points). Since 2000, 11 countries have experienced an increase in their public health spending ratio by 1 percentage point or greater: Canada, Denmark, Finland, Greece, Ireland, Italy, the Netherlands, New Zealand, Luxembourg, the United Kingdom, and the United States (Appendix Figure 2.1). The countries with the smallest increases (0.2 percentage point of GDP or less) were the Czech Republic, Germany, and Norway.

The low correlation between initial per capita GDP in 1980 and the increase in spending ratios over 1980–2008 indicates that income convergence was not a key factor. Furthermore, changes in relative age structures have been slow and are also unlikely to explain this convergence. Indeed, controlling for income and demographics, regression analysis indicates that countries with below-mean ratios of spending to GDP had significantly higher spending growth. This suggests that convergence was driven by "imitation" effects, borrowing from other countries

---

[4]The precise breakdown of the role of these different factors in driving health spending has varied across studies, as very few consider all of these factors simultaneously. The literature has primarily focused on the drivers of total health spending, rather than public health outlays. In Smith, Newhouse, and Freeland (2009), the residual for technological advances explains between one-third and one-half of the increase in total health spending over 1960–2007 for the United States, depending on assumptions about income elasticity and medical care productivity. The remainder is due to changes in income, the Baumol effect, the rise of insurance coverage, and demographics.

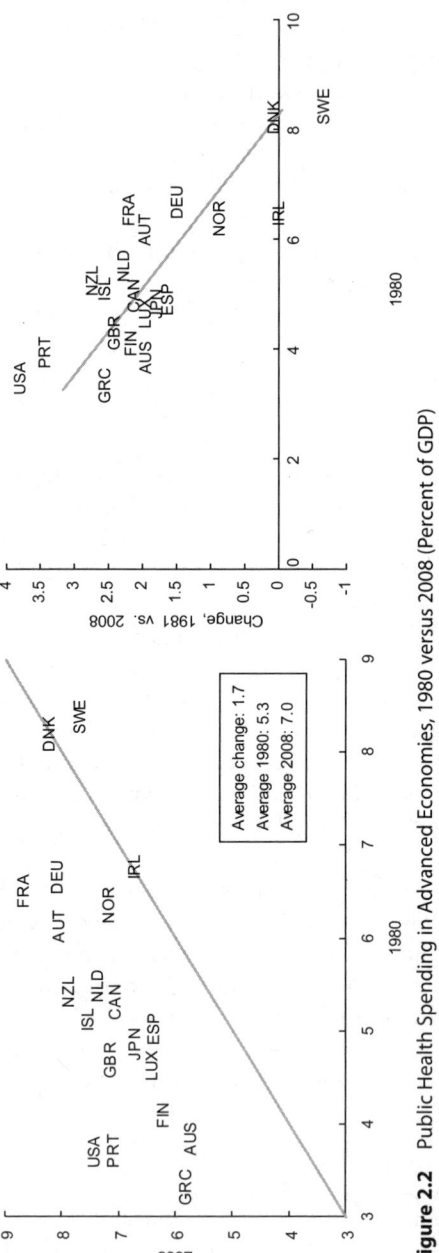

**Figure 2.2** Public Health Spending in Advanced Economies, 1980 versus 2008 (Percent of GDP)

Sources: Organization for Economic Cooperation and Development, OECD Health Data; and IMF staff estimates.

Note: The figures and averages exclude the Republic of Korea, where spending as a share of GDP increased from 0.8 percent in 1980 to 3.6 percent in 2008. Data for 2008 refer to 2008 or latest year available. Averages are unweighted. AUS = Australia; AUT = Austria; CAN = Canada; DEU = Germany; ESP = Spain; FIN = Finland; FRA = France; GBR = United Kingdom; GRC = Greece; IRL = Ireland; ISL = Iceland; JPN = Japan; LUX = Luxembourg; NLD = Netherlands; NOR = Norway; NZL = New Zealand; PRT = Portugal; SWE = Sweden; USA = United States.

some features of the public health system that seemed appealing. This led, for example, to the provision of health services previously not covered. Of course, such imitation required changes in health institutions and policies, including changes in the factors that determine the diffusion of technology. This in turn raises the question whether the rates of increase in spending that were observed during the convergence period will continue in the future (see Box 3.1).

## TRENDS IN EMERGING ECONOMIES

Spending levels and increases have been substantially lower in all the emerging economies. During 1971–95, public health spending increased by ½ percentage point of GDP, to 2 percent. Spending accelerated after that, with an additional ½ percentage point of GDP in the following decade.[5] Public-spending ratios are substantially higher in emerging Europe and Latin America than in emerging Asia, with no evidence of convergence in ratios across emerging economies over time (Figure 2.3). Since 1995, the largest increases in spending have been in Romania, Saudi Arabia, Thailand, and Turkey (by 1–1½ percentage points of GDP), while spending ratios have fallen in Estonia, Hungary, India, Latvia, Russia, and Ukraine. Since 2000—when average public-health-spending-to-GDP ratios started to rise—only six countries have had increases of more than ½ percentage point (Brazil, Bulgaria, Chile, Poland, Thailand, and Ukraine—see Appendix Figure 2.2).

The modest increases in public-health-spending-to-GDP ratios reflect the low priority given to this sector compared with other needs. Public health spending has remained at low levels even in countries where the constraints on higher spending—such as revenue-to-GDP ratios—have eased. For example, between 2000 and 2007, revenue-to-GDP ratios rose in the emerging economies in the sample (excluding Turkey) by 3½ percentage points of GDP, while public health outlays rose by about ½ percentage point. Developing economies allocated half as much of their spending to health as they allocated to education during the 1987–2007 period (Arze del Granado, Gupta, and Hajdenberg, 2010). By contrast, in advanced economies the shares have been approximately equal. Demand-side factors have also kept both total spending and public health spending low, including lower per capita incomes and differences in demographics, such as lower age-dependency ratios. Additionally, many emerging economies have not yet completed an epidemiological transition—from infectious to chronic diseases such as cancer, diabetes, and heart disease—that typically occurs with economic development and raises health care costs.[6]

---

[5]Public health spending in low-income countries, at 2 percent of GDP, is broadly similar to that in emerging economies.

[6]The number of premature deaths from noncommunicable diseases (NCDs) is increasing rapidly. NCDs are the biggest cause of death worldwide. In September 2011, the UN General Assembly held a High-Level Summit to discuss for the first time the prevention and control of NCDs.

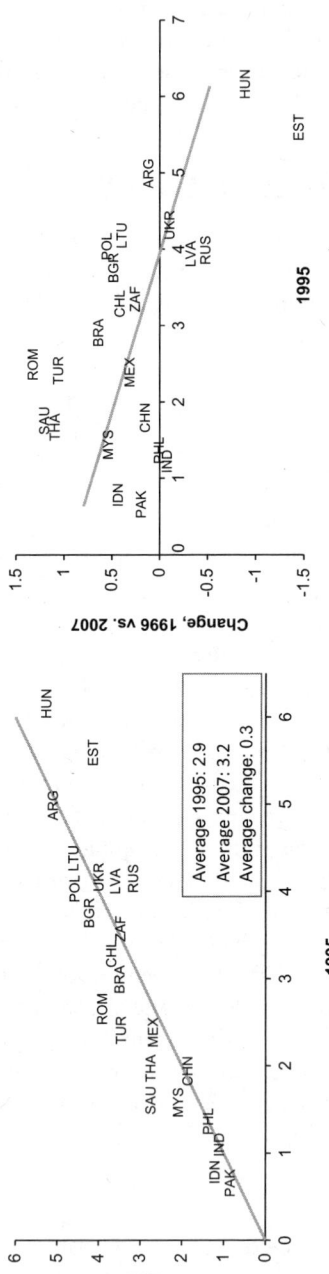

**Figure 2.3** Public Health Spending in Emerging Economies, 1995 versus 2007 (Percent of GDP)

Sources: World Health Organization; and IMF staff estimates.

Note: Averages are unweighted. ARG = Argentina; BGR = Bulgaria; BRA = Brazil; CHL = Chile; CHN = China; EST = Estonia; HUN = Hungary; IDN = Indonesia; IND = India; LTU = Lithuania; LVA = Latvia; MEX = Mexico; MYS = Malaysia; PAK = Pakistan; PHL = Philippines; POL = Poland; ROM = Romania; RUS = Russian Federation; SAU = Saudi Arabia; THA = Thailand; TUR = Turkey; UKR = Ukraine; ZAF = South Africa.

# HEALTH OUTCOMES AND HEALTH SYSTEM EFFICIENCY

Health outcomes vary widely in both advanced and emerging economies. In advanced economies, life expectancy (at birth) averages about 80 years but ranges from a low of 74 years in the Slovak Republic to 83 years in Japan (Joumard, Andre, and Nicq, 2010). The ranking of advanced economies on other health indicators related to longevity, such as life expectancy at age 65 and health-adjusted life expectancy, is similar to that for life expectancy at birth. Infant mortality rates also vary, ranging from a low of three (deaths per thousand) or less in Iceland, Luxembourg, and Sweden to more than five in Canada, the Slovak Republic, and the United States. At 71 years, average life expectancy in emerging economies is about nine years lower than in advanced economies. Among emerging economies, both life expectancy and infant mortality rates are more favorable in emerging Europe, on average, than in other regions. Life expectancy ranges from 52 years in South Africa to 79 years in Chile.

Inefficiencies in public health spending are large. While higher spending can help, improving the efficiency of these outlays is even more critical for improving health outcomes. This can be illustrated by examining the gains from reducing the "efficiency gap" for countries, which provides an estimate of the difference between the life expectancy they achieve—taking account also of the effects of socioeconomic and lifestyle factors—and that of the best-performing country at similar levels of spending.[7] Cutting the efficiency gap of member countries of the Organization for Economic Cooperation and Development (OECD) in half, for example, would increase life expectancy by over one year. Achieving this same gain in life expectancy through higher spending, by contrast, would require a spending increase of over 30 percent. Countries where spending has been identified as the most efficient include Australia, the Republic of Korea, and Switzerland, while Hungary, the Slovak Republic, and the United States are among the least efficient. In developing and emerging countries, health spending is also an important determinant of health outcomes (Baldacci and others, 2008). As in the advanced economies, the efficiency of their outlays varies widely (Gupta and Verhoeven, 2001; Gupta and others, 2008), again suggesting ample room to improve health outcomes without raising spending.

# CONCLUSION

Total health spending in advanced economies has risen by 6 percentage points of GDP since 1970, with two-thirds of the increase due to higher public sector

---

[7]See Appendix 2.2 for a discussion of approaches to measuring the efficiency of health spending. The efficiency results cited here from Joumard, Andre, and Nicq (2010) control for the effects of these nonspending inputs on life expectancy. Still, the limitations of this analysis should be kept in mind, since health spending that leads to improvements in the quality of life but does not affect life expectancy will be measured as inefficient under this approach.

Although life expectancy is only one dimension of health status, it is highly correlated with other widely used health status indicators (Joumard, Andre, and Nicq, 2010).

spending. Public spending increases have been propelled by rising incomes, technology, aging, and public health policies. These outlays experienced distinct periods of accelerated growth, followed by episodes of cost containment. Public spending increases have been more modest in emerging economies than in advanced economies, rising by 1 percentage point of GDP since 1970. This has reflected the lower priority given to health spending relative to other spending needs. There has been some convergence in public health spending ratios in advanced economies over the past several decades, while emerging markets' spending shares do not indicate such a pattern.

Inefficiencies in public health spending are large. This suggests that considerable improvements in health outcomes are possible by tackling these inefficiencies in both advanced and emerging economies.

## APPENDIX 2.1. DATA SOURCES

The data for advanced economies are drawn from the OECD's Health Database. For most countries, data on health expenditure (total, public, and private), as a percentage of GDP and in real per capita terms, are available. The availability of data in earlier years varies, and for most countries, the most complete set of data is available for 2008. The OECD data are subject to a number of structural breaks. To address these and allow for a consistent comparison of spending trends over time, we follow the procedure of Joumard and others (2008). For a year in which a structural break is identified, the average growth rate of real spending over the preceding five years is used to project spending growth in that year.[8] In effect, this predicts spending in the year of the break, based on trend spending increases. The series are interpolated backward in time, based on the growth of spending in the unadjusted series. These adjusted data are used for all charts and tables showing developments in spending over time.

Appendix Table 2.1 provides summary statistics for public health spending for selected OECD countries between 1960 and 2008, unadjusted for these structural breaks. In some cases, data from the adjacent year were used when data were not available. For 1970, the data for Australia refer to 1969 and for the Netherlands to 1972. For the Netherlands, current public spending is used for data from 2003 onward, and for Belgium the entire series refers to current (rather than total) public health spending. Appendix Table 2.2 presents the data adjusting for the structural breaks. These data are also used in the figures and charts in the text. In both tables, Columns 2–8 show public health spending as a share of GDP for selected years, and columns 9–12 in Appendix Table 2.2 show the increase in this ratio over selected years to 2008. For the emerging economies,

---

[8]In the case of Germany, no adjustment was made for the series break in 1991. In France, to address the large structural break in 1995, spending in that year, as a share of GDP, was set equal to the level of 1996. The series was then adjusted in earlier years to be consistent with the new, higher level.

**APPENDIX TABLE 2.1**

### Unadjusted Public Expenditure on Health: Advanced Economies, 1960–2008 (Percent of GDP, unadjusted for structural breaks)

| | 1960 | 1970 | 1980 | 1990 | 2000 | 2007 | 2008 |
|---|---|---|---|---|---|---|---|
| Australia | 1.8 | 2.3 | 3.8 | 4.4 | 5.4 | 5.7 | ... |
| Austria | 3.0 | 3.3 | 5.1 | 6.1 | 7.6 | 7.9 | 8.1 |
| Belgium | ... | ... | ... | 5.7 | 6.1 | 7.3 | 7.4 |
| Canada | 2.3 | 4.8 | 5.3 | 6.6 | 6.2 | 7.1 | 7.3 |
| Czech Republic | ... | ... | ... | 4.6 | 5.9 | 5.8 | 5.9 |
| Denmark | ... | 6.6 | 7.9 | 6.9 | 6.8 | 8.2 | ... |
| Finland | 2.1 | 4.1 | 5.0 | 6.3 | 5.1 | 6.1 | 6.2 |
| France | 2.4 | 4.1 | 5.6 | 6.4 | 8.0 | 8.6 | 8.7 |
| Germany | ... | 4.4 | 6.6 | 6.3 | 8.2 | 8.0 | 8.1 |
| Greece | ... | 2.3 | 3.3 | 3.5 | 4.7 | 5.8 | ... |
| Iceland | 2.0 | 3.1 | 5.5 | 6.8 | 7.7 | 7.5 | 7.6 |
| Ireland | 2.8 | 4.1 | 6.8 | 4.4 | 4.6 | 5.8 | 6.7 |
| Italy | ... | ... | ... | 6.1 | 5.8 | 6.6 | 7.0 |
| Japan | 1.8 | 3.2 | 4.7 | 4.6 | 6.2 | 6.6 | ... |
| Korea, Republic of | ... | ... | 0.8 | 1.5 | 2.2 | 3.5 | 3.6 |
| Luxembourg | ... | 2.8 | 4.8 | 5.0 | 5.2 | 6.6 | ... |
| Netherlands | ... | 4.1 | 5.1 | 5.4 | 5.0 | 7.3 | 7.4 |
| New Zealand | ... | 4.2 | 5.2 | 5.7 | 6.0 | 7.2 | 7.9 |
| Norway | 2.2 | 4.0 | 5.9 | 6.3 | 6.9 | 7.5 | 7.2 |
| Portugal | ... | 1.5 | 3.4 | 3.8 | 6.4 | 7.1 | ... |
| Slovak Republic | ... | ... | ... | ... | 4.9 | 5.2 | 5.4 |
| Slovenia | ... | ... | ... | ... | 6.1 | 5.6 | 6.0 |
| Spain | 0.9 | 2.3 | 4.2 | 5.1 | 5.2 | 6.1 | 6.5 |
| Sweden | ... | 5.8 | 8.2 | 7.4 | 7.0 | 7.4 | 7.7 |
| Switzerland | ... | ... | ... | 4.3 | 5.6 | 6.3 | 6.3 |
| United Kingdom | 3.3 | 3.9 | 5.0 | 4.9 | 5.6 | 6.9 | 7.2 |
| United States | 1.2 | 2.6 | 3.7 | 4.8 | 5.8 | 7.1 | 7.4 |
| | | | | | | | |
| Average | | | | | | | |
| Weighted | 1.7 | 3.3 | 4.6 | 5.2 | 6.1 | 6.9 | 7.3 |
| Unweighted | 2.2 | 3.7 | 5.0 | 5.3 | 5.9 | 6.7 | 6.9 |

Sources: Organization for Economic Cooperation and Development, OECD Health Data; and IMF staff estimates.
Note: See discussion in text for description of data for 1970. For Luxembourg and Portugal data, 2007 refers to 2006.

public expenditure data are derived from the World Health Organization (WHO). Ratios to GDP are calculated on the basis of data from the International Monetary Fund's World Economic Outlook database. For data from 1970 to 1994, public health spending from Sivard (various years) as a share of GDP was used. It was assumed that private spending was a constant share of total spending over the 1970–95 period.

# APPENDIX 2.2. MEASURING THE EFFICIENCY OF PUBLIC HEALTH SPENDING

Efficiency studies provide important insights for health care reform. These studies generally find that there are substantial inefficiencies in many countries, as measured by the relationship between spending inputs and health outcomes. This

**APPENDIX TABLE 2.2**

## Adjusted Public Expenditure on Health: Advanced Economies, 1960–2008 (Percent of GDP, adjusted for structural breaks)

| | 1960 | 1970 | 1980 | 1990 | 2000 | 2007 | 2008 | Changes (Percentage points)[a] | | | |
|---|---|---|---|---|---|---|---|---|---|---|---|
| | | | | | | | | 1960–2008 | 1970–2008 | 1980–2008 | 1990–2008 |
| Australia | 1.8 | 3.0 | 3.8 | 4.4 | 5.4 | 5.7 | ... | 3.9 | 2.7 | 2.0 | 1.3 |
| Austria | 3.5 | 3.9 | 6.1 | 6.1 | 7.6 | 7.9 | 8.1 | 4.5 | 4.2 | 2.0 | 1.9 |
| Belgium | ... | ... | ... | 6.2 | 6.5 | 7.3 | 7.4 | ... | ... | ... | 1.3 |
| Canada | 2.4 | 4.9 | 5.1 | 6.3 | 6.2 | 7.1 | 7.3 | 4.9 | 2.4 | 2.2 | 0.9 |
| Czech Republic | ... | ... | ... | 3.9 | 5.9 | 5.8 | 5.9 | ... | ... | ... | 1.9 |
| Denmark | ... | 6.9 | 8.1 | 7.2 | 7.1 | 8.2 | ... | ... | 1.4 | 0.1 | 1.1 |
| Finland | 1.7 | 3.3 | 4.1 | 5.1 | 5.1 | 6.1 | 6.2 | 4.5 | 2.9 | 2.2 | 1.1 |
| France | 2.8 | 4.7 | 6.5 | 7.4 | 8.0 | 8.6 | 8.7 | 5.9 | 4.0 | 2.2 | 1.3 |
| Germany | ... | 4.4 | 6.6 | 6.3 | 8.2 | 8.0 | 8.1 | ... | 3.7 | 1.5 | 1.8 |
| Greece | ... | 2.3 | 3.3 | 3.5 | 4.7 | 5.8 | ... | ... | 3.5 | 2.6 | 2.3 |
| Iceland | 2.0 | 2.8 | 5.1 | 6.2 | 7.1 | 7.5 | 7.6 | 5.5 | 4.7 | 2.5 | 1.3 |
| Ireland | 3.0 | 4.5 | 6.7 | 4.4 | 4.6 | 5.8 | 6.7 | 3.7 | 2.2 | 0.0 | 2.4 |
| Italy | ... | ... | ... | 6.1 | 5.8 | 6.6 | 7.0 | ... | ... | ... | 0.9 |
| Japan | 1.8 | 3.3 | 4.8 | 4.7 | 6.2 | 6.6 | ... | 4.8 | 3.4 | 1.9 | 1.9 |
| Korea, Rep. of | ... | ... | 0.8 | 1.5 | 2.2 | 3.5 | 3.6 | ... | ... | 2.8 | 2.1 |
| Luxembourg | ... | 2.6 | 4.6 | 4.7 | 5.2 | 6.6 | ... | ... | ... | ... | ... |
| Netherlands | ... | 4.2 | 5.3 | 5.5 | 5.2 | 7.3 | 7.4 | ... | 3.2 | 2.2 | 1.9 |
| New Zealand | ... | 4.2 | 5.2 | 5.7 | 6.0 | 7.2 | 7.9 | ... | 3.7 | 2.7 | 2.2 |
| Norway | 2.4 | 4.3 | 6.3 | 6.7 | 6.9 | 7.5 | 7.2 | 4.8 | 2.9 | 0.9 | 0.4 |
| Portugal | ... | 1.6 | 3.7 | 4.1 | 6.4 | 7.1 | ... | ... | 5.6 | 3.4 | 3.0 |
| Slovak Republic | ... | ... | ... | ... | 4.9 | 5.2 | 5.4 | ... | ... | ... | ... |
| Slovenia | ... | ... | ... | ... | 6.1 | 5.6 | 6.0 | ... | ... | ... | ... |
| Spain | 1.0 | 2.6 | 4.8 | 5.9 | 5.8 | 6.1 | 6.5 | 5.5 | 3.9 | 1.7 | 0.6 |
| Sweden | ... | 5.9 | 8.3 | 7.5 | 7.2 | 7.4 | 7.7 | ... | 1.8 | -0.7 | 0.2 |
| Switzerland | ... | ... | ... | 4.0 | 5.6 | 6.3 | 6.3 | ... | ... | ... | 2.3 |
| United Kingdom | 3.1 | 3.6 | 4.6 | 4.6 | 5.6 | 6.9 | 7.2 | 4.1 | 3.5 | 2.5 | 2.6 |
| United States | 1.2 | 2.6 | 3.7 | 4.8 | 5.8 | 7.1 | 7.4 | 6.2 | 4.9 | 3.8 | 2.7 |
| Average | | | | | | | | | | | |
| Weighted | 1.7 | 3.4 | 4.7 | 5.2 | 6.1 | 7.0 | 7.3 | 5.6 | 4.1 | 2.8 | 2.1 |
| Unweighted | 2.2 | 3.8 | 5.1 | 5.3 | 6.0 | 6.7 | 6.9 | 4.9 | 3.4 | 1.9 | 1.6 |

Sources: Organization for Economic Cooperation and Development, OECD Health Data; and IMF staff estimates.
Note: See text for a description of the methodology for adjusting for structural breaks and for a description of the data for 1970. For Luxembourg and Portugal data, 2007 refers to 2006. The averages for given years (e.g., 1960, 1970) reflect different sample sizes, and comparisons should thus be made with caution.
[a]For comparisons of changes up to 2008, the most recent year with available data is used (in some cases, 2007).

implies that achieving better health outcomes is possible by addressing these inefficiencies, even if spending does not increase.

## Overview of Different Approaches

### Nonparametric methods

Under a nonparametric technique such as data envelopment analysis (DEA), the first step in assessing efficiency is to create a production frontier that links spending inputs and health outcomes (e.g., public health spending per capita and life expectancy). The production frontier indicates the combinations of spending inputs and

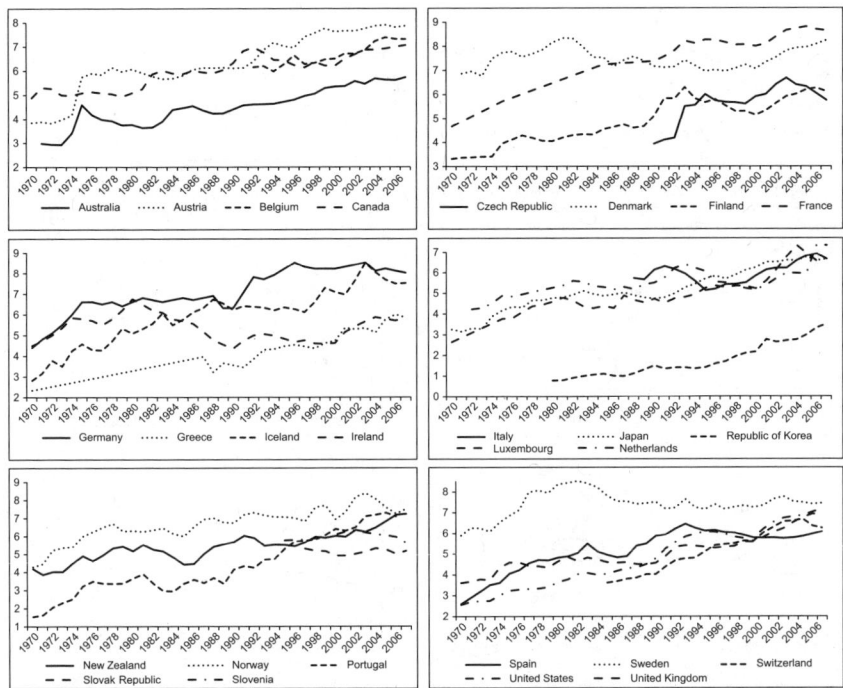

**Appendix Figure 2.1** Public Health Spending in Advanced Economies (Percent of GDP, adjusted for structural breaks)
Sources: Organization for Economic Cooperation and Development, OECD Health Data; and IMF staff estimates.

outputs that are equally efficient. The distance of countries from the frontier is the measure of their inefficiency. Free disposable hull (FDH) analysis is similar to DEA but less restrictive (see Gupta and Verhoeven, 2001, for further discussion).

The major advantage of nonparametric techniques is that no assumption is made about the functional form of the relationship between spending inputs and outputs. The drawback is that the frontier is formed by the outliers that establish "best practices," with a large risk of measurement error.

## Parametric methods

Under a regression (REG) approach, researchers typically take advantage of the panel structure of data (e.g., WHO or OECD health data) to utilize a large number of observations (e.g., Evans and others, 2000; WHO, 2000). This approach allows for the inclusion of a large number of explanatory variables. Efficiency is typically measured in terms of the size of the country fixed effect in the equation. Under stochastic frontier analysis (SFA), regression analysis is used to estimate the production frontier, and the efficiency of spending is measured using the residuals from the estimated equation. The disadvantage of these techniques is that a functional form of the relationship between spending inputs and outputs must be assumed.

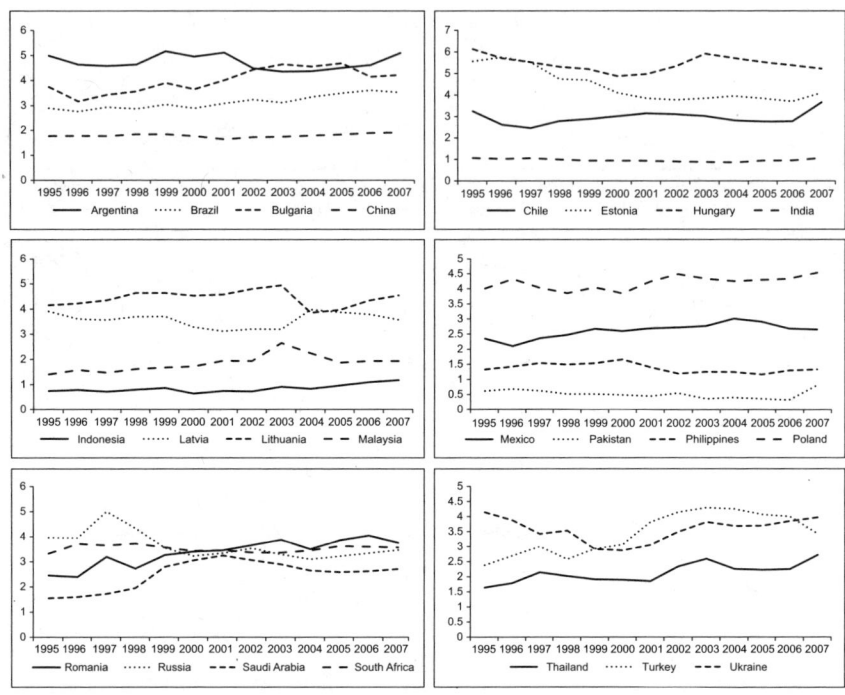

**Appendix Figure 2.2** Public Health Spending in Emerging Economies (Percent of GDP)
Sources: World Health Organization; and IMF staff estimates.

## Empirical Findings

### Nonparametric methods

Joumard and others (2008) and Joumard, Andre, and Nicq (2010) take into account three variables as inputs in explaining cross-country differences in health status in the OECD: health care spending per capita, a proxy for economic status (derived from the Program for International Student Assessment education survey), and a lifestyle variable. The main findings are that population health status could be improved significantly in most OECD countries by raising the efficiency of spending, and that increasing per capita health spending would have smaller effects on life expectancy than improvements in efficiency.

A large number of studies, including those by staff in the IMF's Fiscal Affairs Department, have used DEA and FDH to evaluate the efficiency of education and health care expenditure (Gupta and Verhoeven, 2001; Hauner, 2007; Mattina and Gunnarsson, 2007; Verhoeven, Gunnarsson and Carcillo, 2007; and Gupta and others, 2008). These studies all conclude that there is considerable inefficiency in health spending in many countries.

### Parametric methods

Joumard and others (2008) and Joumard, Andre, and Nicq (2010) estimate a panel regression and find that health care spending, lifestyle, and socioeconomic factors are all important determinants of population health status. Importantly, the ranking of countries (in terms of efficiency) is similar to that obtained using DEA. Evans and others (2000) and WHO (2000) estimate a fixed-effects model by using data from 191 countries from 1993 to 1997. Hollingsworth and Wildman (2003) reexamine WHO's study by using both a time-variant fixed-effects model and DEA. They find that non-OECD countries show more variation in efficiency than OECD countries. Using the same WHO data, Self and Grabowski (2003) find that the comparatively higher life expectancy in wealthier countries is not a result of greater public health expenditures. In middle-income and less-developed countries, however, there is some evidence that public spending does improve health outcomes. Hollingsworth and Wildman (2003) implement an SFA and compare its results with DEA and REG. They find a high degree of correlation in efficiency measures across methods, as in Joumard and others (2008) and Joumard, Andre, and Nicq (2010).

## REFERENCES

Arze del Granado, J., S. Gupta, and A. Hajdenberg, 2010, "Is Social Spending Procyclical?" IMF Working Paper No. 10/234 (Washington: International Monetary Fund).

Baldacci, E., G. Callegari, D. Coady, D. Ding, M. Kumar, P. Tommasino, and J. Woo, 2010, "Public Expenditures on Social Programs and Household Consumption in China," IMF Working Paper No. 10/69 (Washington: International Monetary Fund).

Baldacci, E., B. Clements, S. Gupta, and Q. Cui, 2008, "Social Spending, Human Capital, and Growth in Developing Countries," *World Development*, Vol. 36, No. 8, pp. 1317–41.

Cutler, D., and M. McClellan, 2001, "Is Technological Change in Medicine Worth It?" *Health Affairs*, Vol. 20, No. 5, pp. 11–29.

Evans, D. B., A. Tandon, C. Murray, and J. Lauer, 2000, "The Comparative Efficiency of National Health Systems in Producing Health: An Analysis of 191 Countries," Global Program on Evidence for Health Policy (GPE) Discussion Paper No. 29 (Geneva: World Health Organization).

Gupta, S., G. Schwartz, S. Tareq, R. Allen, I. Adenauer, K. Fletcher, and D. Last, 2008, *Fiscal Management of Scaled-Up Aid* (Washington: International Monetary Fund).

Gupta, S., and M. Verhoeven, 2001, "The Efficiency of Government Expenditures: Experiences from Africa," *Journal of Policy Modeling*, Vol. 23, pp. 433–67.

Hauner, D., 2007, "Benchmarking the Efficiency of Public Expenditure in the Russian Federation," IMF Working Paper No. 07/246 (Washington: International Monetary Fund).

Hollingsworth, B., and J. Wildman, 2003, "The Efficiency of Health Production: Re-estimating the WHO Panel Data Using Parametric and Non-parametric Approaches to Provide Additional Information," *Economics of Health Care Systems*, Vol. 12, pp. 493–504.

International Monetary Fund (IMF), 2010, *From Stimulus to Consolidation: Revenue and Expenditure Policies in Advanced and Emerging Economies*, IMF Departmental Paper (Washington).

Joumard, I., C. Andre, and C. Nicq, 2010, "Health Care Systems: Efficiency and Institutions," Economics Department Working Paper No. 769 (Paris: Organization for Economic Cooperation and Development).

Joumard, I., C. Andre, C. Nicq, and O. Chatal, 2008, "Health Status Determinants: Lifestyle, Environment, Health Care Resources and Efficiency," Economics Department Working Paper No. 627 (Paris: Organization for Economic Cooperation and Development).

Mattina, T., and V. Gunnarsson, 2007, "Budget Rigidity and Expenditure Efficiency in Slovenia," IMF Working Paper No. 07/131 (Washington: International Monetary Fund).

Pomp, M., and S. Vujic, 2008, "Rising Health Spending, New Medical Technology, and the Baumol Effect," Discussion Paper No. 115 (The Hague: CPB [Netherlands Bureau for Economic Policy Analysis]).

Self, S., and R. Grabowski, 2003, "How Effective Is Public Health Expenditure in Improving Overall Health? A Cross-Country Analysis," *Applied Economics*, Vol. 7, pp. 835–45.

Sivard, R., various years, *World Military and Social Expenditures* (Leesburg, VA: WMSE Publications).

Smith, S., J. Newhouse, and M. Freeland, 2009, "Income, Insurance, and Technology: Why Does Health Spending Outpace Economic Growth?" *Health Affairs*, Vol. 28, No. 5, pp. 1276–84.

Verhoeven, M., V. Gunnarsson, and S. Carcillo, 2007, "Education and Health in G-7 Countries: Achieving Better Outcomes with Less Spending," IMF Working Paper No. 07/263 (Washington: International Monetary Fund).

World Health Organization (WHO), 2000, *Health Systems: Improving Performance*, The World Health Report (Geneva).

# CHAPTER 3

# New Projections of Public Health Spending, 2010–50

MAURICIO SOTO, BAOPING SHANG, AND DAVID COADY

Public health spending has been increasing rapidly in advanced economies, but there have been only modest increases in emerging economies in the past decades. Will these trends continue into the future? This chapter provides updated projections of public health spending in advanced and emerging economies, using a methodology that improves upon earlier studies. An appendix describes the methodology used for the projections as well as methodologies used to estimate the effects of reforms that are described in more detail in Chapter 6.

## ADVANCED ECONOMIES

Large increases in public health spending are projected in the advanced economies (Figure 3.1). Public health spending is projected to rise in these countries on average by 3 percentage points of GDP over the next 20 years (Box 3.1 describes the projection methodology). Spending is projected to increase by more than 2 percentage points of GDP in 14 of the 27 advanced economies. About one-third of the increase would be due to the effects of population aging, a slightly higher share than in the past. The remaining two-thirds would be due to excess cost growth, reflecting technological change, income growth, the Baumol effect,[1] and health policies.

The projections suggest that the outlook is grim in the United States, but also in Europe, where the fiscal challenge posed by health spending is sometimes underestimated. In the United States, public health spending is projected to rise by about 5 percentage points of GDP over the next 20 years, the highest of the advanced economies.[2] Spending increases are expected to be driven by continued

---

[1]The Baumol effect refers to the rising unit labor costs in sectors where it is difficult to achieve productivity gains, usually in services. Because salaries rise in these sectors in line with economy-wide averages, while productivity does not, unit labor costs rise in relative terms.

[2]Recent long-term projections by the Congressional Budget Office under the baseline scenario indicate that mandatory federal spending (Medicare and Medicaid) will rise by 3.2 percentage points of

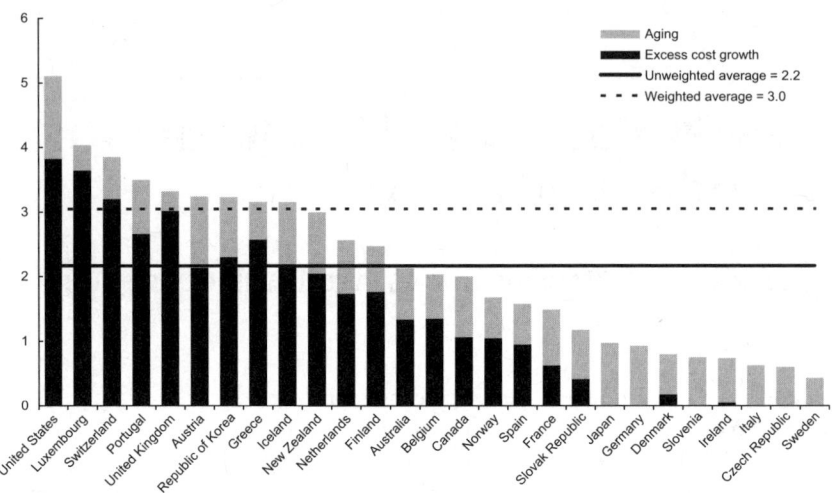

**Figure 3.1** Projected Increases in Public Health Spending in Advanced Economies, 2011–30
(Percent of GDP)

Sources: Organization for Economic Cooperation and Development, OECD Health Data; World Health Organization; and IMF staff estimates.

Note: Excess cost growth is defined as the growth in public health spending in excess of GDP growth after controlling for aging. Weighted averages are based on GDP at purchasing power parity.

high rates of excess cost growth. In Europe, public health spending is also expected to rise substantially, by 2 percentage points of GDP, with spending expected to rise by over 3 percentage points of GDP in seven countries. This stands in marked contrast to the baseline projection of the European Commission's *2009 Ageing Report*, which anticipates that spending will rise by about ¾ percentage point of GDP over the next 20 years (EC and ECP, 2009). This low projected increase reflects a relatively low excess cost growth (about 0.2 percent)—based on the assumption that technology does not increase costs—which would imply a sharp break from past trends (Figure 3.2).[3]

The cumulative fiscal burden of public spending increases will be large. The net present value of the projected increases in public health spending during 2011–30 is 26 percent of today's GDP. This figure rises dramatically—to 98 percent of GDP—when increases over the 2011–50 period are considered, based on

GDP between 2010 and 2030. These projections incorporate the effects of the 2010 health care reform (Box 3.2). Assuming that spending by state governments on Medicaid and nonmandatory federal and state spending (which are not projected by the Congressional Budget Office) would rise in line with mandatory spending, total public health spending would increase by 5.2 percentage points of GDP, which is slightly higher than our model estimates.

[3]The "technology scenario (convergence by 2060)" in *The 2009 Ageing Report* (EC and ECP, 2009, Annex 2) incorporates excess cost growth of about 0.8 percent for all countries and results in a weighted average increase in public health spending of 3 percentage points of GDP over 2010–30 in advanced Europe.

**BOX 3.1**

### Methodology for Public Health Spending Projections

The methodology used for projecting spending ratios for advanced economies improves upon earlier studies by using country-specific estimates of excess cost growth (ECG). The projections are based on an econometric model that explains the growth of real per capita public health spending as a function of the growth of real per capita income, demographic factors, and country-specific effects (Appendix 3.1). This model provides country-specific estimates of ECG (the excess of growth in real per capita health expenditures over the growth in real per capita GDP after controlling for the effect of demographic change). ECG is estimated using 1980–2008 data to reflect the varying success of countries in containing the growth of health spending over the last three decades, which exhibit periods of both accelerated growth and cost containment.[a] More recent years (1995–2008) capture a period of expanding expenditure on both health and nonhealth spending, which may not be representative of longer-term trends. The average ECG arising from this model is about 1.0 percent (Appendix Table 3.1, weighted-average basis), which is comparable to the estimates from previous studies.[b]

The projections reflect the varying success of countries in containing the growth of health spending over the last three decades. The evidence of convergence implies that once convergence has been achieved, spending should decelerate with respect to the convergence period. However, recent trends do not suggest a slowdown in ECG as countries with low spending ratios converge toward the advanced economy mean. Although it is possible that some countries, especially those with initially high spending growth, could have recently introduced reforms to rein in spending growth, this is not supported by the data: ECG has increased, rather than decreased, in more recent periods. Therefore, there is no reason to believe that, absent reforms, the projected ECG—derived from a model in which the convergence term is not included—overstate future spending pressures.[c]

For emerging economies, the projections assume that spending growth will be similar to the average growth in advanced countries over the last three decades. For emerging economies, the short time series of data (1995–2007) resulted in a relatively poor fit of the model and the ECG estimates were judged to be a poor guide of future trends in health spending. The projections are therefore based on a common ECG of 1.0 percent across all countries. This is consistent with the assumption that excess cost growth in these countries will follow the average level observed in advanced economies during 1980–2008. It is also broadly consistent with the average excess growth observed for emerging economies in the raw data (Appendix Table 3.2). The projections incorporate differences across countries in spending by age group, as well as expected changes in the age structure of the population.

---

[a] Since the starting point was set at 1980—when most advanced countries had achieved nearly universal insurance—increases in coverage would not play a major role in these estimates.

[b] For three countries (Norway, Switzerland, and the United States), using more recent data produces slightly lower estimates of ECG, which are incorporated in the projections. See Appendix 3.1 for a description of methodology.

[c] In any case, ECG estimates using a model that includes the convergence term do not differ much from those excluding the convergence term.

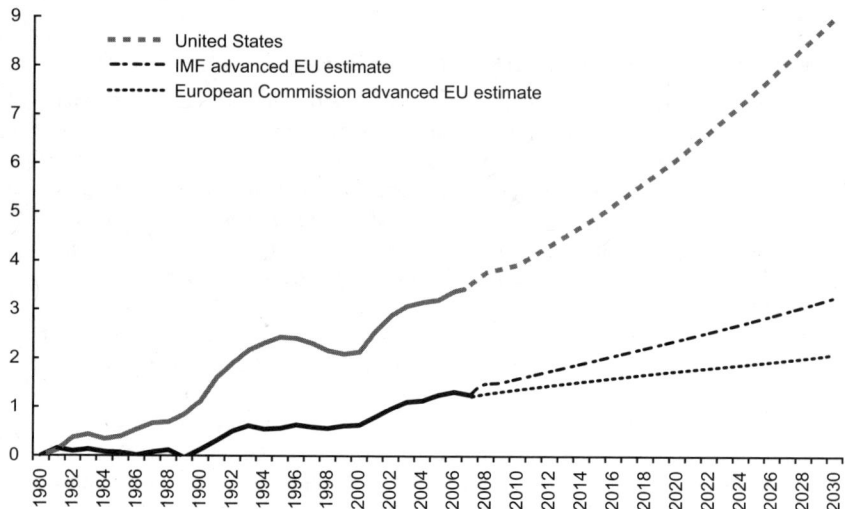

**Figure 3.2**  Actual and Projected Increases in Public Health Spending in the United States and Advanced Europe, 1980–2030 (Percent of GDP)
Sources: European Commission; and IMF staff estimates.
Note: European Commission estimates are based on Organization for Economic Cooperation and Development health spending data for 2008 and changes in the baseline scenario in the European Commission's *2009 Ageing Report* (EC and EPC, 2009).

the staff's longer-term projection of a spending increase of 6½ percentage points of GDP over this period (Appendix Table 3.3).[4]

Recent health care reforms in most countries are unlikely to alter long-term public health spending trends. In the United States, a sweeping reform expanding coverage was introduced and is expected to reduce the budget deficit primarily because of higher payroll and excise taxes on health. The envisaged expenditure savings, however, are small and remain highly uncertain (Box 3.2). In Europe, fiscal adjustment plans affecting general government employment and compensation could have an effect on health spending in the near term, but their long-term effect on excess cost growth is uncertain. Recent reforms have also addressed spending on pharmaceuticals, which constitutes about 15 percent of public health spending. In the United Kingdom, a broader effort to contain spending increases is envisaged, with real health spending budgeted to rise by less than ½ percentage point over the next four years as part of the government's fiscal adjustment efforts. In Germany, health reforms include the reversal of the reduced health care contribution which was approved in November 2010, but spending reductions are expected to be small (0.1 percentage point of GDP). In any case, these reforms in advanced economies, including those being

---

[4]The estimates assume a discount rate of 1 percent.

**BOX 3.2**

### *Recent Health Care Reforms in the Advanced Economies*

The 2010 health care reform in the United States significantly expands health insurance coverage, but its effect on long-term trends in spending is uncertain. Coverage is expected to rise by 11 percentage points to reach 94 percent of the population by 2019. The expansion will be achieved by raising limits on Medicaid eligibility to 133 percent of the poverty line and providing tax breaks and subsidies to individuals between 133 and 400 percent of the poverty line who purchase insurance. The law also forbids insurance companies to deny coverage for preexisting conditions.

The U.S. legislation includes measures for both cost containment and revenue increases, which the Congressional Budget Office projects will result in a reduction of the budget deficit. Congressional Budget Office projections suggest that spending in 2030 would be 0.2 percent of GDP lower than forecast earlier on account of the reforms. Medicare spending growth would be slower, owing to savings from cuts in payments to Medicare health care providers. There is considerable uncertainty regarding the savings from this reform, however, as previous efforts to curtail these payments have been overridden by Congress. Public health spending would rise under the reform with the expansion of eligibility for Medicaid and provision of subsidies to purchase insurance. The reform also includes an increase in payroll taxes for Medicare hospital insurance and introduces an excise tax on expensive employer-provided health plans. Taking into account these revenue measures, the health care reform is expected to reduce the budget deficit by an average of 0.1 percent of GDP per year during 2010–19 and ½ percentage point of GDP per year over 2020–29.[a]

Broader-based efforts to contain spending or raise health care contributions have been implemented in the United Kingdom and Germany, while reductions in employment and compensation across the public sector will also affect health spending in a number of countries. In the United Kingdom, the government has committed to limiting the growth of real health spending to a cumulative ½ percentage point in 2011–15, which is projected to reduce spending by ¾ percentage point of GDP by 2015. Consideration is also being given to a plan to reduce administrative costs by 45 percent, with the savings reinvested in patient care. In Germany, the reform approved by parliament in November 2010 includes the reversal of the reduced health care contribution for stimulus purposes in 2011. The reform aims at saving 0.4 percent of GDP. Fiscal adjustment efforts affecting the government wage bill across all sectors (e.g., in Ireland, Italy, Portugal, and Spain) will also help contain health spending in the near term.

Recent cost containment efforts in Europe have also addressed spending on pharmaceuticals, but this is unlikely to have a major effect on the long-term outlook for spending. Ireland and the United Kingdom have taken steps to effectively reduce the prices paid for pharmaceuticals. Prescription practices were tightened in France, Germany, and Ireland, while reimbursement methods were altered in Germany, Italy, and Ireland. These developments are expected to help reduce spending in the short term, for example with savings of 0.5 percent of GDP in Ireland. They are unlikely to have a major effect on spending over the longer term, especially given the modest share of pharmaceutical outlays in total public health spending (about 15 percent in the OECD).

---

[a] See IMF (2010a, 2010b) for further details on the effect of separate components of the reform.

undertaken in Greece as part of its fiscal adjustment program, have not been incorporated into the projections.

## EMERGING ECONOMIES

Public health spending in emerging economies is projected to rise by 1 percentage point of GDP over the next 20 years, one-third of the increase projected for the advanced economies (Figure 3.3). This is consistent with the assumption that excess cost growth in these countries will follow the average level observed in advanced economies over 1980–2008, and is also consistent with the lower initial health expenditure ratios in emerging economies. In most countries, the increase would range between ½ and 1½ percentage points of GDP. Aging would account for an increase of about ½ percentage point of GDP in this spending and would have the largest effect on spending in Brazil, Chile, and Poland.

Spending pressures in emerging Europe and Latin America are expected to be higher than in emerging Asia. On average, spending would rise by 1½ percentage points of GDP in both emerging Europe and Latin America, with all countries projected to raise spending by at least 1 percentage point of GDP. In emerging Asia, spending increases would be about half this amount, reflecting the low initial spending levels in these countries. The modest increases projected across all regions suggest that rising health spending is unlikely to pose a heavy fiscal

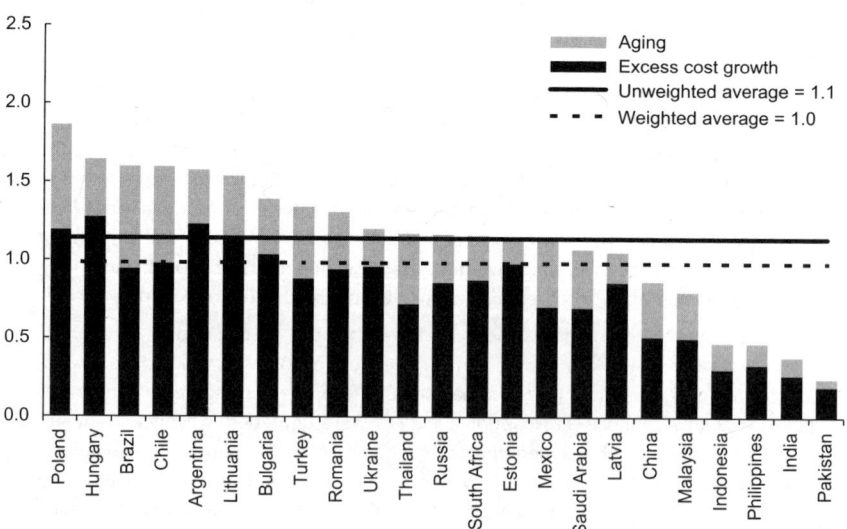

**Figure 3.3** Projected Increases in Public Health Spending in Emerging Economies, 2011–30 (Percent of GDP)
Sources: Organization for Economic Cooperation and Development, OECD Health Data; World Health Organization; and IMF staff estimates.
Note: Excess cost growth is defined as the growth in public health spending in excess of GDP growth after controlling for the effect of aging. Weighted averages are based on GDP at purchasing power parity.

burden in emerging economies over the next 20 years, which is consistent with the view that the primary challenge for these countries is to improve the efficiency of this spending.

## CONCLUSION

Public health spending in advanced economies is projected to rise on average by 3 percentage points of GDP over the next 20 years. About one-third of the increase would be due to the effects of population aging, a slightly higher share than in the past. The remaining two-thirds would be due to excess cost growth, reflecting technological change, income growth, the Baumol effect, and health policies. Spending increases will be especially sharp in the United States, but will also be substantial in Europe. Recent health care reforms in most countries are unlikely to alter long-term public health spending trends. Public health spending in emerging economies is projected to rise by 1 percentage point of GDP over the next 20 years, one-third of the increase projected for the advanced economies. This reflects, in part, the lower initial health expenditure ratios in emerging economies. The large projected increase in spending in advanced economies has made health reform an important priority for fiscal policy.

## APPENDIX 3.1. ECONOMETRIC ESTIMATION OF EXCESS COST GROWTH

This appendix sets out the methodology adopted in the chapter to estimate the excess cost growth of public health expenditures and explains how the results are used in the projections.[5]

### Excess Cost Growth

Excess cost growth (ECG) is defined as the excess of growth in real per capita health expenditures over the growth in real per capita GDP after controlling for the effect of demographic change.

### The Econometric Model

The key determinants of health expenditures are income levels, demographic composition, technology, and other factors that may vary across countries (e.g., climate or diet). The health system adopted in each country determines how these

---

[5]The authors are grateful to Lawrence Kotlikoff for helpful comments on an earlier draft of this appendix.

factors translate into public health expenditures. Reflecting data limitations, the model specification takes the following form:

$$\log\left(\frac{h_{i,t+1}}{h_{i,t}}\right) = \beta_0 + \beta_1 \log\left(\frac{g_{i,t+1}}{g_{i,t}}\right) + \beta_2 \log\left(\frac{x_{i,t+1}}{x_{i,t}}\right) + \beta_{3,i}\mu_i + \varepsilon_{i,t} \quad (3.1)$$

where $h_{i,t}$ denotes real per capita public health spending for country $i$ in year $t$; $g_{i,t}$ denotes the corresponding real per capita GDP; $x_{i,t}$ denotes demographic composition; $\mu_i$ denotes country fixed effects; and $\varepsilon_{i,t}$ is a random error term. This model assumes that public health spending growth (in log terms) is a function of a common growth rate across all countries, GDP growth rate (in log terms), change in demographic composition (in log terms), and a country-specific growth rate.[6] The common growth rate and the country-specific growth rate capture the effects of factors other than income and demographics, such as technology, the Baumol effect, and health policies and institutional settings, to the extent that they do not vary over time. Country-specific ECG can then be expressed as the following (holding demographic composition constant over time):

$$ECG_i = \hat{\beta}_0 + \hat{\beta}_{3i} + (\hat{\beta}_1 - 1)(GDP\ Growth_i) \quad (3.2)$$

Here $\hat{\beta}_0$, $\hat{\beta}_{3i}$, and $\hat{\beta}_1$ are estimates from equation (3.1). Under this specification, a country's ECG is a function of a common spending growth factor, a country-specific spending growth factor, a common income elasticity, and the country's GDP growth rate.

For sensitivity analysis, ECG is also estimated under the ordinary least squares (OLS) specification (without the country fixed effects):

$$\log\left(\frac{h_{i,t+1}}{h_{i,t}}\right) = \alpha_0 + \alpha_1 \log\left(\frac{g_{i,t+1}}{g_{i,t}}\right) + \alpha_2 \log\left(\frac{x_{i,t+1}}{x_{i,t}}\right) + \varepsilon_{i,t} \quad (3.3)$$

The country-specific ECG is calculated as the following:

$$ECG_i = \hat{\alpha}_0 + \frac{1}{T_i}\sum_{t=1}^{T_i} \hat{\varepsilon}_{i,t} + (\hat{\alpha}_1 - 1)(GDP\ Growth_i) \quad (3.4)$$

Here $T_i$ denotes the number of years of data available for country $i$ and $\hat{\varepsilon}_{i,t}$ denotes the residual for country $i$ in time period $t$. After estimating equation (3.3), two steps need to be taken to obtain country-specific ECG: first, calculate the residuals for each observation, and then calculate the average residual for each country for all the time periods (the second term in equation (3.4)).

The fixed-effects and OLS models are estimated separately for advanced economies and emerging economies. The data for advanced economies are taken from the Organization for Economic Cooperation and Development

---

[6] It can be shown that the specification in growth is the first-difference of the following model in levels, which is typically used in the literature, for example, in Smith, Newhouse, and Freeland (2009):

$$\log(h_{i,t}) = \beta_c + \beta_1 \log(g_{i,t}) + \beta_2 \log(x_{i,t}) + \beta_0 t + \beta_{\mu,i}\mu_i + \beta_{3,i}\mu_i t + \varepsilon_{i,t}^*$$

(OECD), while the data for emerging economies are taken from the OECD and World Health Organization (WHO). To address the structural breaks in the OECD data, years with structural breaks have been excluded from the regression analysis.

## Comparison with Earlier Methodologies

The methodology builds on best practice in the literature. Consistent with previous studies, the full panel is used along with common assumptions about some key relationships across countries (e.g., demographics and income). Using pooled data is likely to be superior to country-specific regressions owing to data limitations—only recent data are available for certain countries (Herwartz and Theilen, 2002). Although the focus of the literature has typically been on expenditure levels, here the empirical analysis focuses on first-differences (i.e., on expenditure growth).[7] The choice of the regressions on first differences rather than on levels offers two advantages.

First, the log series of health spending and GDP levels are generally found to be nonstationary, while the first differences are stationary (Blomqvist and Carter, 1997; Dreger and Reimers, 2005). One approach used in the literature to address stationarity has been to use the levels and provide tests suggesting that the series in levels are cointegrated and that they are linked in the long run (Blomqvist and Carter, 1997; Gerdtham and Löthgren, 2000; Hagist and Kotlikoff, 2005; European Commission, 2009; Baltagi and Moscone, 2010; Przywara, 2010). However, these tests are usually less reliable for short series, such as the ones available for health care spending (Herwartz and Theilen, 2002), and structural breaks in the data might also lower the power of these tests (Clemente and others, 2004).

Second, using growth rates provides an easy interpretation in terms of ECG, which is the main focus of this chapter. For example, the constant can be interpreted as an underlying common ECG across countries, while the inclusion of country fixed effects allows for heterogeneity in ECG across countries. Finally, the income elasticity and demographic terms in this model have the same interpretation as in regressions based on levels, which allows for comparisons with previous literature.

## Excess Cost Growth Estimates for Advanced Economies

For advanced economies, the country-specific ECG econometric estimates are based on 1980–2008 data. To assess the sensitivity of the results to different time periods, the results were also estimated on the basis of a shorter period (1995–2008). Of the 27 advanced economies, only in five countries (Germany, Japan, Norway, Switzerland, and the United States) was ECG lower in the more recent period. This is consistent with the acceleration of public health spending observed in most countries since 2000.

Appendix Table 3.1 presents ECG estimates for advanced economies based on the two time periods, 1980–2008 and 1995–2008. Columns 2 and 3 show the

---

[7]This approach is also used by Barros (1998); Herwartz and Theilen (2002); and Okunade, Karakus, and Okeke (2004).

**APPENDIX TABLE 3.1**

## Excess Cost Growth in Advanced Economies

| Country | Difference between public health spending growth and GDP growth | | Fixed effects | |
|---|---|---|---|---|
| | 1980–2008 | 1995–2008 | 1980–2008 | 1995–2008 |
| Australia | 1.5 | 1.6 | 0.9 | 1.8 |
| Austria | 1.1 | 1.0 | 1.0 | 1.3 |
| Belgium | 1.0 | 1.1 | 0.8 | 1.4 |
| Canada | 1.3 | 0.9 | 0.6 | 1.4 |
| Czech Republic | −0.5 | −1.2 | −0.9 | 0.3 |
| Denmark | 0.0 | 1.3 | 0.1 | 1.2 |
| Finland | 1.5 | 0.7 | 1.1 | 1.7 |
| France | 1.4 | 0.8 | 0.3 | 0.3 |
| Germany | −0.1 | −0.1 | −0.1 | −0.3 |
| Greece | 1.9 | 2.2 | 1.6 | 3.5 |
| Iceland | 1.1 | 0.6 | 1.1 | 2.5 |
| Ireland | 0.1 | 2.6 | 0.0 | 3.7 |
| Italy | 1.2 | 2.7 | −0.1 | 1.1 |
| Japan | 1.1 | 1.3 | −0.7 | −0.8 |
| Korea, Republic of | 5.5 | 7.3 | 3.5 | 4.1 |
| Luxembourg | 1.3 | 2.4 | 2.4 | 2.5 |
| Netherlands | 1.3 | 1.8 | 0.9 | 1.9 |
| New Zealand | 1.5 | 2.8 | 1.0 | 2.9 |
| Norway | 0.6 | 0.2 | 0.7 | 0.6 |
| Portugal | 2.1 | 2.4 | 1.4 | 1.9 |
| Slovak Republic | 0.2 | 0.2 | 0.3 | 1.6 |
| Slovenia | 0.2 | 0.2 | −0.1 | 0.9 |
| Spain | 1.3 | 0.8 | 0.6 | 1.1 |
| Sweden | −0.3 | 0.8 | −0.4 | 1.8 |
| Switzerland | 2.3 | 1.6 | 1.9 | 1.8 |
| United Kingdom | 1.5 | 2.2 | 1.7 | 3.1 |
| United States | 2.4 | 1.4 | 2.3 | 1.8 |
| Average | | | | |
| _Weighted_ | 1.7 | 1.5 | 1.2 | 1.3 |
| _Unweighted_ | 1.2 | 1.5 | 0.8 | 1.7 |

Regression (dependent variable: log of real per capita public health spending)[a]

| | | | | |
|---|---|---|---|---|
| _Log of GDP per capita_ | | | 0.303*** | 0.097 |
| | | | (0.079) | (0.110) |
| _Log of age 14 and under_ | | | 0.104 | 0.450 |
| | | | (0.193) | (0.321) |
| _Log of age 65 plus_ | | | 0.638*** | 0.614** |
| | | | (0.201) | (0.273) |
| _Constant_ | | | 0.023*** | 0.035*** |
| $R^2$ | | | 0.040 | 0.021 |
| $N$ | | | 618 | 324 |

Sources: Organization for Economic Cooperation and Development, OECD Health Data; and IMF staff estimates.

Note: Standard errors in parentheses.

[a] All variables are expressed in first-differences except the constant. The coefficients of these sets of regressions are robust to different specifications. The relatively low $R^2$ reflects the large variability in the annual changes observed in the data. Using a model with five-year differences produces similar results but increases $R^2$ from 0.02 to 0.16.

*$p < .1$; **$p < .05$; ***$p < .01$.

ECG estimates without adjusting for changes in demographics—subtracting per capita GDP growth from per capita health spending growth—with an average of about 1.2 and 1.5 percent (unweighted), respectively, for the periods 1980–2008 and 1995–2008. Under the country fixed-effects model, equation (3.2) is used to calculate country-specific ECG by applying coefficient estimates from equation (3.1)—the coefficient estimates are shown in the bottom panel of Appendix Table 3.1. The average of ECG estimates from country fixed effects (columns 4 and 5) are 0.8 percent and 1.7 percent, respectively, for the periods 1980–2008 and 1995–2008.[8]

The estimates of ECG from the econometric analysis are comparable to those in the literature. OECD (2006) finds ECG to be 1.0 percent for 1980–2005 using a decomposition approach, and its baseline assumes that ECG would decline from 1.0 percent in 2005 to 0 percent in 2050, with an average of 0.7 percent from 2011–2030. Hagist and Kotlikoff (2005) estimate ECG at about 1.5 percent over 1970–2002 for 10 OECD countries. A recent report by the European Commission finds an ECG of 1.4 percent in its econometric analysis, but it is only used in its technology scenario, which assumes ECG declines from 1.4 percent in 2007 to 0 percent in 2060 (EC and EPC, 2009). ECG estimates from other studies (O'Connell, 1996; Christiansen and others, 2006; Blomqvist and Carter, 1997; Przywara, 2010) are broadly consistent with those in the above studies.

## Excess Cost Growth Estimates for Emerging Economies

For emerging economies, the average ECG without adjusting for changes in demographics is 1.1 percent, and the average ECG under the fixed-effects model, adjusting for demographic changes, is −1.8 percent (Appendix Table 3.2). The results show that the estimates of country-specific ECG in emerging economies display considerable variation for two reasons.[9] First, reliable data for emerging economies are available only for recent years. Second, the experiences of emerging economies are very diverse: some countries have recently completed economic and political transitions, while others are still in transition; some countries have achieved universal coverage (including most emerging eastern European countries, Thailand, and Chile), while others are still in the process of doing so. As a result, the econometric estimates of ECG from historical data may not be a reliable source for projecting forward. Instead, an ECG of 1 percent, which is close to the emerging economy average without adjusting for changes in demographics, is assumed in the projections of public health spending.

There have been relatively few estimates of ECG in emerging economies. *The 2009 Ageing Report* (EC and EPC, 2009) assumes that ECG in emerging European countries (Bulgaria, Estonia, Hungary, Latvia, Lithuania, Poland, and

---

[8]The ECG estimates under an alternative OLS specification (not shown) are, on average, lower than the estimates under the fixed-effects model. This indicates that the simple OLS estimates are biased downward, as too much of the spending growth is attributed to demographic variables.

[9]The ECG estimates, under an alternative OLS model (not shown), also display a large degree of variation, with an average of −0.1 percent.

**APPENDIX TABLE 3.2**

## Excess Cost Growth in Emerging Economies

| Country | Difference between public health spending growth and GDP growth | Fixed effects |
|---|---|---|
| Argentina | 0.2 | −1.2 |
| Brazil | 1.7 | −1.3 |
| Bulgaria | 1.0 | −1.6 |
| China | 0.6 | −3.8 |
| Chile | 1.0 | −2.2 |
| Estonia | −2.5 | −6.6 |
| Hungary | −1.3 | −3.0 |
| India | 0.0 | −2.2 |
| Indonesia | 3.8 | 0.2 |
| Latvia | −0.8 | −5.1 |
| Lithuania | 0.7 | −3.5 |
| Malaysia | 2.7 | 0.0 |
| Mexico | 1.0 | −2.3 |
| Pakistan | 2.1 | 1.0 |
| Philippines | 0.0 | −1.8 |
| Poland | 1.1 | −2.7 |
| Romania | 3.6 | 0.3 |
| Russia | −1.1 | −4.9 |
| Saudi Arabia | 4.7 | 4.6 |
| South Africa | 0.6 | −2.5 |
| Thailand | 4.3 | −0.3 |
| Turkey | 3.1 | 0.4 |
| Ukraine | −0.3 | −3.8 |
| Average | | |
| Weighted | 0.9 | −2.4 |
| Unweighted | 1.1 | −1.8 |

Regression (dependent variable: log of real per capita public health spending)[a]

| | |
|---|---|
| Log of GDP per capita | 0.545*** |
| Log of age 14 and under | −0.758 |
| Log of age 65 plus | 0.908 |
| Constant | 0.006 |
| $R^2$ | 0.285 |
| N | 276 |

Sources: World Health Organization; and IMF staff estimates.
[a]All variables are expressed in first-differences except the constant.
*$p < .1$; **$p < .05$; ***$p < .01$.

Romania) would be similar to ECG in other European countries. Its baseline scenario assumes an ECG of 0.2, while its "technology convergence" scenario assumes that ECG would decline from 1.4 percent in 2007 to 0 percent in 2060, with an average ECG of 1.1 percent between 2010 and 2030. An OECD (2006) study assumes that ECG for emerging OECD economies (Hungary, Mexico, Poland, and Turkey) would decline from 1.0 percent in 2005 to 0 percent in 2050 in the baseline scenario, with an average of 0.7 percent between 2010 and 2030, and a constant ECG of 1.0 percent in the cost pressure scenario. A recent (2010) World Bank study takes into account future increases in coverage in its total health spending projections for four representative economies, but does not provide country-specific projections (World Bank, 2010). That study's implicit ECG is above 1.0, given the large increase in spending-to-GDP ratios (a doubling over 2010–30). Projections by Jackson, Howe, and Nakashima (2010) assume a catch-up factor[10] for emerging economies (Chile, China, India, Mexico, Poland, and Russia). However, their projections involve only public health spending for the elderly population, so the ECG figures are not comparable to those used in our study. The ECG that is implicit in their projections assumptions appears high, as spending-to-GDP ratios triple (from 1 percent of GDP in 2007 to 3 percent of GDP in 2040).

## Excess Cost Growth Estimates and Health Projections

The ECG estimates are combined with projected changes in demographic composition to project future public health spending (Appendix Table 3.3). The projections incorporate country-specific assumptions for spending patterns by different age groups. In most countries, for example, spending rises substantially toward the end of life, although the extent to which this occurs varies. In using these age-spending profiles, an important assumption is whether projected increases in life expectancy will result in years of good health and lower spending (typically associated with younger years of life) or years of relatively poor health and higher spending (associated with later years of life). Following the European Commission (EC and EPC, 2009) and its baseline (reference) scenario, it is assumed that one-half of the gains in longevity are spent in good health. For the emerging economies, because of data limitations, a common age-spending profile is used, based on the OECD average.

Figures for 2010 are estimated on the basis of 2008 figures and the reported ECG estimates. As such, the 2010 figures can be interpreted as an estimate of health spending as a share of potential GDP. This provides a better basis for projections than more recent data, in which spending-to-GDP ratios would reflect the effect of the recent economic crisis.

For advanced economies, ECG estimates from country fixed-effects regressions based on 1980–2008 data are used. However, the ECG estimates are capped between 0 and 2.0 percent, as the estimates from the econometric model are less reliable for outliers.[11] The results are largely consistent with previous estimates (IMF, 2010b). Public health spending in advanced economies is projected to increase, on average, by 3 percentage points of GDP between 2010 and 2030.

---

[10]If per capita health spending as a share of GDP in a country is less than two-thirds of the developed-country average, the gap is assumed to narrow by 5 percent per year until spending reaches two-thirds of the developed-country average.

[11]For three countries (Norway, Switzerland, and the United States), more recent ECG estimates from 1995–2008 were used in the projections, as staff judged these to be a better predictor of future spending pressures.

**APPENDIX TABLE 3.3**

## Projections of Public Health Spending, 2010–50 (*Percent of GDP*)

| Country | 2010 | 2015 | 2020 | 2025 | 2030 | 2035 | 2040 | 2045 | 2050 | Baseline | Optimistic | Pessimistic |
|---|---|---|---|---|---|---|---|---|---|---|---|---|
| *Advanced economies* | | | | | | | | | | | | |
| Australia | 6.0 | 6.4 | 6.9 | 7.5 | 8.1 | 8.7 | 9.3 | 9.8 | 10.3 | 2.1 | 1.4 | 3.0 |
| Austria | 8.3 | 9.1 | 9.8 | 10.7 | 11.6 | 12.5 | 13.5 | 14.4 | 15.2 | 3.2 | 2.2 | 4.4 |
| Belgium | 7.6 | 8.1 | 8.5 | 9.1 | 9.6 | 10.2 | 10.8 | 11.3 | 11.7 | 2.0 | 1.1 | 3.0 |
| Canada | 7.4 | 7.9 | 8.4 | 8.9 | 9.4 | 9.9 | 10.4 | 10.8 | 11.1 | 2.0 | 1.1 | 3.0 |
| Czech Republic | 5.8 | 6.0 | 6.1 | 6.3 | 6.4 | 6.6 | 6.7 | 6.8 | 6.8 | 0.6 | 0.0 | 1.3 |
| Denmark | 8.6 | 8.8 | 9.0 | 9.2 | 9.4 | 9.5 | 9.6 | 9.6 | 9.6 | 0.8 | −0.1 | 1.8 |
| Finland | 6.4 | 7.0 | 7.6 | 8.3 | 8.9 | 9.5 | 10.1 | 10.7 | 11.2 | 2.5 | 1.6 | 3.4 |
| France | 9.0 | 9.4 | 9.7 | 10.1 | 10.5 | 10.8 | 11.1 | 11.4 | 11.6 | 1.5 | 0.5 | 2.6 |
| Germany | 8.1 | 8.4 | 8.6 | 8.8 | 9.0 | 9.3 | 9.4 | 9.6 | 9.6 | 0.9 | 0.1 | 1.9 |
| Greece | 6.2 | 6.9 | 7.6 | 8.4 | 9.4 | 10.4 | 11.5 | 12.7 | 13.9 | 3.2 | 2.3 | 4.1 |
| Iceland | 7.8 | 8.4 | 9.1 | 9.9 | 10.9 | 12.0 | 13.0 | 14.1 | 15.2 | 3.2 | 2.1 | 4.3 |
| Ireland | 6.8 | 6.9 | 7.0 | 7.2 | 7.5 | 7.7 | 7.9 | 8.1 | 8.3 | 0.7 | 0.0 | 1.5 |
| Italy | 6.9 | 7.0 | 7.2 | 7.3 | 7.5 | 7.7 | 7.8 | 7.9 | 8.0 | 0.6 | −0.1 | 1.4 |
| Japan | 6.8 | 7.1 | 7.3 | 7.6 | 7.8 | 7.9 | 8.0 | 8.1 | 8.2 | 1.0 | 0.2 | 1.8 |
| Korea, Rep. of | 3.9 | 4.5 | 5.2 | 6.1 | 7.1 | 8.2 | 9.5 | 10.9 | 12.3 | 3.2 | 2.6 | 4.0 |
| Luxembourg | 7.1 | 7.9 | 8.9 | 9.9 | 11.2 | 12.5 | 14.1 | 15.7 | 17.5 | 4.0 | 3.0 | 5.2 |
| Netherlands | 7.6 | 8.2 | 8.9 | 9.5 | 10.2 | 10.8 | 11.4 | 12.0 | 12.5 | 2.6 | 1.6 | 3.6 |
| New Zealand | 8.1 | 8.8 | 9.5 | 10.3 | 11.1 | 12.0 | 12.9 | 13.7 | 14.5 | 3.0 | 1.9 | 4.1 |
| Norway | 7.2 | 7.5 | 7.9 | 8.4 | 8.8 | 9.3 | 9.7 | 10.1 | 10.5 | 1.7 | 0.8 | 2.6 |
| Portugal | 7.6 | 8.4 | 9.2 | 10.1 | 11.1 | 12.2 | 13.4 | 14.7 | 15.9 | 3.5 | 2.5 | 4.6 |
| Slovak Rep. | 5.5 | 5.7 | 6.0 | 6.3 | 6.7 | 7.0 | 7.3 | 7.6 | 7.9 | 1.2 | 0.5 | 1.9 |
| Slovenia | 6.1 | 6.3 | 6.5 | 6.6 | 6.8 | 7.0 | 7.2 | 7.3 | 7.3 | 0.7 | 0.1 | 1.5 |
| Spain | 6.6 | 6.9 | 7.3 | 7.7 | 8.2 | 8.7 | 9.3 | 9.7 | 10.1 | 1.6 | 0.8 | 2.4 |
| Sweden | 7.8 | 7.9 | 8.0 | 8.1 | 8.2 | 8.3 | 8.3 | 8.3 | 8.3 | 0.4 | −0.4 | 1.3 |
| Switzerland | 6.6 | 7.4 | 8.4 | 9.4 | 10.5 | 11.7 | 13.0 | 14.3 | 15.6 | 3.9 | 2.9 | 4.9 |
| United Kingdom | 7.3 | 8.0 | 8.7 | 9.6 | 10.6 | 11.7 | 12.9 | 14.2 | 15.5 | 3.3 | 2.3 | 4.4 |
| United States | 7.6 | 8.6 | 9.8 | 11.2 | 12.7 | 14.2 | 15.7 | 17.3 | 18.9 | 5.1 | 3.9 | 6.4 |
| | | | | | | | | | | | | |
| *Emerging economies* | | | | | | | | | | | | |
| Argentina | 5.1 | 5.4 | 5.8 | 6.2 | 6.6 | 7.1 | 7.7 | 8.2 | 8.9 | 1.5 | 0.9 | 2.2 |
| Brazil | 3.6 | 3.9 | 4.2 | 4.7 | 5.1 | 5.6 | 6.2 | 6.7 | 7.3 | 1.6 | 1.1 | 2.1 |
| Bulgaria | 4.2 | 4.5 | 4.8 | 5.2 | 5.6 | 6.0 | 6.5 | 6.9 | 7.4 | 1.3 | 0.8 | 1.9 |
| China | 1.9 | 2.1 | 2.3 | 2.5 | 2.8 | 3.1 | 3.3 | 3.6 | 3.9 | 0.8 | 0.6 | 1.1 |
| Chile | 3.7 | 4.1 | 4.5 | 4.9 | 5.3 | 5.8 | 6.2 | 6.7 | 7.2 | 1.5 | 1.1 | 2.1 |
| Estonia | 4.2 | 4.4 | 4.7 | 5.0 | 5.3 | 5.6 | 6.0 | 6.4 | 6.7 | 1.1 | 0.6 | 1.7 |
| Hungary | 5.3 | 5.6 | 6.0 | 6.4 | 6.9 | 7.3 | 7.8 | 8.3 | 8.9 | 1.6 | 0.9 | 2.3 |
| India | 1.1 | 1.2 | 1.2 | 1.3 | 1.5 | 1.6 | 1.7 | 1.9 | 2.0 | 0.4 | 0.2 | 0.5 |
| Indonesia | 1.2 | 1.3 | 1.4 | 1.5 | 1.7 | 1.8 | 2.0 | 2.1 | 2.3 | 0.5 | 0.3 | 0.6 |
| Latvia | 3.6 | 3.9 | 4.1 | 4.3 | 4.6 | 5.0 | 5.4 | 5.7 | 6.1 | 1.0 | 0.6 | 1.5 |
| Lithuania | 4.6 | 5.0 | 5.3 | 5.7 | 6.1 | 6.6 | 7.1 | 7.5 | 8.0 | 1.5 | 0.9 | 2.1 |
| Malaysia | 2.0 | 2.1 | 2.3 | 2.5 | 2.7 | 3.0 | 3.2 | 3.5 | 3.8 | 0.8 | 0.5 | 1.1 |
| Mexico | 2.7 | 2.9 | 3.2 | 3.5 | 3.8 | 4.2 | 4.6 | 5.0 | 5.4 | 1.1 | 0.8 | 1.5 |
| Pakistan | 0.8 | 0.9 | 0.9 | 1.0 | 1.1 | 1.1 | 1.2 | 1.3 | 1.4 | 0.2 | 0.1 | 0.3 |
| Philippines | 1.4 | 1.4 | 1.6 | 1.7 | 1.8 | 2.0 | 2.1 | 2.3 | 2.5 | 0.5 | 0.3 | 0.6 |
| Poland | 4.6 | 5.0 | 5.4 | 5.9 | 6.4 | 7.0 | 7.5 | 8.1 | 8.7 | 1.8 | 1.2 | 2.5 |
| Romania | 3.8 | 4.1 | 4.4 | 4.7 | 5.1 | 5.5 | 6.0 | 6.4 | 6.9 | 1.3 | 0.8 | 1.8 |
| Russia | 3.5 | 3.8 | 4.0 | 4.3 | 4.6 | 5.0 | 5.3 | 5.7 | 6.0 | 1.1 | 0.7 | 1.6 |

*(continued)*

**APPENDIX TABLE 3.3**

## Projections of Public Health Spending, 2010–50 *(Percent of GDP) (continued)*

| Country | Baseline projections | | | | | | | | | Change, 2010–30 | | |
|---|---|---|---|---|---|---|---|---|---|---|---|---|
| | 2010 | 2015 | 2020 | 2025 | 2030 | 2035 | 2040 | 2045 | 2050 | Baseline | Optimistic | Pessimistic |
| Saudi Arabia | 2.7 | 3.0 | 3.2 | 3.5 | 3.8 | 4.1 | 4.5 | 4.9 | 5.4 | 1.0 | 0.7 | 1.4 |
| South Africa | 3.6 | 3.9 | 4.1 | 4.4 | 4.7 | 5.0 | 5.4 | 5.7 | 6.1 | 1.1 | 0.7 | 1.6 |
| Thailand | 2.8 | 3.0 | 3.3 | 3.6 | 3.9 | 4.3 | 4.6 | 4.9 | 5.2 | 1.1 | 0.8 | 1.5 |
| Turkey | 3.5 | 3.7 | 4.0 | 4.4 | 4.8 | 5.2 | 5.7 | 6.2 | 6.7 | 1.3 | 0.9 | 1.8 |
| Ukraine | 4.0 | 4.3 | 4.5 | 4.8 | 5.2 | 5.6 | 6.0 | 6.3 | 6.7 | 1.2 | 0.7 | 1.7 |
| Average | 5.4 | 5.9 | 6.4 | 7.0 | 7.6 | 8.3 | 8.9 | 9.6 | 10.3 | 2.2 | 1.5 | 3.0 |
| *Advanced* | 7.3 | 7.9 | 8.7 | 9.5 | 10.4 | 11.2 | 12.1 | 13.0 | 13.9 | 3.0 | 2.1 | 4.1 |
| *Emerging* | 2.5 | 2.7 | 2.9 | 3.2 | 3.5 | 3.8 | 4.1 | 4.4 | 4.7 | 1.0 | 0.6 | 1.3 |

Sources: Organization for Economic Cooperation and Development, OECD Health Data; World Health Organization; and IMF staff estimates.

Note: The optimistic (pessimistic) scenario assumes excess cost growth that is 0.5 percentage point lower (higher) than in the baseline.

# REFERENCES

Baltagi, B.H., and F. Moscone, 2010, "Health Care Expenditure and Income in the OECD Reconsidered: Evidence from Panel Data," IZA Discussion Paper No. 4851 (Bonn: Institute for the Study of Labor).

Barros, P.P., 1998, "The Black Box of Health Care Expenditure Growth Determinants," *Health Economics*, Vol. 7, pp. 533–44.

Blomqvist, A., and R. Carter, 1997, "Is Health Care Really a Luxury?" *Journal of Health Economics*, Vol. 16, No. 2, pp. 207–29.

Christiansen, T., M. Bech, J. Lauridsen, and P. Nielsen, 2006, "Demographic Changes and Aggregate Health-Care Expenditure in Europe," Research Report No. 32 (Brussels: European Network of Economic Policy Research Institutes).

Clemente, J., C. Marcuello, A. Montañes, and F. Pueyo, 2004, "On the International Stability of Health Care Expenditure Functions: Are Government and Private Functions Similar?" *Journal of Health Economics*, Vol. 23, pp. 569–613.

Congressional Budget Office (CBO), 2008, *Evidence on the Costs and Benefits of Health Information Technology*, Publication No. 2976 (Washington: U.S. Government Printing Office).

Dreger, C., and H.E. Reimers, 2005, "Health Care Expenditures in OECD Countries: A Panel Unit Root and Cointegration Analysis," IZA Discussion Paper 1469 (Bonn: Institute for the Study of Labor).

European Commission (EC) and Economic Policy Committee (EPC), 2009, *The 2009 Ageing Report: Economic and Budgetary Projections for the EU-27 Member States, 2008–2060*, European Economy Paper No. 2 (Brussels).

Gerdtham, U.G., and M. Löthgren, 2000, "On Stationarity and Cointegration of International Health Expenditure and GDP," *Journal of Health Economics*, Vol. 19, pp. 461–75.

Hagist, C., and L. Kotlikoff, 2005, "Who's Going Broke? Comparing Health Care Costs in Ten OECD Countries," Working Paper No. 11833 (Cambridge: National Bureau of Economic Research).

Herwartz, H., and B. Theilen, 2002, "The Determinants of Health Care Expenditure: Testing Pooling Restrictions in Small Samples," *Journal of Health Economics*, Vol. 12, pp. 113–24.

International Monetary Fund, 2010a, *From Stimulus to Consolidation: Revenue and Expenditure Policies in Advanced and Emerging Economies*, IMF Departmental Paper (Washington).

———, 2010b, "United States: Staff Report for the 2010 Article IV Consultation," IMF Country Report 10/249 (Washington).

Jackson, R., N. Howe, and K. Nakashima, 2010, *The Global Aging Preparedness Index* (Washington: Center for Strategic & International Studies).

O'Connell, J.M., 1996, "The Relationship between Health Expenditures and the Age Structure of the Population in OECD Countries," *Journal of Health Economics*, Vol. 5, No. 6, pp. 573–78.

Okunade, A.A., M.C. Karakus, and C. Okeke, 2004, "Determinants of Health Expenditure Growth of the OECD Countries: Jackknife Resampling Plan Estimates," *Health Care Management Science*, Vol. 7, No. 3, pp. 173–83.

Organization for Economic Cooperation and Development (OECD), 2006, "Projecting OECD Health and Long-Term Care Expenditures: What Are the Main Drivers?" Economic Department Working Paper No. 477 (Paris).

Przywara, B., 2010, "Projecting Future Health Care Expenditure at European Level: Drivers, Methodology, and Main Results," European Economy Economic Paper No. 417 (Brussels: European Commission and Economic Policy Committee).

Smith, S., J. Newhouse, and M. Freeland, 2009, "Income, Insurance, and Technology: Why Does Health Spending Outpace Economic Growth?" *Health Affairs*, Vol. 28, No. 5, pp. 1276–84.

World Bank, 2010, "Population Aging and Fiscal Sustainability in APEC Economies: Simulations of Pension and Health Care Expenditures," unpublished.

# PART II

# The Role of the Private Sector in Health Care Financing and Delivery

# CHAPTER 4

# The Future of Public and Private Health Care Insurance in Asia

LUDWIG KANZLER AND ALEXANDER NG

Globally, both public and private health care systems are facing major fiscal challenges. New technologies provide patients with more-sophisticated diagnostic and treatment methods, but they also significantly increase costs. Simultaneously, the number of patients who are elderly or have chronic diseases is surging worldwide, straining health care budgets. Paradoxically, in many countries, including emerging markets, the situation is exacerbated by an increase in wealth levels. As expendable income rises in these locations, patients are more likely to seek health care, since high copayments and out-of-pocket (OOP) expenses are less of a deterrent. Similarly, they may expect a higher quality of care, such as greater access to expensive new drugs. Even in cases in which patients pay for the majority of their treatment, payers must often cover some costs associated with the higher utilization.

Asia is no exception. In this region, governments have primary responsibility for providing care, and private insurance remains a small niche market, mainly reserved for those with expendable income. In response to spiraling health care costs, many governments—even in the wealthiest countries—have analyzed or begun implementing reforms to reduce spending. Consider a few examples:

- As part of a widespread effort to reduce health care spending, the Japanese government has kept spending increases to about 2 percent annually, which is far below the level seen in other OECD countries (McKinsey & Company, 2008).

- China is moving away from fee-for-service reimbursement to models that do not reward providers for high utilization; it is also capping the prices that hospitals and other facilities can charge for certain drugs (Süssmuth-Dyckerhoff and Wang, 2010; Kyburg and Stuker, 2007).

- The Philippines is also moving away from fee-for-service reimbursement and has introduced legislation to decrease hospital costs, including a bill that encourages cooperation between tertiary and specialized facilities to eliminate duplication of expensive services (Philippines, State Senate, 2004).

The authors would like to acknowledge the contributions to this effort of their McKinsey colleagues, Jeffrey Livingston, Claudia Süssmuth-Dyckerhoff, Scott Lichtenberger, Jean Drouin, and Saum Sutaria.

Such reform efforts will intensify throughout Asia as fiscal pressures increase, but the diverse nature of the region makes it impossible to offer a single solution—each country differs in terms of economic development, political systems, social values, and health care priorities. However, all governments should consider whether private insurance can play a greater role in alleviating fiscal burdens and resolving other issues, such as the widespread lack of health care coverage in developing countries and the increasing demand for higher-quality services.

If private health care insurance does become more common, governments will need to consider several important questions. Should private insurers largely replace public payers or work in coordination with them? What are the pros and cons of private insurance? What regulations are needed to promote sustainability and guarantee that all citizens have equal access to quality care? And what measures can public and private payers implement to ensure that they remain financially strong?

In answering these questions, we will focus on the role that private insurance can play in one basic area: providing reimbursement for services. While private payers in the United States and some other locations are well established and have assumed more complex responsibilities—serving as provider network managers, for instance—such capabilities take years to develop. Since private payers have only a small presence in Asia and lack infrastructure in the region, we expect that their initial growth efforts will concentrate on reimbursement.

## HEALTH CARE SYSTEMS IN ASIA: A WIDE DIVERSITY OF MODELS, CHALLENGES, AND BENEFITS

To understand the current health care systems in Asia, we looked at 13 major countries, examining government budgets, the role of private payers, and typical OOP costs. In all cases, private health insurance represented less than 10 percent of total health expenditures, ranging from a low of 1.6 percent in Singapore to a high of 8.3 percent in Australia. But there were significant differences among countries in other respects, including total health expenditures and GDP per capita. Looking at these two variables, we divided Asian countries into three major groups favored by macroeconomic analysis (Figure 4.1):

- *Developed countries*: Australia, Japan, New Zealand, Singapore, and the Republic of Korea. All countries in this cohort provide near-universal public health care coverage, although benefits may be fairly basic. Health care spending is high—an average of 7.4 percent of GDP—but still lower than the OECD average of 9.5 percent in 2009. OOP expenses account for about 28 percent of total health expenditures.

- *Emerging markets*: China, Malaysia, and Thailand. As in the developed markets, these countries have achieved near universal coverage under public health plans. However, consumers in emerging markets face a greater burden from OOP expenses—about 33 percent of total health expenditures. Health

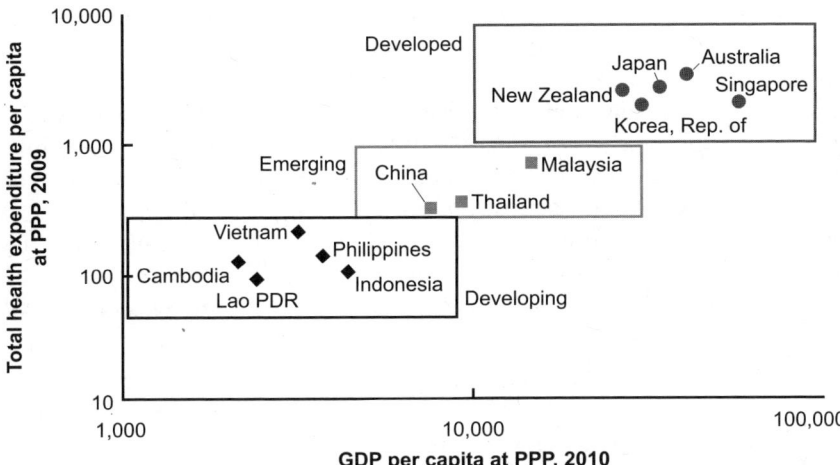

**Figure 4.1** Categorization of Health Care Systems in the Asia Pacific Region
Sources: World Health Organization; and IMF staff estimates.
Note: PPP = purchasing power parity.

care spending is lower (4.6 percent of GDP) than in developed countries, and patients may not have as much access to sophisticated treatments.

- *Developing countries*: Cambodia, Indonesia, the Lao People's Democratic Republic, the Philippines, and Vietnam. For these countries, access to health care is still a major problem, with many people lacking sufficient coverage for various reasons. For instance, the Philippines, Indonesia, the Lao People's Democratic Republic, and Vietnam have public insurance for workers, with mandatory payments taken from both employers and employees. (Some governments may make additional contributions.) But many people in these countries, such as taxi drivers and street vendors, do not have a "formal" employer; this segment of the population often lacks the ability to pay premiums, and it is difficult for the government to enforce collection (Tangcharoensathien and others, 2011). And while governments in developing countries subsidize insurance for the poor with tax revenues, the scope and quality of care is often extremely limited (Tangcharoensathien and others, 2011). In fact, OOP expenses may be high at all levels of society because of coverage restrictions. However, health care spending in this cohort is similar to that of emerging markets (4.7 percent of GDP), and many countries have been increasing health care significantly to improve coverage and provision.

Not surprisingly, health outcomes also vary significantly by cohort, with developed countries scoring the highest on key metrics and developing countries the lowest. For instance, people in developed countries can expect to live four years longer than those in emerging markets and eight years longer than those in developing markets.

Box 4.1 provides more detail about the opportunities and challenges in developed, emerging, and developing markets, using selected countries as examples.

Given the variations among developing, emerging, and developed countries, each cohort will naturally have different priorities regarding the three fundamentals of health care: cost effectiveness/sustainability, equal access to treatment for all citizens, and quality of care (Angrisano and others, 2006). But in all locations, private insurance could potentially play a role in solving many problems. For instance, it could help reduce OOP expenses in emerging and developing countries, thereby making health care more affordable and accessible.

**BOX 4.1**

### Variations Within Asia: Patterns of Health Care Coverage

#### Developed-Country Example: Japan

Japan requires its citizens to pay premiums to receive public insurance coverage. While this should theoretically provide universal access, about 10 percent of households do not pay the mandatory premiums (McKinsey & Company, 2008). Copayments are also high, representing 30 percent of treatment costs for most people and 10 percent for those over 70 (McKinsey & Company, 2008). (Some intractable diseases are not subject to any copayment, and expenses may be capped for other conditions, but not until patients have already incurred rather high costs.) There are over 4,000 public insurers in Japan, but patients must enroll in the one that serves their employer or, if not employed, their prefecture (Henke, Kadonaga, and Kanzler, 2009). With a guaranteed customer base, payers have no incentive to improve quality or offer better services to attract patients.

#### Emerging Market Example: China

Over the last few years, China has enrolled significantly more people in public insurance plans, with about 95 percent of the population now covered (China, Office of State Council, 2007). But public insurance focuses on coverage for catastrophic diseases and inpatient services, and patients still have little assistance with basic outpatient care, a factor that will become more problematic as the rate of chronic diseases continues to rise. OOP expenses have fallen in recent years but remain high at 41 percent of total health expenditures.

#### Developing-Country Example: Vietnam

Like most developing countries, Vietnam provides all services through a public health insurance system. The government pays about two-thirds of the premiums, and employers or consumers contribute the remaining amount. Given the significant financial burden, many people—about 45 percent—lack health care coverage (Tangcharoensathien and others, 2011). OOP payments remain high, at about 55 percent of total health expenditures, and have decreased only modestly in recent years (Tangcharoensathien and others, 2011).

# A WINDOW OF OPPORTUNITY FOR PRIVATE INSURANCE IN ASIA

Worldwide, in developing and developed countries, health care spending has been growing for decades at a rate of 2 percent above GDP. This pattern is occurring, in part, because income levels are rising globally, promoting greater health care utilization. The increased spending will produce many benefits, such as greater longevity, but unrelenting high growth will also raise costs to ultimately unsustainable levels that could bankrupt health care systems.

Although Asia trails the United States and many other Western countries in health care spending, the situation in this region is still serious and will become increasingly problematic, even if the growth rate declines to a more modest rate of 1 percent above GDP growth (Figure 4.2).

Many of the forces that are raising health care costs in Asia are similar to those at work in other countries, such as greater use of sophisticated and costly technologies, a growing elderly population, and an increase in the number of patients suffering from chronic disease. But perhaps one factor—rising incomes and the growth of the middle class—is having a greater effect in Asia than in the rest of the world. For the first time, many patients in China and other emerging markets have expendable income to devote to health care. While they may have ignored a minor ailment or accepted a place on a waiting list in the past, they are now more

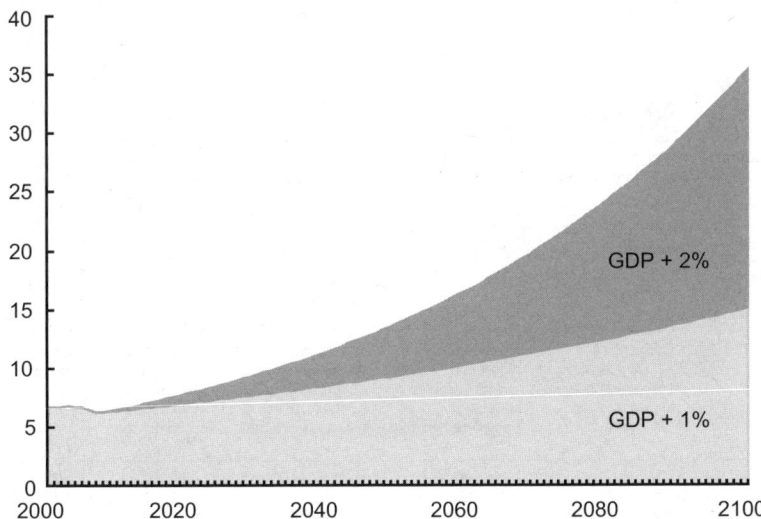

Health care as percentage of GDP, Asia-Pacific[a]

**Figure 4.2** Projected Rise in Health Care Costs in Asia
Sources: World Bank; and McKinsey analysis.
Note: 1995–2009 compound annual growth rate (CAGR): GDP = 4.13%, health care spending = 4.49%; if Japan is excluded: GDP = 9.55%, health care spending = 11.25%.
[a]Includes 13 major countries: Australia, Cambodia, China, Indonesia, Japan, the Republic of Korea, the Lao People's Democratic Republic, Malaysia, New Zealand, the Philippines, Singapore, Thailand, and Vietnam.

likely to seek immediate treatment or make more frequent visits to providers, increasing utilization. In addition, patients may expect access to the latest diagnostic and treatment methods, even if the new technologies are more expensive than traditional methods.

Traditionally, Asian governments have taken a laissez-faire approach to private health insurance. While private payers have been free to offer products, generally through employers or as a rider to existing life or property and casualty insurance policies, governments have not actively promoted the industry. But the current fiscal environment and the rising expectations of the new middle class may prompt Asian countries to encourage a greater role for private payers, since they could relieve some of the financial burdens on the public sector.

## THE ASIAN HEALTH INSURANCE MODEL

If private insurance does become more common in Asia, what form will it take? To answer this question, we reviewed the current health care paradigms throughout Asia and in other regions. Our research showed that health care models vary greatly worldwide, with some countries offering only public or only private coverage, and others providing a mix of the two (Figure 4.3). Historically, countries have been reluctant to change their existing models, so attempts at health care reform tend to proceed slowly.

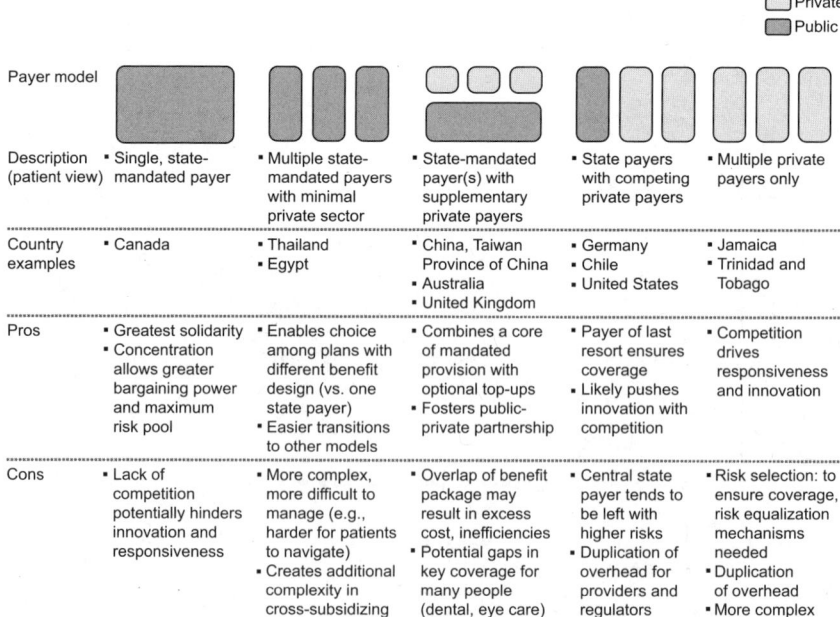

| | | | | |
|---|---|---|---|---|
| **Description** (patient view) | • Single, state-mandated payer | • Multiple state-mandated payers with minimal private sector | • State-mandated payer(s) with supplementary private payers | • State payers with competing private payers | • Multiple private payers only |
| **Country examples** | • Canada | • Thailand<br>• Egypt | • China, Taiwan Province of China<br>• Australia<br>• United Kingdom | • Germany<br>• Chile<br>• United States | • Jamaica<br>• Trinidad and Tobago |
| **Pros** | • Greatest solidarity<br>• Concentration allows greater bargaining power and maximum risk pool | • Enables choice among plans with different benefit design (vs. one state payer)<br>• Easier transitions to other models | • Combines a core of mandated provision with optional top-ups<br>• Fosters public-private partnership | • Payer of last resort ensures coverage<br>• Likely pushes innovation with competition | • Competition drives responsiveness and innovation |
| **Cons** | • Lack of competition potentially hinders innovation and responsiveness | • More complex, more difficult to manage (e.g., harder for patients to navigate)<br>• Creates additional complexity in cross-subsidizing | • Overlap of benefit package may result in excess cost, inefficiencies<br>• Potential gaps in key coverage for many people (dental, eye care) | • Central state payer tends to be left with higher risks<br>• Duplication of overhead for providers and regulators | • Risk selection: to ensure coverage, risk equalization mechanisms needed<br>• Duplication of overhead<br>• More complex |

**Figure 4.3** Common Health Care Coverage Models across the World
Source: McKinsey analysis.

At present, most Asian countries mandate state coverage but allow patients to purchase private insurance as a supplement—for instance, to receive a better hospital room or additional services that are not included as part of the public benefit package.

Overall, we do not expect the Asian paradigm to change significantly, largely because of social beliefs. Even in the most free-market countries, politicians and the general population value the role of public payers in ensuring access to care and providing some degree of financial protection for all citizens. A system in which the private sector has primary responsibility for health care, as in the United States, would be greeted warily, unless it was to assume the same broad and mandatory coverage as public insurance. Given these beliefs, we expect Asian governments to continue to offer or aspire to have universal public coverage, and private insurance to be used largely as a supplement that allows patients to receive more extensive or frequent services or some other type of upgrade.

There will be some variations in the extent to which different Asian countries incorporate private insurance into their systems, mostly because of differences in health care priorities and economic standing. As one example, developed countries may see private insurance as a tool for improving quality or expanding the depth of services provided, such as by providing reimbursement for sophisticated new diagnostic and treatment methods that public plans do not cover. By contrast, developing countries and emerging markets may be primarily interested in private insurance as a tool to increase access to health care, since large segments of the population lack any form of coverage. For instance, developing countries and emerging markets could encourage private payers to offer low-cost policies that reduce OOP expenses, thereby removing some financial barriers to treatment. These countries might also be interested in the ability of private insurance to solve basic health care problems that developed countries have already addressed, such as the spread of communicable diseases and high infant mortality rates.

## POSSIBLE BENEFITS—AND CHALLENGES— RESULTING FROM AN INCREASED ROLE FOR PRIVATE INSURANCE IN ASIA

Governments in Asia may welcome private insurance, believing that it will improve care and ease financial strains on the public sector. But what can private insurance realistically provide in terms of cost control/sustainability, equal access to treatment for all citizens, and quality improvement, especially if, as expected, it continues to serve as a supplement to public coverage? And what potential problems may arise as private insurance becomes more common?

### Cost Control/Sustainability

A few facts suggest that private payers might be better able to control costs than public payers. For instance, private payers are more likely to undertake cost control initiatives to improve profitability—as one example, by hiring pharmacy benefit managers to negotiate discounts for drugs. In addition, most public plans start off with fee-for-service reimbursement, which encourages providers to see as many patients as possible. While private payers may follow fee-for-service schemes when establishing themselves in new markets, most eventually gravitate toward systems that reward providers for judiciously conserving resources more quickly than public plans do. These include capitation models (known as managed care in some locations), in which providers are paid a set amount for each patient, and diagnosis-related group models, in which reimbursement fees are based solely on a patient's diagnosis. Both of these methods give providers a financial incentive to avoid unnecessary treatments.

In reality, however, private payers typically need to differentiate themselves from competitors and attract subscribers based on the services that they reimburse. As such, their ability to manage cost is severely limited. By contrast, public payers that dominate or monopolize a health care system have more power to set reimbursement limits, since patients have few or no other alternatives for coverage. For the same reason, public payers can exert more influence over providers, since hospitals and physician groups cannot opt to align themselves with other health plans. Finally, private payers are also associated with higher administrative costs, which increase overall expenses (Hacker, 2008).

Given these facts, the introduction of private payers into Asia will not automatically control rising costs. However, it will produce some financial benefits for both the public sector and providers. For instance, supplemental private insurance will inject money into the health care system by freeing latent demand for a higher level of care than most public plans provide, such as an upgrade to a better hospital room or the ability to get a CT scan or other expensive tests that public payers deem medically unnecessary (McKinsey & Company, 2008). The additional income that providers receive for these services may become even more important as cash-strapped governments continue to reduce reimbursements and set limits on covered services. And supplemental private plans can relieve some financial pressures on governments by assuming reimbursement responsibility for expensive new treatments that would pose additional burdens for public plans or for other services that patients expect but that governments cannot afford to cover.

Later in this chapter, we will discuss how public and private payers can be more effective in controlling costs, since both groups have had limited success in their efforts to date.

## Equal Access to Care

The health care issues that plague the United States and other countries that lack a strong public option are well known. For instance, patients who cannot afford private coverage may forsake treatment or preventive care—a problem that will have even greater implications as the rate of chronic disease rises. Other patients face financial hardship because of high premiums or OOP expenses for services not covered under their private plans. And most disturbingly, some patients find it difficult or impossible to get private insurance because of preexisting conditions or other factors that make them a high financial risk.

If private insurance continues to play a supplemental role in Asia, as expected, the risk of such problems is more limited. But it could still introduce some degree of inequity between those willing and able to pay for additional services and those who opt out or cannot afford this option (McKinsey & Company, 2008). Such a development could raise major concerns, since, as noted, social values throughout Asia strongly emphasize the importance of equal access to health care.

As we discuss in the next section, however, Asian countries can minimize problems by enacting strong regulations that keep private insurance affordable and require payers to accept all patients regardless of health status. In fact, we believe that private insurance may increase access to care, especially in emerging and developed markets, by decreasing OOP expenses.

## Quality of Care

Among its greatest benefits, private insurance has the potential to contribute to an increase in health care quality. Since private payers have to compete for patients, they want the best provider networks—those that offer the widest range of innovative treatments and demonstrate the best outcomes. To win contracts with private payers, providers may need to prove their worth by monitoring quality and measuring outcomes. In addition, private insurance typically provides greater reimbursement for advanced care than public insurance, which can have many benefits. For instance, it gives medical facilities an incentive to specialize in particular areas and become true centers of excellence. Such facilities are rare in countries like Japan, which lack a private option and provide the same compensation for specialists and generalist physicians (McKinsey & Company, 2008).

In Asia, private insurance could also help provide the quality services that patients in the growing middle class increasingly expect. As one example, public payers sometimes limit reimbursement for new and innovative therapies until they have been proven to be more cost effective than traditional treatments. If private payers assume more responsibility for these costs to attract subscribers, they will reduce the financial burden on the public sector while simultaneously raising patient satisfaction.

Private insurance may also encourage quality improvements beyond the provider sphere. Looking broadly at the health care industry, for instance, both pharmaceutical companies and medical device manufacturers will have greater incentives to introduce new treatments into the market if they know that private payers will provide reimbursement.

## REGULATING PRIVATE INSURANCE: WHAT NEEDS TO BE DONE

Given the risk of inequity associated with private insurance, how can Asian countries maximize its benefits while still protecting payers from financial hardship? The answer lies in a strong regulatory system that should, at minimum, include guidelines related to the following:

- *Fixed premiums*: Regulators should consider setting fixed private insurance premiums for basic coverage. In addition to keeping health care affordable, fixed premiums will encourage payers to differentiate themselves from the competition based on quality, rather than cost, which may improve outcomes.

- *Mandatory acceptance of all patients*: Regulators should consider instituting a law that requires private insurers to accept all patients, regardless of preexisting conditions. Mandatory acceptance will eliminate the paradoxical situation that occurs in the United States, where the seriously ill patients who most need health insurance are least likely to qualify for it.

- *Creation of risk equalization funds*: If regulators are to block insurers from screening out high-risk patients, the health care burden may be unfairly distributed, with some payers having responsibility for a high proportion of subscribers with expensive medical needs. To ensure fairness, regulators should establish a fund that reimburses insurers for all high-risk patients that they cover. Among other benefits, this fund would eliminate financial incentives for selectively targeting lower-risk populations (e.g., by creating advertisements or promotions designed to appeal to young, healthy patients).

In Asia, such regulations could make supplemental private insurance a feasible option for most patients while protecting payers from financial hardship. In fact, the regulations have already been highly effective in countries where private insurance dominates. For instance, the Netherlands does not offer any form of public insurance but instead mandates that citizens must purchase private plans that provide a basic range of services—a system described as "private health insurance with social conditions" (Netherlands, MoHWS, 2009). (Patients may opt for additional coverage at an added cost.) Overall, Dutch patients express a high degree of satisfaction with the health system. The risk-sharing provisions have also made the Netherlands more attractive to private insurers, resulting in a higher degree of competition than might otherwise be expected.

To guarantee impartiality, regulators should be fully independent, free from undue influence from both government officials and private industry executives. They should emphasize pricing transparency, since health care plans often have fine print that makes it difficult to determine the exact cost of coverage. In addition, regulators should monitor the quality of each payer's health care network and make this information publicly available, also as part of an effort to increase transparency. For instance, the regulator in the Netherlands has a website that ranks payers based on health care quality.

In some cases, regulators may look beyond payers to other participants in the health care value chain in their efforts to protect patients. As one example, they may consider setting laws regarding the amount that pharmaceutical or medical device companies can charge for their products to ensure that treatments remain affordable to all, while also preserving those companies' right to profit.

## ENSURING SUSTAINABILITY OF PUBLIC AND PRIVATE HEALTH CARE BY CONTROLLING COSTS AND UTILIZATION

As we noted, the introduction of private payers into the Asian market will not automatically solve the fiscal challenges facing the health care system. Public payers, who will continue to dominate the market, will still need to take proactive steps to reduce their costs. But what measures will be most effective? And how can private payers entering this region develop better cost containment methods and avoid the financial problems that they have encountered elsewhere?

While many payers have instituted copayments to discourage patients from seeking unnecessary treatment and thus reduce costs, evidence suggests that they have little impact. For instance, Japan increased its copayment rate from 20 percent to 30 percent for patients under 70 seeking inpatient services in 2003. However, hospital utilization fell by only 2 percent, and even this modest benefit disappeared within 12 months (Japan, MoHLW, 2007). Furthermore, spending per patient actually rose after the copayment increased (Japan, MoHLW, 2007).

Copayments are largely ineffectual because patients do not regard health care as an optional expenditure. If they are concerned about their health, or if a physician directs them to have a certain procedure performed, a small copayment will not discourage them from seeking care. Research does suggest that if copayments are set at a very high level, utilization will be reduced and financial sustainability promoted—but they also burden patients and potentially limit access to care.

As an alternative to copayments, public and private payers in Asia may want to consider the following:

- ensuring that they have access to outcomes data from providers; in addition to promoting quality, as noted previously, this will allow payers to create reimbursement formulas that promote cost effectiveness and improve care;

- following capitation or diagnosis-related-group-based reimbursement models, rather than fee-for-service models;

- providing incentives or penalties to encourage hospitals to merge or take other action to reduce costs; and

- mandating flat fees, based on diagnosis, to reduce the length of hospital stays.

Public and private payers could also significantly reduce costs through patient education, because misconceptions and long-ingrained habits about seeking treatment often increase costs in this region. For instance:

- Some Chinese patients ask to receive expensive intravenous drugs for common colds because they believe that represents the best value for their money.

- Japanese patients visit physicians about 14 times each year—three times the rate in other developed countries (Henke, Kadonaga, and Kanzler, 2009).

- In Taiwan Province of China, native citizens and Chinese patients spend about $1.40 on treatment for every $1 premium paid in public or private insurance, compared to 40 cents for every $1 premium paid for foreigners living in the country who have comparable plans (Chang, 2011).[1]

---

[1]Here and throughout this volume, the $ symbol always indicates U.S. dollars.

Among other initiatives, payers could actively monitor patients with chronic diseases and ensure that they visit their general practitioners. While payers have to fund such programs, they ultimately benefit from decreased health care costs.

## THE EVOLUTION OF PRIVATE HEALTH CARE IN ASIA

Well-established private payers in Western countries often play a sophisticated role in the health care system, having responsibilities that extend far beyond provider reimbursement (Figure 4.4). For instance, private payers may purchase hospitals or other health care facilities or acquire physician groups, allowing them to serve as network managers. In this role, they can exert more influence over provider quality and efficiency (e.g., by providing financial rewards to providers with the best health outcomes, or setting care guidelines). At an even more advanced level, some private payers play a role in disease management, working directly with patients, providers, and other stakeholders to improve care. As one example, a payer could appoint a disease management facilitator to identify patients with diabetes who are at risk of high-cost complications and help them proactively receive preventive care. Such measures increase short-term costs but have long-term benefits.

Although private payers will become more common in Asia over the next few years, we expect that their responsibilities will initially be restricted to provider reimbursement because of infrastructure issues. For instance, most private payers in Asia have a list of preferred providers but do not own any physician networks or facilities, making it impossible for them to serve as network managers. And it could be difficult for payers to acquire hospitals in Asia, especially in developing or emerging markets, because of a lack of existing facilities that are available for purchase, since most are owned by the public sector. Construction of new hospitals, the only other option, is time

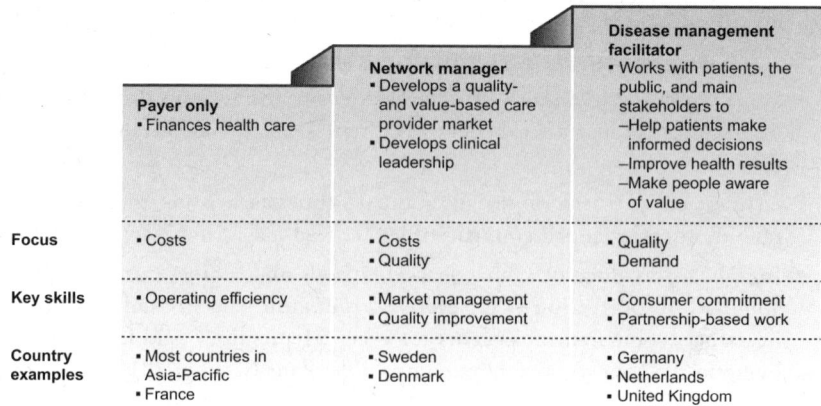

**Figure 4.4** Possible Roles for Payers
Source: McKinsey analysis.

consuming. As another complication, payers in emerging markets or developing countries might first need to make significant investments in provider education and training, since there may not be enough qualified personnel available to staff a network.

Despite these complications, private payers in Asia could eventually assume the role of network managers or disease management facilitators, following the path taken in Western countries. Such advances, however, probably will not be seen for many years.

While the growth of private health care in Asia is a welcome development, both governments and payers should proceed with caution. As recent experience in the United States shows, any efforts to reform a health care system may be met with distrust and violent objections. To avoid such problems, all reforms should support a country's long-standing social values, political goals, and health care priorities.

## APPENDIX 4.1. MAJOR HEALTH INSURANCE MODELS IN ASIA

Appendix Figure 4.1 summarizes the major health insurance models in Asia.

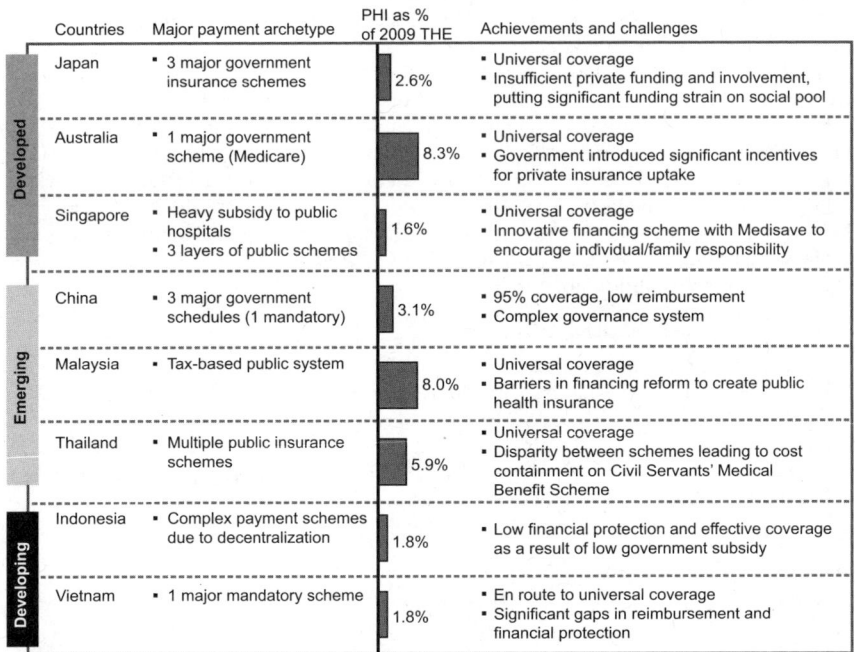

| | Countries | Major payment archetype | PHI as % of 2009 THE | Achievements and challenges |
|---|---|---|---|---|
| Developed | Japan | • 3 major government insurance schemes | 2.6% | • Universal coverage<br>• Insufficient private funding and involvement, putting significant funding strain on social pool |
| | Australia | • 1 major government scheme (Medicare) | 8.3% | • Universal coverage<br>• Government introduced significant incentives for private insurance uptake |
| | Singapore | • Heavy subsidy to public hospitals<br>• 3 layers of public schemes | 1.6% | • Universal coverage<br>• Innovative financing scheme with Medisave to encourage individual/family responsibility |
| Emerging | China | • 3 major government schedules (1 mandatory) | 3.1% | • 95% coverage, low reimbursement<br>• Complex governance system |
| | Malaysia | • Tax-based public system | 8.0% | • Universal coverage<br>• Barriers in financing reform to create public health insurance |
| | Thailand | • Multiple public insurance schemes | 5.9% | • Universal coverage<br>• Disparity between schemes leading to cost containment on Civil Servants' Medical Benefit Scheme |
| Developing | Indonesia | • Complex payment schemes due to decentralization | 1.8% | • Low financial protection and effective coverage as a result of low government subsidy |
| | Vietnam | • 1 major mandatory scheme | 1.8% | • En route to universal coverage<br>• Significant gaps in reimbursement and financial protection |

**Appendix Figure 4.1** Asian Insurance Models
Note: Coverage of figure is not exhaustive. PHI = private health insurance; THE = total health expenditure.

# REFERENCES

Angrisano, C., Y. Elbaz, D. Farrell, L. Fiorito, N. Henke, K. Khajavi, B. Kocher, M. Laboissiere, A. Loat, P. Mango, D. Nuzum, and J. Wettke, 2006, *A Framework to Guide Health Care System Reform* (New York: McKinsey Global Institute, McKinsey & Co.).

Angrisano, C., D. Farrell, B. Kocher, M. Laboissiere, and S. Parker, 2007, *Accounting for the Cost of Health Care in the United States* (New York: McKinsey Global Institute, McKinsey & Co.).

Chang, V., 2011, "Utilizing Health Care Insurance—Experience from Taiwan." Presentation at the Shanghai Medical Association's Fourth Annual Premium Health Care Conference, Shanghai, October 21.

China, Office of State Council, 2007, "Chinese Health Care Reform," press release, Beijing, July 7.

Fukawa, T., 2002, *Public Health Insurance in Japan* (Washington: World Bank Institute).

Hacker, J., 2008, The Case for Public Plan Choice in National Health Reform" (Washington: Institute for America's Future). Available at http://institute.ourfuture.org/files/Jacob_Hacker_Public_Plan_Choice.pdf.

Henke, N., S. Kadonaga, and L. Kanzler, 2009, "Improving Japan's Health Care System," *McKinsey Quarterly*, March.

Japan, Ministry of Health, Labor, and Welfare Statistics (MoHLW), 2007, "Detailed Forecast of Health Care Expenditure," PowerPoint presentation, Tokyo, February.

Kyburg, L., and H. Stuker, 2007, "Feasibility Study: DRG System as Cost Containment Method—Medical Insurance Scheme in China," EU-China Social Security Reform Cooperation Project, November. Available at http://www.eucss.org.cn/fileadmin/research_papers/policy/Medical_insurance/Feasibility_DRG_Final_maintext_20071126.pdf.

Lin, W., G. Liu, and G. Chen, 2009, "Urban Resident Basic Medical Insurance: A Landmark Reform Toward Universal Coverage in China," *Health Economics*, Vol. 18, No. S2, pp. S83–S96.

Ma, S., and N. Sood, 2008, "A Comparison of the Health Systems in China and India," Occasional Paper, Rand Center for Asia Pacific Policy (Arlington, VA). Available at http://www.rand.org/pubs/occasional_papers/2008/RAND_OP212.pdf.

McKinsey & Company, 2008, *The Challenge Of Funding Japan's Future Health Care Needs* (New York: McKinsey Global Institute, McKinsey & Co.).

Netherlands, Ministry of Health, Welfare, and Sport (MoHWS), 2009, "Health Insurance System." Available at http://english.minvws.nl/en/themes/health-insurance-system/.

Philippines, Department of Health (DoH), 2010, "Toward Financial Risk Protection: Health Care Financing Strategy 2010–2020," Health Sector Reform Agenda Monograph No. 10. Available at http://www.scribd.com/doc/35105401/Health-Care-Financing-Strategy-2010-2020-Philippines.

Philippines, State Senate, 2004, "An Act to Reduce Health Care Costs by Requiring Tertiary and Specialized Hospitals to Share Certain Services and Equipment," Bill No. 60. Available at http://erbl.pids.gov.ph/listbills.phtml?id=233.

Süssmuth-Dyckerhoff, C., and J. Wang, 2010, "Identifying Private-Sector Opportunities in Chinese Health Care," *McKinsey Quarterly*, November.

Tangcharoensathien, V., W. Patcharanarumol, P. Ir, S. Aljunid, A. Mukti, K. Akkhavong, E. Banzon, D. Huong, H. Thabrany, and A. Mills, 2011, "Health-Financing Reforms in Southeast Asia: Challenges in Achieving Universal Coverage," *Lancet*, Vol. 377, No. 9768, pp. 863–73.

Xu, K., P. Saksena, X. Fu, H. Lei, N. Chen, and G. Carrin, 2009, "Health Care Financing in Rural China: New Rural Cooperative Medical Scheme," Technical Brief for Policy-Makers No. 3/2009 (Geneva: World Health Organization).

# CHAPTER 5

# Perspective on the Appropriate Role of the Private Sector in Meeting Health Care Needs

TSUNG-MEI CHENG AND UWE E. REINHARDT

Throughout the post–World War II decades, health policy advisors and health policymakers in modern health systems have argued inconclusively over the question "government versus market" or "regulation versus competition." Because the empirical evidence on this issue has been inconclusive, the debate has proceeded and continues to proceed mainly on the basis of ideology and not evidence. And because political power changes hands in any country, health systems have meandered forward, slouching either toward "market" or toward "government."

We do not purport to settle the issue in this chapter. Our intent merely is to survey the factors one should consider in this debate—especially the distributive social ethic that a health system is to observe. We offer some of our own conclusions in the summary section.

The chapter begins with a listing of the basic functions any health system must perform, along with the agents who might perform each function. The second section presents a brief survey of the distinct distributive social ethics nations may wish to impose on their health system. The third section turns to the potential role of private markets in health systems, followed in the fourth section by a taxonomy of different mixes of health insurance and health care delivery that nations around the world have adopted. The chapter concludes with a distillate of our own conclusions on the subject.

Our overarching conclusion is that a health system certainly can enlist the power and ingenuity of the private sector, as long as the latter is regulated and provided with incentives that will naturally lead it to stay within the social moral norms that society wishes its health system to observe.

## THE BASIC FUNCTIONS OF A HEALTH SYSTEM

To explore the role that the private sector can play in meeting the health care needs of a nation, it is useful to list first the common functions that any health care system must perform:

1. financing health care (through taxes, insurance premiums, or out-of-pocket payments);

2. producing and delivering health care services;

3. purchasing and paying for health care (by either patients or insurers);

4. regulating and monitoring the health system (governance);

5. making sure the system has adequate human capital (e.g., physicians, nurses, medical technicians) and physical capital;

6. making sure every citizen has access to timely, needed health care; and

7. protecting individuals and families from the risk of high expenses for serious illness (risk pooling through health insurance) that can leave households in financial distress or even financial bankruptcy—a circumstance not unknown in the United States.

## THE GOALS OF A HEALTH SYSTEM

Presumably, if one asked the man and woman in the street about the goal to be posed for these functions of a health system, it would be "maintaining and enhancing the health of the population." An ancillary goal would be to protect individuals and families from financial catastrophe in case of illness. But such broadly stated goals leave much room for alternative approaches.

For example, suppose a given national budget were set aside to pursue these goals, and suppose one measured the output produced by a health system crudely by "quality-adjusted life-years" (QALYs) added through medical care.[1] Should the fixed budget then be allocated among the people it covers to maximize the algebraic sum of QALYs attainable from the budget, regardless of who does and does not get these QALYs? If not, how else should the budget be allocated? To the sickest people? Or on the basis of willingness and ability to pay?

Similarly, when speaking about "Protecting individuals and families from the risk of high expenses for serious illness," how far should that protection go? Suppose one expressed it as the maximum fraction $X$ of its budget that a family should be asked to contribute to health insurance and health care in a given year. How large should $X$ be? Should it vary progressively with income? And if so, how?

Already we are touching with these questions on issues of social ethics and notions of fairness, a subject on which more will be said in the next section.

---

[1] To develop the adjustment for "quality of life," a representative sample of individuals is asked how many life-years in perfect health would be equivalent in their minds to, say, 10 years of life in a specified, less-than-perfect health status. For example, if the survey respondents say, on average, that they would rank 8 years of life in perfect health equally with 10 years of life in the specified, less-than-perfect health status, then each life-year in that less-than-perfect health status is counted as 0.8 QALYs. See, for example, http://www.medicine.ox.ac.uk/bandolier/painres/download/whatis/QALY.pdf.

## POTENTIAL AGENTS FOR PERFORMING THE HEALTH SYSTEM'S FUNCTIONS

In principle, each of the seven functions listed above could be performed by the following actors:

- patients themselves (in countries that treat health care as just another personal consumption good);
- private, for-profit commercial entities;
- private not-for-profit entities;
- government entities; or
- quasi-governmental entities, that is, private bodies endowed by government with a set of specified regulatory authorities (as, e.g., the Federal Joint Committee of Germany, which promulgates the specific, binding regulations required by federal legislation for all of German health care) (Gemeinsamer Bundesausschuss, 2007).

As this list makes clear, the term "private sector" could refer to both the *not-for-profit* and the *for-profit sectors*. In microeconomic theory, these two private sector actors are thought to pursue different objectives in the conduct of their enterprises, which implies that they will behave differently in the same market setting (Folland, Goodman, and Stano, 2010, Chap. 13). In the hospital and nursing home sector, for example, the not-for-profit institutions are thought to seek high quality, high occupancy, and merely "satisfactory" profits, while for-profit hospitals and nursing homes are thought to maximize the singular goal of profits. In practice, however, both forms of ownership tend to pursue mainly profits and behave similarly, especially in highly competitive markets with some excess capacity.

For-profit enterprises seek profits to enhance the wealth of owners. Not-for-profits seek "excess of revenue over expenses"—their delicate term for "profits"—to enhance the power and prestige of the institution by reinvesting these funds in the enterprise for further growth and more prestige. In fact, "growth," meaning growth in revenues, becomes the mantra for both for-profit and not-for-profit institutions. Therefore, in this chapter we shall think of "private sector" as a synonym for "commercial sector."

## THE DISTRIBUTIVE SOCIAL ETHICS IMPOSED ON THE HEALTH SYSTEM

Different nations may have rather different ideas on what distribution of health care among the citizenry is considered "fair" and "appropriate," as do different citizens within nations. These ideas are fundamental to the way in which health systems are financed and structured and how they evolve under successive health reforms. Failure to articulate these ideas about social justice explicitly before undertaking any health reform usually leads to either failure of reform or an inability to implement reform. The long struggle of the United States in this regard is a prime example of what happens when this important first step is disregarded, as it routinely is in the United States.[2]

There are at least three distinct notions on how health care ought to be distributed within society, and many mixtures in between. These distinct notions are described below, followed by a discussion on social ethics and the concept of "efficiency."

## The Different Notions of a "Just" Distribution of Health Care

*Social Ethic I: Pure Egalitarianism. The health system should be financed and structured so that the entire health care experience a person has in response to a given illness should be the same regardless of that individual's socioeconomic status in society, and the financial burden of health insurance and out-of-pocket spending for health care should be at least proportional to income if not progressive.*

Canada and several Asian nations—Japan, the Republic of Korea, and Taiwan Province of China—have officially adopted this ethic, although high out-of-pocket spending in some Asian health systems does reduce the attained degree of egalitarianism somewhat. All of these systems operate through a government-run, single-payer health insurance system that pays physicians, hospitals, and other providers of health care the same fees for every citizen and is financed largely on the basis of ability to pay.

A common fee schedule, by design, encourages egalitarianism on the delivery side. By contrast, in the United States fees paid to providers by the government-run Medicaid insurance program for the poor are much lower than those paid by commercial insurance. This has led many U.S. physicians to refuse to treat poor people covered by the Medicaid program. In effect, Medicaid signals physicians that their professional work has a lower value when applied to poor people covered by Medicaid than it has when applied to commercially insured patients. U.S. policymakers should ask themselves if that is the signal they wish to send.

*Social Ethic II: Two-Tiered Health Care. Most of the citizenry should share the same health care experience in response to a given illness, although a small, wealthy elite can buy out of this social contract and have its own, more expensive health insurance and health care system.*

One finds that approach in the United Kingdom and in some countries in continental Europe—for example, Germany—although Germany's privately insured well-to-do actually receive about the same clinical care as does the rest of the population, and the privately insured constitute but a small percentage of the total population.[3] These European nations adopt the two-tiered approach mainly to provide an escape valve for the discontent that the well-to-do may develop with more egalitarian approaches that could, but do not always, entail some restrictions on health care and some rationing. Canada does not have an official safety valve of this sort, but the U.S. health system serves as an informal upper tier for

---

[2]For a fuller discussion of this facet of health system, see Roberts and others (2003) and Ruger (2010), especially Chapter 1.

[3]For more on the German health system, see Busse (2010).

Canadians with the ability to pay out of pocket for the more expensive U.S. care that is available on demand. So far, however, these nations tend to keep the private upper-tier health system relatively small, by various regulatory means.

In the United Kingdom, about 11 percent of the population has private health insurance coverage, on top of being automatically entitled to treatment under the government-run National Health System (NHS). Those privately insured patients pay premiums to the private insurers of their choice but do not receive a tax refund for their share of the taxes paid toward the NHS care financed out of general taxation. In effect, this approach means that people who opt for private health insurance and health care pay for both the NHS and the private health insurance plans they choose.

Germans who elect to opt out of their country's statutory health insurance (SHI) system in favor of private commercial health insurance avoid having to pay the payroll taxes that finance the statutory system (on average about 13–14 percent of gross payroll).[4] The role of the private insurance sector is kept small, however, by stipulating under the law that people who leave the highly government-regulated, egalitarian SHI system for the private insurance sector cannot ever return to the SHI system unless they became paupers. This stipulation makes switching to the private system much more risky for the individual, because under private insurance, premiums are set on commercial, actuarial principles and rise with age much more rapidly than they do under the SHI system.

In sum, many of the European two-tiered health systems provide fairly egalitarian health care for 90 percent or more of the population, keeping the fraction of fully privately insured individuals at or below 10 percent of the population.

*Social Ethic III: Multitiered Health Care.* *Health care is really just another private consumption good for which the patient should be financially responsible. Thus, it is perfectly alright to let the quality of health care and of the entire health care experience vary by income class.*

No developed country currently follows this social ethic *completely*—not even the United States—although for some low-income population groups the United States increasingly does lean in that direction, side by side with the basically egalitarian private employer-based health insurance systems managed by large employers and the private health insurers they contract with to provide health insurance for their employees. One may further note that the current enthusiasm among some American policymakers for very high-deductible health insurance, coupled with tax-favored health savings accounts (patterned after Singapore's medical savings accounts), also leans in the direction of more nonegalitarian health care. (More on this approach will be said further on.)

There are, of course, many different mixtures of these social ethics in between that are now being practiced by different countries. The point here is that, for any health reform to be successful, one should begin with a political consensus on

---

[4]Germany's SHI system is financed by a proportional payroll tax, and by general federal revenue for children only, and is administered by some 200 self-regulating not-for-profit sickness funds that are very tightly regulated under federal law.

what ethical goal the health system is to achieve. Once that ethical goal is agreed upon and articulated, health policy analysts can design policies that can achieve the chosen goal.

A second point is that political leaders should not pay any attention to health reform proposals, and especially those proposed by foreign consultants, that do *not* explicitly state up front what ethical goals their proposal is structured to achieve and whether those goals are consistent with those of the country they presume to advise. It is an effective way to control what might easily turn into a cultural or ideological hegemonic takeover.

## Social Ethics and the Concept of "Efficiency"

It is often argued that there exists a conflict between "equity" and "efficiency" in health care and that, therefore, trade-offs must be made between these two major features of a health system. We find this unhelpful—indeed, misleading—imagery.

The concept of "efficiency" is most easily taught and understood with reference to the textbook model of the production of imaginary, unidimensional, standard "widgets" that are sold in perfectly competitive markets, *without any one caring who in particular does and does not receive any of the produced widgets*, that is, *in the absence of a distinct social ethic on the desirable distribution of the widgets among members of society*. In real life, the concept of efficiency is much more complex and intellectually challenging. Figure 5.1 illustrates the many facets of the concept.

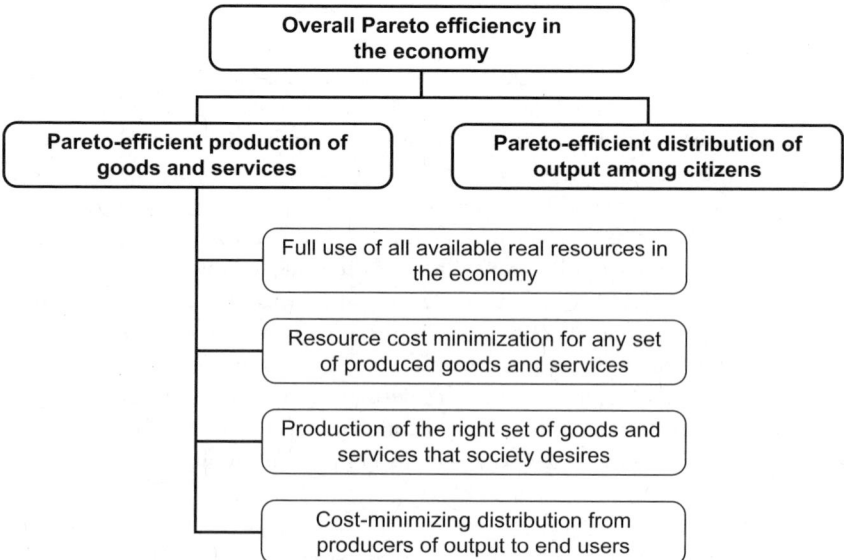

**Figure 5.1**  Facets of "Economic Efficiency" in an Economy

First, a distinction must be made between *efficiency in production* and *efficiency in distribution*. Efficiency in production has at least three distinct facets:

1. It requires that no real resources available to society are left idle (which makes unemployment, by definition, inefficient).

2. It requires that for any given bundle of real-resource inputs, the "value" of output to society is maximized or, conversely, that for any given set of outputs with a given "value," the opportunity cost of the real resources used to achieve that output has been minimized.

3. It requires that all producers in society collectively produce the right combination of outputs desired by society.

Efficiency in distribution has at least two distinct facets:

1. The channels of distributing output from producers to end users should be so configured as to minimize the opportunity cost of the real resources used to move the output.

2. The distribution of the available output among members of society, for any given initial distribution of income, should be "Pareto efficient," that is, should be such that it is not possible to reallocate the output among members of society so as to make some people feel better off without making someone feel worse off.

These criteria can be made more rigorous with mathematical notation, but for present purposes, Figure 5.1 suffices.

There is much loose talk in health policy and health politics about the "value of health care" and "efficiency." Our experience over many years is that these terms are hardly ever rigorously defined by people who use them, which leaves such discussions nebulous.

First, what is actually meant by the "value" of health care? Consider the implantation of a coronary stent or of a defibrillator into a patient. Does that device have the same "value" whether it is implanted into a wealthy person able to pay for it with his or her own resources as it does if implanted into a low-income person who would be unable to pay for it with his or her own financial resources? Classical welfare economists would answer "no," because they measure the value of a thing by the maximum price someone would bid for it. The idea is that the higher the price bid, the more the bidder "values" the thing. Virtually all of applied welfare economic analysis one sees in textbooks and in practice is based on this valuation principle. In health care, it would mean that the total social value of health care is maximized if health care is rationed strictly on the basis of price and ability to pay.

But is that valuation principle for health care shared by the population at large—or by the politicians who represent the population? Would any politician, journalist or, for that matter, even economist openly announce that a stent implanted in a rich person has higher value than one implanted in a poor person—that health care should be rationed by price and ability to pay? If not, how then do we define and measure what is "value" in health care? It remains an unsolved challenge in health economics. Cost-utility analysis does not get one out of this fix, because it only helps to define quality-adjusted units of output (e.g., quality-adjusted life-years or disability-adjusted life-years lost). Someone still has to put a monetary value on that measured output.

Consider next the concept of Pareto efficiency. One of the great shocks to first-year students in economics is that an allocation of resources in society under which most people are starving while others live in gluttony may nevertheless calmly be certified by economists as Pareto efficient, if those living in gluttony would resent giving up some of their benefits for the sake of bestowing them on the starving masses. Does that conform to popular notions of an efficient resource allocation in a nation? Thus, it can be asked how useful the much-hallowed criterion of Pareto efficiency actually is in applied health policy or, for that matter, in public policy in general.[5]

This excursion into theoretical concepts should make it clear just how intellectually challenging it is to noneconomists—that is, the majority of people—to speak about "value," "efficiency," and the much-discussed but rarely clearly articulated trade-off between "equity" and "efficiency." That said, however, one surely can explore whether a hospital or medical clinic or long-term care facility minimizes the real-resource costs to treat a given patient load, whether the combination of health services produced by a health system meets the clinical needs of patients as determined by expert clinicians (rather than economists), and whether distribution channels are efficient, or whether a public or private insurer minimizes the real-resource cost and the premium of providing coverage for a given benefit package. From what is known, it can be said that many components of virtually any operating health system today operate inefficiently in this sense.

Matters become much more intractable, however, if one wishes to apply the term "efficiency" to the distribution of health care among members of society. For example, suppose one defined and measured the output to be had from a given health care budget by the much-used metric of QALYs. Would it then be "efficient" to maximize the QALYs one could extract from that budget, regardless of who receives those QALYs? Would it be efficient if the QALYs were auctioned off to the highest bidders in an efficiently conducted auction? There is empirical evidence from surveys that citizens generally would prefer to see health care resources go to the sickest and most-suffering fellow citizens rather than have the number of QALYs maximized. This may confuse economists. But should that matter to policymakers? Similarly, would it be most efficient to have a completely free market in the donation and use of transplantable organs, with available organs allocated to the highest bidders?

Finally, a statement that Canada's government-run health insurance system is less efficient than America's commercial insurance system is not particularly helpful, because Canadians impose upon their system strict egalitarian principles that are not imposed on the system in the United States. The two systems do not pursue the same social goals. One could, of course, imagine in theory two systems begetting the same clinical outcomes and equitable distributions of these out-

---

[5]For a more extensive discussion of this proposition, see Reinhardt (2001).

comes among citizens, but with one using more real resources to achieve that outcome than the other. Clearly the one using less resources would dominate the other in terms of relative efficiency. Unfortunately, we cannot readily think of a practical context that matches this ideal.

These are important points to keep in mind in health reform discussions of league tables for health systems, of which more will be said further on.

## IS PRIVATE ENTERPRISE INVARIABLY MORE EFFICIENT THAN GOVERNMENT ENTERPRISE?

There is a strong presumption, especially among economists, that any economic activity organized and managed by private enterprise—especially by investor-owned, for-profit enterprise—is invariably more efficient in production than would be a government enterprise entrusted with organizing and managing that activity. The assumption here is that profit-driven private enterprise has every incentive to minimize the real-resource costs of production, while these incentives are lacking in government-run enterprise which, in addition, frequently becomes a victim of political patronage. In the abstract, it is a persuasive argument. In the context of health care, however, one must be mindful of two caveats.

First, while a private enterprise has strong incentives to minimize costs, it also has every incentive to maximize the claim it makes on the nation's GDP, that is, the prices it charges for its output. Quite often these two facets of enterprises—production costs and output prices—are confused in the discussion. More efficient production does not necessarily lead to lower prices.

Second, as noted earlier, efficiency in production requires that the right quantity and combination of output be produced. One can assume it in markets in which potential buyers are well informed about the quality dimensions of the product traded, have adequate countervailing power vis-à-vis sellers, and pay 100 percent of the price charged for the product. Those conditions do not generally apply in health care, however, where profit-chasing for-profit and not-for-profit enterprises have powerful incentives to deliver more care to patients than is clinically needed or provide a profit-enhancing but clinically inappropriate mix of procedures. This is especially so when distant third parties (health insurance) foot the bill.

Policymakers in most of the fully developed world as well as in emerging market economies are convinced that their health systems waste huge fractions of total health spending in this way. It is one of the major challenges facing health policymakers around the world.

## THE POTENTIAL ROLE OF PRIVATE MARKETS IN HEALTH SYSTEMS

As the comparative history of different economic systems amply showed during the twentieth century, an economic system based on clearly defined rights to private, productive property, in which profit-seeking producers of goods and services compete for customers in markets regulated by government to be competitive and in which contracts among private parties are reliably and fairly enforced by law, tends to endow members of society *on average* with far more goods and services and greater personal wealth than does any other economic system. That by now well-established fact has led to the idea that all or most social problems can be solved through a competitive free-market approach, even the production and distribution of health care. Among some policy analysts and management consultants, the idea is like a religious belief that need not be questioned. But for all its power to unleash human energy and imagination, a market approach to solving social problems does have at least two serious limitations:

1. Some economic activity does not meet the basic conditions for a properly functioning market, and much of health care (along with education and the administration of justice) is among these activities.

2. The distribution of goods and services among members of society brought about by markets may violate the ethical goals society wishes to achieve for certain activities, such as health care, education, and justice.

Too many advocates of a "market approach" to health care seem unaware—or lose sight—of these serious limitations of markets. These limitations do not mean that market forces should never be enlisted here and there in a health care system. But they do mean that great care must be taken by policymakers in deciding when to enlist market forces and when to use other mechanisms to guide and control economic activity.

Let us briefly elaborate on these two limitations of a market approach.

## Conditions for a Properly Functioning Market

Among the *requirements* that must be met for a market for traded goods and services to function efficiently and in society's best interest are the following:

1. Buyers must be technically and intellectually competent to judge the merits of the goods and services being offered them by the sellers. This means that the buyers must fully understand the various quality attributes of these goods and services and what benefits they personally might derive from them.

2. *Before* making a decision to buy, the potential buyers must know the full price they have to pay per unit of the good and service.

3. Buyers should bear the full price charged by the producer of the good or service being sold to the buyers, and producers should bear the full cost of producing them.

4. No seller or buyer should have a monopoly in the market for traded goods or services.

5. Neither the buy side nor the sell side of the market should be able to collude to fix prices or other terms of trade.

6. There must be completely free entry for buyers and sellers to interact in the marketplace.

Let us explore how well these conditions are met in health care.

## The Problem of Asymmetric Information

The first condition—full knowledge and understanding on the part of buyers of the services or goods sold them by sellers (providers)—typically is not met in modern medicine, where the traded goods or services usually are of a highly technical nature. It is the reason why patients visit physicians who have spent years acquiring the superior, specialized knowledge they have in this regard. Economists call this problem an "asymmetry of information." Markets do not function well under conditions of asymmetric information. In any market with asymmetric information on the buy or sell sides, the party with superior information can easily exploit the other party.

In principle, physicians act as the agents of patients paid to formulate the patients' demand for the goods and services that go into the treatment of a medical illness. A major problem in health care is that physicians may not fulfill that agency function properly, for a number of reasons.

First, when patients come to see them, physicians themselves may not know the best current treatment for a medical condition, and patients may not be aware of that fact, trusting that their physician does know the best clinical practice for any condition. The physician's knowledge base may be obsolete or, alternatively, the medical profession might not have agreed on what is the best response to a given medical condition. This can explain, for example, why there are huge variations in practice style and per capita health spending across the United States for similar populations.[6] Regional variations in practice styles and per capita health spending exist in any health system, but probably not with quite the high variance one observes in the United States. For example, the cost of health spending by the federal Medicare program for the elderly, measured per insured elderly person during the last two years of their lives, can vary inexplicably by a factor of three across a small state, such as New Jersey.[7]

Second, when physicians profit from every one of their services given to patients, for example, in a fee-for-service payment environment, and profit more from some services than from others, they may persuade patients to accept and pay for services that patients do not need—a problem economists call "supplier induced demand."

Third, in some instances physicians may be paid financial rewards (kickbacks or bribes) from health care producers to whom physicians might refer patients— for example, from hospitals, or pharmaceutical companies, or medical device companies, and so on. Given their power to induce demand for health care, physicians may induce their patients to accept and pay for those referral services when they are not truly needed.

## Transparency on Prices

The second condition—full information on prices—also is only rarely met in health care, even in the most economically developed nations. More typically, in

---

[6]In this connection, see http://www.dartmouthatlas.org.
[7]See New Jersey Commission (2008), Table 6.1.

the United States and elsewhere, patients enter the health care market like blind-folded shoppers groping their way through a department store. In fact, in the United States the prices negotiated between individual private insurers and individual providers of health care typically are proprietary and kept as trade secrets. Very little is officially known about these prices, even to the research community.

Furthermore, in the United States the fee schedule for physicians has more than 9,000 separate items in it, and that for hospitals has more than 20,000 (Reinhardt, 2006). Even if there were a published price list, with so many prices for items patients cannot possibly understand, it would not be helpful to patients. For competition to work, prices have to be meaningful to patients.

### Monopoly Power or Collusion

The presence of health insurance violates the third condition of properly functioning markets. Consolidation among hospitals and collusion among physicians through professional associations violates the fourth condition listed above. Professional licensing and the restrictions that come with it—for example, the prohibition on nurses' competing with doctors for patients and to prescribe medicine—violate the sixth condition.

Given these shortfalls from the competitive ideal—asymmetry of information, lack of user-friendly information on quality and prices, and monopoly power on the supply side—it would take an enormous regulatory effort to move health care markets closer to the competitive ideal. Indeed, one invariably sees attempts to move the health system closer to "more market" accompanied with a whole host of government regulations, including price regulation, that belie the move to a free market. We see this clearly in the Dutch, German, and Swiss health systems.[8]

In 2006, for example, the government of the Netherlands embarked on a bold experiment to abandon its erstwhile system, in which 60 percent of the population had been enrolled in a mandatory social insurance scheme, in favor of a system based on competing private insurance companies only that must compete under a regime of "managed competition." A recent interim assessment of this experiment in *The New England Journal of Medicine* by Okma, Marmor, and Oberlander (2011) is not encouraging about the ability of that approach to control growth in health spending. Health spending in the Netherlands has been rising rapidly since 2006. Furthermore, as the authors emphasize, to make the "managed competition" approach work within a framework of social solidarity, the system remains highly regulated by the government:

> Notwithstanding the rhetoric of competition, the Netherlands still relies heavily on regulation. Indeed, the Dutch case shows that competitive systems that seek to escape supposedly centralized, bureaucratic control of medical care paradoxically require sophisticated regulation and government intervention in order to work. The government has not abandoned its traditional tools,

---

[8]For more information on the Dutch and Swiss health systems, see Leu and others (2009).

including global budgets and constraints on prices and patient cost sharing. It sets fees for independent specialists and general practitioners and controls prices for most hospital services. In 2010, for example, payments to specialists were reduced in response to budget overruns. (p. 289)

The Swiss health system presents a similar case of tight government regulation over the private health insurance market, in which 84 private insurers compete for enrollees. Switzerland has no government-run health insurance plan. The Swiss health reform of 1996 imposed a mandate on all Swiss to enroll in a private insurance plan for a specified national uniform benefit package, regardless of preexisting conditions. Private insurers could no longer cherry-pick patients who were low risks. Private insurers compete for enrollees based on the various policies with varied deductibles they offer, but according to the former Swiss federal minister of public health, Thomas Zeltner, in a published interview in *Health Affairs*, each insurer "must charge all of its customers the same premium for that policy, regardless of the customer's health status and age" (Cheng, 2010a, p. 1443).

We regard both the Swiss system and the Dutch experiment as ones worth following closely over the next decade, as they can tell us much about the feasibility and relative merits of private markets in health care.

## What Actually Is Meant by "Competition" in Health Care?

Frequently, when competition is mentioned during the health policy debate, the speakers do not clearly describe (1) who is to compete and (2) on what instrument they are to compete. This adds to the confusion around health policy. We might be talking here about either *health insurers* or *providers of health care*—or both. The instruments on which they compete might be *prices* or *quality*—or both.

One gains the impression that when people speak about competition they naturally have in mind competition on the basis of price. But the providers of health care could be made to compete strictly on quality under fixed prices determined elsewhere—perhaps by government regulation (e.g., Medicare in the United States or Taiwan Province of China's single-payer National Health Insurance)[9] or by negotiations among associations of insurers with associations of providers (as in Germany and Switzerland).

### Competition among Health Insurers

For starters, it must be understood how private health insurers set the premiums they charge the insured, unless government dictates that the insurer must charge all customers the same premium regardless of gender, age or health status, a stricture called "community rating." Absent such a government regulation, an insurer will try to obtain information on any applicant's health status, using age, gender, income, and prior use of health care as data. Using actuarial methods that rely on large databases

---

[9]For Taiwan Province of China, see Cheng (2009).

of health care utilization in previous years, the insurer's actuaries will then calculate the mathematically expected cost of procuring insured benefits for an insured individual falling into this age, gender, and health status category. That mathematically expected cost becomes the "actuarially fair" premium for the insured.

To that actuarially fair premium is then added a load factor to cover the costs of marketing and administration, such as claims processing, cost controls, and so on, and a hoped-for margin of profits, to arrive at the total premium for that individual. Insurers call the fraction of the premium that buys health care proper the "medical loss ratio," because that part of the premium is "lost," so to speak, to the providers of health care.

For large private health insurers in the United States, for example, between 15 and 25 percent of the premium charged goes for marketing, administration, and profits. For smaller insurers selling policies to individuals or groups of employees of small employers, between 35 and 45 percent of the premium is absorbed by marketing, administrative expense, and profits. Insurers compete for clients on total premiums, of course, which means they do have an incentive to constrain the cost of marketing, administration, and even profit margins. But the bulk of the premium they charge is driven by the prices that the providers of health care charge them.

It is often thought that the more health insurers compete for enrollees living in a given market area, the lower will be the insurance premiums charged to the insured. If these prices are *externally* set—either through government regulation or through negotiations between regional associations of insurers and regional associations of providers—then the premiums charged by individual insurers to the insured may be lower than they would be with fewer insurers, for two reasons. First, competitive pressures may force each insurer to put more effort into controlling the utilization of health care through "managed care" techniques. Second, each insurer will be forced to seek the utmost in reducing marketing and administrative expenses and profit margins.

On the other hand, if *individual* insurers themselves must negotiate prices with *individual* providers of care—as is the case in the U.S. private commercial insurance sector—then having more insurers in a market area will weaken each insurer vis-à-vis providers, especially hospitals, in bargaining over prices. The more insurers there are in a market area, the smaller will be, on average, the fraction of a provider's total revenue that comes from each insurer and the more leverage the provider will have over the insurer. That can cause rapid inflation in health care prices (Reinhardt, 2010).

Furthermore, a system of individually negotiated prices results in rampant price discrimination, as is the case in the United States, where a given insurer may pay several dozen different prices for the same procedure and an individual insurer will pay dozens of different prices to different providers for the same service. A recent study, for example, revealed that in 2007 a large California commercial insurer paid anywhere from $1,300 to $13,700 for an appendectomy, depending on which hospital performed it. For a coronary artery bypass graft, prices paid by the insurer varied from $33,000 to $99,800. Similarly, a large not-for-profit insurer in

New Jersey in 2007 paid different hospitals prices ranging from \$716 to \$3,717 for the facilities component of a colonoscopy; the corresponding fees for the physician ranged from \$178 to \$431. Neither total nor marginal costs could explain such differences.[10]

We know of no empirical research that links this enormous range of prices to a commensurate variation in quality. In fact, it would be hard to imagine, because a given hospital or doctor receives different prices from different insurers and, indeed, different prices from the same insurer under different types of policies sold by that insurer.

It is difficult to see what benefit society derives from such price discrimination, with prices varying solely on the basis of relative market power among payers and providers. Certainly it has not been able to control the annual growth in U.S. health spending. As Porter and Teisberg (2006) have argued in their *Redefining Health Care,* "the dysfunctional competition that has been created by price discrimination [in the United States] far outweighs any short-term advantages that individual system participants gain from it, even for those participants who currently enjoy the biggest discounts [of list prices]" (p. 66).

We agree with that assessment of price discrimination in the current U.S. health system and we do not recommend it to any other nation. Instead, we favor the so-called all-payer systems of, say, Germany and Switzerland, under which prices are negotiated by regional associations of insurers and providers, subject to overall budget caps set by government based on macroeconomic criteria.

## Competition among Providers

The effect of competition among providers also depends on who sets the prices that providers are paid. If those prices are *externally* set and identical for the same service for all providers competing in an area and, moreover, are the same for given procedures in a given market area, then competition among them will be mainly on the basis of the quality patients attribute to each hospital—either by word of mouth or through publicly available quality metrics. A very recent paper on competition in the United Kingdom, for example, found that under an externally set, fixed-price regime, competition for patients among hospitals appears to lead to an improvement in quality (Cooper, Gibbons, and McGuire, 2011). Likewise, providers in Taiwan Province of China, where fees are set by the government, compete for patients on the basis of the quality of services they deliver and not on price (Cheng, 2009). Once again, if individual providers negotiate fees with individual health insurers, the result will be pervasive price discrimination.

## Markets and Distributive Social Ethics in Health Care

Finally, while on the topic of private markets in health systems, it must be noted that, quite aside from the stringent conditions that must be met for a market approach to health care to function properly, the use of market systems

---

[10]New Jersey Commission (2008), Tables 6.3 and 6.4.

in an economy brings with it distinct ethical consequences for the distribution of economic privilege in society. As every first-year student of economics knows, a market that functions properly (as economics textbooks would define "properly") will allocate society's scarce resources to those individuals who are willing and able to outbid with money other individuals bidding for the same resources. This is how private markets *ration* scarce resources among members of society. The idea that market-based health systems do not ration health care, a proposition sometimes put forth by advocates of that approach, is non-sense.[11] This basic fact of markets explains why, in a free-market economy even as rich as the United States, there are millions of homeless people living side by side with families who own two or three homes, why millions of people go hungry while most of their fellow citizens eat too much, and why millions of poor people go without timely health care while others may consume too much care.

It is the present authors' experience that advocates of a free-market solution for health care—especially business-oriented management consulting firms—abstract unduly from distributive ethics. Instead, they talk about the "efficiency" of markets without acknowledging that the word "efficiency," as noted earlier, actually has no operative meaning unless it is defined in terms of specific social goals society wishes to reach with an economic sector such as health care (Reinhardt, 2001).

As the distinguished Nobel Laureate economist Kenneth J. Arrow pointed out in his famous 1963 article on health economics, in theory one could solve the problem of distributing health care equitably simply by redistributing money among members of society and then letting the free markets rule. Arrow quickly added, however, that in practice two obstacles stand in the way of this ideal solution. First, because of the great uncertainty surrounding health care—including knowledge of what might and might not work in treating a given illness—and the agency problem with physicians discussed earlier in this chapter, the conditions for a properly functioning market would still not be present in health care. Second, it is difficult in the political process of most modern nations to make the desired redistribution of income for this market solution.

One effective way to make this redistribution possible, however, is a system of so-called social health insurance (to be discussed more fully in the next section). For example, if all members of society were included in a large risk pool and paid into that pool premiums based on their ability to pay (based on their income), then every member's insurance card would, in effect, represent the purchasing power needed to purchase health care in an equitable manner.

Let us now turn to the various approaches by which different nations have sought to achieve a roughly equitable distribution of health care among their citizens.

---

[11]See, for example, Katz and Rosen (1991), Chapter 1, and Reinhardt (2007), which explores Canada's and the United States' different styles of rationing health care.

**TABLE 5.1**

A Taxonomy of Health Systems

| Ownership of delivery system | Social insurance (ability-to-pay financing) | | Private insurance (actuarially fair financing) | | No health insurance |
| --- | --- | --- | --- | --- | --- |
| | FINANCING AND HEALTH INSURANCE | | | | |
| | Single payer | Multiple payers | Nonprofit | For-profit | (Out of pocket) |
| Government | A | D | G | J | M |
| Private nonprofit | B | E | H | K | N |
| Private for-profit | C | F | I | L | O |

# A TAXONOMY OF DIFFERENT NATIONAL HEALTH SYSTEMS

In thinking about the structure of national health systems, it is useful to make a distinction between two major facets of such systems:

- the structure, ownership, and control of the *health insurance carriers* that pay for much of health care (that is, how health care is financed); and
- the structure, ownership, and control of the facilities that *produce and deliver* health care.

Table 5.1 shows various combinations of these two facets. Different countries in the developed world use different combinations of the cells in the table. Which combination is chosen depends mainly on the social distributive ethic that a nation wishes to impose on its health care system. That ethic, it must be noted, is translated into practice mainly through the health insurance facet of the system. In general, the more fragmented and unregulated that insurance facet is, the more likely the entire health system will lean toward a multitiered, nonegalitarian health system.

Furthermore, as we have argued earlier, the more fragmented the payment side is, the weaker it will be vis-à-vis the supply side of the health care market and the higher will be the administrative overhead of the system. Here, too, the United States provides ample data to support this assertion. In its recent, fairly sophisticated analysis of U.S. health spending relative to value received for that spending, the Business Roundtable (2009b) concluded that in "a new measure of the 'value' (cost and performance) of the U.S. health care system relative to our competitors' systems on a 100-point scale, the United States faces a 23-point 'value gap' relative to five leading economic competitors—Canada, Japan, Germany, the United Kingdom and France (the 'G-5 Group')—and a 46-point 'value gap' compared to emerging competitors Brazil, India, and China ('the BIC group')" (p. 2).

## Purely Socialized Medicine (Cell A)

The purest form of what is called "socialized medicine" is a health system defined as A in Table 5.1. The inpatient facilities of the British NHS and the Hong Kong Hospital Authority are examples of such systems, as are most of the Scandinavian systems, in which health care is financed and managed by the countries. Finally, the huge health system of the U.S. Department of Veterans Affairs—known as the VA Health Care System—is socialized health care in its purest form.

On the surface, there is a great irony in the fact that Americans, who routinely speak disparagingly of "socialized medicine," reserve precisely such a system for their veterans, whom they claim to admire. In fact, of course, the VA health system is now widely acknowledged to be America's most advanced health care system in the area of smart application of electronic information systems and of quality control. In a study by researchers at the Rand Corporation it was found that patients in the VA health system receive higher-quality care overall than do patients in the rest of the U.S. health system (Asch and others, 2004). This vast improvement in the VA system happened during the 1990s, after the Clinton administration threatened to subject the then less well-run VA health system to competition from private health maintenance organizations under the Clinton health reform plan (which, however, itself failed to become reality).

For developing countries with government-owned health care delivery systems, the recent history of the U.S. VA health system holds two important lessons. First, a government-run health system can, indeed, deliver first-rate health care, if its leadership is motivated to do so. Second, the leadership of a government-run health care system is most likely to be motivated to achieve first-rate health care if it is threatened by competition from other systems, as was the case with the VA in the 1990s. The challenge in health policy is to provide this competitive force without destroying the social ethic a nation's leaders may wish to impose on their health system.

## Other Forms of Social Insurance (Combinations ABC or DEF)

*Social insurance* can be defined in various ways. In this chapter, a social insurance system is thought to have the following characteristic:

> *The individual's or family's contribution to financing health care is based on ability to pay—for example, wages or all income—and is in no way related to the individual's health status.*

The strictest definition also divorces the contribution from age and gender.

Canada's and Taiwan Province of China's systems implement this approach through government-run, single-payer health insurance (for Taiwan Province of China, see Cheng, 2003). Other countries allow multiple health insurance carriers, although they impose very tight government regulations that force those private nonprofit or for-profit insurers to work under a common social ethic, common fee schedules and terms, and risk pooling over the entire population. Such is the case under the so-called Bismarck model, most clearly exemplified by Germany's statutory health insurance system and by the Swiss system, which pools risks over the entire population in a canton (Busse, 2010; Cheng, 2010a).

These systems differ from purely socialized medicine, such as the Hong Kong Hospital Authority or the U.S. VA system, in that the delivery of health care is not in the hands of government but under the control of a variety of nongovernmental facilities, including investor-owned for-profit providers (hospitals, clinics, private physician practices, and pharmacies), community-owned or religious facilities, and government-owned, public facilities that compete for patients side by side, under identical terms and payments. The single-payer systems of Taiwan Province of China and the Republic of Korea, for example, fall under this rubric. In Taiwan Province of China, the central government owns and operates the National Health Insurance system through its Bureau of National Health Insurance under the Department of Health, but the health care delivery system is mixed. In fact, it is predominantly private (Cheng, 2010b). By law, hospitals in Taiwan Province of China are all not for profit. But as discussed earlier, the difference between for profit and not for profit is in name only.

Canada's single-payer health insurance system (cells ABC) falls under this rubric as well. There the provincial governments each run the provincial health insurance system under federal guidelines; the health care delivery systems in the provinces are mixed, though predominantly private.

Germany's multiple-payer, not-for-profit SHI system is represented by cells DEF. The country still has several hundred nonprofit, nongovernmental "sickness funds" (Krankenkassen) that originated in the labor movement in the late nineteenth century. However, these sickness funds operate under a very tight regulatory framework (the Reichsversicherungsverordnung) first legislated under the German Chancellor Otto von Bismarck in the1880s, which is still in force after a century's worth of amendments. Germany's health care delivery system, once again, is mixed, with for-profit and not-for-profit hospitals competing side by side, on the same terms and fees.

Finally, in the United States, the government-run Medicare program for the elderly and Medicaid program for the poor are funded through taxes of various sorts and perform the financing and risk-pooling functions, but they contract out to private for-profit and not-for-profit insurance carriers the purchasing, claims processing, and cost control functions. Private carriers compete for these contracts on the basis of premiums charged to the government and quality of services delivered. Countries interested in adopting a model that combines social health insurance with managed care administered by private nonprofit or for-profit enterprises would do well in perusing the website of the U.S. Medicaid and Children's Health Insurance Program (CHIP) Payment and Access Commission.[12] The commission is a body of stakeholders—providers of health care, private managed-care companies, policy analysts, and so on—established in 2010 to advise the U.S. Congress and state governments on Medicaid and CHIP. These insurance programs provide tax-financed insurance coverage for low-income adults and children. They are administered by the state governments, with heavy cost sharing (on average over 60 percent) by the federal government. Thus, they are pure social health insurance.

But more than 70 percent of the insured in these public health insurance programs are enrolled in private nonprofit or for-profit managed-care plans that compete for contracts with the state governments on the basis of cost and quality.[13] Once such a company has won a contract with a state government, it

---

[12]See http://www.macpac.gov/home.
[13]One of the authors serves on the Board of Directors of such a company.

negotiates over fees and other matters with providers of health care to establish the networks of doctors, hospitals, pharmacies, nursing homes, home care agencies, and other providers of health care. Many state governments hold these insurance plans to stringent quality standards.

The advantages to the state governments come from the competitive bidding for managed-care contracts and also from the fact that after the contract is signed, these private organizations assume full financial risk for the health care of the uninsured. The state governments thus have full budget certainty concerning these two programs *at the beginning* of the fiscal year. Under the alternative, where these insurance programs are administered by the states themselves, they tend to be open-ended financial commitments, in good part because they are still typically based on fee-for-service payments of providers, which are known to encourage providers to expand the volume of services.

In this regard, readers may find of interest the Medicaid and CHIP Payment and Access Commission's report to Congress dated June 2011, which provides great detail on this arrangement across the states. Readers might also follow the ongoing work and reports of the commission.[14]

Cells DEF in Table 5.1 represent one possible approach to combining social solidarity in the financing and risk-pooling functions with private sector competition in the production, delivery, and purchasing of health care.

## Relatively Unregulated Private Insurance (Combinations GHI or JKL)

As used here, the term "unregulated" is not meant to convey that insurance carriers face no regulation at all. It merely means that they are not regulated to achieve an egalitarian health system. Instead, the insured typically are segmented to a substantial degree by risk class (health status), and the premiums paid by the insured tend to reflect their health status.

Few if any private health insurance carriers anywhere in the world are completely free from government regulation, even in the United States. For example, they are almost always subject to strict government rules of accounting and solvency (reserve requirements). In some states of the United States, their benefit packages may be regulated, or the structure of their premiums, or the terms under which they enroll the insured. A state may require, for example, that a given private health insurer must charge all customers the same insurance premium, regardless of age and health status, a requirement known as "community rating."[15]

However, if premiums are community-rated for the individual, but the latter is free to choose whether or not to purchase insurance, "community rating" will inexorably make relatively healthy individuals go without health insurance. Over

---

[14]The reports are available at http://docs.google.com/viewer?a=v&pid=sites&srcid=bWFjcGFjLmdvdnxtYWNwYWN8Z3g6NTM4OGNmMTJlNjdkMDZiYw.

[15]"Community rating" means that the premium paid by the individual insured is divorced from that individual's health status, age, and gender. It is based on the average health care cost experience of entire communities—be they geographic regions or employers.

time, the proportion of relatively sicker enrollees in community-rated pools will increase, insurance premiums will rise rapidly, and eventually the pool will dwindle and collapse. Actuaries call this the death spiral of insurance (Monheit and others, 2004).

In practice, community-rated health insurance premiums work only if they are coupled with a strict mandate upon the individual to purchase at least a minimum specified health insurance package. Germany and Switzerland, which rely on community rating, do impose such mandates.

## Out-of-Pocket Payments (Combination MNO)

As a general rule, the higher the per capita income of nations, the smaller will be the fraction of their total national health spending borne by individuals in the form of out-of-pocket (OOP) spending. In some low-income countries, that spending can represent 80 to 90 percent of total national health spending. Obviously, nations with very high ratios of OOP spending cannot achieve an egalitarian or near-egalitarian distribution of real health care resources across their citizenry.

According to the most recent (2009) Organization for Economic Coooperation and Development (OECD) data, OOP is 36.3 percent in the Republic of Korea, 16.0 percent in Japan, 12.5 percent in Germany, 15.4 percent in Canada, and 13.3 percent in the United States, even though absolute spending per capita in the United States ($7,960 in 2009, in international purchasing power parity dollars) is close to twice that in Canada or most European health systems, with the exception of Switzerland, which spends about 64 percent of the U.S. level.[16] Furthermore, in the United States some 50 million Americans at any point in time are without any health insurance coverage at all (while others have very comprehensive coverage).

According to the latest estimates, OOP health spending is 37 percent in Taiwan Province of China (Cheng, 2009). However, as it is not a member state of OECD, Taiwan Province of China does not calculate OOP according to the methods of the OECD National Health Accounts but includes such things as diapers, infant formula, and herbal medicine.[17] Thus, in all likelihood its reported OOP is artificially higher than it is according to the OECD methods and thus is misleading.

Currently fashionable among some U.S. policymakers, policy analysts, and management consulting firms is a construct they market under the label "consumer-directed health care" (CDHC). CDHC American style consists mainly of health insurance policies with very high annual deductibles of $2,000 to $10,000 a year for a family, which the insured must spend out of pocket before insurance coverage sets in. Unfortunately, in most localities in the United States, "consumers" (formerly "patients") have no accurate and meaningful information on the prices charged by competing providers of health care or on the quality of

---

[16]See OECD.Stats Extracts, available at http://stats.oecd.org/index.aspx.

[17]This information is based on author Cheng's meeting with Cheng-Hua Lee, Deputy Director General of the Bureau of National Health Insurance, Department of Health, October 6, 2011, Taipei.

their services. Here it must be recalled that the U.S. health system is beset by pervasive price discrimination which, along with the thousands of items in fee schedules, makes it very difficult even to construct meaningful prices for price comparisons by consumers.

Under CDHC, individuals and families, or their employers, may deposit annually money into a health savings account (HSA), like the Singapore or Chinese medical savings accounts, to help insured individual and families meet their deductible OOP expenses. The enticement to do so is that these deposits are *tax-deductible* from ordinary, taxable income. Practically, the tax-deductibility of deposits into HSAs means that a high-income family facing a marginal income tax rate of, say, 45 percent saves $450 in taxes for every $1,000 it deposits into the HSA. By contrast, a low-income worker facing a marginal income tax rate of only 10 percent saves only $100 in taxes for every $1,000 he or she deposits in the HSA.

The objective stated for CDHC is to make patients more conscious of the true cost of their health care. It is hoped that this will lead them to not waste health care resources by engaging in wasteful utilization and thus help reduce the annual growth in U.S. national health spending. Perhaps it will do that. An added objective often mentioned by the proponents of this approach is that it will put patients "in the driver's seat" for their health care, which is why these proponents market the idea under the label "consumer-directed health care." That nice label, however, is more fiction than reality, unless patients actually have the information on the prices charged and quality of care given by different physicians and hospitals.

It should be recognized, however, that this CDHC system has a number of distinct ethical implications. For high-income families, even a deductible of $5,000 or $10,000 is not likely to change their health care behavior. They will use whatever health care they desire, because the deductible (OOP) is not a major item in their budget. By contrast, a waitress or taxi driver will find such a deductible a heavy burden on the household budget and, therefore, may not use even important early care in case of illness. In reality, proponents of CDHC would saddle the lower income classes with most of the belt tightening and self-rationing in American health care. Furthermore, under this scheme chronically ill people may have to spend all of the deductible year after year, while chronically healthy people can save that money.

There is no question in our mind that high-deductible health insurance leans in the direction of rationing health care by income class. A nation may want to do that, but its leaders should be honest about it. It would, of course, be possible to make this approach more equitable. Thus, one could tie the annual deductible to a family's income, letting it rise with family income. One could also give chronically ill people higher government subsidies.

## Mixed Health Systems: The United States

Very few countries have pure health systems. Most of them have a mixture of two or more of the systems discussed above, and none more so than the United States, which literally has subsystems in every cell of Table 5.1, each subsystem for a different group of Americans.

As noted, for its veterans the United States relies on the purest form of socialized medicine (the VA health system), an approach American politicians routinely claim to abhor. It is one of the great ironies of that complicated country. For its elderly and poor, Americans have social insurance (Medicare and Medicaid), traditionally based on single-payer, government-run systems, but in recent years also with commercial insurers contracted to perform the purchasing, claims processing, cost control, and quality assurance functions.

The majority of employed Americans rely on what one may call "private social insurance," that is, health insurance sponsored by their employer, with premiums that reflect the health status of the firm's employees as a group (group experience rating), but with the employees' own direct contribution to the premium completely divorced from age and health status, albeit not from family size. Health insurance so attached to an individual's employment status changes or is lost when people change jobs.

Americans under age 65 who do not receive health insurance as part of their employment contract can purchase private, commercial insurance, if they can afford the usually very high premiums, which are based on the individual's age, gender, and health status (an approach called "medically underwritten"). Finally, there are some 50 million or so uninsured Americans who forego much timely primary and secondary health care but will receive critically needed tertiary care for what is called an "emergency medical condition" from hospitals under a federal law, the Emergency Medical Treatment and Active Labor Act, enacted in 1986 by the U.S. Congress. Typically, lacking any market power vis-à-vis hospitals, these patients are billed afterward at the highest prices by the hospitals for their inpatient care. But if the patients cannot pay those bills, the hospital will write them off, often after harsh collection attempts by collection agencies or the courts.

So in a way, the uninsured are protected against catastrophically high bills for very serious illness by an informal catastrophic health insurance system mandated upon hospitals by federal law. Hospitals recover the cost of that uncompensated care from other, insured patients, if the uninsured themselves cannot pay.

At its best, the United States arguably has the best clinical health care in the world, although on average the record appears to be more mixed (Squires, 2011). The American health insurance system, on the other hand, grew haphazardly during the twentieth century, without any coherent guidance from government.

We certainly do not recommend such a complicated health insurance system like the U.S. system to any other country that still has the option of choosing a system. As noted earlier, the U.S. system is enormously expensive. That high cost is now displacing other priorities in government budgets and pushing many households to the brink of financial bankruptcy. Indeed, as former Office of Management and Budget Director Peter Orszag writes in his recent (2011) article, "How Health Care Can Save or Sink America," the high and rapidly rising cost of American health care is one of the nation's most serious macroeconomic problems, threatening fiscal stability and the future growth of the U.S. economy.

Because of its high degree of complexity, the U.S. system is also very confusing and, therefore, cannot be easily reformed. Few citizens understand how the system works, what it costs overall, or what it costs them personally.

Finally, the system leaves millions of Americans without the protection and peace of mind of health insurance. The recently passed health insurance reform law, the Affordable Care Act, will most probably cover less than half of the current 50 million uninsured (out of a total U.S. population of 310 million) over a 10-year period beginning in 2014.

Without government interference, any purely market-based commercial health insurance system inevitably will lead to that result.

## Citizens' Satisfaction with Their Nations' Health Systems

From the perspective of political policymakers, enhancing the health of the population and protecting families from the financial risk of illness are not the only objectives. Presumably, they also seek a health system with which the citizenry is satisfied.

So far, for example, the citizens of Taiwan Province of China have been reported in survey after survey to be highly satisfied with their national health insurance system, whatever the shortcomings of that system may be (Cheng, 2009). By contrast, U.S. citizens have consistently expressed dissatisfaction with their system.[18] Blendon, Kim, and Benson (2001) had earlier reported on a survey during the mid-1990s showing that citizens in many of the European countries with government-run or government-regulated health systems declare themselves quite satisfied with their health system. Only 40 percent of U.S. citizens declared themselves "satisfied with the current health system." The comparable number for Canada was 46 percent, for France 65 percent, for Germany 58 percent, and for the government-run Danish system 91 percent. The overall impression left by the study is that a more market-based health insurance system offering its citizens multiple choices among health insurance plans appears to entail much higher health care costs per citizen, even after adjustment for differences in GNP per capita, but does not necessarily create commensurately higher satisfaction with the health system among the citizenry (Squires, 2011).

## Is There an Evidently "Best" Health System?

The question naturally arises whether one constructs league tables of different health systems to identify the best one among them. Because health systems have multiple clinical, socioeconomic, and ethical dimensions, league tables are attempts at ranking vectors. Although we are skeptics on this point, it has been tried. Table 5.2, for example, developed by the Commonwealth Fund, represents such an attempt (Davis, Schoen, and Stremikis, 2010). In this table, the numbers in each row denote the rankings of countries for the criterion represented by that row. (For example, on the criterion "Overall Ranking (2010)," the Netherlands ranked best, with 1, and the United States worst, with 7.)

Inevitably, such a league table is partly objective and partly subjective and hence quite controversial. Politically conservative health economists in the United

---

[18]See, for example, FoxNews.com, "U.S. Trails Others in Health Care Satisfaction," at http://www.foxnews.com/story/0,2933,136990,00.html.

TABLE 5.2

## Commonwealth Fund Ranking of Health Systems

|  | AUS | CAN | GER | NETH | NZ | UK | US |
|---|---|---|---|---|---|---|---|
| **Overall ranking** | 3 | 6 | 4 | 1 | 5 | 2 | 7 |
| **Quality of care** | 4 | 7 | 5 | 2 | 1 | 3 | 6 |
| *Effective care* | 2 | 7 | 6 | 3 | 5 | 1 | 4 |
| *Safe care* | 6 | 5 | 3 | 1 | 4 | 2 | 7 |
| *Coordinated care* | 4 | 5 | 7 | 2 | 1 | 3 | 6 |
| *Patient-centered care* | 2 | 5 | 3 | 6 | 1 | 7 | 4 |
| **Access** | 6.5 | 5 | 3 | 1 | 4 | 2 | 6.5 |
| *Cost-related problems* | 6 | 3.5 | 3.5 | 2 | 5 | 1 | 7 |
| *Timeliness of care* | 6 | 7 | 2 | 1 | 3 | 4 | 5 |
| **Efficiency** | 2 | 6 | 5 | 3 | 4 | 1 | 7 |
| **Equity** | 4 | 5 | 3 | 1 | 6 | 2 | 7 |
| **Long, healthy, productive lives** | 1 | 2 | 3 | 4 | 5 | 6 | 7 |
| **Health expenditures per capita, 2007** | $3,357 | $3,895 | $3,588 | $3,837 | $2,454 | $2,992 | $7,290 |

Sources: Calculated by The Commonwealth Fund based on 2007 International Health Policy Survey; 2008 International Health Policy Survey of Sicker Adults; 2009 International Health Policy Survey of Primary Care Physicians; Commonwealth Fund Commission on a High Performance Health Systems National Scorecard; and Organization for Economic Cooperation and Development, OECD Health Data 2009.

Note: Expenditure data are in U.S. dollars at purchasing power parity (figure for the Netherlands is an estimate).

AUS = Australia; CAN = Canada; GER = Germany; NETH = Netherlands; NZ = New Zealand; UK = United Kingdom; US = United States.

States who are supporters of a private market approach to health care do not concur with this ranking, nor would one expect experts from the ranked nations to concur.

In another attempt at cross-national evaluation of health systems, as mentioned earlier, the U.S. Business Roundtable, composed of the chief executives of major U.S. corporations, sought to evaluate whether, relative to other nations, Americans get their money's worth in health care (Business Roundtable, 2009a). That study was guided by over a dozen distinguished health economists and medical experts. Its overall conclusion was that

> Combining 19 internationally reported measures in a weighted 100-point scale that takes both the spending on, and performance of, our health care system into account, the U.S. stands at a 23-point disadvantage relative to five leading economic competitors—Canada, Japan, Germany, the United Kingdom and France (the "G-5 group")—and a 46-point disadvantage relative to the emerging competitors of Brazil, India and China (the "BIC group"). (p. 2)

Finally, in a recent study by Pritchard and Wallace (2011), the authors sought to compare the United States, the United Kingdom, and 17 other Western nations in terms of cost-effectiveness in reducing mortality. The authors' overall conclusion was that "in cost-effective terms, i.e. economic input versus clinical output, the USA health care system was one of the least cost-effective in reducing mortality rates whereas the UK was one of the most cost-effective over the period." Once again, however, one can always take issue with studies that seek to attribute observed differences in health status and mortality rates to differences in the performance of health systems, as these variables are driven by many other socioeconomic and cultural factors as well.

Our recommendation would be that, first, instead of relying on controversial league tables of this sort, any developing nation or emerging market economy seeking to build a health system should start by articulating the distributive social ethic the system is to observe and what fraction of GDP the nation might be able to afford to devote to health care. Next, the country's policy analysts should explore which well-known and more fully developed national health systems most closely match those constraints, and then visit those nations to study each system in detail. Finally, from insights learned abroad, the analysts should design their own system, one that fits their culture, social ethic, and budget. This is exactly how Taiwan Province of China decided to develop its now highly regarded National Health Insurance system during the late 1980s and early 1990s. As one high official put it, the National Health Insurance system was like a car designed and produced there but with many component parts imported from abroad (Cheng, 2003).

## SUMMARY AND CONCLUSIONS

Our study of national health systems and the relevant literature leads us to a series of conclusions that can be distilled into the following points.

*The degree to which a health system can be delegated to the play of freely competitive private markets is constrained by the distributive social ethic that dominates in the nation's culture.* Depending upon that ethic, particular functions that any health system must perform can or cannot be delegated to private markets.

Most nations do in fact preface their health reforms with an explicit recitation of that ethic. Europeans subject their health policy and health systems to the *principle of social solidarity.* Canada routinely affirms its commitment to social solidarity and, therefore, to a national health system.[19] In Taiwan Province of China, National Health Insurance is protected by specific provisions in the constitution.[20] The structure of these nations' health system and their national health policies reflect that articulated social ethic.

Remarkably, citizens and their representatives in the United States have never been able to articulate a consensus on a distributive social ethic for U.S. health care, which is why health reform in the United States has always been so difficult and incoherent. Nations aspiring to a health system that will leave the citizenry highly satisfied cannot avoid as a first crucial step in health reform the articulation of the social ethic the system is to obey. It is fundamental to sound policy.

*If a nation is willing to let health care be rationed among its citizens by price and ability to pay, it can delegate most health system functions to the private market.*

---

[19]See Romanow (2002), especially Chapter 2.
[20]Constitution of the Republic of China, Amendment Article 10, 2005. Also see Cheng (2003).

Just as other basic commodities, such as food and shelter, can be rationed among citizens by price and ability to pay, guaranteeing at most a bare minimum to all citizens, a nation can delegate most of the functions to be performed by the health system to the play of private market forces, with only the standard regulations required to make private markets function honestly and efficiently.

In such a system, the guaranteed minimum health care services probably had best be delivered through budgeted public or private facilities dedicated to low-income citizens, for example, public hospitals and neighborhood clinics. It will lead to a sharply delineated, two- or multiclass health system, as has been the case in India (Anand, 2011).

*If a nation aspires to a roughly egalitarian health system, government inevitably will perform some of the functions that a health system must perform—notably the financing of health care and risk pooling.* Furthermore, government will strictly monitor and regulate the performance of whatever functions are delegated to private markets. The Dutch, German, and Swiss health systems are clear examples of this approach. The more recently introduced Dutch experiment, in which private health insurance operates under managed competition, bears close following in the years ahead.

*It is quite feasible to combine a distributive social ethic of social solidarity implemented through government-run health insurance with a mixed public-private health care delivery system.* Such a mixed system would include for-profit hospitals, clinics, and nursing homes, but every provider of care must deliver health care to patients under the same terms and at identical prices, that is, common fee schedules that apply to *all* providers. Examples of that approach can be found in the United States in its social insurance, single-payer Medicare program for the elderly and Medicaid program for the poor, and in Taiwan Province of China's single-payer universal National Health Insurance, which covers the entire population.

*Under social solidarity, private health insurers can still be productively engaged but not in extracting contributions to health care from households.* While under social solidarity, private health insurers cannot properly perform the function of extracting contributions to health care (usually income-based premiums) from households and risk pooling, they can be productively engaged to perform the purchasing, claims-processing, and quality as well as cost control functions under competitive contracting.

This is a form of "regulated competition"—regulated, because the competitively bid contracts under which the private insurers perform their functions are strictly supervised by government, with a variety of performance metrics (Reinhardt, 2011). Once again, the U.S. Medicare and Medicaid programs provide working examples of this model, as do the health systems of Switzerland and the Netherlands (to some extent). Such systems tend to be more expensive on a per capita basis than are fully government-run national health service or government-run single-payer systems, but they allow for greater flexibility and innovation.

*We could not recommend in good conscience that any other nation adopt the overall structure of the U.S. health insurance system.* Although the U.S. health system is a giant labyrinth of subsystems experimenting with different approaches to health care delivery and cost and quality controls from which other nations can learn, we could not recommend in good conscience that any other nation adopt the overall structure of the U.S. health insurance system. It strikes us as an excessively complex and highly inefficient approach to financing health care and protecting households from the financial risk of illness, which it has done quite imperfectly.

Our overarching conclusion, then, is that even under the goal of social solidarity, a health system certainly can enlist the power and ingenuity of the private sector, as long as the latter is regulated and provided with incentives that will naturally lead it to stay within the social moral norms that society wishes its health system to follow.

# REFERENCES

Anand, G., 2011, "India's Public Health Crisis: The Government Responds," *Wall Street Journal,* July 30.

Arrow, K.J., 1963, "Uncertainty and the Welfare Economics of Medical Care," *American Economic Review,* Vol. 53, No. 5, pp. 942–73.

Asch, S., E. McGlynn, M. Hogan, R. Hayward, P. Shekelle, L. Rubenstein, J. Keesey, J. Adams, and E. Kerr, 2004, "Comparison of Quality of Care for Patients in the Veteran Health Administration and Patients in a National Sample," *Annals of Internal Medicine,* Vol. 14, No. 12, pp. 938–45.

Blendon, R.J., M. Kim, and J.M. Benson, 2001, "The Public versus the World Health Organization on Health Systems Performance," *Health Affairs,* May/June, pp. 10–20.

Business Roundtable, 2009a, *Tracking the Contribution of U.S. Health Care to the Global Competitiveness of American Employers and Workers: 2009 Business Roundtable Health Care Value Comparability Study.* Available at http://businessroundtable.org/studies-and-reports/health-care-value-comparability-study-full-report/.

———, 2009b, "The Business Round Table Health Care Value Index Executive Summary." Available at http://businessroundtable.org/uploads/studies-reports/downloads/The_Business_Roundtable_Health_Care_Value_Index_Executive_Summary.pdf.

Busse, R., 2010, "The German Health Care System," in *International Profiles of Health Care Systems,* pp. 28–31 (New York: The Commonwealth Fund).

Cheng, T.M., 2003, "Taiwan's New National Health Insurance Program: Genesis and Experience So Far," *Health Affairs*, Vol. 22, No. 3, pp. 61–76.

———, 2009, "Lessons from Taiwan's Universal National Health Insurance: A Conversation with Taiwan's Health Minister Ching-Chuan Yeh," *Health Affairs,* Vol. 28, No. 4, pp. 1035–44.

———, 2010a, "Understanding the 'Swiss Watch' Function of Switzerland's Health System," *Health Affairs,* Vol. 29, No. 8, pp. 1442–51. Available at http://content.healthaffairs.org/content/29/8/1442.full.pdf1html?sid5c083dca2-0cc3-4940-804b-3ab8a190e678.

———, 2010b, "Taiwan's National Health Insurance System: High Value for the Dollar," in *Six Countries, Six Reform Models: The Healthcare Reform Experience of Israel, The Netherlands, New Zealand, Singapore, Switzerland and Taiwan,* ed. by K.G. Okma and L. Crivelli (Singapore: World Scientific Publishing).

Commonwealth Fund, 2011, "The U.S. Health System in Perspective: A Comparison of Twelve Industrialized Nations" (New York). Available at http://www.commonwealthfund.org/Content/Publications/Issue-Briefs/2011/Jul/US-Health-System-in-Perspective.aspx.

Cooper, Z., S. Gibbons, and A. McGuire, 2011, "Does Hospital Competition Save Lives? Evidence from the English NHS Patient Choice Reforms," *Economic Journal,* Vol. 121, pp. F228–60.

Dartmouth Institute for Health Policy and Clinical Practice, *The Dartmouth Atlas of Health Care.* Available at http://www.dartmouthatlas.org/.

Davis, K., C. Schoen, and K. Stremikis, 2010, *Mirror, Mirror on the Wall: How Performance of the U.S. Health System Compares Internationally* (New York: Commonwealth Fund). Available at http://www.commonwealthfund.org/Publications/Fund-Reports/2010/Jun/Mirror-Mirror-Update.aspx.

Folland, S., A.C. Goodman, and M. Stano, 2010, *The Economics of Health and Health Care,* 6th ed. (Englewood Cliffs, NJ: Prentice Hall).

FoxNews.com, 2004, "U.S. Trails Others in Health Care Satisfaction," October 29. Available at http://www.foxnews.com/story/0,2933,136990,00.html.

Gemeinsamer Bundesausschuss, 2007, *The German Health Care System and the Federal Joint Committee.* Powerpoint presentation, September. Available at http://www.g-ba.de/downloads/17-98-2449/2007-10-08-General_Presentation_G-BA.pdf.

Katz, M.L., and H.S. Rosen, 1990, *Microeconomics* (Homewood, IL: Irwin).

Leu, R., R. Rutten, W. Brouwer, P. Matter, and C. Rütschi, 2009, "The Swiss and Dutch Health Insurance Systems: Universal Coverage and Regulated Competitive Insurance Markets" (New York: The Commonwealth Fund). Available at http://www.commonwealthfund.org/~/media/Files/Publications/Fund%20Report/2009/Jan/The%20Swiss%20and%20Dutch%20Health%20Insurance%20Systems%20%20Universal%20Coverage%20and%20Regulated%20Competitive%20Insurance/Leu_swissdutchhltinssystems_1220%20pdf.pdf.

Monheit, A.C., J.C. Cantor, M. Koller, and K. Fox, 2004, "Community Rating and Sustainable Individual Health Insurance Markets: Trends in the New Jersey Individual Health Coverage Program," *Health Affairs,* Vol. 23, No. 4, pp. 167–75.

New Jersey Commission on Rationalizing Health Care Resources, 2008, *Final Report* (Trenton, NJ). Available at http://www.nj.gov/health/rhc/finalreport/documents/entire_finalreport.pdf.

Nord, E., J. Pinto, J. Richardson, P. Menzel, and P. Ubel, 1999, "Incorporating Societal Concerns for Fairness in Numerical Valuations of Health Programmes," *Health Economics,* Vol. 8, pp. 25–39.

Okma, K.G., T.R. Marmor, and J. Oberlander, 2011, "Managed Competition for Medicare? Sobering Lessons from the Netherlands," *New England Journal of Medicine,* Vol. 365, No. 4, pp. 287–89.

Orszag, P., 2011, "How Health Care Can Save or Sink America," *Foreign Affairs,* Vol. 90, No. 4, pp. 42–56.

Porter, M.E., and E.O. Teisberg, 2006, *Redefining Health Care: Creating Value-Based Competition on Results* (Cambridge, MA: Harvard Business Press).

Pritchard, C., and M.S. Wallace, 2011, "Comparing the USA, UK and 17 Western Countries' Efficiency and Effectiveness in Reducing Mortality," *Journal of the Royal Society of Medicine,* Short Reports, Vol. 2, pp. 1–10.

Reinhardt, U.E., 2001, "Can Efficiency in Health Care Be Left to the Market?" *Journal of Health Policy, Politics and Law,* Vol. 26, No. 5, pp. 967–92.

———, 2006, "The Pricing of U.S. Hospital Services: Chaos behind a Veil of Secrecy," *Health Affairs,* Vol. 25, No. 1, pp. 57–69.

———, 2007, "Keeping Health Care Afloat: The United States versus Canada," *Milken Institute Review,* Second Quarter, pp. 36–43.

———, 2010, "Will More Insurers Control Health Spending Better?" *Health Affairs Blog,* July 9. Available at http://healthaffairs.org/blog/2010/07/09/will-more-insurers-control-health-care-costs-better/.

———, 2011, "The Wyden-Ryan Plan: Déjà vu All Over Again," The New York Times Economix, December 23. Available at http://economix.blogs.nytimes.com/2011/12/23/the-wyden-ryan-plan-deja-vu-all-over-again/.

Roberts, M., W. Hsiao, P. Berman, and M. Reich, 2003, *Getting Health Reform Right: A Guide to Improving Performance and Equity* (Oxford, UK: Oxford University Press).

Romanow, R.J., 2002, *Building on Values: The Future of Health Care in Canada,* Final Report (Saskatoon, Saskatchewan: Commission on the Future of Health Care in Canada).

Ruger, J.P., 2010, *Health and Social Justice* (Oxford, UK: Oxford University Press).

Squires, D.A., 2011, "The U.S. Health System in Perspective: A Comparison of Twelve Industrialized Nations" (New York: The Commonwealth Fund). Available at http://www.commonwealthfund.org/~/media/Files/Publications/Issue%20Brief/2011/Jul/1532_Squires_US_hlt_sys_comparison_12_nations_intl_brief_v2.pdf.

U.S. Medicaid and CHIP Payment and Access Commission, 2011, "Report to the Congress: The Evolution of Managed Care in Medicaid" (Washington: Government Printing Office). Available at http://docs.google.com/viewer?a=v&pid=sites&srcid=bWFjcGFjLmdvdnxtY WNwYWN8Z3g6NTM4OGNmMTJlNjdkMDZiYw.

# PART III

# Cross-Country Studies

# CHAPTER 6

# Containing Public Health Spending: Lessons from Experiences of Advanced Economies

Justin Tyson, Kenichiro Kashiwase, Mauricio Soto, and Benedict Clements

Public health spending in advanced economies is projected to rise by an average of 3 percentage points of GDP over the next 20 years and by 6½ percentage points of GDP in the next 40 years. These increases will occur at a time when countries need to undertake large fiscal adjustments to reduce public debt ratios in the wake of the global financial crisis, and they present a daunting fiscal challenge for many of these countries (IMF, 2010). Health care reforms to contain public health spending growth are needed, as part of the fiscal adjustments, to stabilize age-related-spending-to-GDP ratios. This chapter examines the health care reform experiences in advanced economies and identifies the most promising strategies to contain public health spending growth.

## OVERVIEW

Country case studies, event study analysis, and econometric analysis are used here to gain insights into the policy options available to contain the growth of public health spending.[1] Data limitations and the fact that various policy reforms are often implemented together and in response to spending pressures make the identification of reform impacts difficult. Therefore, this chapter uses three complementary methodologies:

- *Case studies:* Eight episodes of successful containment of health expenditure in advanced economies are examined. In each of these episodes, countries achieved a sustained reduction in the ratio of public health spending to GDP and a moderation in real spending growth rates. The advanced economies and time periods covered are Canada (late 1970s and 1990s); Finland (1990s); Germany (2000–07); Italy (1990s); the Netherlands

---

[1]Detailed results are provided in Appendix 6.1 (econometric analysis) and chapters covering case studies.

(early 1980s and 1990s); Sweden (1980s and early 1990s); the United Kingdom (1980s); and the United States (1990s) (see chapters 10 and 13 for detailed case studies).

- *Event analysis:* The event analysis focuses on the impact of reforms in 24 countries. It assesses developments in public health spending before and after specific reforms. Thus, unlike the case studies, this analysis is not confined to reforms that were successful in reducing spending as a share of GDP. Spending trends of nonreforming countries during the same period are also used as a basis of comparison.

- *Econometric analysis:* The econometric analysis uses recently compiled OECD data on key indicators of health care systems (Joumard, Andre, and Nicq, 2010) to evaluate the relationship between these characteristics (such as the extent of private health care provision, degree of regulation, patient choice, and stringency of budget constraints) and the growth of public health spending. The impact of particular reforms on the growth rate of public health expenditure is then simulated by changing a country's rating on these indices.

Reforms are grouped into three categories: macro constraints on available resources, micro reforms to improve efficiency, and demand-side reforms (Box 6.1). Many governments have experimented with macro-level controls (e.g., budget caps, volume controls on inputs and outputs, and price controls on inputs and health services) to restrain public health spending, often as part of broader fiscal consolidation efforts. While these reforms were initially effective at reducing costs, they sometimes shifted spending to areas not covered by the controls or led to undesired side effects (e.g., waiting lists for essential procedures). To reduce the resulting pressures on cost containment, many countries turned to micro-level reforms that targeted not only cost containment, but also higher efficiency and continued high-quality provision of health care. These reforms included improving the organizational arrangements between different parts of the health care system, reimbursing providers through contracts specifying services and prices, and greater reliance on market mechanisms that increase the choices available to purchasers and patients. On the demand side, the most prominent reform has been to increase cost sharing.

The econometric results suggest that a range of options has proven effective in reducing the growth of public health expenditures. Table 6.1 shows the estimated impact on excess cost growth of a country moving up one unit in any given Organization for Economic Cooperation and Development (OECD) index, keeping all other indices fixed. Scores on the OECD indices range from 0 to 6, with a mean score for the different indices of 2.6 (see Appendix Table 6.1). The results suggest that substantial reductions in excess cost growth (ECG) could be obtained from extending market mechanisms (−0.50), improving public sector management and coordination (−0.30), and strengthening budget caps (−0.24)—relative to the 1.0 average ECG under the baseline. Some measures appear ineffective in controlling health spending; price controls, for example, are associated with higher excess cost growth (+0.11). In what follows, the effects of specific reforms on health spending are described in greater detail, drawing also on the complementary findings provided by the case studies and event study analysis.

BOX 6.1

## Reforms in Advanced Economies: A Typology

Reforms implemented in advanced countries over the past three decades can be grouped into three categories (Oxley and MacFarlan, 1995):

### Macro-level controls

- *Budget caps*: These are the bluntest instrument for restraining resources allocated to the public health sector. They can be expressed as limits on overall health care spending or on subsectors, such as hospitals or pharmaceuticals. Examples include global budgets for hospitals and expenditure ceilings for general practitioners.

- *Supply constraints*: Here the focus is on regulating the volume of either inputs into or outputs from the health care system. Input controls include limits on admittance to physician training colleges, defining positive lists for drugs, or rationing of high-tech capital equipment. Output controls include delisting of certain treatments, such as eye tests and dental treatment.

- *Price controls*: Price controls regulate prices of inputs or outputs. They include wage controls for health care professionals, reference pricing for pharmaceutical products, and price controls on specific treatments.

### Micro-level reforms

- *Public management and coordination*: These reforms seek to alter the organizational arrangements between different parts of the health care system in order to reduce costs through improved coordination, alignment of responsibility and accountability, better incentive structures, and/or reduction in overlap or redundancy. Examples of such changes include abolition of managerial levels, decentralization of health care functions, and introduction of gatekeeping arrangements (i.e., a physician who manages a patient's health care services, coordinates referrals to secondary and tertiary levels, and helps control health care costs by screening out unnecessary services).

- *Contracting*: How providers are reimbursed is one of the most important factors affecting the micro-level efficiency of health spending. There are many different ways to pay physicians, hospitals, and other providers, but three of the most general methods are (1) salaries or budgets, (2) case-based payment such as capitation or diagnosis-related groups, and (3) fee for service.

- *Market mechanisms*: These reforms seek to improve micro-level efficiency and/or control costs by introducing varying degrees of market mechanisms into the health sector. These reforms operate not so much on the supply side as on the nexus between supply and demand. Examples include creating internal markets (e.g., where primary care physicians purchase services from hospitals), separating the purchase of health services from provision (thus allowing competition among providers), and promoting patient choice (e.g., where patients can choose among primary care providers and hospitals).

### Demand-side reforms

These reforms include policies intended to increase the share of health care costs borne by patients, often with the objective of avoiding excessive consumption of specific health services. The two important issues on the demand side are the level of patient cost sharing (this can take the form of lump sum or percentage copayments) and the tax treatment of private health insurance.

TABLE 6.1

## Relationship between System Characteristics and Excess Cost Growth

| Reform areas and indices | Impact of a one-unit change in index on excess cost growth[a] |
|---|---|
| **Budget caps** | −0.24 |
| Of which: | |
| *Budget constraint:* rules and/or targets to fix the health budget and its allocation across subsectors and/or regions | −0.03 |
| *Central government oversight:* number of key decisions overseen by central government | −0.22 |
| **Supply constraints** | −0.06 |
| Of which: | |
| *Regulation of workforce and equipment:* degree of regulation on the number and distribution of health care workforce and hospital high-tech equipment and activities, and control of recruitment and remuneration of hospital staff | −0.05 |
| *Priority setting:* definition of health benefit basket, effective use of health technology assessment, and definition and monitoring of public health objectives | −0.01 |
| **Price controls** | 0.11 |
| Of which: | |
| *Regulation of providers' prices:* regulation of drug prices and of prices billed by physicians and hospitals | 0.05 |
| *Regulation of prices paid by third-party payers:* regulation of prices paid by third-party payers for primary care physicians, specialists, hospital services, and drugs | 0.06 |
| **Public management and coordination** | −0.30 |
| Of which: | |
| *Gatekeeping:* obligation or incentive to register with a general practitioner and/or to get referrals to access secondary care | −0.04 |
| *Subnational government involvement:* number of key decisions made at the subnational level | −0.36 |
| *Delegation:* number of key decisions made at the insurer level | 0.10 |
| **Contracting methods** | 0.09 |
| Of which: | |
| *Volume incentives:* degree of payment modes to incentivize less services | 0.09 |
| **Market mechanisms** | −0.50 |
| Of which: | |
| *Choice of insurers:* ability of people to choose their insurer for basic coverage | −0.22 |
| *Insurer levers:* ability of insurers to compete and availability of insurer information for consumers | −0.17 |
| *User information:* availability of information on quality and prices of health care services | 0.11 |
| *Private provision:* degree of private provision of physician and hospital services | −0.14 |
| *Choice among providers:* degree of freedom in choosing among primary care physicians, specialists, and hospitals | −0.08 |
| **Demand-side reforms** | −0.09 |
| Of which: | |
| *Over-the-basic coverage:* share of the population covered by nonprimary insurance, share of health care expenditures financed out of private insurance, and degree of market concentration | −0.10 |
| *Price signals on users:* extent to which patients face out-of-pocket expenses | 0.01 |

Sources: Joumard, Andre, and Nicq (2010); and IMF staff estimates.

[a]Impact on excess cost growth of public health spending due to one-unit change in each OECD index. OECD indicators range between 0 and 6. In the regression analysis, the effect of each individual reform option is estimated keeping all other indices fixed. In practice, some reforms may require offsetting changes in other indices. In addition, simultaneous reforms across different health system characteristics may be undesirable.

# COUNTRY EXPERIENCE WITH DIFFERENT REFORM INSTRUMENTS

## Macro-Level Controls

### Budget Caps

Budget caps and central oversight have been effective in reducing spending growth. According to the econometric analysis, the combined effect of a one-unit improvement in the budget constraint index and central government oversight of key decisions, such as the total health care budget or the financing of high-cost equipment, reduces excess cost growth by ¼ percentage point.[2] Event studies confirm the potential of budget caps to contribute to cost containment: in the 19 episodes (in 13 countries) in which a budget cap was implemented, increases in spending-to-GDP ratios slowed substantially, while spending ratios continued to rise in countries without caps (Figure 6.1). In six out of the eight successful reform episodes covered by the case studies, budget caps were used to contain cost increases. Budget caps were also typically employed before or during periods of broader fiscal consolidation.

Nevertheless, even effective budget caps may suffer from some drawbacks: they can limit access to health care, as evidenced by growing waiting times for elective surgery in Canada, Sweden, and the United Kingdom during the period of expenditure consolidation. They may also be inequitable, as rich households can often circumvent waiting lists by purchasing private health care. Furthermore, budget caps alone are unlikely to incentivize greater efficiency, as they are most often based on historical costs.

Budget caps are most effective when applied to broad health expenditure aggregates. Budget constraints that are applied partially (e.g., only to inpatient care spending) can lead to expenditure increases in areas that are not controlled. In the Netherlands, the partial budget cap on inpatient care was unwound by subsequent reform efforts to introduce a managed-care model, and in Italy partial caps on capital investment proved ineffective. In Finland, the introduction of fixed transfers to municipalities to finance health care, alongside other constraints, was successful in containing the costs of inpatient care; however, it was offset by higher pharmaceutical expenditure, much of which was financed through a different source and not subject to the cap on transfers.

### Supply and Price Controls

Supply and price controls appear to have only modest effects on the growth of public health spending. According to the econometric analysis, limiting the supply

---

[2]"Central government oversight" is based on the OECD's "consistency" index, with a low score for consistency implying a high score for central government oversight. In the econometric estimates, increasing a country's score on the consistency index increases excess cost growth. This owes to the construction of the OECD index on consistency, which gives countries a low rating on consistency if several levels of government are involved in decisions, which is interpreted here as a type of budget constraint imposed under decentralized systems. According to the OECD indices, highly decentralized systems with low consistency generally reflect the involvement of the central government in key health decisions.

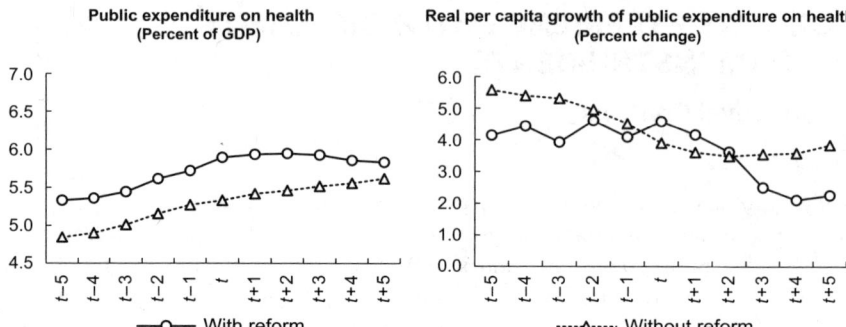

**Figure 6.1** Reform Episodes of Budget Caps or Constraints
Sources: Organization for Economic Cooperation and Development, OECD Health Data; and IMF staff calculations.

of health services—for example, by imposing regulatory controls on the health workforce and equipment—lowered excess cost growth only slightly (by less than 0.1 percentage point). Event studies also reinforce this finding (Figure 6.2). In practice, supply constraints are often combined with budget caps as a way of targeting cost containment measures. Restrictions on supply were used in Canada (hospital closures, mergers, and reduction in the number of beds), Finland (reduction in the number of hospital beds), Germany (delisting ineffective treatments and positive drug lists), Italy (positive list for pharmaceuticals), and the Netherlands (delisting certain treatments). Price controls, on the other hand, have been ineffective (see below), and the econometric results suggest that increased reliance on these measures actually increases excess cost growth. Price controls were implemented mainly in those countries where the public sector contracts with the private sector to provide services: Canada (with regulated fees for physicians), and Germany and the Netherlands (both with reference pricing for pharmaceuticals).

The mixed success of price and volume controls is due to supplier responses that have circumvented or offset the effect of controls. For example, the impact of price controls can be eroded by supplier responses such as increasing volumes or directing patients to higher-cost services (Docteur and Oxley, 2003). Country case studies also find variable levels of effectiveness. In Germany, the reduction in

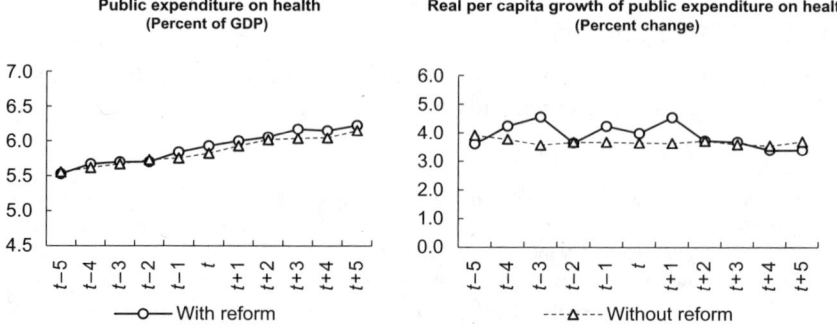

**Figure 6.2** Reform Episodes of Supply and Price Controls
Sources: Organization for Economic Cooperation and Development, OECD Health Data; and IMF staff calculations.

pharmaceutical expenditure was short-lived, as drug companies were successful in working around the controls so that pharmaceutical spending did not decrease over the longer term. In contrast, in the Netherlands real per capita expenditure on pharmaceuticals declined over five years.

### Cost-Effectiveness Evaluations to Control Supply

More recently, governments have sought to use cost-effectiveness evaluations to determine what treatments should be financed from public funds. Many countries (such as Australia, Finland, the Netherlands, Sweden, and the United Kingdom) have established government bodies that assess the cost-effectiveness of new and existing technologies. In some countries, such as the United States, formal cost-effectiveness analysis is not used to make public reimbursement decisions. However, the United States is moving in this direction by supporting comparative effectiveness research in its 2010 health care reform. Similarly, more effective and cheaper health care can be achieved through greater efforts to define and promote "best practice" medicine and updating this in line with technology advancements. This approach can also provide greater incentives for the private sector to develop technologies that are cost-effective and cost-reducing.

## Micro-Level Reforms

### Strengthened Public Management and Contracting Methods

Greater involvement of subnational governments in key health care decisions can reduce expenditure growth if central oversight is maintained. According to the econometric analysis, a one-unit increase in the index measuring involvement of local and regional governments in key health care decisions reduces excess cost growth by about 0.30 percentage point. This impact, however, would be smaller if oversight were loosened—a one-unit reduction in the central oversight index would offset the majority of the impact—suggesting that checks and balances are necessary to control spending growth in decentralized systems. Health systems that score high on subnational involvement and central government oversight (Canada, Sweden) tend to have lower excess cost growth than those with relatively weak oversight (Spain).[3] As indicated in the case studies of Canada and Sweden, the decentralization of additional responsibilities to lower levels of government was accompanied by measures to enhance accountability for respecting resource ceilings, contributing to success in containing spending growth.

The econometric evidence on other public management and contracting reforms is mixed. Changes in the gatekeeping index have a small effect on excess cost growth. However, incentives to reduce volumes (such as reduced reliance on fee-for-service payments) and increased delegation to insurers are associated with higher excess cost growth. The event and case studies provide more resounding

---

[3]Thornton and Mati (2008) also emphasize the role of institutional arrangements, such as administrative controls and fiscal rules, in ensuring good performance under decentralization. Recent work on decentralization and health spending underscores the detrimental effect of soft budget constraints (Crivelli, Leive, and Stratmann, 2010).

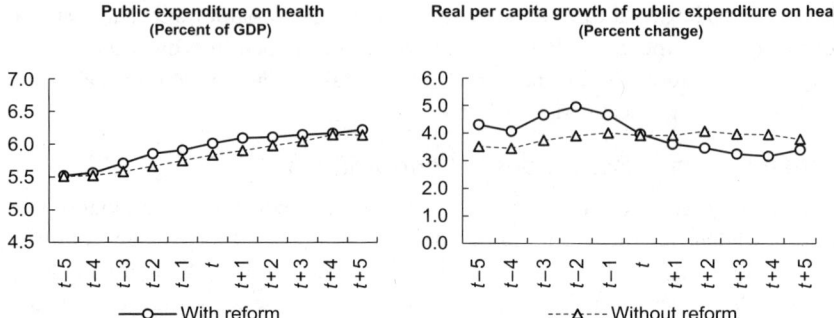

**Figure 6.3** Reform Episodes of Public Management and Contracting
Sources: Organization for Economic Cooperation and Development, OECD Health Data; and IMF staff calculations.

evidence in favor of these contracting reforms that improve incentives to provide cost-effective care. The event studies show that in the aggregate, management and contracting reforms have helped slow the growth of spending (Figure 6.3). In many cases, this has reflected innovations in contracting.

In the United States, the major change in this area was the adoption of managed care.[4] Cost containment approaches used by managed care include requiring preauthorization for services (a type of gatekeeping) and selective contracting with providers who are willing to accept a particular plan's payment arrangements and utilization reviews. Additionally, in many countries there are now explicit contracts that target cost control, efficiency, and quality of care (Docteur and Oxley, 2003). To contain spending, payment methods have shifted from traditional fee-for-service methods to case-based payments, such as the diagnosis-related groups (DRGs) used in Finland, Germany, Italy, and the United Kingdom.[5] Case-based payment methods, however, can be less effective if providers affect quantities by increasing admissions.[6] Other countries have moved from paying the provider on the basis of costs toward prospective or forward-looking budgets, often as part of aggregate budget control (Finland and Sweden). Forward-looking budgets constrain spending by providing a hard budget constraint based on projected demand and average cost per patient or per case.

## Market Mechanisms

Market mechanisms can also slow the growth of health expenditures. The econometric analysis shows that a one-unit increase in the indices for choice of

---

[4]"Managed care" is a general term for health plans that are proactive in seeking to affect the type or amount of care their enrollees receive. Unlike traditional insurance-based plans, they tend to have detailed contractual or employment relationships with health care providers.

[5]DRGs specify treatment protocols for medical conditions and provide an associated price schedule.

[6]Changes in payment methods can be combined with budget ceilings to help address these concerns. For example, in some Canadian provinces, individual physicians are reimbursed according to a fee-for-service schedule. However, once certain billing thresholds are reached, a declining fraction of the negotiated fees are reimbursed.

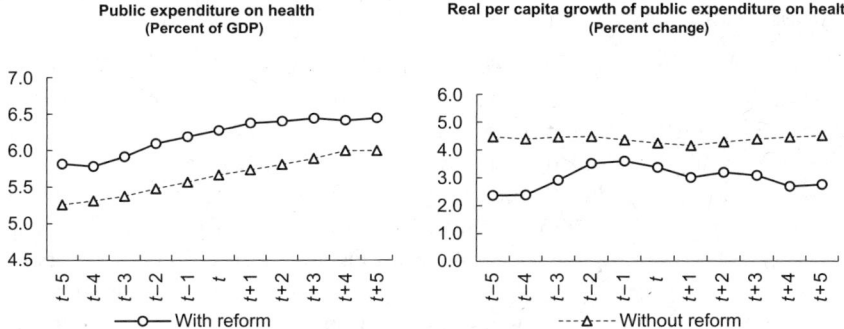

**Figure 6.4** Reform Episodes of Market Mechanisms
Sources: Organization for Economic Cooperation and Development, OECD Health Data; and IMF staff calculations.

providers and insurers, private provision, and the ability of insurers to compete would altogether reduce excess cost growth by about ½ percentage point.[7] Event studies also find that the growth in public health spending as a share of GDP slowed after reforms that increased the use of market mechanisms, especially relative to countries not adopting them (Figure 6.4).

Market-oriented reforms have to be carefully designed if cost containment is to be achieved. Italy, Sweden, and the United Kingdom separated the roles, within government, of purchasing and providing health care services. These arrangements allow for more active contracting for health care services from primary care providers. The United Kingdom and Sweden also allowed greater competition among hospitals in order to improve responsiveness and efficiency, but evidence from these two experiments is mixed. In the United Kingdom there are some indications that primary care physicians who contracted health services from competing NHS Trusts (hospitals) were more successful in controlling costs, but there is little evidence of improved hospital outcomes. Introducing competition in Sweden, alongside the introduction of case-based (DRG) payment methods, initially increased the volume of hospital care and raised expenditure (Docteur and Oxley, 2003). To address these effects, DRG rates were reduced, and penalties imposed on providers. Sweden also introduced charges for municipalities that were not ready to receive discharged hospital patients (e.g., if a nursing home was not available) and this has been effective in reducing the number of long-term care patients treated in hospitals, as opposed to nursing homes.

---

[7]Providing greater information on the quality and prices of health care services appears to be associated with higher excess cost growth. In theory, more information should help users choose the most effective providers. However, research indicates the difficulty health consumers have in understanding this information, as medical treatments are often very complex and consumers rely more on health professionals for advice. More importantly, this information may not provide incentives to reduce costs, because patients could choose high-quality (high-cost) services over low-quality (low-cost) services, especially as they do not bear the full costs of treatment.

## Demand-Side Reforms

Demand-side reforms can also help curtail spending growth. The econometric results indicate that extending the use of supplementary and complementary private insurance has a dampening effect on excess cost growth (−0.10 percentage point). The evidence on the effects of raising copayments is mixed, although this reflects the small share of spending covered by copayments (such as pharmaceuticals) to date. Event studies of 17 reforms in which cost sharing was increased show that they were successful in slowing the growth of health spending relative to GDP for about a year after the reform, but this decline was reversed by subsequent increases (Figure 6.5). The potential for reducing costs from higher copayments is potentially large, given the substantial share of outpatient spending (30 percent). Other demand-side reforms include abolishing tax deductions for medical expenses, as in Finland. The size of these tax expenditures can be large and often benefit the rich the most. The issue is often discussed in the context of the United States, where these benefits amount to 2 percent of GDP. Tax subsidies for private insurance also exist in a number of countries, although the size of these subsidies is small owing to the predominant role of the public sector in health care financing in most countries.

Demand-side policies can raise equity and access concerns. Sweden and Finland helped increase the political acceptability of these reforms by allowing lower levels of government greater discretion on copayments for health services along with increased responsibility for health care provision. While patient cost sharing may discourage moral hazard, it can raise concerns about equity and access for poor households. To address this concern, cost sharing can be linked to income. Similarly, to avoid adverse health consequences, chronic medical conditions are also often exempted from cost sharing (Newhouse and the Insurance Experiment Group, 1993; Gruber, 2006; Chernew, Rosen, and Fendrick, 2007). Cost sharing can also be allowed to vary according to the cost-effectiveness of services or treatments, through so-called value-based benefit design (Chernew, Rosen, and Fendrick, 2007). Although the financial contribution of these changes is often small, when appropriately directed they can decrease cost pressures.

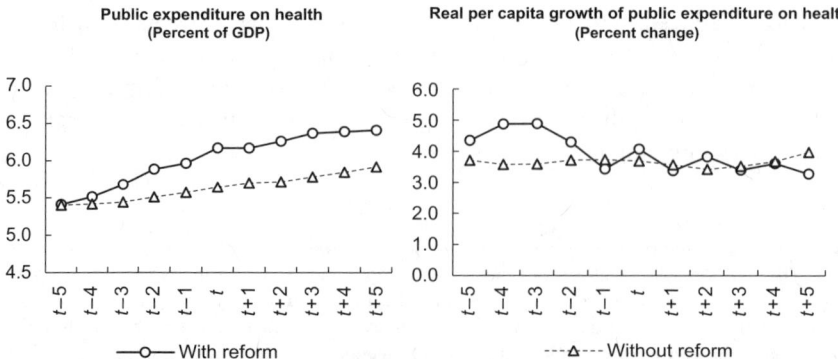

**Figure 6.5** Reform Episodes of Demand-Side Measures (Patient Cost Sharing)
Sources: Organization for Economic Cooperation and Development, OECD Health Data; and IMF staff calculations.

## Other Lessons

Continued monitoring and refinement of health reforms, based on real-time data on the behavior of providers and patients, is required to contain cost pressures over the long term. Success appears to be linked to a continuous tweaking and reformulation of reform initiatives as players adapt to the rules of the game and find ways around them. The effectiveness of reforms needs to be continuously monitored to ensure that providers, insurers, and patients are responding to incentives as expected.

Better use of health information technology can help improve efficiency by increasing adherence to clinical guidelines, enhancing disease surveillance, decreasing medication errors, and reducing service duplication (OECD, 2009). However, the benefits have yet to be fully exploited, as the use of health information technology varies widely across advanced economies.

Raising the emphasis on preventive care could also contribute to decreasing health spending. Health outcomes are driven by factors other than public health spending, including income and the behavior of individuals. While governments can play an important role in promoting behaviors conducive to improved health outcomes (e.g., smoking cessation, drinking less alcohol, improving diet, exercising more, and driving more safely), market mechanisms can also play a crucial role. For example, linking cost sharing or insurance premiums to having regular checkups can reinforce a preventive approach to health care.

Access to a basket of basic health care services by the poor should be maintained during health reforms as part of advanced economies' social safety nets. Countries with less dispersion in health outcomes tend to have better aggregate outcomes (Joumard, Andre, and Nicq, 2010), suggesting that improving the health care outcomes of the most disadvantaged may be an efficient way to improve overall population health. Thus, cost containment reforms need to be carefully formulated to minimize any potential adverse effects on the poor by maintaining means-tested programs during and after reforms. Most advanced economies have achieved universal access to basic health services. Health reforms should seek to maintain this pillar of the safety net.

## Key Conclusions

- Effective reforms combine a mix of macro-level instruments to contain costs and micro-level reforms to improve the efficiency of spending.

- Among macro instruments, budget caps and central oversight are powerful tools for reducing spending growth.

- Among micro-level reforms, strengthening market mechanisms—increasing patient choice of insurers, allowing greater competition between insurers, relying on a greater degree of private provision, and allowing more competition between providers—is particularly important to contain costs.

Management and contracting reforms, such as extending the use of managed care or shifting toward case-based payments, are central to improving the efficiency of spending.

- Although used less extensively, demand-side reforms—such as expanding private insurance and increasing the level of cost sharing—have also been successful in containing the growth of spending. However, demand-side policies can raise equity and access concerns.

- Price controls appear to be among the less successful approaches for containing health care costs. These controls are often eroded by supplier responses, such as increasing volumes or directing patients to higher-cost services. Furthermore, some types of public management and contracting reforms, as well as reforms to market mechanisms, do not appear effective. In particular, increasing the extent to which key decisions are made at the insurer level, providing greater user information on the quality and price of health care services, and creating incentives to reduce the volume of services are all associated with higher excess cost growth. These reforms may nevertheless be desirable from the perspective of increasing the quality of health care.

These conclusions help explain the varying success of countries in containing the growth of public health spending in recent decades.

- Italy, Japan, and Sweden, with above-average scores in the indices related to budget caps and central oversight, are among the countries projected to experience the lowest excess cost growth. Macro instruments also played key roles in the successful containment episodes in Canada, Sweden, and the United Kingdom.

- The use of market mechanisms in Germany and Japan is an important factor in explaining the low excess cost growth observed in these countries—both of which score relatively high in the indices for choice of insurer, choice of provider, and private provision.

- Countries that have been less successful at controlling the growth of spending tend to use macro- and micro-level instruments less extensively. These countries score low in several health system indices, implying that room for reform exists. Luxembourg and Greece, for example, score below average in the majority of the indices evaluated; Switzerland and the United States score low on the budget caps; and Portugal and the United Kingdom score below average on market mechanisms.

## IMPACT OF FURTHER REFORMS

Health reforms could help slow the growth of spending over the next 20 years. The focus in this analysis has been on reforms that are effective in containing the growth of spending based on the analysis presented in Table 6.1. As an illustration, Figure 6.6 shows the average impact of reforms on

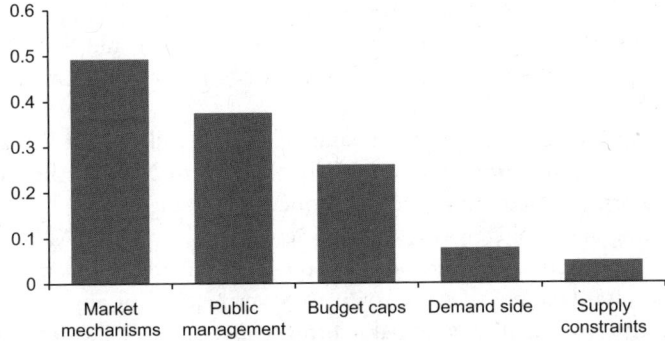

**Figure 6.6**    Average Impact of Reform Components on Health Spending, 2030
(Decrease relative to the baseline, percent of GDP)
Sources: Organization for Economic Cooperation and Development, OECD Health Data; and IMF staff estimates.
Note: Unweighted averages of the impact of reforms.

public-health-spending-to-GDP ratios in 2030, grouped in the following five categories:

- budget caps—including budget constraints and central oversight;
- public management and coordination—including gatekeeping and greater subnational government involvement;
- market mechanisms—including choice of insurers and providers, the degree of private provision, and the ability of insurers to compete;
- demand-side reforms—including expansion of private insurance and cost-sharing; and
- supply controls—including regulation of the health care workforce and the use of a well-defined health basket.

The figure shows the combined effect of raising countries to the mean score in each of these indices.[8] The results suggest that reforms of market mechanisms can be powerful, yielding a reduction in spending of 0.5 percentage point of GDP.[9] This exercise also underscores the importance of budget caps, which can reduce spending by 0.25 percentage point. Finally, the simulated impacts of demand-side reforms (–0.10) and supply constraints (–0.05) are small, but not negligible.

The possible savings under reforms are subject to uncertainty. Simultaneous reforms across different aspects of the health system may be undesirable or counterproductive. For example, efforts to increase central government oversight could be inconsistent with attempts to promote greater subnational involvement.

---

[8]For the United States, the simulations show only the impact of an increase in this index for a strengthening of budget constraints and supply constraints. The United States was not included in the OECD study of health institutions, as it did not respond to the OECD questionnaire. For this exercise, the value of the budget caps and supply constraints indices for the United States is set equal to the average for countries that are below the sample average in each of these indices.

[9]In the regression analysis, the effect of each individual reform is estimated keeping all other indices fixed.

Thus, the effect of the reforms across the categories described in Figure 6.6 cannot necessarily be aggregated. Some reforms, however, could be complementary, implying that the estimates of savings under a particular individual reform are understated.

Reform options and the appropriate mix of reforms will depend on a country's characteristics and the projected outlook for the growth of public health spending. The reform impacts simulated above focus on strengthening health system characteristics and policies where countries score below the OECD mean (Appendix Table 6.3). Of course, not all of the identified reforms using this methodology necessarily apply to every country. Nevertheless, this approach provides a systematic way to identify potential reforms that could have a significant payoff in their effect on the growth of public health care spending. The recommendations under this approach are broadly consistent with a recent OECD assessment on health systems. The OECD study, using a different methodology, focuses on priorities for improving the efficiency of health systems (Joumard, Andre, and Nicq, 2010), and covers both the private and public sectors.[10]

Among the group of countries that rely more heavily on market mechanisms:

- Canada, the Czech Republic, France, Germany, Japan, and the Slovak Republic are projected to have relatively low excess cost growth. For these countries, staying the course with marginal reforms would be enough to keep ECG low, although bolder reforms might still be needed to offset the effects of demographics on health spending. The Slovak Republic's relatively low efficiency ranking also suggests that room for reform exists there.

- In Australia, Austria, Belgium, and the Netherlands, the projected ECG is moderate (¾ to 1 percentage point). These countries tend to combine macro-level components (some central oversight and tight regulations for work force and equipment) and micro-level components (extensive private provision and over-the-basic insurance). Possible strategies to curb the growth of spending in these countries include tightening budget constraints, strengthening gatekeeping, and increasing cost sharing.

- Greece, the Republic of Korea, Luxembourg, Switzerland, and the United States are projected to have relatively high ECG, indicating the need for future reforms, especially in those countries that score low on efficiency measures (Greece and Luxembourg).[11] These five countries score relatively low on macro-level instruments—they tend to have less stringent budget constraints, minimal central oversight (especially Korea and Luxembourg),

---

[10]For one variable, the focus of the OECD study (on efficiency)—compared with the focus in this chapter on reducing expenditure growth—produces different results. In the OECD study, a high degree of central government oversight of spending in decentralized systems (a high score on consistency) is considered to be positive from the standpoint of efficiency. In our study, the empirical results indicate that this oversight helps reduce excess cost growth. This points to a potential trade-off between cost containment and efficiency in this area.

[11]The assessment does not take into account reforms in Greece as part of its fiscal adjustment program initiated in 2010.

lax regulations of the workforce and equipment, and little gatekeeping. Future efforts to contain spending growth in these countries should address these weaknesses.

Among the group of countries that rely more heavily on public insurance and provision:

- Denmark, Ireland, Italy, and Sweden are projected to have a relatively low ECG. Of these countries, Denmark and Ireland could focus on efficiency-enhancing reforms to reduce ECG further. Denmark could also consider using budget caps to reduce its growth in spending. Italy and Sweden, both of which score high on efficiency and have low ECG, could improve their score on priority setting (for example, by better monitoring public health objectives and the composition of the public health package).

- Norway and Spain are projected to have a moderate growth in health spending—with ECG of 0.6 and 0.7 percentage point, respectively. In these countries, containing the future growth of spending could require tightening macro controls (including increasing central oversight), broadening insurance for over-the-basic care (Norway), and improving priority setting (Spain).

- Iceland, Finland, New Zealand, Portugal, and the United Kingdom have the highest ECG in this group—all above 1 percentage point. This group of countries could also strengthen supply constraints on workforce and equipment. In addition, these countries could benefit from extending the role of private health insurance for over-the-basic health care and increasing choice among providers (especially in Finland, New Zealand, and the United Kingdom).

The impact of the simulated reforms is substantial, but may still fall short of what would be needed in some countries to stabilize public-spending-to-GDP ratios at current levels. Therefore, additional efforts may be needed to achieve that target. If this is not sufficient, fiscal adjustment may need to rely more on cuts in other areas or on further increases in revenue.[12]

- A successful implementation of reforms might not yield enough savings to offset projected increases in public health spending in some countries of advanced Europe. This is especially important in countries with relatively high projected growth in public health spending, such as Austria, Portugal, Switzerland, and the United Kingdom.

- In the United States, the challenge would be even larger. The illustrative savings from an assumed increase to the mean in the category of budget caps would yield savings of about 1 percentage point of GDP, which is consistent

---

[12]As discussed in the first section of this chapter, in order to lower the general-government-debt-to-GDP ratio to 60 percent by 2030, advanced economies would have to increase their cyclically adjusted primary balance by some 8 percentage points of GDP, on average, during 2011–30. To the extent that some spending is allowed to increase as a ratio of GDP, other spending would have to be cut correspondingly, or revenues would have to increase more.

with recent reform proposals.[13] Other options for reducing spending, beyond those captured in the econometric analysis, include the extension of health information technology, which would yield savings of 0.2 percent of GDP (Hillestad and others, 2005; CBO, 2008). Curtailing the favorable tax treatment of health insurance contributions (these tax expenditures are about 2 percent of GDP) could potentially yield large savings, and recent proposals in this area would yield an additional 0.5 percentage point of GDP on an annual basis.[14] All told, these reforms, including those simulated in the econometric analysis, would reduce spending (including tax expenditures) by about 2 percentage points of GDP. This would still leave health spending rising by 3 percentage points of GDP.

These reform scenarios raise two important questions: first, whether the impact of cost-reducing reforms on health outcomes will be adverse; second, whether they imply a fundamental change in the role of the state in the provision of health care services.

The relationship between cost containment and the provision of high-quality health services varies by reform. For example, there is strong evidence that the expansion of managed care in the United States in the 1990s, while reducing spending growth, did not have large deleterious impacts on health outcomes, compared to fee for services (Cutler, 2004). The general practitioner fund-holding scheme in the United Kingdom, whereby general practitioners receive a fixed and predetermined amount to provide or purchase care for their patients and keep any surplus that they generate, reduced patient waiting times, but the evidence on costs, referral rates, patient satisfaction, and inequality is mixed (Brereton and Vasoodaven, 2010). While a few studies show that the introduction of DRGs has led to higher readmission rates or slower quality gains (Forgione and others, 2004; Busato and von Below, 2010), most studies find no evidence of the adverse effects of DRGs on health outcomes (Or and Hakkinen, 2010). Greater cost sharing, on the other hand, reduces both essential and nonessential health services and is found to be associated with worse health outcomes for individuals in poor health (Newhouse and the Insurance Experiment Group, 1993; Gruber, 2006).

More generally, continued high levels of inefficiency in health spending suggest ample opportunities to improve health outcomes without raising spending. Research on spending efficiency implies that the potential gains from improving efficiency are very large (see Chapter 2 and Appendix 2.2). Most micro-level efficiency reforms, such as the introduction of competition, can improve the

---

[13]A recent reform proposal, sometimes referred to as the Rivlin-Ryan proposal, is based on a voucher system for Medicare (which is similar to a stringent budget cap with some market mechanism reforms) and an increase in the age of eligibility for Medicare. This reform is estimated to save up to 1¼ percentage points of GDP by 2030 (CBO, 2010). See also Committee for a Responsible Federal Budget (2010).

[14]See U.S. Senate, Joint Committee on Taxation (2008). It is estimated that a recent proposal to replace the employer-sponsored health insurance tax exclusion in the United States with a credit indexed to the CPI would save a little over 5 percent of GDP cumulatively over the next 10 years (Committee for a Responsible Federal Budget, 2010).

responsiveness of the health system to patient needs and also reduce excess cost growth. It is thus possible to control costs without adverse effects on health outcomes with an appropriate mix of reforms. This said, because of the limited research to date, it will be necessary to closely monitor the impact of cost containment reforms on health outcomes during the course of implementation. Reform measures may need to be fine-tuned to prevent adverse effects on health outcomes.

The above reforms have implications for the range of services or products financed by the public sector. If containing increases in public spending is a key feature of consolidation efforts, countries may need to eliminate some health services or products that are currently part of the public benefit package (e.g., dental services, nongeneric pharmaceuticals) or rely more heavily on the private sector for their financing. For predominately public sector systems, this could be achieved through much greater reliance on cost sharing than has typically been the case in many countries.

Alternatively, these countries could increase the role of private insurance. For example, private health insurance could be available to cover health services not covered by the public package, as is already the case in Australia, Canada, France, Ireland, Italy, Spain, and the United Kingdom. As indicated earlier, the econometric evidence suggests that greater shares of private insurance are associated with lower excess cost growth. However, there are considerable market failures associated with private insurance markets, such as adverse selection[15] and risk selection.[16] The expansion of private insurance thus needs to be accompanied by appropriate regulations to ensure access, equity, and efficiency. For example, health insurers should be required to offer coverage to all individuals, regardless of their health status or claims history, and insurance premiums should be allowed to vary only in relation to certain demographic characteristics—such as age—but not in relation to health status. Regulators also need to ensure adequate competition in the private insurance market.

## CONCLUSION

Effective reforms combine a mix of both macro-level instruments to contain costs and more micro-level reforms to improve the efficiency of spending. Reform options and the appropriate mix of reforms will depend on country characteristics and the projected outlook for the growth of public health spending.

Health reforms could help slow the growth of spending over the next 20 years. The simulation results reported in this chapter suggest that reforms of market mechanisms can be especially powerful and that budget caps are an important tool for containing spending growth. The simulated impacts of demand-side reforms and supply constraints are small, but not negligible.

While the impact of the simulated reforms is substantial, it may still fall short of what would be needed in some countries to stabilize age-related-spending-

---

[15]High-risk individuals drive up insurance premiums to such an extent that low-risk individuals leave the market, which may result in limited risk pooling and, at the extreme, the collapse of the insurance market.
[16]Health insurers selectively offer insurance coverage only to those with favorable risks, which may result in no market for those with less favorable risks.

to-GDP ratios at current levels. Therefore, additional efforts would be needed to achieve that target. If this is not sufficient, fiscal adjustment may need to rely more on cuts in other areas or on revenue increases.

# APPENDIX 6.1. ESTIMATION OF REFORM IMPACTS IN ADVANCED ECONOMIES

This appendix describes measures of health institutions and policies, econometric estimates of the impacts of these measures on excess cost growth, and the simulated impacts of potential reforms based on these measures.

## OECD Indicators on Health Institutions and Policies

A recent OECD report provides comprehensive and systematic measures of health institutions and policies in advanced economies. Joumard, Andre, and Nicq (2010) collected information on 269 key qualitative characteristics of health institutions and policies, and transformed these characteristics into 20 indicators related to market signals and regulations affecting users, providers, and insurers; the extent of insurance coverage; budget and management approaches affecting the level of available resources; and the degree of delegation of decision making. All advanced economies (except the United States, for which data were not provided) were scored according to these indicators on a scale of 0 to 6. Of the 20 indicators, 17 were used in the principal component analyses in the OECD report to create four composite indices that capture most of the variation across countries—"reliance on market mechanisms," "intensity of regulation," "intensity of budget constraint," and "degree of decentralization"—and three were not mapped because of lack of variation across countries.[17] In Appendix Table 6.1, the first column shows the mapping of the 17 characteristics to the reforms identified in Box 6.1. Columns 2 and 3 show the mean and standard deviations of the 17 indicators, and columns 4–7 show the principal component analysis weights of the 17 indicators in constructing the four composite indices.

---

[17]Principal component analysis condenses the information contained in a set of indicators into a smaller number of uncorrelated principal components, which are linear combinations of the original indicators. The first principal component accounts for as much of the variability in the data as possible, and each succeeding component accounts for as much of the remaining variability as possible. In the OECD study, two principal component analyses were performed, and only the top two components were selected for subsequent analysis. "Reliance on market mechanisms" and "intensity of regulation" are the two principal components from the first principal component analysis, and input variables are "choice of insurers," "insurer levers," "over-the-basic coverage," "private provision," "volume incentives," "regulation of provider prices," "user information," "regulation of the workforce and equipment," "choice among providers," "gatekeeping," and "price signal on users." "Intensity of budget constraint" and "degree of decentralization" are the two principal components from the second principal component analysis, and input variables are "priority setting," "budget constraint," "regulation of workforce and equipment," "regulation of prices paid by third-party payers," "decentralization," "delegation," and "consistency."

**APPENDIX TABLE 6.1**

## Description of OECD Indicators on Health Institutions and Policies

| Reform areas/OECD indicators | Descriptive statistics | | Principal component analysis weights | | | |
|---|---|---|---|---|---|---|
| | Average | Standard deviation | Intensity of regulation | Reliance on market mechanism | Stringency of budget constraint | Degree of centralization |
| **Budget caps** | | | | | | |
| *Budget constraint* | 2.90 | 2.06 | — | — | 0.75 | 0.55 |
| *Consistency*[a] | 4.62 | 1.51 | — | — | -0.41 | 0.29 |
| **Price controls** | | | | | | |
| *Regulation of providers' prices* | 4.26 | 1.05 | 0.04 | -0.12 | 0.00 | 0.19 |
| *Regulation of prices paid by third-party payers* | 4.55 | 0.75 | — | — | — | — |
| **Supply constraints** | | | | | | |
| *Regulation of workforce and equipment* | 2.92 | 1.32 | 0.23 | 0.03 | 0.17 | -0.09 |
| *Priority setting* | 3.02 | 1.16 | — | — | — | — |
| **Public management and coordination** | | | | | | |
| *Gatekeeping* | 3.07 | 2.40 | 0.68 | 0.48 | 0.06 | 0.02 |
| *Decentralization* | 1.92 | 1.72 | — | — | 0.36 | -0.75 |
| *Delegation* | 0.89 | 0.98 | — | — | -0.32 | 0.03 |
| **Contracting methods** | | | | | | |
| *Volume incentives* | 3.14 | 1.13 | -0.18 | 0.19 | — | — |
| **Market mechanisms** | | | | | | |
| *Choice of insurers* | 1.31 | 1.77 | -0.24 | 0.53 | — | — |
| *Insurer levers* | 0.74 | 1.44 | -0.22 | 0.40 | — | — |
| *User information* | 1.08 | 1.28 | -0.05 | 0.31 | — | — |
| *Private provision* | 2.77 | 1.34 | -0.28 | 0.28 | — | — |
| *Choice among providers* | 4.43 | 2.05 | -0.51 | -0.02 | — | — |
| **Demand-side reforms** | | | | | | |
| *Over-the-basic coverage* | 1.51 | 1.58 | 0.01 | 0.31 | — | — |
| *Price signals on users* | 1.16 | 0.59 | 0.03 | -0.02 | — | — |

Sources: Joumard, Andre, and Nicq (2010); and IMF staff estimates.

[a] This is referred to as central government oversight in Table 6.1.

## Econometric Estimation of Reform Impacts

The econometric analysis estimates the effects of each of the four composite indices on public health spending growth. It includes the four composite indices as explanatory variables (along with additional variables for GDP and demographic composition) in the regression model:

$$\log\left(\frac{h_{i,t+1}}{h_{i,t}}\right) = \gamma_0 + \gamma_1 \log\left(\frac{g_{i,t+1}}{g_{i,t}}\right) + \gamma_2 \log\left(\frac{X_{i,t+1}}{X_{i,t}}\right) + \gamma_{3,j} I_{i,j} + \varepsilon''_{i,t} \qquad (6.1)$$

Here $I_{i,j}$ denotes the score of country $i$ on composite indices $j$. Since these indices are time invariant, it is not possible to also include country fixed effects. Excess cost growth can thus be calculated as the following:

$$ECG_i = \hat{\gamma_0} + \sum_{j=1}^{4} \hat{\gamma_{3,j}} I_{i,j} + (\hat{\gamma_1} - 1)\, (GDP\ Growth_i) \qquad (6.2)$$

Country observations with structural breaks in the data have been excluded from the econometric analysis. Given that the indicators and composite indices provide a snapshot of health institutions and policies in 2009, more recent years (1995–2008) are used to estimate the impact of health reforms on public health spending growth. The coefficients should be interpreted as indicating the relationship between health system characteristics in 2009 and spending growth in 1995–2008. The exercise thus assumes that the 2009 snapshot provides an accurate characterization of the health care system over 1995–2008. The results indicate that reliance on market mechanisms and the stringency of budget constraints are negatively related to public health spending growth, while intensity of regulations and degree of centralization are positively related to public health spending growth (Appendix Table 6.2).

**APPENDIX TABLE 6.2**

## Impact Estimates of Health Institutions and Policies

**Dependent variable: log of real per capita public health spending**

|  | 1995–2008 | |
|---|---|---|
| Log of GDP per capita[a] | 0.2954** | (0.1124) |
| Log of age 14 and under[a] | 0.1953 | (0.1953) |
| Log of age 65 plus[a] | 0.6766*** | (0.2424) |
| Intensity of regulations | 0.0017 | (0.0011) |
| Reliance on market mechanisms | −0.0033** | (0.0013) |
| Stringency of budget constraint | −0.0029* | (0.0017) |
| Degree of centralization | 0.0034* | (0.0017) |
| $R^2$ | 0.135 | |
| $N$ | 345 | |

Sources: Joumard, Andre, and Nicq (2010); and IMF staff estimates.
Note: Standard errors in parentheses.
[a]All variables are expressed as first-differences. The coefficients are robust to different specifications. The relatively low $R^2$ reflects the large variability in the annual changes observed in the data. Using a model with five-year differences produces similar results but increases $R^2$ from 0.13 to 0.40.
*$p < .1$; **$p < .05$; ***$p < .01$.

**APPENDIX TABLE 6.3**

## Potential Reform Strategies for Different Country Groupings

| Countries scoring below mean | Potential reform strategies |
|---|---|
| ***Budget caps: budget constraint***<br>Australia, Austria, Belgium, Czech Republic, Denmark, Finland, France, Germany, Greece, Iceland, Japan, Korea, Luxembourg, Netherlands, Slovak Republic, Spain, Switzerland, United States | Make health sector budgets more stringent. Introduce prospective budget caps for the most critical health services where there are none, reduce flexibility on over-runs for existing caps, or target caps at the entire health sector. |
| ***Budget caps: central oversight of key decisions***<br>Belgium, Czech Republic, Finland, France, Germany, Greece, Iceland, Ireland, Korea, Luxembourg, Netherlands, New Zealand, Norway, Slovak Republic, Spain, Switzerland, United States | Increase the role of the center in oversight of macro-level decisions related to resource allocation—for example, the total budget dedicated to health care and level of social contributions. Although consistency declines when several levels of government are involved in key decisions, this is correlated with low cost growth. |
| ***Supply constraints: regulation of workforce and equipment***<br>Czech Republic, Finland, Germany, Greece, Iceland, Japan, Korea, Luxembourg, Netherlands, New Zealand, Sweden, Switzerland, United Kingdom, United States | Exert greater central control over physician numbers and hospital activities and staff. For example, move from hospitals with full autonomy toward negotiating capacity and staffing levels with government. |
| ***Supply constraints: priority setting***<br>Austria, Canada, Czech Republic, Finland, Germany, Greece, Iceland, Italy, Luxembourg, Portugal, Spain, Sweden, United States | Put more emphasis on affordability in terms of deciding the publicly funded benefit package. For example, complement cost-effectiveness evaluation with a consideration of budget impact, use positive lists, and regulate the coverage of new procedures by the state via guidelines. |
| ***Public management: subnational government involvement***<br>Belgium, Czech Republic, France, Germany, Greece, Iceland, Ireland, Korea, Luxembourg, Netherlands, Portugal, Slovak Republic | Increase the number of health policy decisions made at a subnational level, such as decisions on remuneration methods and financing new facilities. For example, involve lower levels of government in health policy decisions alongside central government or delegate policy responsibility to regions/states. |
| ***Public management: gatekeeping***<br>Australia, Austria, Belgium, Czech Republic, Greece, Ireland, Japan, Korea, Luxembourg, Sweden, Switzerland | Create incentives to steer demand to more appropriate resources. For example, encourage patients to register with a primary care physician, or require a compulsory referral to access secondary care. |
| ***Market mechanisms: user choice of insurers***<br>Australia, Belgium, Canada, Denmark, Finland, Iceland, Ireland, Italy, Korea, Luxembourg, New Zealand, Norway, Portugal, Spain, Sweden, United Kingdom | Increase the degree of user choice over insurers (including not-for-profit public insurers)—for example, by increasing the number of insurers. Most relevant for public contract health care systems. |
| ***Market mechanisms: insurance levers***<br>Australia, Austria, Belgium, Canada, Czech Republic, Denmark, Finland, France, Germany, Greece, Iceland, Ireland, Italy, Japan, Korea, Luxembourg, Netherlands, New Zealand, Norway, Portugal, Slovak Republic | Allow greater freedom to insurers to vary the scope, premium, etc., for basic insurance packages and more freedom in negotiating with health providers. Most relevant for public contract and private insurance health care systems. |
| ***Market mechanisms: private provision***<br>Czech Republic, Finland, Iceland, Ireland, Italy, New Zealand, Portugal, Spain, Sweden, United Kingdom | Foster contestability by allowing/encouraging greater private provision of both primary and acute care (regardless of financing source). |
| ***Market mechanisms: choice among providers***<br>Austria, Denmark, Finland, Greece, New Zealand, Portugal, Spain | Allow greater patient choice over primary care physicians, specialists, and hospitals, even if some limitations remain. |
| ***Demand-side reforms: over-the-basic coverage***<br>Austria, Czech Republic, Denmark, Finland, Greece, Iceland, Italy, Japan, Korea, Luxembourg, Norway, Portugal, Slovak Republic, Sweden, United Kingdom | Encourage insurers to offer complementary (e.g., reimburs-ing patients for cost sharing required by the public system) and supplementary (e.g., filling gaps not covered by the public system) insurance over the basic packages. |

Sources: Joumard, Andre, and Nicq (2010); and IMF staff estimates.

Note: The policy reform strategies indicate the characteristics of countries that score highly in each index. Hence, not all of the identified reforms may necessarily apply to every country scoring below the mean. For Greece, the assessment does not take into account the effect of recent reforms.

## Simulations of Reform Impacts

To estimate the impacts of these reforms on excess cost growth, a one-unit increase is applied to each of the 17 variables underlying the four composite indices; the resulting changes in the four composite indices are calculated based on the principal component analysis weights in Appendix Table 6.1. These changes are then multiplied by the coefficients from the regression analysis (Appendix Table 6.2) to get the impacts on ECG, with a negative sign indicating a decrease in ECG (Table 6.1).

To further illustrate the potential impacts of these reforms on public health spending growth in each country, in all of the variables that are shown to reduce ECG, country scores are raised to the mean if their scores are below the mean. This provides the basis of the estimates of the savings under each of the categories in Figure 6.6. Appendix Table 6.3 provides a list of countries scoring below the mean in different categories and the types of reform strategies that would help them improve performance in these areas.

## REFERENCES

Brereton, L., and V. Vasoodaven, 2010, *The Impact of the NHS Market: An Overview of the Literature* (London: Civitas—Institute for the Study of Civil Society).

Busato, A., and G. von Below, 2010, "The Implementation of DRG-Based Hospital Reimbursement in Switzerland: A Population-Based Perspective," *Health Research Policy and Systems* [online], Vol. 8, Art. 31 (Oct. 16).

Chernew, E.M., A.B. Rosen, and A.M. Fendrick, 2007, "Value-Based Insurance Design," *Health Affairs*, Vol. 26, No. 2, pp. 195–203.

Committee for a Responsible Federal Budget, 2010, "Principle #5: Continued Vigilance in Health Reform" (Washington).

Congressional Budget Office (CBO), 2008, *Evidence on the Costs and Benefits of Health Information Technology*, Publication No. 2976 (Washington: U.S. Government Printing Office).

———, 2010, "Preliminary Analysis of the Rivlin-Ryan Health Care Proposal," analysis transmitted by letter to Rep. Paul Ryan (Washington).

Crivelli, E., A. Leive, and T. Stratmann, 2010, "Subnational Health Spending and Soft Budget Constraints in OECD Countries," IMF Working Paper No. 10/147 (Washington: International Monetary Fund).

Cutler, D., 2004, *Your Money or Your Life* (New York: Oxford University Press).

Cutler, D., and M. McClellan, 2001, "Is Technological Change in Medicine Worth It?" *Health Affairs*, Vol. 20, No. 5, pp. 11–29.

Docteur, E., and H. Oxley, 2003, "Health-Care Systems: Lessons from the Reform Experience," OECD Health Working Paper No. 9 (Paris: Organization for Economic Cooperation and Development).

Evans, D., A. Tandon, C. Murray, and J. Lauer, 2000, "The Comparative Efficiency of National Health Systems in Producing Health: An Analysis of 191 Countries," GPE Discussion Paper No. 29 (Geneva: World Health Organization).

Forgione, D., T. Vermeer, K. Surysekar, J. Wrieden, and C. Plante, 2004, "The Impact of DRG-Based Payment Systems on Quality of Health Care in OECD Countries," *Journal of Health Care Finance*, Vol. 31, No. 1, pp. 41–54.

Gruber, J., 2006, "The Role of Consumer Copayments for Health Care: Lessons from the RAND Health Insurance Experiment and Beyond" (Washington: Kaiser Family Foundation).

Gupta, S., G. Schwartz, S. Tareq, R. Allen, I. Adenauer, K. Fletcher, and D. Last, 2008, *Fiscal Management of Scaled-Up Aid* (Washington: International Monetary Fund).

Gupta, S., and M. Verhoeven, 2001, "The Efficiency of Government Expenditures: Experiences from Africa," *Journal of Policy Modeling*, Vol. 23, pp. 433–67.

Hauner, D., 2007, "Benchmarking the Efficiency of Public Expenditure in the Russian Federation," IMF Working Paper No. 07/246 (Washington: International Monetary Fund).

Hillestad, R., J. Bigelow, A. Bower, F. Girosi, R. Meili, R. Scoville, and R. Taylor, 2005, "Can Electronic Medical Record Systems Transform Healthcare? An Assessment of Potential Health Benefits, Savings, and Costs," *Health Affairs*, Vol. 24, No. 5, pp. 1103–17.

Hollingsworth, B., and J. Wildman, 2003, "The Efficiency of Health Production: Re-estimating the WHO Panel Data Using Parametric and Non-parametric Approaches to Provide Additional Information," *Economics of Health Care Systems*, Vol. 12, pp. 493–504.

International Monetary Fund (IMF), 2010, *From Stimulus to Consolidation: Revenue and Expenditure Policies in Advanced and Emerging Economies,* IMF Departmental Paper (Washington).

Joumard, I., C. Andre, and C. Nicq, 2010, "Health Care Systems: Efficiency and Institutions," Economics Department Working Paper No. 769 (Paris: Organization for Economic Cooperation and Development).

Joumard, I., C. Andre, C. Nicq, and O. Chatal, 2008, "Health Status Determinants: Lifestyle, Environment, Health Care Resources and Efficiency," OECD Economics Department Working Paper No. 627 (Paris: Organization for Economic Cooperation and Development).

Mattina, T., and V. Gunnarsson, 2007, "Budget Rigidity and Expenditure Efficiency in Slovenia," IMF Working Paper No. 07/131 (Washington: International Monetary Fund).

Newhouse, J., and the Insurance Experiment Group, 1993, *Free for All? Lessons from the RAND Health Insurance Experiment* (Cambridge, MA: MIT Press).

Or, Z., and U. Hakkinen, 2010, "DRGs and Quality: For Better or Worse," presentation at the Eighth European Conference on Health Economics, Helsinki, July 7–10.

Organization for Economic Cooperation and Development (OECD), 2006, "Projecting OECD Health and Long-Term Care Expenditures: What Are the Main Drivers?" Economics Department Working Paper No. 477 (Paris).

———, 2009, *Achieving Better Value for Money in Health Care* (Paris).

Oxley, H., and M. MacFarlan, 1995, "Health Care Reform: Controlling Spending and Increasing Efficiency," OECD Economic Study No. 24 (Paris: Organization for Economic Cooperation and Development).

Thornton, J., and A. Mati, 2008, "Fiscal Institutions and the Relation between Central and Sub-national Government Fiscal Balances," *Public Finance Review*, Vol. 36, No. 2, pp. 243–54.

United States Senate, Joint Committee on Taxation, 2008, "Tax Expenditures for Health Care: Hearing before the Senate Committee on Finance, July 30, 2008," JCX-66-08 (Washington: Government Printing Office).

Verhoeven, M., V. Gunnarsson, and S. Carcillo, 2007, "Education and Health in G-7 Countries: Achieving Better Outcomes with Less Spending," IMF Working Paper No. 07/263 (Washington: International Monetary Fund).

World Health Organization (WHO), 2000, "Health Systems: Improving Performance," in *The World Health Report* (Geneva).

# CHAPTER 7

# Health Reform Lessons from Experiences of Emerging Economies

EVA JENKNER, BAOPING SHANG, AND BENEDICT CLEMENTS

This chapter draws on the general lessons of the literature to assess the challenges of health care reform in emerging economies. It begins by assessing how challenges differ between the advanced and emerging economies, then follows with a discussion of reform options.

## EMERGING ECONOMIES: A DIVERSE SET OF CHALLENGES

The challenges facing emerging economies are different from those in advanced economies. Average life expectancy in emerging economies is about nine years lower than that in advanced economies, and infant mortality rates are significantly higher (Table 7.1). In emerging Europe, health spending is relatively high by emerging economy standards, as coverage of the population is nearly universal and disease patterns mirror those of advanced economies. However, overall health outcomes there remain relatively poor, so the challenge is to enhance the efficiency of spending to improve lagging health outcomes and the quality of service delivery. In most emerging economies of Asia and Latin America, the main challenge remains to expand basic coverage to a larger share of the population without generating undue fiscal pressures over the medium term as incomes rise and these systems expand. In these economies, increased public spending could not only improve health indicators, but also catalyze economic growth (Baldacci and others, 2010). These economies should aim to expand their systems in a way that avoids the inefficiencies and resulting high costs of health systems in the advanced economies.

The fiscal space in emerging economies needed to increase public health spending varies. This can be assessed with reference to the adjustment required for them to reduce debt to an illustrative target of 40 percent of GDP over the next 20 years.[1] Figure 7.1 indicates the adjustment required in each country to meet

---

[1]See IMF (2010a, 2010b) for a further description of the methodology used for these estimates.

**TABLE 7.1**

**Selected Expenditure and Social Indicators by Country Group, 2007**

| | | Emerging | | |
| --- | --- | --- | --- | --- |
| | Advanced | All | Europe | Other |
| GDP per capita | 36,567 | 11,981 | 14,408 | 10,542 |
| Total health expenditures | | | | |
| Per capita | 3,351 | 728 | 935 | 612 |
| Percent of GDP | 9.2 | 5.8 | 6.5 | 5.4 |
| Public health expenditures | | | | |
| Per capita | 2,446 | 424 | 651 | 295 |
| Percent of GDP | 6.7 | 3.2 | 4.2 | 2.5 |
| Percent of government expenditures | 15.8 | 9.8 | 11.0 | 8.6 |
| Out-of-pocket expenditures | | | | |
| Per capita | 533 | 198 | 273 | 164 |
| Percent of total health expenditures | 17.2 | 33.0 | 29.3 | 37.1 |
| Percent of population above 60 | 21.2 | 13.5 | 21.3 | 9.0 |
| Life expectancy | 80 | 71 | 73 | 69 |
| Infant mortality | 3.7 | 18.9 | 8.0 | 27.0 |

Sources: World Health Organization; and IMF staff calculations.
Note: Estimates based on simple averages.

this target, as well as the projected increase in public health spending, in percent of GDP, for the 2011–30 period. For some countries (Argentina, Indonesia), only a small fiscal adjustment would be needed to achieve the illustrative target, thus making it easier for these countries to accommodate the projected rise in health spending. However, adjustment needs are high in a number of emerging European countries (Lithuania, Poland, Romania, Russia, and Ukraine) that are projected to have above-average increases in health spending. While all countries should be targeting improvements in efficiency, doing so is especially important for countries with limited fiscal space.

In emerging Asia, adjustment needs are generally lower. Whereas fiscal conditions are conducive to expanding public health spending in some countries with relatively low current levels (Indonesia, Philippines), they limit the room for increases in others (India, Malaysia). Countries with high projected economic growth will also be in a better position to expand health spending, owing to its favorable effects on fiscal sustainability. Countries with more moderate growth prospects will need to take a more gradual approach.

## REFORM OPTIONS FOR EMERGING ECONOMIES

Given limited fiscal space, most of emerging Europe will need to rely on additional micro-level reforms to improve health outcomes, rather than on increasing spending. Most of these countries (including Estonia, Hungary, Latvia, Russia, and Ukraine) have successfully contained spending, in some cases implementing reforms similar to those of the advanced economies. Estonia and Hungary, for example, implemented a single insurance fund and a global budget, which helped contain spending growth and reduced transaction costs.

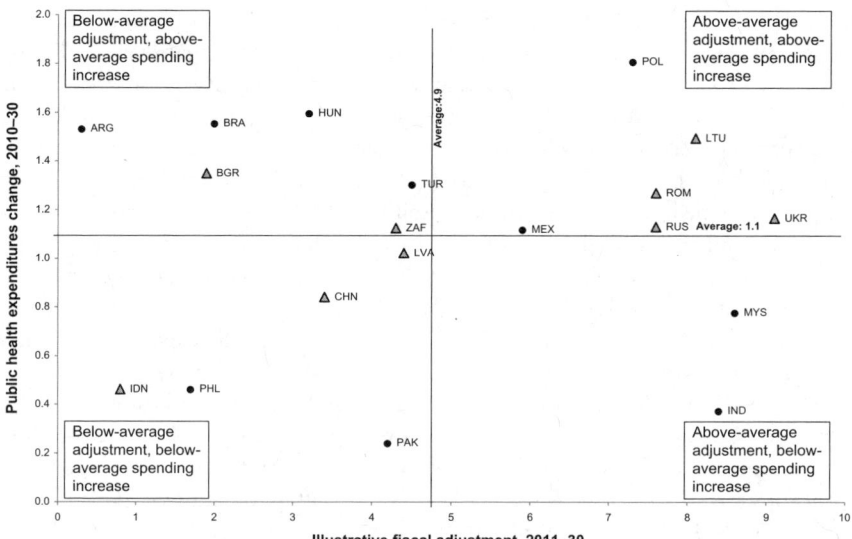

**Figure 7.1** Emerging Economies: Illustrative Fiscal Adjustment and Projected Public Health Expenditure Increase, 2011–30 (Percent of GDP)

Sources: IMF (2010b); and IMF staff estimates.

Note: "Illustrative fiscal adjustment" refers to the change in the cyclically adjusted primary balance (CAPB) needed to reduce public-debt-to-GDP ratios to 40 percent by 2030 or stabilize debt-to-GDP ratios at the end-2012 levels. See IMF (2010b, Table 5b) for details. Circles indicate debt ratios above 40 percent projected at end-2012. Triangles indicate debt ratios below 40 percent projected at end-2012. The vertical and horizontal lines represent unweighted averages. CAPB is reported in percent of nominal GDP. In the illustrative fiscal adjustment strategy, the CAPB is assumed to improve in line with IMF *World Economic Outlook* projections in 2011–12 and gradually from 2013 until 2020; thereafter, the CAPB is maintained constant until 2030. The analysis is illustrative and makes some simplifying assumptions: in particular, up to 2015, an interest rate–growth rate differential of 0 percentage points is assumed, broadly in line with *World Economic Outlook* assumptions, and 1 percentage point afterward, regardless of country-specific circumstances. For large commodity-producing countries, even larger fiscal balances might be called for in the medium term than shown in the illustrative scenario, given the high volatility of revenues and the exhaustibility of natural resources. ARG = Argentina; BGR = Bulgaria; BRA = Brazil; CHN = China; HUN = Hungary; IDN = Indonesia; IND = India; LTU = Lithuania; LVA = Latvia; MEX = Mexico; MYS = Malaysia; PAK = Pakistan; PHL = Philippines; POL = Poland; ROM = Romania; RUS = Russia; TUR = Turkey; UKR = Ukraine; ZAF = South Africa.

There is nonetheless scope for additional micro-level reforms, as many countries are still hampered by provider payment systems that do not ensure the appropriate incentives for cost-effective medical care. In Hungary, for example, primary care doctors are paid on the basis of capitation fees alone and have little incentive to treat patients. This has led to excessively high referral rates to specialists. Estonia provides a positive example of how to modify incentives to improve the efficiency of spending, using a mix of payment methods (capitation, fee for service, and lump sum) to promote provision of preventive care by primary care physicians.

Emerging economies in Latin America and Asia have more scope to increase spending but will need to avoid putting health systems on a fiscally unsustainable path as they expand coverage. In many of these economies, the public system provides coverage for only a small share of the population, and in some cases the benefit package, even for those covered, is insufficient to protect against all key health risks. Thailand and Chile have successfully expanded basic coverage at a low fiscal cost and provide valuable lessons for other countries. By extending benefits to a wide share of the population, health risks can be pooled for much of the population. This can lead to a substantial improvement in aggregate social welfare and equity, as it helps reduce the burden of catastrophic health events on low-income groups.

The country case studies underscore the advantages of extending coverage to a wide share of the population with a fiscally sustainable benefit package. In order to keep costs low, including over the longer term, it is essential to restrict the benefit package to the most essential health services until the capacity to finance higher public spending increases. More efficient use of resources, such as improvements in the composition of spending, can lead to better health outcomes without incurring additional costs. For example, in some countries the allocation of spending to combat infectious diseases is too low, with the benefits of spending concentrated in urban areas with relatively well-off populations (Wagstaff and others, 2009; Hsiao and Heller, 2007).

The experiences of advanced economies that successfully expanded health insurance coverage in the recent past provide valuable lessons for emerging economies on the road ahead. The experiences of Taiwan Province of China and the Republic of Korea are instructive in this regard:[2]

- Cost containment is one of the biggest challenges following a successful coverage expansion. The profit-seeking behavior of health care providers during an expansion of coverage can put considerable pressure on public health spending. It is important to put in place mechanisms that ensure that the increase in outlays is consistent with the government's long-term expenditure plans. For example, to achieve this objective, Taiwan Province of China adopted a global budget system (Lu and Hsiao, 2003). Successful emerging economy reforms have followed a similar route. Chile, for instance, has used explicit annual budgetary ceilings and eliminated direct budget support to public providers to help achieve broad coverage at a reasonable fiscal cost.

- A judicious mix of roles for the public and private sectors in the postreform era can help contain the level of public expenditures. Even after a swift and broad expansion of coverage, public spending in the Republic of Korea remains well below the Organization for Economic Cooperation and Development (OECD) average, with private spending accounting for about 45 percent of total health spending (Jones, 2010).

---

[2]The Republic of Korea gradually expanded health insurance coverage to different segments of its population. The coverage rate was 30 percent in 1980 and reached 100 percent in 1988. Public health spending as a share of GDP increased from 0.8 percent in 1980 to 3.6 percent in 2008. Taiwan Province of China expanded its social insurance program from 57 percent of the population in 1994 to 90 percent in 1995. Public health spending as a share of GDP increased from 2.7 percent in 1994 to 4.1 percent in 2005 (IMF staff estimates based on Wen, Tsai, and Chung, 2008; and Iwamoto and others, 2005).

- Improving efficiency is the key to long-term health system performance. Taiwan Province of China and the Republic of Korea undertook important reforms to better align provider incentives, promote primary and preventive care, and improve public management and coordination. Both have introduced case-based (diagnosis-related groups) payment methods for reimbursement for certain diseases and treatments. Taiwan Province of China has also initiated a fee-for-outcome program, in which physicians receive bonus payments based on clinical outcomes. In Mexico, by contrast, the health care system remains highly fragmented and vertically integrated. This has ruled out competition and contributed to the highest public health administrative costs in the OECD (OECD, 2009). Similarly, in China, reforms to the provider payment system are needed to encourage greater use of preventive and primary care.

An expansion of benefits financed by taxes, rather than by social insurance, should be the first option for most countries seeking to expand coverage where labor market informality is high. Social insurance systems can help contain spending by limiting benefits to contributors. However, if the goal is to expand coverage and labor market informality is high—as it is in many emerging economies—tax-financed provision of universal basic health care (such as in Thailand) may be the best starting point (Box 7.1).

For countries where labor market informality is limited and revenue administration is of high quality, an expansion of social-insurance-based systems could be considered. The experience of Chile suggests that sustainable financing flows can be achieved through a combination of mandatory contributions in the formal labor market, individual cost sharing through copayments, and supplementary budget financing (especially where subsidization is necessary and in the public interest).

In emerging Asia, higher public health care spending could also help reduce household precautionary savings and stimulate growth. Empirical evidence suggests that increasing public health expenditures could have a powerful effect in reducing precautionary savings that are accumulated to finance large out-of-pocket health spending (Box 7.2). This would assist countries in this region in their efforts to make domestic demand a stronger engine of growth.

## CONCLUSION

The health care reform challenges facing emerging economies are different from those facing advanced economies. Across emerging economies—a heterogeneous group—challenges also vary, as does the fiscal space they have available to increase public health spending. Most of emerging Europe will need to rely on additional micro-level reforms rather than on increasing spending to improve health outcomes, such as reforms that strengthen incentives for cost-effective medical care. Emerging economies in Latin America and, especially, in Asia have low coverage levels and more scope to expand spending. In order to maintain fiscal sustainability, it is essential to restrict the benefit package to the most essential health services until the capacity to finance higher public health spending increases.

**BOX 7.1**

### *Health Care Financing: Is Taxation Better than Social Insurance?*

In a social insurance system, the receipt of benefits is, at least in principle, contingent on the payment of mandatory contributions (usually from both employers and employees). In a tax-financed system, the receipt of benefits is not contingent. In practice, however, it is often impossible to deny the provision of health services to those who need them. This has implications for the choice between the tax and social insurance model.

Tax-financed systems can be most appropriate when informality is high and the objective is to provide universal coverage of a basic package of health services. A tax-financed system can draw on a broad revenue base for raising resources. In Thailand, general revenue financing played a key role in enabling the achievement of universal coverage. Relying on contributions would not work unless the threat of nonprovision of health services were credible so as to induce informal workers to join the formal work force. But such a threat is unlikely to be credible, at least for essential services.

Social insurance schemes can be an effective way of providing coverage when labor market informality is low. Such schemes often cover only a limited population (for example, those who work in large formal sector enterprises), at least at their early stages, and provide a source of nondistortionary financing, as contributors see a strong link between contributions and benefits (Gottret and Schieber, 2006). Additional benefits include their potential for pooling funds and risk. However, expanding coverage to vulnerable groups, such as those in the informal sector and pensioners, could be difficult under social insurance schemes, especially when labor market informality is high. Social insurance systems are also often more complex and expensive to manage than tax-based systems.

In practice, many countries have hybrid systems. The system chosen should fit the specific socioeconomic and institutional context. For countries where labor market informality remains high, a tax-based system with a focus on primary health services is important in order to ensure universal access to basic health care without excessively high labor taxes. In many countries, social insurance does not cover the majority of the population, contributions are insufficient to cover public health expenditures, and the system effectively relies on fiscal transfers to be sustainable. In these countries, expansion of the social insurance system should occur only if accompanied by greater formalization of the labor market, and fiscal resources should be oriented toward providing a basic package of services.

**BOX 7.2**

### Public Health Expenditure and Household Consumption in Emerging Asia

Precautionary motives play an important role in explaining household savings and consumption behavior. This is an especially relevant consideration for countries where out-of-pocket health payments are high and where households need to accumulate savings to pay for lumpy health expenditures. In China, for example, households facing high health expenditure risk tend to have a savings rate 20 percentage points higher than that of households not facing these risks (Chamon and Prasad, 2008).

Higher public expenditure on health could increase household consumption rates. In 2007, average public health expenditure for six emerging Asia economies (China, India, Indonesia, Malaysia, the Philippines, and Thailand) was about 1.5 percent of GDP, well below the average of 7.0 percent for advanced economies. Raising these public outlays in emerging Asia could help raise private household consumption. For China, Baldacci and others (2010) find that a 1 percent of GDP increase in public health spending would raise consumption by 1.3 percent, while Barnett and Brooks (2010) find a slightly larger effect. The 1995 introduction of National Health Insurance in Taiwan Province of China was found to have reduced household savings rates by 9–14 percent (Chou, Liu, and Hammitt, 2003). Cross-country econometric estimates from Baldacci and others (2010) imply that, for these emerging Asia countries, an increase in public health spending of 1 percent of GDP would result in an average increase in household consumption of more than 1 percent of GDP.

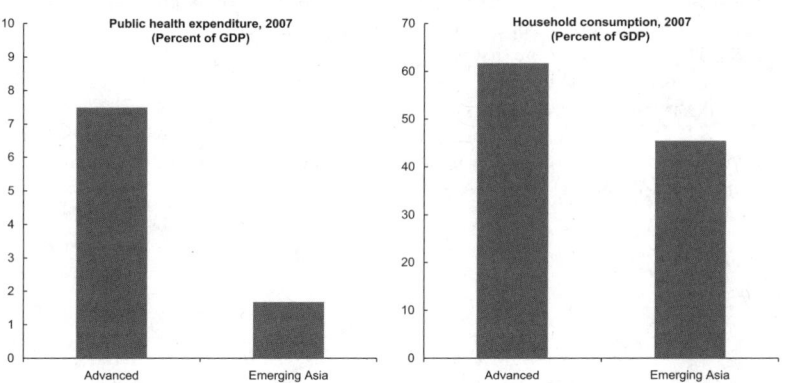

Sources: Organization for Economic Cooperation and Development; World Health Organization; and IMF staff estimates.
Note: Estimates are purchasing power parity weighted. Emerging Asia comprises China, India, Indonesia, Malaysia, the Philippines, and Thailand.

# REFERENCES

Baldacci, E., G. Callegari, D. Coady, D. Ding, M. Kumar, P. Tommasini, and J. Woo, 2010, "Public Expenditures on Social Programs and Household Consumption in China," IMF Working Paper No. 10/69 (Washington: International Monetary Fund).

Barnett, S., and R. Brooks, 2010, "China: Does Government Health and Education Spending Boost Consumption?" IMF Working Paper No. 10/16 (Washington: International Monetary Fund).

Chamon, M., and E. Prasad, 2008, "Why Are Saving Rates of Urban Households in China Rising?" *American Economic Journal,* Vol. 2, No. 1, pp. 93–130.

Chou, S.-Y., J.-T. Liu, and J. K. Hammitt, 2003, "National Health Insurance and Precautionary Saving: Evidence from Taiwan," *Journal of Public Economics*, Vol. 87, pp. 1873–94.

Gottret, P., and G. Schieber, 2006, *Health Financing Revisited: A Practioner's Guide* (Washington: World Bank).

Hsiao, W., and P. Heller, 2007, *What Macroeconomists Should Know about Health Care Policy* (Washington: International Monetary Fund).

International Monetary Fund, 2010a, *From Stimulus to Consolidation: Revenue and Expenditure Policies in Advanced and Emerging Economies*, IMF Departmental Paper (Washington).

———, 2010b, "Addressing Fiscal Challenges to Reduce Economic Risks," *Fiscal Monitor*, September (Washington).

Iwamoto, Y., T. Fukui, M. Ii, H. Kawaguchi, M. Kohara, and M. Saito, 2005, "Policy Options for Health Insurance and Long-Term Care Insurance" (Tokyo: Economic and Social Research Institute).

Jones, R.S., 2010, "Health-Care Reform in Korea," Economics Department Working Paper No. 797 (Paris: Organization for Economic Cooperation and Development).

Lu, J.-F., and W.C. Hsiao, 2003, "Does Universal Health Insurance Make Health Care Unaffordable? Lessons from Taiwan," *Health Affairs*, Vol. 22, No. 3, pp. 77–88.

Organization for Economic Cooperation and Development (OECD), 2009, *Achieving Better Value for Money in Health Care* (Paris).

Wagstaff, A., W. Yip, M. Lindelow, and W. Hsiao, 2009, "China's Health System and Its Reform: A Review of Recent Studies," *Health Economics*, Vol. 18, pp. S7–S23.

Wen, C.P., S.P. Tsai, and W.-S.I. Chung, 2008, "A 10-Year Experience with Universal Health Insurance in Taiwan: Measuring Changes in Health and Health Disparity," *Annals of Internal Medicine*, Vol. 148, No. 4, pp. 259–66.

# CHAPTER 8

# Health Financing Systems in East Asia and the Pacific: Early Successes and Current Challenges

## JOHN C. LANGENBRUNNER AND AJAY TANDON

This chapter provides an overview of health financing systems in the East Asia and Pacific (EAP) region of the World Bank.[1] The success of health financing systems depends upon the performance of three important functions, namely: revenue collection, pooling and management of resources, and purchasing of services and interventions. Following an assessment of the current macroeconomic, health status, and health sector situation in the region, the chapter then follows with a discussion of these functions in the EAP context. It also discusses current reform initiatives related to universal health coverage with general patterns and examples from specific EAP country cases. Finally, the chapter looks ahead to future challenges for the health sector in the region related to population aging and changing disease profiles.

## OVERVIEW

The EAP region is extremely diverse, perhaps more so than other regions of the world. The region contains great variations in size and population, from small Pacific islands with fewer than 100,000 people to countries such as China and Indonesia, respectively the largest and fourth-largest countries in the world in terms of population.[2] Relative to other regions of the world, the EAP region is the most populous, containing more than two billion people. It includes some of the world's fastest-growing economies, as well as the second-largest number of fragile states after Africa. It contains a wide spectrum of political systems and forms of government organizations, from democracies to military dictatorships. While many countries are highly centralized, fiscal and political decentralization is an important trend in many EAP countries.

The authors wish to thank George Schieber for his review and comment on an earlier draft.

[1]Unless otherwise noted, front sections draw on Langenbrunner and Somanathan (2011).

[2]The World Bank's classification includes over 20 developing countries as part of the EAP region, including Cambodia, China, Fiji, Kiribati, the Republic of Korea, the Lao People's Democratic Republic, Malaysia, Marshall Islands, the Federated States of Micronesia, Mongolia, Palau, Papua New Guinea, the Philippines, Samoa, the Solomon Islands, Thailand, Timor-Leste, Tonga, Vanuatu, and Vietnam.

The region is extremely dynamic: the estimated average growth rate in developing EAP countries in 2010 was 9.6 percent (in seven countries it was above 7 percent), up from 7.4 percent in 2009 and 8.4 percent in 2008 (World Bank, 2011a). The region has demonstrated resilience to the adverse global economic developments of 2008-09. Although several countries in the region, including Cambodia, China, Malaysia, the Philippines, the Republic of Korea, and Thailand, saw a significant slowdown in growth in 2009, almost all the major economies of the region rebounded by 2010 and are projected to continue to grow at a rapid pace through 2015 (Figure 8.1).

Improvements in the business environment continue to facilitate private sector growth in the region. However, the effects of prolonged rapid growth and the amassing of large foreign exchange reserves from strong exports and rising capital inflows are being felt by the larger economies, with risks of overheating, the formation of asset bubbles, and the emergence of financial sector and macroeconomic vulnerabilities (as in the Western countries in 2008 and 2009). Managing the extraordinary volatility in real commodity prices, in particular, those for energy and food, as well as the recent natural disasters in China and Myanmar, presents new challenges. Most recently, the severe downturn in commodities will present other types of challenges, such as loss of revenues from copper mining in Mongolia (Bredenkamp, Lie, and Brenzel, 2010).

Income inequality in the region has grown despite sustained growth and policies that have provided opportunities to the poor and produced dramatic advances in poverty reduction. A study by the Asian Development Bank (2007) found that income inequality rose significantly over the past decade in many EAP

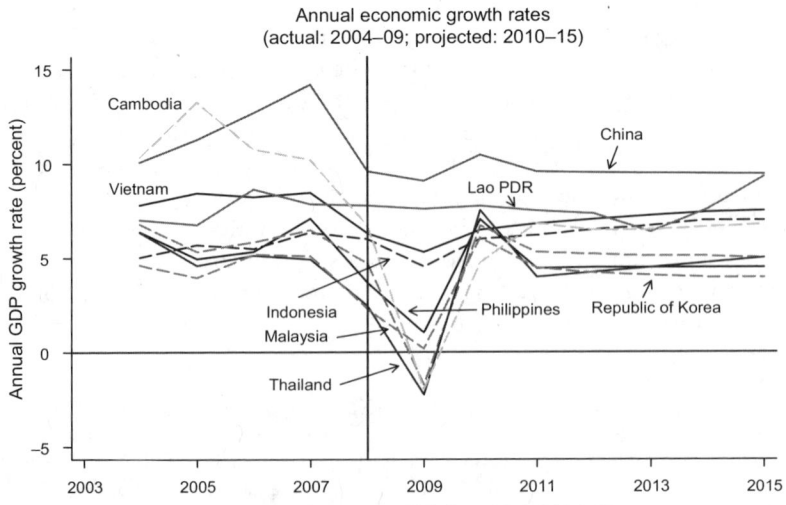

**Figure 8.1**  Annual Economic Growth Rates in EAP Countries, 2004–15
Source: IMF, World Economic Outlook database.

countries. Middle-income countries in the region, such as China and the Philippines, and emerging middle-income countries, such as Vietnam, have seen income inequality rise dramatically in their domestic economies over the past decade, as have lower-income countries such as Cambodia and the Lao People's Democratic Republic (PDR). There has been rapid urbanization, although some countries in the region remain predominantly rural. The region also contains fragile states (such as Timor-Leste) and many conflict-affected areas, but these have tended to be limited to relatively small geographic zones.

## HEALTH STATUS AND OUTCOMES

The recent history of the region presents a surprising profile of relatively good health outcomes while at the same time relatively modest expenditures for health. EAP countries perform relatively well in global comparisons of commonly used health and expenditure indicators.

In general, the region does well on health outcomes when compared with other countries of the world with similar income and health spending levels. Outcomes on infant mortality, under-five mortality (Figure 8.2), life expectancy, and maternal mortality (Figure 8.3) are generally better than expected when regressed on levels of income and levels of health spending. (Nevertheless, there are some notable exceptions, such as Cambodia for infant and under-five mortality and Lao PDR and Indonesia for maternal mortality.)

At present, EAP countries spend relatively less on health, both as a share of GDP and in per capita terms, relative to other countries at comparable levels

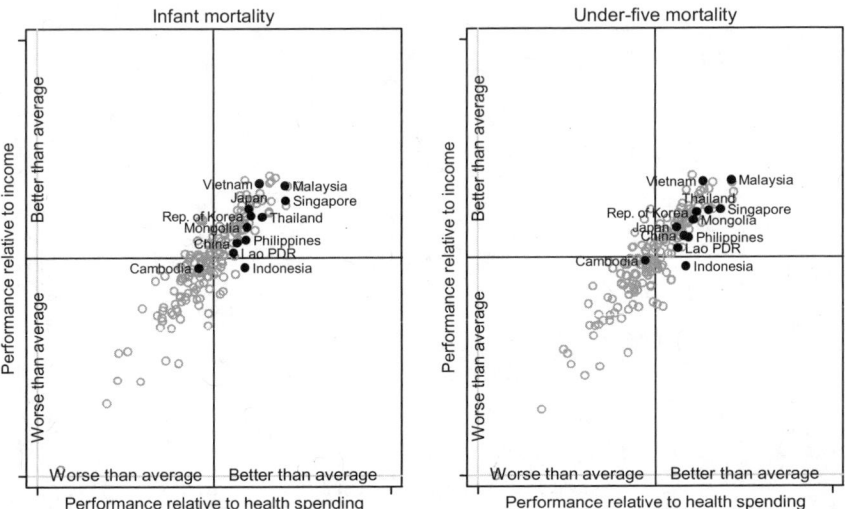

**Figure 8.2** Infant and Under-Five Mortality Relative to Income and Health Spending, 2009
Sources: World Bank Institute; and World Health Organization.
Note: Plots are residuals of regressions of outcome on income and health spending separately.

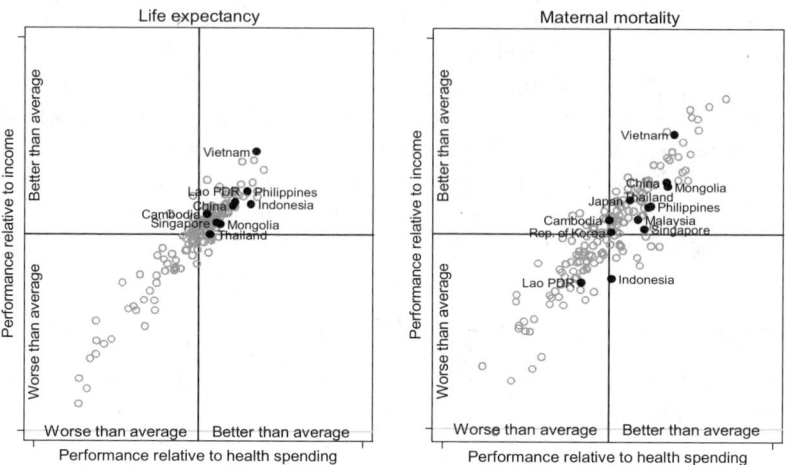

**Figure 8.3** Life Expectancy and Maternal Mortality Relative to Income and Health Spending, 2008
Sources: World Bank Institute; and World Health Organization.
Note: Plots are residuals of regressions of outcome on income and health spending separately.

of income. Although there are some exceptions, in general in EAP the levels of total and public (government) health spending (Figure 8.4) are lower than expected. The lower levels of health spending reflect generally lower levels of health system inputs such as doctors, nurses, and beds per capita. And as shown below, lower public spending further correlates with relatively high levels of out-of-pocket (OOP) expenditures and poor levels of financial protection in many EAP countries, even in some high-income ones such as Singapore.

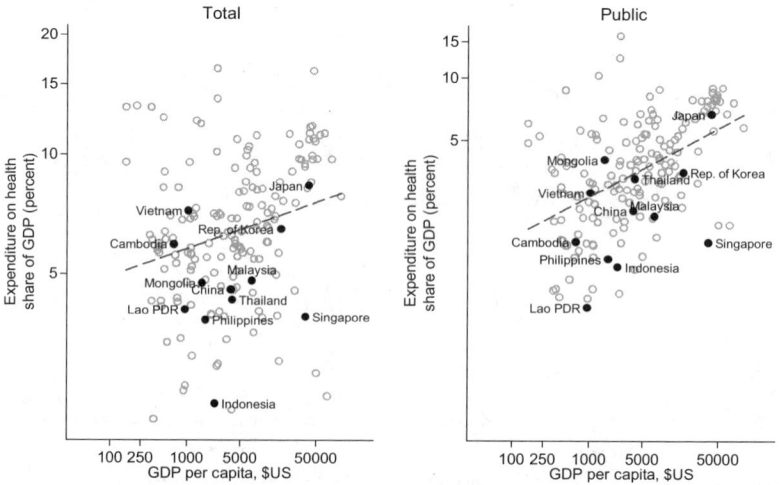

**Figure 8.4** Health Spending versus Income, 2009
Sources: World Bank, *World Development Indicators*; and World Health Organization.

**Figure 8.5** Disability-Adjusted Life-Years per Capita in East Asia and Pacific versus Global Comparators, 2004
Source: World Health Organization.

EAP countries generally have fewer disability-adjusted life-years (DALYs)[3] per capita than other countries (Figure 8.5), which correlates with the generally higher literacy and education levels found in the region. The burden-of-disease figures for the region indicate that, for communicable diseases, maternal, perinatal, and nutritional conditions, the burden of disease (in thousands of DALYs) is greatest in China (31,878)—as a result of its large population size—and Indonesia (15,382). For noncommunicable diseases, again China exhibits the highest level (141,016), followed by Indonesia (25,623), Japan (10,961), and the Philippines (9,188).[4] This "good performance" to date of fewer DALYs per person and relatively good outcomes, coupled with relatively modest expenditures, may be attributable to historic levels of investments in related sectors such as (women's) education, clean water and sanitation, basic public health, good housing, and roads.

Despite significant progress in terms of levels, many EAP countries are still characterized by large and persistent inequalities in health outcomes. Evidence from demographic and health survey data across countries indicates that in some EAP countries—such as Cambodia, the Philippines, and Vietnam—under-five mortality rates are three times higher among the lowest economic quintiles than among the highest quintiles. Similarly, under-five mortality rates are one-and-a-half to two times higher in rural areas than in urban areas (Table 8.1). In some

---

[3]A disability-adjusted life-year is a time-based measure that combines years of life lost through premature mortality and years of life lost as the result of time lived in states of less than full health.
[4]The DALY numbers are from the World Health Organization's Global Burden of Disease database.

**TABLE 8.1**

| Under-Five Mortality in Selected EAP Countries | | | | |
|---|---|---|---|---|
| Country | Year | Under-five mortality rate (per 1,000 live births) | Ratio of lowest to highest economic quintiles | Rural-urban ratio |
| Cambodia | 2005 | 106 | 3.0 | 1.5 |
| Indonesia | 2007 | 51 | 2.4 | 1.6 |
| Philippines | 2008 | 37 | 3.4 | 1.7 |
| Vietnam | 2007 | 33 | 3.3 | 2.2 |

Source: World Bank estimates, based on U.S. Agency for International Development, Demographic and Health Surveys.

countries, such as China, even though interprovincial health outcomes have converged, there is evidence that rural-urban health inequalities have increased substantially (Zhang and Kanbur, 2005; Tandon, Zhuang, and Chatterji, 2006).

Underlying these differences in outcomes are large inequalities in the financing and delivery of health care. Improved averages in health outcomes could have very well been achieved through a pattern that benefits primarily the better-off while largely bypassing the poor (Moser, Leon, and Gwatkin, 2005). Despite relatively low levels of health spending and good outcomes, efficiency improvements—including, as discussed below, making public spending allocations more pro-poor—will be critical for generating additional public sector resources for health care in the EAP region in order to tackle inequalities.[5]

## HEALTH EXPENDITURE PATTERNS AND ALLOCATIONS

Total health expenditures as a share of GDP ranged from 2 to 8 percent in the region in 2009. These numbers have generally been increasing modestly every year, on average, over the past decade in most countries in the region. This increase in spending has been driven largely by sustained increases in public sector spending in countries such as China, Japan, Malaysia, and Thailand. By contrast, in Cambodia, Lao PDR, and the Pacific Island countries, increased donor spending explains a large proportion of the growth in overall spending. Only in Vietnam, with the initiation of user fees, has the increase in overall health spending been driven by an increase in OOP spending.

Per capita health expenditures in the region have tended to reflect GDP per capita levels, both over time and relative to global comparators at any given point

---

[5]Efficiency and equity are two dimensions used to assess health sector performance in the region. *Efficiency* is typically defined as maximizing outcomes from inputs, although there are many dimensions to it. In the EAP region, there is suggestive evidence of poor allocative efficiency (for example, relatively low shares of expenditures on primary and outpatient care, low hospital occupancy rates) as well as poor technical efficiency (relatively long lengths of stay), but there is limited data and information with which to understand the problem of efficiency in greater depth.

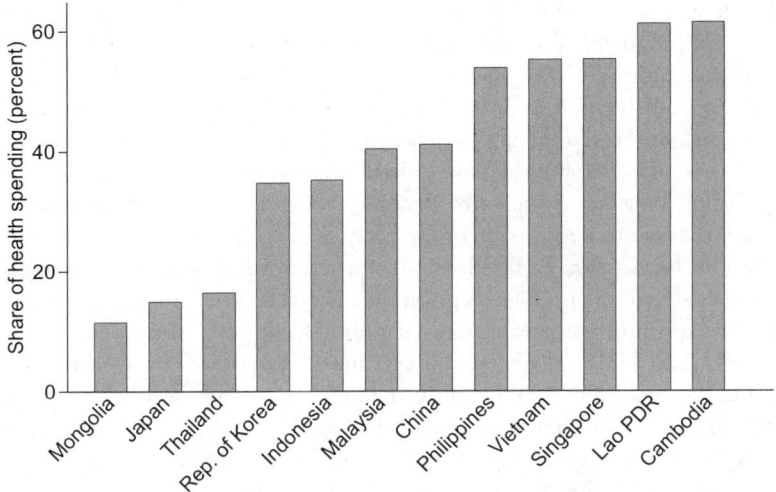

**Figure 8.6** Out-of-Pocket Spending Share of Total Expenditure, 2009
Source: World Health Organization.

in time, although there are some outliers, such as Cambodia. For instance, using global comparators, per capita health spending levels in Indonesia, Malaysia, the Philippines, and Thailand are low relative to these countries' income levels. Cambodia and Vietnam are above the expected levels of spending on health relative to income. Both GDP per capita and health expenditure per capita are in a middle range compared to other regions. On both indicators, the regions of Europe, Central Asia, Latin America and the Caribbean, and the Middle East and North Africa are higher on average, and South Asia and Africa are lower.

EAP countries and territories generally conform with the global pattern, namely, with reliance on OOP declining and government's share of total financing increasing as national income rises. The government share of total health financing ranges from 20 to 30 percent in low-income EAP countries such as Cambodia, Lao PDR, and Vietnam, compared to 50 to 60 percent in middle-income countries such as Malaysia and Thailand. Meanwhile, OOP spending finances 50 to 60 percent of total expenditures in most low-income countries in Asia and 40 percent or less of expenditures in middle- and upper-income countries (Figure 8.6).

Significant evidence exists of pro-rich differentials in health care allocation and utilization in the EAP region. The use of public sector inpatient services is strongly pro-poor[6] in Hong Kong Special Administrative Region (SAR), moderately pro-poor in Malaysia, and pro-rich in China, Indonesia, the Republic of Korea, Taiwan Province of China, Thailand, and Vietnam. Use of outpatient care

---

[6]Public services are regarded as "pro-poor" when the proportion of the poor who use them is greater than the proportion of poor in the population. For example, if more than 20 percent of all users of public health care facilities are poor but only 20 percent of the population is poor, then public health care is deemed pro-poor.

services, particularly nonhospital outpatient care services, is moderately pro-poor or relatively proportional to income in most countries.

In low-income countries, inequalities in access to services are caused by deficiencies in both breadth and depth in coverage. The unemployed, agricultural workers, and workers in the informal sector either have no coverage (for example, in Indonesia and Vietnam) or have partial coverage that entitles them to a relatively shallow benefits package (for example, in China and the Philippines). This may be due either to poor design of the package or to affordability within a country's current fiscal space. In tax-financed systems in which universal coverage has not been achieved, the poor face significant financial barriers to access in the form of formal and informal user charges at public health facilities (for example, in Cambodia, Lao PDR, and Papua New Guinea). Targeted fee waiver/exemption schemes (for example, health cards in Indonesia) and health equity funds (Cambodia, Lao PDR) have been established to help the poor overcome financial barriers to access. However, there is little compelling evidence that these targeting mechanisms succeed in improving equity in access to care.

In high-income countries, where universal coverage has been achieved, inequalities still exist due to shallow coverage. The more catastrophic expenditures may be outside the domain of health insurance, or there may be wide variations among benefits packages offered under different insurance schemes. Where the social insurance law mandates the same benefits for all (for example, Japan) there are fewer inequities. Similarly, in high-income, tax-financed countries/territories where universal coverage has been achieved (for example, Hong Kong SAR, Malaysia), inequalities are not as widespread because there are fewer restrictions on who has access to which services.

Benefit-incidence studies in Asia have typically found that public health spending in low- and middle-income countries is not pro-poor. Public subsidies for inpatient care are especially pro-rich, although there are some exceptions. The distribution of public subsidies is considerably more pro-poor in higher-income Hong Kong SAR, Malaysia, and Thailand, for both hospital and nonhospital care. What are the potential explanations for the unusually pro-poor distribution of subsidies in these countries? While the level of national income is a critical factor in improving the distribution of public subsidies, the mix of public and private services that are offered also plays a role. Targeting the poor is successful in richer countries because they can afford a system of universal public health care funded from general taxation with minimal user charges.

An alternative explanation for the pro-poor distribution of public health subsidies lies in the types of private sector alternatives available to the rich. In these territories, the combination of universal public provision, a private sector offering an attractive alternative to the basic package, and incomes that make demand for this alternative effective all lead to redistribution through public provision in precisely the way that theory predicts (e.g., Hong Kong SAR). This suggests that effective targeting of public spending on health care depends not only upon policies concerning the publicly run system but also upon the scale, locations, and allocation of public spending.

# HEALTH CARE FINANCING

## Sources of Revenues

Underlying the push for health financing reform in the EAP region is a growing concern among policymakers that the current levels of resources available for health expenditures are inadequate for meeting emergent health needs and achieving universal coverage. Other factors underlying these calls for reform are a high reliance on donor funding in low-income countries and OOP sources of financing in both low- and middle-income countries, as well as a perceived lack of sustainability of current sources of public financing.

As in many OECD countries, public prepayment, composed of taxes and social insurance, accounts for the largest share of health financing in high-income EAP countries. A large portion of prepayment revenues in social insurance systems is raised through wage-related contributions, shared between employers and employees. Hong Kong SAR is the only high-income country in the EAP region that collects more than half of its publicly funded prepayment through taxation rather than social insurance. Voluntary (or private) health insurance accounts for a relatively small share of overall health expenditures in high-income EAP countries and territories.

Despite the significance of public prepayments in total financing, the share of OOP payments in total health expenditures is relatively high in high-income EAP countries/territories compared to other OECD countries. In the Republic of Korea, for instance, copayments account for 20 percent of expenditures for inpatient care and 30 to 55 percent for outpatient care. In tax-financed countries like Hong Kong SAR, OOP payments are predominantly used to pay for services obtained from private health care providers, while in social-insurance-financed countries, OOPs consist of copayments, coinsurance, and deductibles.

Public prepayments account for a higher share of health financing in middle-income EAP countries compared to other middle-income countries globally, thanks in part to stronger economic growth in recent years. A significant portion of public prepayment in these middle-income EAP countries is accounted for by general government revenues, regardless of the type of health financing model or system. The majority of these countries also have social health insurance for civil servants and other formal sector workers, financed through payroll contributions. Private health insurance plays a minor role in middle-income EAP countries, somewhat surprising given the high OOP share of total spending, the existence of a middle class, and a viable financial market that is conducive to private health insurance growth.

Low-income countries in the EAP region, as elsewhere, are characterized by low public health spending and limited ability to mobilize domestic resources to increase the share of public prepayments for health care. On average across the EAP region, public prepayment for health accounts for 30 percent or less of total health expenditure; most of the remaining 70 percent from private sources is in the form of OOP payments.

Historically, general government revenues have financed public prepayment for health care in low-income EAP countries (Figure 8.7). Low economic growth,

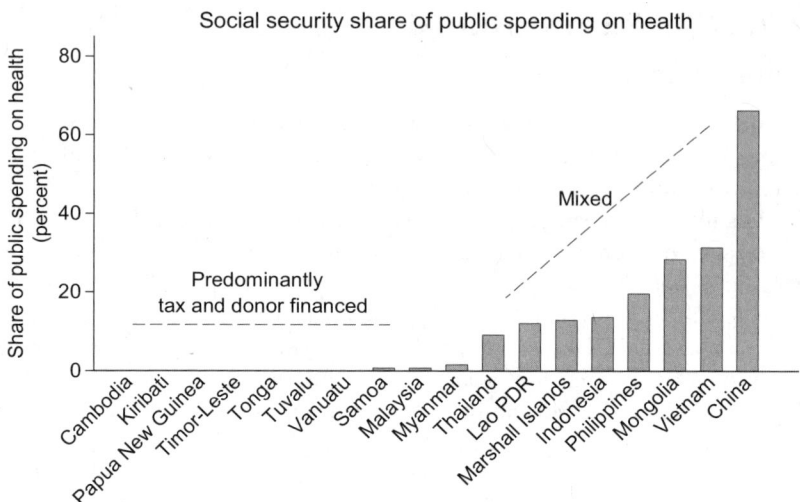

**Figure 8.7** Share of Tax and Donor Financing versus Social Insurance in Public Spending on Health in East Asia and Pacific Countries, 2009
Source: World Health Organization.

weak tax administration capacity, and limited potential for increasing government revenues have led to the imposition of fees. In recent years, a range of social insurance schemes and community-based insurance schemes have been introduced, partly to diversify the revenue base for health care (for example, social health insurance in Vietnam) and partly to provide low-income households with a means of financial protection in the face of rising user fees (for example, health equity funds in Cambodia and Lao PDR). Voluntary health insurance accounts for less than 5 percent of total health expenditures in low-income countries in the region and is mainly to supplement private care for middle- and upper-income groups. Donor financing accounts for a significant share of health spending in low-income countries, yet complete, consistent data on donor spending are rarely available.

OOP payments are the principal means of financing health care throughout much of the EAP region and are a significant burden on household resources in many low- and middle-income countries. The proportion of households incurring catastrophic payments for health care (defined at three thresholds, namely 15 percent, 25 percent, and 40 percent of both food and nonfood expenditures) is highest in China and Vietnam.

Many countries continue to assess the relative merits of different options for improving public prepayment levels. For example, Hong Kong SAR and Malaysia have each considered a move to a social health insurance model from a general government revenue model. The sustainability of social health insurance financing depends on economic growth, which is essential for ensuring the sustainability of payroll taxes as well as the existence of a large formal labor market, administrative capacity for collection, good regulatory and oversight structures, and appropriate incentive structures. In middle-income countries in EAP, economic growth has been strong in recent years, but many of the other enabling factors are not present.

Low- and middle-income countries in EAP are characterized by large rural populations and small formal labor markets. Even in the context of the limited formal labor market, the collection of social insurance contributions is constrained by weak administrative capacity and the lack of good regulatory oversight and incentive structures. The nonenrollment of formal sector workers in insurance schemes, and the full or partial evasion of payments among those who are enrolled, mean that the collection of social insurance contributions is no more efficient than the collection of tax revenues in most middle-income countries (for example, China and Vietnam). Evasion exists even where enrollment is mandatory, as workers and employers can take advantage of lax enforcement but do not enroll in the scheme at all (for example, Indonesia). Furthermore, in many EAP countries—despite robust economic growth—the share of the formal sector in the labor market has not increased significantly (Figure 8.8 shows the example of Indonesia over the period 1990–2007).

Some forms of taxes, such as taxes on tobacco, cigarettes, and alcohol, represent an alternative source of revenues whose potential remains relatively untapped in most EAP countries. The tobacco tax rate is less than 50 percent of the price of cigarettes in all Asian countries with the exception of Singapore and Thailand. In EU-15 countries, taxes on the price of cigarettes average 58 percent, although the proportion of smokers in the population is quite similar in both regions. One key consideration regarding taxation of tobacco is that in most EAP countries the incidence of tobacco consumption tends to be higher among poorer quintiles, for whom elasticities tend to be higher.

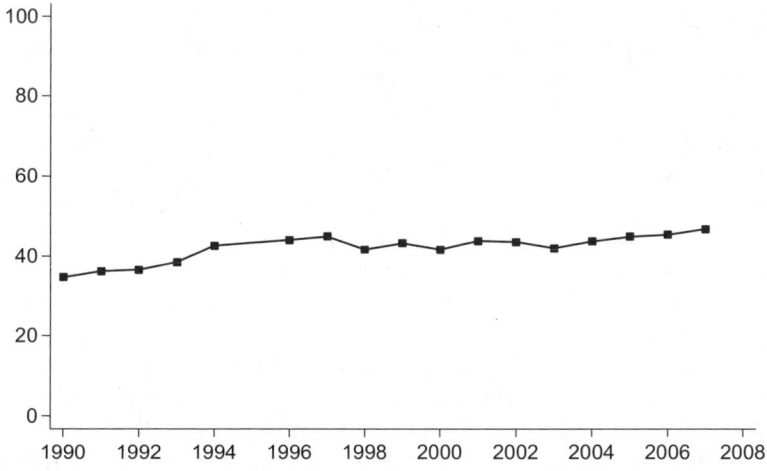

**Figure 8.8** Formal Sector Share of Employment in Indonesia, 1990–2007
(Percent)
Source: World Bank staff estimates.

There is some greater understanding of the dimension of equity in financing revenues across health sectors in the region. The incidence of the health care financing burden in high-income countries/territories in the EAP region is similar to that in the European countries: tax financing is the most progressive and social insurance is slightly regressive, while direct OOP payments are proportional (Hong Kong SAR) or regressive (Japan, Taiwan Province of China). The incidence is quite different in low- and middle-income EAP countries. There, both tax and social insurance financing are highly progressive, because their incidence is limited to skilled, professional groups and levied on a narrow tax base. Direct payments are also progressive in all low- and middle-income EAP countries, with the exception of China.

Fiscal capacity and policy priorities are twin dimensions in improving levels of public prepayment for health. Regardless of the options (above) chosen, overall levels of public prepayment tend to track a country's GDP per capita. This is true both globally and in the EAP region. At the same time, there is significant variation in public spending as a share of GDP for countries with similar GDP (for example, Lao PDR has much higher levels of prepayment than Cambodia, even though both are low-income countries). This variation may be due to variation in fiscal capacity and/or in different public sector priorities regarding investing in health spending as a share of the public budget. Analysts will want to disentangle these two factors in order to understand how much is fiscal "context" versus how much is public policy "priorities."[7]

## POOLING AND MANAGEMENT OF FUNDS

Pooling of funds is a major challenge in the region, which is characterized by numerous small pools in many countries. This fragmentation limits the potential for cross-subsidy, while perhaps unnecessarily increasing administrative costs in very limited funding contexts. Many countries in the region—Indonesia, Mongolia, the Philippines, and Vietnam—have established, or are in the process of establishing, a national social health insurance program as a way to pool funds, while Cambodia is also developing a blueprint.

Fragmentation can also involve planned segmentation in any country, leading to "inequity by design." This has been the experience of many low- and middle-income countries, especially in Latin America. Cambodia plans a separate administrative structure in the short run for its civil servants and formal sector workers. This approach has been administratively unsuccessful in Thailand and other countries with fragmented insurance pools. The decision is more political than technical. The government in Thailand, for example, has not been able to "take on" the civil servants politically.

Similarly, it is important to integrate new health insurance funds for poorer groups into the broader pooling of funds. New health equity funds for the poor are now well established institutionally in Cambodia and Lao PDR and could be used to make contributions to social health insurance for the poor. A similar

---

[7]For more on fiscal space for health see Tandon and Cashin (2010).

challenge is faced by Indonesia's health insurance program for the poor (Jamkesmas). Similarly in China, the medical assistance programs, which subsidize lower-income groups with current coverage, could be folded into larger social insurance pools. Perhaps China's biggest challenge will be to pool funds across geographic areas within provinces to pool urban and rural populations.

Regionally, there are different approaches to pooling that EAP countries might adapt, including consolidation of a multipool system and establishment of a single national pool. The Republic of Korea went from more than 380 funds to one national fund over a 12-year time span, from the 1990s to the early part of this decade. Taiwan Province of China moved from three insurance funds to a single insurance fund model as well. Japan is an interesting model from the region, as it effectively has a single fund. In Japan, a single pooling fund was created in 1983 so that costs would be shared equally by the multiple insurers that developed over time. This single pool pays for 70 percent of all costs.

Globally, there are also useful models for pooling, such as those in Europe, Canada, and Latin America that adjust risks prospectively or retrospectively into insurance pools, or pool geographically by province. Since decentralization is a popular option in the EAP region, such geographic-based pooling mechanisms could serve as models or interim models for several countries such as China and Indonesia.

In EAP countries with multiple pools, pooling might follow two tracks related to the time frame available. In the short term, the health sector should assess disparities across risk pools and develop a risk adjustment mechanism across payers. Some regulatory framework and stewardship capacity would be needed, but this would increase equity and better spread risks as well as encourage purchasers to better manage purchasing arrangements. How the low-income countries (for example, Cambodia and Lao PDR) provide the necessary regulatory framework and stewardship capacity will be an important challenge.

Bureaucratically, there are also hurdles in several EAP countries. In many countries, such as Cambodia, China, Lao PDR, and Mongolia, different government ministries manage different funds. For example, a total of 16 ministries handle health policy in China. A decision would need to be made in each country about whether the Ministry of Social Security or Ministry of Health (or some other ministry) would bring various funds under one umbrella.

## STRATEGIC PURCHASING OF SERVICES

Many countries have adopted a general "strategic purchasing" of health services framework which recognizes a number of components of purchasing, or "policy levers." These can be used by purchasers to better allocate resources across geographic areas or directly to providers. They include

- coverage and targeting of funds;
- setting the benefits package;
- contracting; and
- setting payment rates and the incentive framework for providers.

While elements of strategic purchasing are emerging in the region, capturing value for money expended remains a significant unfinished agenda.

## Benefits Package

Given low levels of health spending in low-income countries, a widely held view is that the state should first finance a small package of services for universal coverage, essentially encompassing public goods, goods with externalities, and other interventions that have a proven impact. All other clinical care and catastrophic expenditures would be financed for the poor using some targeting mechanism. In reality, decisions about which package of services the government should buy are based not only on economic criteria, but also on social and political criteria. While cost-effectiveness of spending is referred to frequently in policy documents in many of the low-income EAP countries, almost no country has a benefit package defined purely on this basis. Globally, tradition, corruption, and political pressures mean that increased health resources are often allocated to tertiary care centers and urban health facilities. The regional experience follows this global pattern.

For most middle-income countries in Eastern Europe and Latin America, concerns about the design of the package relate more to the depth of coverage than to its breadth. However, the same is not true of all middle-income countries in the EAP region. For instance, China and the Philippines have yet to achieve high levels of coverage of publicly financed services. Underinsurance is a key problem even for those countries that are expanding to universal coverage over time. This is also true for upper-income countries, such as the Republic of Korea.

There is a further problem stemming from variations in packages across insurance schemes within a country. Formal sector and urban-based programs or insurance schemes tend to have richer packages relative to parallel programs (for example, Cambodia, China, Indonesia, Lao PDR, and Thailand). In most tax-financed systems, in both Europe and Asia, the benefits package is not explicitly defined. High-income tax-financed systems in Asia, like those in Hong Kong SAR and Malaysia, whose systems were based on the UK National Health Service (NHS), are no different. Low-income tax-financed systems in the EAP region, such as those in the Pacific Island nations, also do not explicitly define benefits.

As the burden of disease in EAP increasingly shifts to noncommunicable and chronic diseases, preventive and promotive services—as well as screening services—become more important. The benefit packages need to be continually updated to address the changing disease profile and coordinated with basic public health programs, with due consideration for fiscal sustainability issues. The provision of early treatment can prevent longer-term complications and can help reduce costs overall.

## Contracting

There is significant external contracting with providers across most countries in the EAP region, and this seems to occur across all income groups. Indeed, there is a rich and well-documented tradition of this in some countries, including

Cambodia. An important issue in contracting in many EAP countries is whether the payer is to contract with both the public sector and the emergent private sector. There is a growing private sector in health care delivery, and while it remains small in some countries, it has grown significantly in Cambodia (mostly nongovernmental organizations), Indonesia, Mongolia, and the Philippines. Growth in contracting both public and private providers can be found in countries such as Malaysia, Mongolia, and Thailand in addition to such high-income countries as Japan, the Republic of Korea, and Taiwan Province of China. For contracting to succeed, the regulators will need to "level the playing field," since many public facilities receive separate subsidies for salaries and capital investment.

Some countries, including Mongolia and Thailand, also utilize the element of gatekeeping in contracts with primary care providers. This model can be used to better encourage the use of primary care and more cost-effective outpatient services. However, there is little in the way of contract evaluation in any of the countries in the region, and outside of Cambodia there is no evidence of selective contracting on the basis of quality, costs, and performance. More often, the situation is one of soft, relational contracts in which both sides (purchaser and provider) expect that a contract will be automatically extended in ensuing years. Selective contracting should be on the agenda for many countries in the region in the next few years.

## Provider Payment

The EAP region displays a rich variety of provider payment systems, and many countries would appear to be in transition. Currently, though, there is an over-reliance on fee for service. Outside of high-income countries, fee for service is often utilized in conjunction with supply-side financing with line-item budgets, as in China, Lao PDR, the Philippines, and Vietnam. This can create a toxic mix of incentives. On the one hand, line-item budgets are often unresponsive to patient needs and demands. The fee-for-service overlay can encourage unnecessary demand, often becoming a way of generating new revenues for underfunded line-item budgets or for reallocating revenues across line-item budgets. The impact can be borne by the purchaser as unnecessary outlays or fall on consumers in the form of OOP costs.

At the same time, many countries are now looking to move beyond fee for service, especially as they grapple with increased health expenditures and cost containment and efficiency are becoming higher priorities. New provider payment strategies and new provider payment pilots are emerging in several countries (China, Indonesia, Mongolia, and Vietnam) regardless of income. Thailand is perhaps the regional leader in moving beyond fee for service, with a sophisticated mix of geographic caps, hospital global budgets, and case mix (often referred to as diagnosis-related groups, or DRGs) adjusters for hospital admissions.

Governments in the EAP region with multiple purchasers (Cambodia, China, Indonesia, and Lao PDR) will also need to strongly consider new and more consistent sets of payment rules and systems across insurers. Variations across payers can distort the incentives providers face, and thus distort practice patterns by encouraging overuse of highly paid services by some payers while, at the same time, discouraging access to relatively poorly paid services and discouraging equitable treatment for groups under some payers relative to others. New payment systems need to restructure incentives, but more uniform rules across payers will also help improve equity across groups.

## Profiles in the Push for Reform and for Universal Health Coverage

Many governments in the EAP region have made great strides in extending coverage step by step on a path to universal health coverage. For example, Thailand achieved it earlier in the last decade through its general-revenues-based 30-baht insurance scheme.

Challenges for covering all of the populations in EAP region countries are often linked to formalization of labor and payment of the payroll tax. As mentioned above, one of the challenges faced by the region is the persistence of informality in the labor market, despite rapid economic growth (Felipe and Hasan, 2006). As dynamic economies expand in EAP, several countries have begun to assess or commit to use of general revenues to bring in newly covered. In several cases, funds have been well targeted to prioritize lower-income groups and the poorest.

China has gone from near-zero coverage to almost universal coverage (more than 90 percent) for its population of more than 700 million citizens in rural areas since the early part of this decade. It is also scaling up for nonemployed segments in urban areas and estimates coverage currently at 1.2 billion (out of 1.4 billion total population). Utilization has increased dramatically. Hospital admissions per capita have effectively doubled in most geographic areas from 2005 to 2010. This doubling of admissions per capita over just 5 years may be unprecedented globally. But is the increase due to unmet need or to induced demand? Most studies (Ping, 2010) estimate the number of unnecessary admissions to be as high as 51 percent. The Ministry of Health estimates unnecessary admissions at 29.4 percent using its national survey from 2008. Secondly, OOPs as a share of total expenditures have decreased to as low as 40 percent (from 60 percent over the last five years), but OOPs as a share of average patient income have not improved. This is true for urban and rural areas, and for all income quintiles (MOH National Health Survey, 2008). In great part, the incentives under fee for service appear to be driving up costs per admission at equal or faster levels than at the rate of benefit package coverage increases.

Increases in national expenditures for health have been estimated at 20 percent and 16.3 percent over 2009 and 2010, roughly double the GDP growth.[8] In the short term, government surpluses funding health reform may be good politics and good macroeconomics (see Barnett and Brooks, 2010). In the medium term,

---

[8]Personal communication, Ministry of Finance, Beijing, China, 2011.

China will need to address its fee-for-service incentive structure with improved policies aimed at efficiencies and cost containment.

More recently, Vietnam, Indonesia, and the Philippines have also made commitments to reaching universal health coverage (UHC). Each country is at a relatively early stage. Vietnam (Figure 8.9) initiated coverage for the formal sector in the 1990s and followed with a focus on the poor and near poor. Recent estimates indicate about 55 percent of the population has some form of coverage (Tangcharoensathien and others, 2011). To date there has been increased utilization of hospital services, substitution away from private sector, and some muted impact on OOP spending, with reduced incidence of catastrophic OOPs for the poor (currently 3–5 percent), but no impact on OOPs on drugs. But financial sustainability has quickly become an issue. In 2009, the health insurance fund starting running deficits due to rising unit costs and utilization. There was also some evidence of adverse selection by the informal sector and self-employed. Vietnam has also accelerated its effort toward provider incentives reform, wanting to move from fee for service to hospital DRGs and outpatient capitation. Institutional implementation of the reforms will also be a challenge with current dual management of health financing by the Ministry of Health and the Social Security Board.

In Indonesia, a UHC law was passed in 2004, and implementation was immediately started by covering first the poor, and then by 2008 both the poor and near poor (with a target of over 70 million citizens) under the Jamkesmas insurance scheme program. Survey data estimates indicate that about a quarter of Indonesia's population is covered by Jamkesmas, but that the coverage rate among the bottom three economic deciles of the population was only about 42 percent in 2009 (Figure 8.10). Beneficiaries tend to have a lower incidence and intensity of catastrophic expenditure and higher rates of outpatient and inpatient utilization. Some 50 percent of the population, however, largely informal (but also many formal) sector workers, remained uncovered through 2010.

In the Philippines, the new president has committed to reaching UHC by 2016. There are two issues: making care accessible to the currently enrolled (estimated at around 42 percent of the population) and, secondly, extending coverage to those currently not enrolled (recent estimates from the U.S. Agency for International Development's Demographic and Health Survey indicate that about 58 percent of the population—and 80 percent of the poorest quintile—had no insurance coverage). The benefit package is being restructured to include both outpatient and inpatient services. Actuarial models have been developed and estimates of reaching UHC by 2016 depend upon the specifics of the new benefit structure and the levels of copayments and policies to improve efficiency such as gatekeeping. Nevertheless, the overall incremental change estimates remain less than 1 percent of GDP overall (under an assumed 5 percent GDP growth per year). Fiscal sustainability will be driven by both efficiency gains in organization of care and payment reforms, and by new "sin taxes" on tobacco products going into general revenues. Table 8.2 provides an overview of a recent fiscal space analysis in the context of UHC for the Philippines.

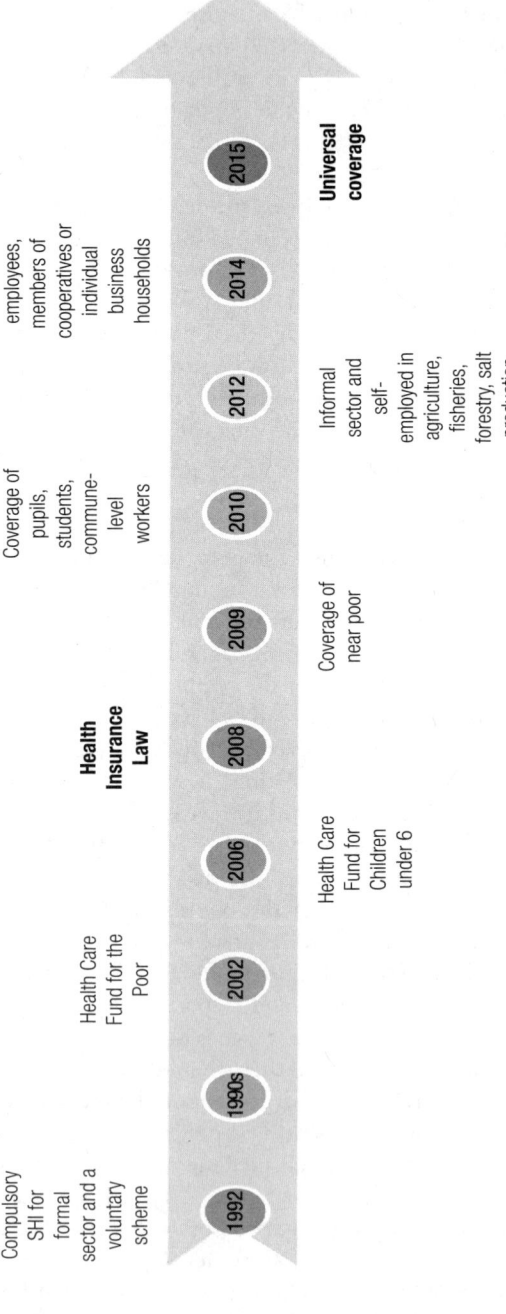

**Figure 8.9.** The Road to Universal Health Coverage in Vietnam, 1992–2015

Source: World Bank (2011b).

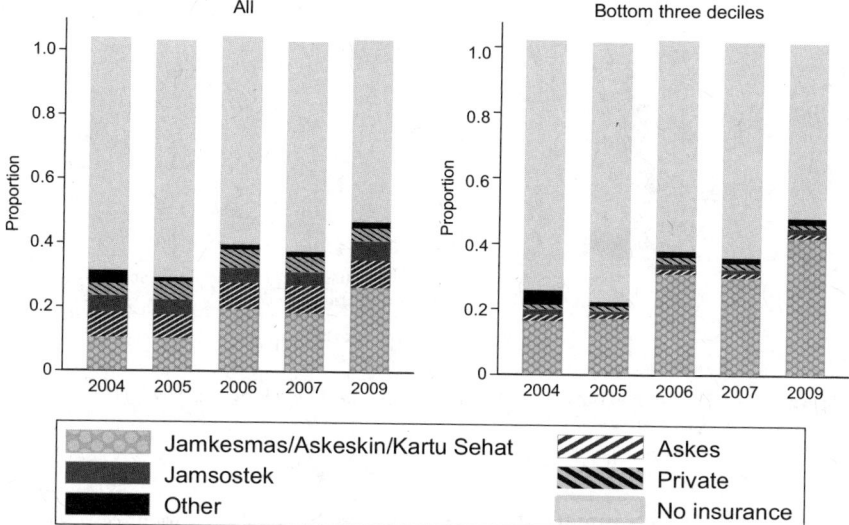

**Figure 8.10.** Trends in Insurance Coverage in Indonesia, 2004–09
Source: SUSENAS (2004–09).

**TABLE 8.2**

## Fiscal Space Analysis for the Philippines, 2010

| Fiscal space source | Key information | Prospects for fiscal space |
|---|---|---|
| Macroeconomic conditions | GDP growth rates (reduced from 7 percent to 1 percent between 2007 and 2009), declining revenue shares and low elasticity of public expenditures on health to GDP limit likelihood of additional public resources for health, but will rebound in 2011 to 7 percent with IMF estimates of 5 percent per year to 2015. | Moderate |
| Reprioritization of health in the government budget | Public spending on health is low relative to revenue efforts in the country and relative to the regional average. There are some indications that the priority accorded to health may be increasing. | Moderate |
| Health-sector-specific resources | The Philippines currently earmarks excise taxes on tobacco and alcohol for health as well as a portion of incremental revenues from VAT. Gaining further fiscal space from increased social health insurance contributions is unlikely given large informal sector. | Limited |
| Health-sector-specific grants and foreign aid | ODA for health is 2.9 percent of total health spending. External dependence is relatively low and irregular and likely to remain so given current global economic crisis. | Limited |
| Efficiency gains | Improvements in revenue collection efforts and governance, better allocation of health resources, quality improvements and more cost-effective interventions could create additional resources for health. | Good |

Source: World Bank (2011c).

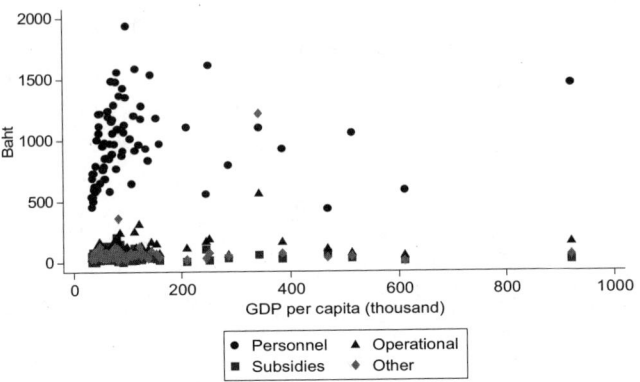

**Figure 8.11.** Thailand: Variations in Per Capita Expenditure by Province
Source: World Bank (2011d).

In low-income Cambodia, there is the promise by the government of universal coverage by 2015 (Cambodia, BHEF, 2008) as new insurance schemes emerge for the formal sector and civil servants, but together this covers only about 15 percent of the population. Nearly 50 health equity funds funded by donors are covering 5–10 percent of the poor, and multiple community-based health insurance funds are being nurtured as well. The challenge will be to scale up these programs and make sustainable, but also integrate and coordinate, these multiple schemes for reasons of both efficiency and equity.

Cutler (2002) has observed that in many member countries of the Organization for Economic Cooperation and Development (OECD), three consecutive waves of reforms can be discerned: (1) universal coverage and equal access, (2) controls, rationing, and expenditure caps, and (3) incentives and competition. The pattern in EAP is similar, at least emerging now for many of the middle-income countries. At the level of wave 1, there is a push for UHC, though in the most successful countries such as Thailand and China some insured groups and some regions may not be receiving equity of funding relative to need or demand and thus there may be a mismatch of equity of access and equity to quality of services. This can be a particular issue in the region where so many countries—China, Indonesia, Malaysia, the Philippines, Thailand, and Vietnam—utilize some form of fiscal decentralization. For example, the ratio of per capita spending between urban and rural is ten to one in China (Wagstaff and others, 2009). Variations in per capita spending for Thailand are shown in Figure 8.11. In the short term, the easiest approach technically for countries might be to move toward more population-based allocation methods.

In the medium term, cost containment and efficiencies will be increasingly important, especially with the changing disease profile in the region. Thailand has embarked on relatively sophisticated payment reforms,[9] and perhaps China,

_____

[9]But Thailand now seems stuck in moving to greater pooling and integration of insurance schemes, as outlined in the last sections.

Indonesia, the Philippines, Malaysia, and Vietnam are not far behind. In Indonesia, providers are paid capitation at primary level and DRGs for inpatient care. Although capitation or DRGs are used in some instances, Vietnam reimburses most providers primarily on a fee-for-service basis. Hospital case payments for up to 50 groups are slated to be introduced in the Philippines on a pilot basis in 2011 (Wagstaff, 2011). Even Cambodia is developing a payment reform strategy for 2011–12.

Reducing inefficiencies in health financing and provision can also generate additional resources for health. Improved revenue-raising capacity, while important, will not be sufficient by itself to increase allocations for health. The EAP countries generally commit a lower percentage of overall public funding for health relative to other countries in similar income categories. Reforms and the commitment to UHC have increased the short-term increment. But alternatively, fiscal space for health may need to be generated by improving the efficiency of sector outlays. Improvements in efficiency can increase effective fiscal space, and at the same time, improved performance and the promise of impact can attract additional resources from Ministries of Finance.

Finally, as noted recently by Wagstaff (2011), most countries in the region appear to be moving toward a greater role for government in the finance of health care and a smaller emphasis on government provision of health care. For example, in Indonesia 30 percent of hospitals contracted by the Jamkesmas scheme are private. In the Philippines and Thailand, private hospitals provide care to those covered by tax-financed insurance schemes. Similar trends can be observed in Vietnam as well as in China, although in these countries the public-private split is not as clearly demarcated (Wagstaff, 2011).[10]

## LOOKING AHEAD: THE CHANGING POPULATION AND EMERGENT DISEASE PROFILE

Looking to the future, changes in the demographic and epidemiological profile of EAP countries are likely to be key determinants of health care costs and needs in the medium to long term, whereas actual public expenditures will be constrained by the overall fiscal envelope available. Demographic and epidemiological profiles and changing patterns in these profiles are important drivers of the demand for health care and thus also of the patterns of health spending and financing within a macroeconomic environment wherein several middle-income EAP countries are projected to undergo fiscal consolidation and reductions in deficits (Table 8.3).

Within the EAP region, the total fertility rate has decreased and individuals are living longer, as exhibited by increases in life expectancy from about 52 years in 1960 to 66 years in 1990 to almost 72 years in 2008. In the short term, there will be relatively more of both genders of working age, and if workers are in relatively good health, this could provide a "demographic dividend" whereby the workforce will have a lower dependency ratio and will be able to support

---

[10]See, for example, World Bank (2010).

**TABLE 8.3**

### General Government Balance and Expenditure, 2010 and 2015

| Country | General government balance (percent of GDP) | | General government expenditure (percent of GDP) | |
|---|---|---|---|---|
| | **2010** | **2015** | **2010** | **2015** |
| Cambodia | −2.9 | 0.1 | 22.3 | 21.9 |
| Indonesia | −1.5 | −1.4 | 17.3 | 18.1 |
| Philippines | −4.6 | −4.6 | 30.5 | 30.4 |
| Vietnam | −3.9 | −1.9 | 18.9 | 19.4 |

Source: IMF (2010).

economic expansions and help improve overall productivity. For the 22 EAP countries for which data were available, all (with the exception of Timor-Leste) exhibited a decline in the age-dependency ratio from 1960 to 2009.

Notably, however, over the next 50 years, the age-dependency ratios for many EAP countries are expected to increase dramatically from their 2005 levels. This will be the case in current higher-income countries such as Japan, the Republic of Korea, and Singapore, as well as middle-income countries such as China. In the medium term, with an aging population, the role of noncommunicable diseases in the overall disease burden profile can also be expected to increase in EAP. This will effectively place greater challenges on meeting growing demands for care for primary and secondary prevention and in the treatment of chronic diseases. As individuals live longer, there can be greater demands (on average) on the health system, particularly in the later years of life when medical needs increase.

Together, the combination of population growth, nutritional transition, an aging population, and a shifting epidemiological profile suggests that policymakers will need to be concerned about the overall macro-level efficiency of heath care expenditures. While general revenues have powered the recent push for universal

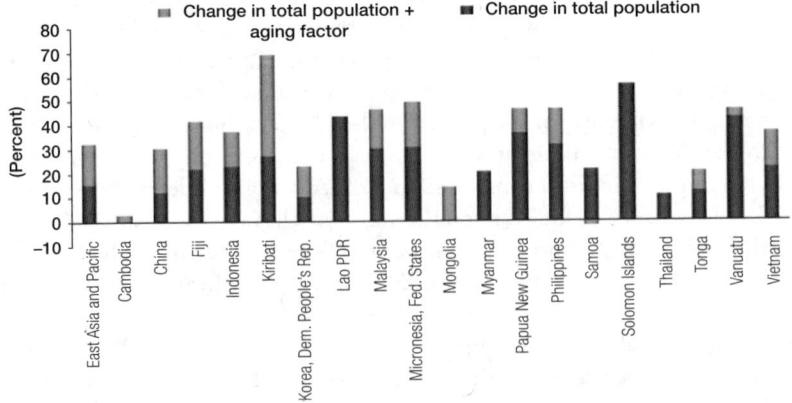

**Figure 8.12.** Expected Increases in Health Expenditures from 2000 to 2020 Due to Population and Epidemiological Dynamics
Source: Gottret and Schieber (2006).

coverage, there could be increased pressure on the economically productive segments of the population to provide revenues for the health sector. Demand will grow significantly by the year 2020 because of population dynamics alone, and this growth will be even more explosive because of changes in patterns of aging. Overall, most countries in the region could see expenditures grow by 20–40 percent between 2000 and 2020 (Figure 8.12). The initiation, then, of micro-level reforms through purchasing reforms and the use of a public-private mix of providers can be expected to continue if not expand in the years ahead.

# REFERENCES

Asian Development Bank (ADB), 2007, *Key Indicators: Inequality in Asia* (Manila).

Barnett, S., and R. Brooks, 2010, "China: Does Government Health and Education Spending Boost Consumption?" IMF Working Paper No. 1016 (Washington: International Monetary Fund).

Bredenkamp, C., G.S.S. Lie, and L. Brenzel, 2010, "Rapid Assessment of the Effects of the Economic Crisis on Health Spending in Mongolia," HNP Discussion Paper No. 58556 (Washington: World Bank).

Cambodia, Bureau of Health Economics and Financing (BHEF), Department of Planning and Health Information, 2008, *Strategic Framework for Health Financing* 2008–2015 (Phnom Penh).

Cutler, D., 2002, "Equality, Efficiency, and Market Fundamentals: The Dynamics of International Medical Care Reform," *Journal of Economic Literature*, Vol. 40, pp. 881–906.

Felipe, J., and R. Hasan, 2006, *Labor Markets in Asia: Issues and Perspectives* (New York: Palgrave Macmillan).

Gottret, P., and G. Schieber, 2006, *Health Financing Revisited: A Practitioner's Guide* (Washington: World Bank).

International Monetary Fund (IMF), 2010, "Fiscal Exit: From Strategy to Implementation," *Fiscal Monitor*, November (Washington).

Langenbrunner, J., and A. Somanathan, 2011, *Financing Health Care in East Asia and Pacific Region: Best Practices, Remaining Challenges* (Washington: World Bank).

Moser, K.A., D.A. Leon, and D.R. Gwatkin, 2005, "How Does Progress towards the Child Mortality Millennium Development Goal Affect Inequalities between the Poorest and Least Poor? Analysis of Demographic and Health Survey Data," *BMJ*, Vol. 331, pp. 1180–83.

Ping, H., 2010, "Chongqing Study on Inappropriate Admissions" (unpublished).

Tandon, A., and C. Cashin, 2010, "Assessing Public Expenditures on Health from a Fiscal Space Perspective," Health, Nutrition, and Population Discussion Paper (Washington: World Bank).

Tandon, A., J. Zhuang, and S. Chatterji, 2006, "Inclusiveness of Economic Growth in the People's Republic of China: What Do Population Health Outcomes Tell Us?" *Asian Development Review*, Vol. 23, No. 2, pp. 53–69.

Tangcharoensathien, V., W. Patcharanarumol, P. Ir, S.M. Alijunid, K. Akkhavong, E. Banzon, D.B. Huong, H. Thabrany, and A. Mills, 2011, "Health-Financing Reforms in Southeast Asia: Challenges in Achieving Universal Coverage," *Lancet*, Vol. 377, No. 9768, pp. 863–73.

Wagstaff, A., 2011, *Health Reform in Asia*, World Bank blog. Available at http://blogs.worldbank.org/developmenttalk;/blogs/adam-wagstaff .

Wagstaff, A., M. Lindelow, S. Wang, and S. Zhang, 2009, *Reforming China's Rural Health System* (Washington: World Bank).

World Bank, 2011a, *East Asia and Pacific Economic Update* (Washington).

———, 2011b, "Vietnam Health Reform Directions and Challenges," PowerPoint presentation by Toomas Palu, Human Development Week, March, Washington, D.C.

———, 2011c, *Transforming the Philippines Health Sector: Challenges and Future Directions* (Manila).

———, 2011d, "Thailand: Public Expenditure Review, Health Sector," internal draft, May 15 (Washington).

Zhang, X., and R. Kanbur, 2005, "Spatial Inequality in Education and Health Care in China," *China Economic Review*, Vol. 16, pp. 189–204.

# CHAPTER 9

# Measuring the Health Effects of Health Care Reform

Jonathan Skinner and Catherine Suarez

All countries around the world are struggling with the financial strain of rising health care costs. For example, public health care spending relative to GDP rose from 5.2 percent of GDP in 1990 to 7.3 percent in 2008 in advanced economies, while in emerging economies it is predicted to rise by roughly 1 percent of GDP over the next 20 years (Clements and others, 2010). While technological gains in health care are anticipated to bring wider health benefits, the additional costs will also place considerable pressure on already overstressed tax systems. Patient user fees or private insurance could in theory help to pay for some of these additional expenditures, but most countries will seek to restrain (and in the United States, perhaps even cut back on) health care costs through a variety of approaches.

These health care reforms may include imposing restrictions on budgets, quantity restrictions, price cuts, improved coordination of treatments, changes in the incentive structure of provider payments, and demand-side increases in cost sharing. As more countries confront rising health care costs with a variety of cost-saving strategies, we are learning more about which of these specific reforms are most effective at actually saving money (Clements and others, 2010). But how do they affect health outcomes? Unfortunately, this is a difficult question to answer. What is different about health care is the dramatic variation in the cost-effectiveness of specific treatments, ranging from a few dollars per life saved for highly effective care—such as aspirin for heart attack patients—to tens of thousands of dollars for treatments with no established value. Thus cutting back on (or not going ahead with) one million euros' worth of expenditures could have vastly different effects on health, depending on what the money would have been spent on. As we show below, the remarkable degree of inefficiency in health care systems in all countries leads naturally to the elusive Holy Grail of health care reform: changes that both improve health outcomes *and* cut costs—or cost-saving productivity gains.

The authors thank Amitabh Chandra, Benedict Clements, and participants at the IMF Conference on Public Health Care Reform in Asia for helpful suggestions. We are grateful to the National Institute on Aging (PO1-AG-19783) and the Robert Wood Johnson Foundation for financial support.

How do we know whether health care reforms have yielded improved or diminished productivity? While it is straightforward to measure budgetary savings arising from health care reform, monitoring the health effect is more difficult. Ideally, one would measure health endpoints, but health issues often take time to accumulate in the absence of good treatment—for example, poor outcomes for chronically ill people, or rates of lung cancer and cardiovascular disease, may not appear for years following an adverse change in the health care system. A different approach we suggest here is to develop *process* measures of care that, if collected on a real-time basis, can be used to monitor changes in types of treatments across countries, regions, and socioeconomic status.

We further rely on earlier work to categorize health care treatments into three broad categories, defined in terms of cost-effectiveness. These range from effective (Category I) care, such as immunization programs, checklists in hospitals, and aspirin for heart attacks, to ineffective (Category III) treatments, such as an excess use of branded drugs when generics are available. Unfortunately, many of these monitoring approaches are still in their infancy and stymied by a lack of data, particularly across emerging economies. We draw on data both from the Organization for Economic Cooperation and Development (OECD) and the Institute for Health Metrics and Evaluation at the University of Washington to illustrate how health care reform and health care systems more generally can be evaluated with regard to the potential underuse of effective care—of the type that might (and should) rise over time—and the potential overuse of ineffective care.

## THE PRODUCTIVITY OF HEALTH CARE VARIES WIDELY ACROSS TREATMENTS

Cost-effectiveness is a commonly used analytic tool for the analysis of economic value in health care. It measures the cost of increasing, in the aggregate, by one life-year, typically adjusted for quality of life, for a specific treatment or procedure.[1] For example, insecticide-soaked bed nets in regions with endemic malaria typically lead to one quality-adjusted life-year for less than $50—highly cost effective (Wiseman and others, 2003). By contrast, minimally invasive (but still expensive) arthroscopic surgery to treat patients with osteoarthritis of the knee was shown to provide no benefit at all (Moseley and others, 2002).

Chandra and Skinner (forthcoming) have developed three general categories for health care treatments, ranked according to their cost-effectiveness or equivalently to the importance of their contribution to aggregate productivity.[2] The first is Category I or "home-run" treatments with very high cost-effectiveness ratios;

---

[1] This approach has also been used to assess health care systems; see Chandra, Jena, and Skinner (2011).
[2] These in turn follow closely on Wennberg, Fisher, and Skinner's (2002) categories of effective, preference-sensitive, and supply-sensitive treatments.

these include improved health behaviors (e.g., a drop in smoking), low-cost but highly effective drugs such as aspirin for heart attack patients, and (as noted above) highly cost-effective interventions such as insecticide-soaked bed nets in regions with endemic malaria. In some cases, the treatment may save money as well as save lives, for example, the introduction of surfactants to treat neonatal acute respiratory distress for newborns. In other cases, Category I treatments are costly, for example, anti-retroviral drugs for the treatment of HIV patients. But for any advanced economy, there is a natural limit on diffusion—no one without HIV or AIDS would ever take anti-retroviral drugs because of side effects, limiting their inappropriate use. And while for emerging countries these expensive but effective drugs could overwhelm health ministry budgets, their high effectiveness also encourages incremental funding from international organizations.

Category II is for treatments that are cost-effective in some patients—at least by advanced economy standards—but that have modest or even adverse consequences in others. Perhaps the best example is angioplasty, in which a cardiologist inserts a very small balloon into blocked cardiac arteries in order to restore blood flow to the heart muscle. Typically, the cardiologist then inserts a stent, a small wire mesh cylinder, to maintain blood flow following the procedure.[3] These procedures are typically very expensive (in the United States, the cost is at least $15,000) in part because of the necessity to maintain a dedicated catheterization laboratory and often backup cardiac surgical facilities for complications during the procedure. They have been proven to be highly effective and cost-efficient when used within 12 hours for patients who have just had a heart attack (Boden and the COURAGE Trial Group, 2002; Hartwell and others, 2005). By contrast, when stents are used to treat stable angina, a common condition in which stress or physical activity causes chest pain, there is no reduction in mortality and no reduction in the chance of another heart attack, but there is temporary improvement in functioning for several years following the procedure (Weintraub and the COURAGE Trial Group, 2008), implying a cost-effectiveness ratio (or spending per quality-adjusted life-year) reaching as much as $400,000. In other words, an additional $1 million can either improve health outcomes by 2,000 life-years through the expansion of a bed net program or by 2.5 life-years through the insertion of stents for stable angina.[4]

This heterogeneity of treatment effects is shown graphically in Figure 9.1.[5] Assume that patients are ordered from left to right with regard to appropriateness of care, with patients gaining the highest incremental benefit of the treatment receiving it first. The figure's vertical axis measures both the cost per procedure

---

[3]Because the stents are inserted into an artery with a needle puncture, they are also sometimes referred to by their more general description of percutaneous coronary interventions (PCIs). This subcutaneous approach is in contrast to an "open" approach, such as bypass surgery, involving a scalpel.

[4]This simple calculation assumes that incremental bed nets (or stents) yield the average benefit, and that other countries face the same costs as in the United States. Clearly, lower-cost providers of stents would yield more appealing cost-effectiveness.

[5]This discussion draws heavily from Chandra and Skinner (forthcoming).

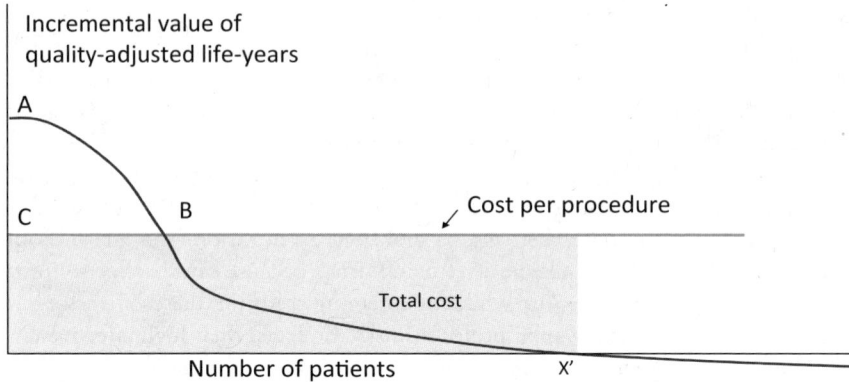

**Figure 9.1**   The Productivity of "Category II" Treatments

(the horizontal line—assumed constant) and the dollar incremental value of the health benefit. That is, wealthier countries may place a greater "price" on health, which would shift the benefit curve upward.

For some patients, there are clear net benefits where the benefit curve is above the cost curve. If only the patients up to point B in Figure 9.1 were to receive the treatment, net benefits would be given by ABC. But in the United States, where physicians are typically paid on a fee-for-service basis (and where all physicians are taught to provide care where it will help their patient), a different solution occurs, where the marginal patient yields zero gross benefits, at point X′. This maximizes total health benefits (the area under the curve), but does not maximize net benefits or productivity. On net, the total cost at point X′ is given by the shaded rectangle and is about the same as the area under the treatment benefit curve. In other words, despite the demonstrated benefit of the treatment among a subgroup of the population, *net* benefit, averaged across all patients, is roughly zero. One can find similar poor-productivity outcomes in emerging economies if subsidized malaria treatments, for example, are consumed by people who do not have malaria or where access to scarce treatments depends more on income or geography than on the appropriateness for the patient.

Category III includes treatments with either (1) very poor or nonexistent cost-effectiveness or (2) benefits that are simply not known. One example, as noted above, is the use of arthroscopic surgery for osteoarthritis of the knee (Moseley and others, 2002). (This study is also notable because the control group received "placebo surgery"—skin incisions and simulated surgery.) Other Category III intensity measures include aggressive cancer treatment for metastatic cancers. For example, patients treated aggressively in the hospital for advanced lung cancer experienced worse quality of life, higher hospital use, and *shorter* life expectancy relative to those treated with palliative care (Temel and others, 2010). As well, there is no evidence that screening for prostate cancer is useful after age 75, yet rates of screening for older men are as high as 37 percent annually in some sections of the United States (Bynum, Song, and Fisher, 2010).

# THE IMPACT OF HEALTH CARE REFORM ON HEALTH: A PRODUCTION FUNCTION APPROACH

While we may not observe ideal health care systems in practice, economists can still assume a health care production possibility frontier, as shown in Figure 9.2. On the horizontal axis is the aggregate level of spending (measured on a per capita basis) for health care; this may include both private and public sources of funds. The vertical axis is an aggregate measure of life expectancy (or survival rates) combined with quality of life. Thus, a higher point on the vertical axis will reflect, for example, better functioning after knee replacements for appropriate patients, even without any improvement in life expectancy (Garber and Skinner, 2008).

The curved line PF* represents the production possibility frontier, or the first-best combination of treatments and choice of appropriate patients. The curve is traced out by assuming that the country begins with the most cost-effective treatments for the most appropriate patients—for example, aspirin for hospital patients who have just had a heart attack—and proceeds down the cost-effectiveness list as the country spends additional funds. This is why the production function is concave; the slope of the line—or the gain in survival and quality of care per euro spent—declines as the health care system works its way down to successive treatment options.

In practice, all countries fall short of efficient care. For example, one study suggested that just over half of the recommended care was provided during primary care visits in the United States (McGlynn and others, 2003). Similarly, average rates of influenza vaccinations for the elderly—a commonly used quality measure whose rate should be near 100 percent—were just 55.9 percent across all OECD countries in 2007. Country-specific rates ranged from 23.7 percent in the

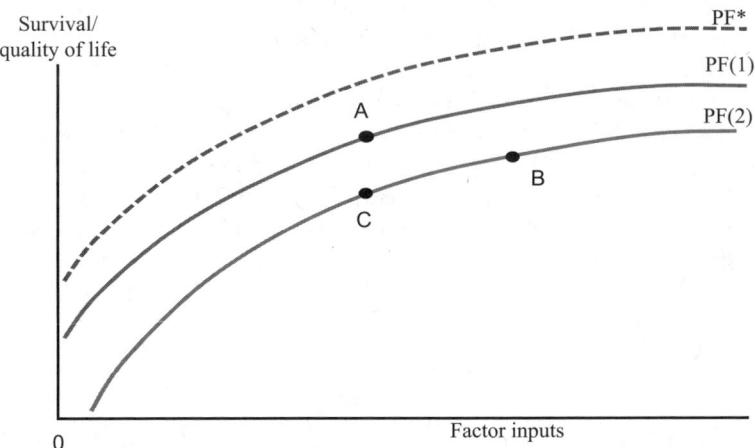

**Figure 9.2**  Different Country-Specific Production Functions
PF(1) represents the production possibility for country 1, and PF(2) for country 2. The two production functions can differ because of underlying health status or different degrees of inefficiency in each country. The positions of point A and point B illustrate a potentially negative association between spending and outcomes—at a point in time—as shown by the broken line, even while in each country spending is positively associated with outcomes.

Czech Republic and 36.1 percent in Austria to more than 77 percent in the Netherlands, the Republic of Korea, and Australia (OECD, 2009a). At the same time, low-value Category III spending was estimated to comprise a large fraction of health care spending, at least in the United States (Chandra and Skinner, forthcoming). Thus one can trace out production functions specific to different countries, such as PF(1) and PF(2) in the figure, that reflect the association between spending and outcomes (at least locally) for health care systems with different degrees of efficiency or inefficiency in providing care.

This approach can help to make sense of the perplexing lack of association between spending and health outcomes, whether across countries or across regions within the United States (e.g., Fisher and others, 2003a, 2003b). Points A and B in Figure 9.2 each represent combinations of spending and outcomes for, say, two countries. The production functions may differ because one system is more efficient than the other (as above) or because the underlying health status of one country is worse, leading to a production function everywhere below that of the other. Note that the slope of each country-specific production function is positive, so more spending yields better outcomes in either country. But a comparison of the two countries implies a negative correlation between spending and outcomes (Garber and Skinner, 2008). This negative correlation might be used to support the view that health care costs can be cut in the more expensive region without a health penalty; after all, Country 1 attains better health outcomes at lower costs. But assuming that Country 2 continues to provide health care in its conventional way and does not restructure the health care system, it might then be likely to end up at point C in the figure, with worse health outcomes. The larger point is that comparisons of countries or regions at a point in time cannot be used to infer properties of the production function in a given country. Even when the correlation between spending and outcomes might be faintly positive for 12-month survival following surgery, as in Silber and others (2010), this does not mean that spending more *at a given hospital* will yield better outcomes.

The impact of health cost cutbacks is illustrated in Figure 9.3. Consider next the impact of a health care reform that is designed to save money. As noted by Clements and others (2010), there are a variety of approaches used by health care systems to reduce cost growth, particularly for the public sector. If we ignore for the moment the distinction between public and private expenditures, consider a successful reform that achieves its goal of actually saving money relative to trend. Suppose for example that point A in the figure is next year's anticipated outcome and spending level, in the absence of any system-level change in the health care system. That is, anticipated costs are given by $X$ in the figure. A new and successful health care reform is implemented that changes how the government pays for services, changes how much is paid, or changes demand-side incentives for care. Now the economy is spending $Z$ instead of $X$, leading to net savings of $(X - Z)$.[6]

---

[6]Most, but not all, health care reforms attempt to simply slow down the growth of health care expenditure—this is why $X$ is anticipated spending given the status quo, and $Z$ is the counterfactual. But $Z$ could still be higher than current $(t - 1)$ spending.

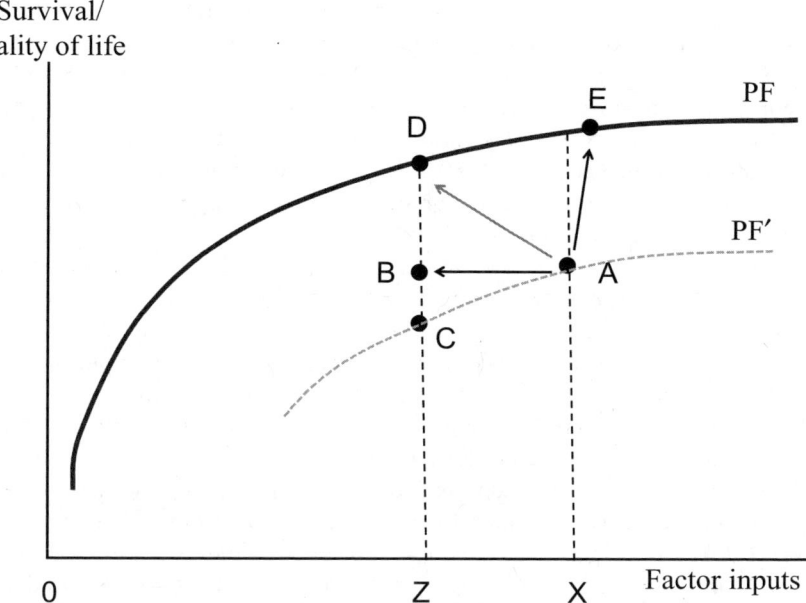

**Figure 9.3** Hypothetical Effects of Budgetary Cutbacks on Health Outcomes
For example, consider a scaling back of spending from anticipated levels (*X*) to actual levels (*Z*). One cannot assume that this shift will move along the production possibility frontier PF. Instead, the budgetary cuts could be attained with a significant decline in health by getting rid of the most useful procedures or treatments (from point A to point C) or by completely restructuring the health care system and using more efficient methods to attain even better health levels (from point A to point D).

But how might the reform affect health outcomes? If we suppose that spending cuts occur by simply squeezing all government budgets by a common percentage and letting individual providers make their own decision, corresponding to the dotted line through point A, then one might observe clinics in poor neighborhoods closing, perhaps according to political priorities within the budgetary constraints. In this case, aggregate health drops again to point C.

Suppose instead that the reform is carefully designed to target Category III care—care that has little or no value. In this case, the economy would move from point A to point B with no loss in health outcomes. In a much more favorable scenario, the health care reform not only cuts costs, but also reforms priorities and pushes the new outcome measure to point D on the production possibility frontier—and for the same cost *Z*.

One can of course question the plausibility of a reform that results in point D. If the solution was to spend less and get better outcomes, then why had it not happened originally? This puzzle has been addressed empirically since Leibenstein (1966) first proposed the idea of "X-efficiency"—that apparently similar petroleum factories in Egypt, for example, could experience twofold productivity differences. The resolution might just be new management (as in the example in Egypt), but this alone seems unlikely to solve the rampant inefficiency in the United States and in other countries.

Making the problem more complicated is the fact that if the goal of health care reform is to improve health (for example, to introduce new developments in health care delivery), costs may actually rise. A hypothetical shift in Figure 9.3 from point A to point E will cost more, but in this case it is most likely "worth it" because the extra cost—for example, from putting in an electronic health system—yields such large benefits. In this case, one can make a case for spending more, rather than less, even in the presence of a high marginal cost of funds.

One may question how much variation in inefficiency (or efficiency) is observed in health care systems—that is, how much better can health care systems become at the same cost? There is an increasing realization that the quality of care (Category I treatments) may not be closely correlated to how much is spent on Category III treatments. Baicker and Chandra (2004), for example, showed a *negative* association between Medicare expenditures and the "process quality" of care, in the sense of administering beta blockers and aspirin after heart attacks. And while other studies have illustrated a modest positive association (e.g., for tourists, but not residents, admitted to Florida emergency rooms, as in Doyle [2011], or for 30-day outcomes following surgical procedures, as in Silber and others [2010]), the general pattern for all of these studies is that the correlation between spending and outcomes is generally modest. That is, there is considerable variation in the extent of total factor productivity across health care institutions, even within a country (Skinner and Staiger, 2009). This is reflected not simply in the wide variation in utilization rates and expenditures, but also in the very wide variation in risk-adjusted outcomes. Country-level comparisons of spending and outcomes are even more tricky, simply because it is so hard to adjust for underlying health status and the way money is spent in each country (Garber and Skinner, 2008).

In sum, evaluating the success of a specific health care reform requires more than measuring the revenue savings—it also requires measuring the impact on health. Ideally, one should attempt to measure health outcomes directly as a consequence of health reform change. Yet measuring health at the population level is challenging, even in advanced economies. Another approach is to consider the utilization of health care services directly. This is often difficult as well, but at least more feasible, particularly in the context of a nationally coordinated health care accounting system. In the next section, we consider how one might measure such changes over a period of time to guard against the prospect of health care reforms cutting rather too close to the bone.

## DATA ANALYSIS

While health care expenditures have been rising across developed and developing countries, there is considerable difference in growth rates. The OECD data in Figure 9.4 show the trend in health care expenditures as a percentage of GDP for a variety of countries. Some countries are growing more rapidly relative to others, and while it is not surprising that Turkey should be catching up to other developed economies, it is surprising that the United States, historically a high-cost

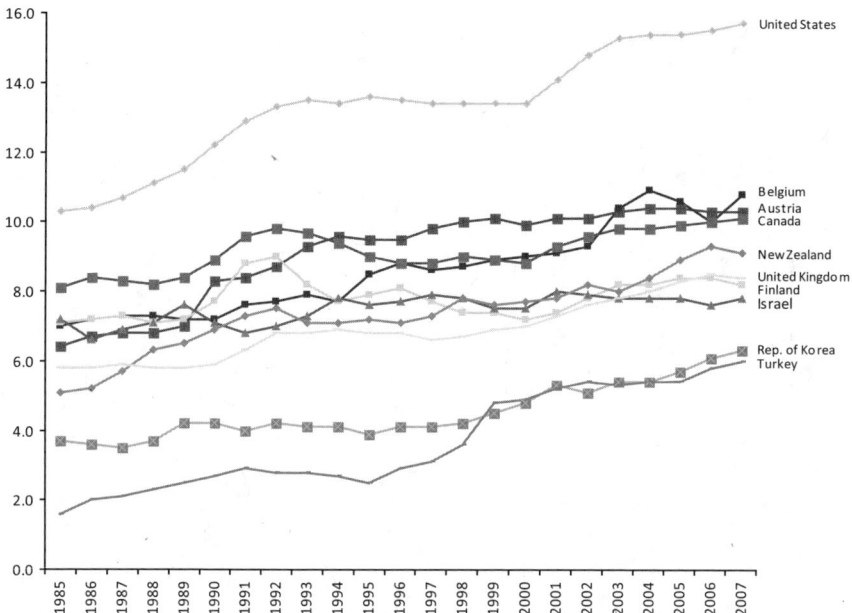

**Figure 9.4** Total Expenditure on Health as a Percentage of GDP, 1985–2007
Source: Organization for Economic Cooperation and Development Health Database.

country, should also be breaking away from the pack with more rapid growth (Chandra and Skinner, forthcoming).[7]

Table 9.1 compares a select group of countries (chosen primarily for their relative strength in reporting relevant data) with regard to overall health expenditures, underlying health status, and the extent to which the countries may have underinvested in Category I effective procedures, or overinvested in Category II or Category III procedures. Not surprisingly, there are large differences in real spending (in U.S. dollars) across the OECD countries, ranging from $852 per capita in Mexico to $7,538 in the United States. Second, higher health expenditures per capita do not necessarily correlate with health outcomes such as life expectancy, as noted in the preceding section. In part, this lack of correlation may reflect the wide variance in underlying health status, as shown by obesity rates and tobacco consumption levels in Table 9.1. Still, despite high rates of both obesity and tobacco consumption in Finland and the United States, the United States spends two and a half times as much per capita on health care and more than twice as much on pharmaceuticals per capita and performs 50 percent more stenting procedures. The fact that life expectancy is higher in Finland is consistent with the notion (but does not imply) that costly branded prescription drugs and stents are overused in the United States.

---

[7]Clements and others (2010) consider growth in public sector spending; generally the results are similar except in the United States, where a large fraction of the growth is accounted for by increases in private spending.

**TABLE 9.1**

## Health Expenditure and Utilization Differences across Selected OECD Countries

| | Canada | Finland | France | Germany | Israel | Mexico | Poland | Switzerland | United Kingdom | United States |
|---|---|---|---|---|---|---|---|---|---|---|
| Total health expenditure per capita, $US puchasing power parity[a] | 4,079 | 3,008 | 3,696 | 3,737 | 2,165 | 852 | 1,213 | 4,627 | 3,129 | 7,538 |
| Life expectancy at birth, years[b] | 81.4 | 79.3 | 81.2 | 80.1 | 81.0 | 76.5 | 76.1 | 81.1 | 80.1 | 78.4 |
| Obesity, percentage of adult population with a body mass index >30 kg/m², based on self-reports[c] | 15.9 | 15.7 | 11.2 | 16 | 13.6 | | | 8.1 | | 27.5 |
| Tobacco consumption, percentage of adult population who are daily smokers[c] | 17.5 | 20.4 | 26.2 | | 22.2 | | | 20.4 | 22 | 16.5 |
| Percentage of population 65 and over vaccinated against influenza[c] | 64 | 51 | 69 | 56 | 56 | 35 | | 56 | 74 | 67 |
| Total MRI units per million population[a] | 6.7 | 15.3 | | | | 1.8 | 1.5 | 2.7 | 5.6 | 25.9 |
| Total CT scanners per million population[a] | 12.7 | 16.5 | | | 7 | 4 | 9.7 | 31.4 | 7.5 | 34.3 |
| Percutaneous coronary intervention (stenting) per 100,000 (inpatient)[d] | 135.9 | 152.2 | 186.3 | 536.1 | 254.6 | 1.8 | 207.6 | 112.8 | 93.3 | 436.8 |
| Coronary bypass procedures per 100,000 (inpatient)[d] | 72.7 | 66.2 | 30.2 | 129.1 | 62.5 | 2.8 | 52.6 | 33.8 | 43.5 | 84.5 |
| Prostatectomy procedures per 100,000 males (inpatient)[e] | 161 | 181 | 286 | 287 | 141 | 32 | | 205 | 117 | 114 |
| Hip and knee replacements per 100,000 (inpatient)[d] | 259.2 | 379.5 | 317.4 | 448.2 | 95.7 | 10.2 | | 384.3 | 288.4 | 345 |
| Pharmaceutical expenditure per capita, $US at purchasing power parity[c] | 665 | 408 | 595 | 545 | | 232 | 257 | 461 | 365 | 876 |
| Practicing physicians, density per 1,000 population[c] | | 2.7 | 3.6 | 3.6 | 3.4 | 2 | 2.2 | 3.9 | 2.6 | 2.4 |
| Ratio of remuneration of GPs (specialists) to average wage[f] | 3.1 (4.7) | 1.8 (2.5) | 2.6 (4.4) | 3.3 (4.1) | 3.9 (4.2) | 3.9 (4.2) | | 2.7 (3.0) | 4.2 (4.3) | 3.7 (5.6) |

Note: Obesity data for Germany and Switzerland are for 2009; tobacco consumption data for Switzerland are for 2007.

[a]Source: 2007 OECD Health Data.

[b]Source: 2011 CIA World Factbook.

[c]Source: 2008 OECD Health Data.

[d]Source: 2006 OECD Health Data.

[e]Most recent data, 2006–08.

[f]When both salaried and self-employed physician data are reported, self-employed salary ratio has been used.

The extreme variation in procedure utilization suggests that physician choices and treatment decisions reflect wide differences in incentive systems across countries. The fact that Germany performs 536 percutaneous coronary procedures per 100,000 people compared to the United Kingdom's 93 procedures, or that Switzerland has 31.4 CT scanners per million people compared to Israel's 7 scanners raises the well-known question of "Which rate is right?" Does Israel have too few CT scans, or Switzerland (or the United States) too many? While the correct number of CT scanners and stents for a given country is unknown a priori, physician decision making appears to adjust practice style to local norms and the supply of resources available.

In some cases, rates of utilization may appear to be low but actually reflect incomplete data on all procedures. For example, rates of prostatectomy are quite low in the United States at 114 per 100,000 men as compared to 287 in France. This could reflect differences in underlying rates of prostate cancer, or in detection rates, although the United States is well known to screen more actively for prostate cancer. Another possibility is that the United States also uses other methods for treating prostate cancer, such as radiation therapy. Thus, a full accounting of all treatment modalities is desirable to measure overall utilization.

There is also a concern that countries with much higher remuneration for specialists as compared to general practitioners (GPs) end up with more specialists than is socially optimal. Studies show that GPs provide better preventive care and therefore more cost-effective care. Nevertheless, in the OECD countries, the number of specialists grew by 60 percent between 1990 and 2007, as compared with 23 percent growth in GPs, and in 2007 on average there were twice as many specialists as GPs (OECD, 2009b).

One question that naturally arises is the importance of highly remunerated physicians in explaining higher (or lower) expenditures across countries. Again limiting ourselves to just selected countries, we report OECD estimates of the ratio of practicing physicians to the population, and physician salaries relative to the average salary in each country (see the last two rows of Table 9.1). The latter adjustment implicitly adjusts for differences in GDP per capita across countries. Neither the supply of physicians nor their relative salary appears to explain patterns of expenditures across regions. For example, relative salaries in the United Kingdom are slightly higher than in the United States for general practitioners (4.2 versus 3.7) and somewhat lower for specialists (4.3 versus 5.6), but on average there are more physicians per population in the United Kingdom (2.6 per thousand) than in the United States (2.4). But these modest differences in overall physician payments cannot explain the enormous gap between the countries in health care spending: 16.0 percent of GDP in the United States versus 7.0 percent in the United Kingdom. Similarly, Belgium and the Netherlands have the highest number of specialists per capita (OECD, 2010) as well as the highest specialist remuneration ratios when compared to average national wages, yet their health care spending lags far behind that in the United States.

While we might look to differences in the structure of payment and the fraction of fee-for-service physician practices to explain differences in physician compensation and workforce, it seems more likely that spending differences across countries reflect differences not just in quantities of services, but also in the type of service and the workforce devoted to those services. Thus, higher prices per procedure or per admission in, say, the United States relative to other countries, as found by Koechlin, Lorenzoni, and Schreyer (2010), are unlikely to reflect solely higher wages paid to health care providers—physicians in the United States would need to be paid far more than their current salary to absorb the much higher costs in U.S. inpatient care. Instead, it is likely to reflect quantities of what is done inside a typical hospital, such as more testing prior to and after a procedure, larger numbers of clerical workers needed for billing, more pleasant private rooms, or more nursing staff. In some cases, of course, aggregate spending on health care will be the consequence of real price differences; for example, the higher price of branded pharmaceuticals in the United States leading to higher overall expenditures for pharmaceuticals in that country (see Table 9.1).

The cross-country comparisons highlight a key point: there is dramatic variation among developed and developing countries in their utilization of health care treatments, suggesting an overutilization of Category III procedures in high-cost regions. Moreover, there is likely to be an underutilization of Category I and effective Category II treatments in emerging countries, for example, as reflected in the very low rate of cardiovascular procedures in Mexico. Health care costs are growing at a much slower rate in lower-income countries, and for many of these countries, the primary concern is to expand coverage. Such countries must avoid building the unsustainable cost structures seen, to a varying extent, in some developed countries.

Figure 9.5 draws on data from Institute for Health Metrics and Evaluation (IHME) (2008), based on Lim and others (2008), to provide a comprehensive picture of rates of DTP3[8] immunization rates for various countries over time. The IHME has created time-series cross-sectional data sets, although their comprehensiveness also means that they make wide use of imputation methods to fill in the blanks. (One might also be concerned about reporting standards of some countries.) Nonetheless, these provide a remarkable time-series snapshot of how countries are spending their health care resources. Mexico has made a steady and dramatic improvement in DTP3 immunization rates over the past 20 years, even if these rates do not show the same miraculous jump in 2008 indicated by the OECD data. While not all developing countries have given immunization the same high priority, these measures could in theory be used to monitor the country-level performance of Category I treatments.

Figure 9.6 shows a related measure of Category I treatment, insecticide-treated bed nets relative to the number of people living in wet regions of countries with endemic malaria (IHME, 2010). While all countries in the sample have experienced rising use of bed nets, the extent of growth differs dramatically across countries, with some countries still exhibiting minimal use. These measures could

---

[8] The DTP3 vaccination protects against three infectious diseases: diphtheria, tetanus, and pertussis or whooping cough.

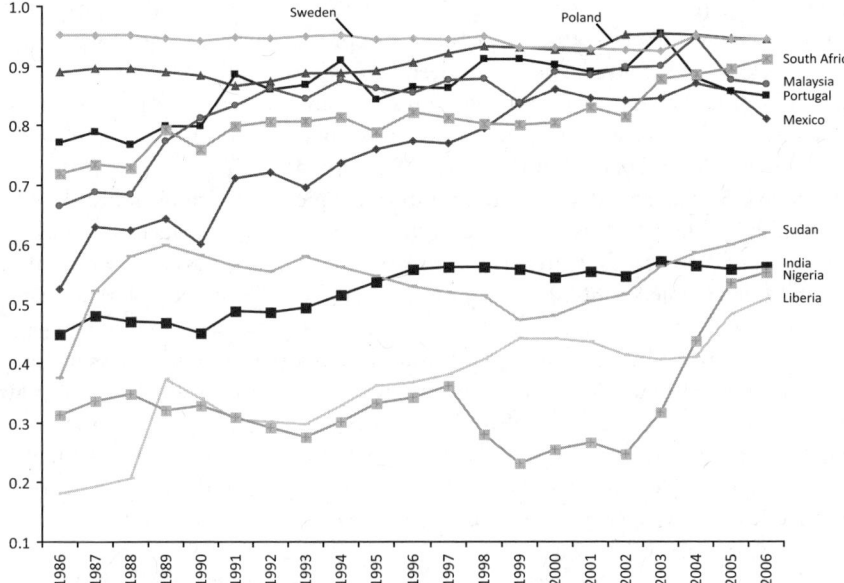

**Figure 9.5** DTP3 Immunization Rates, 1986–2006
Source: IHME (2008).

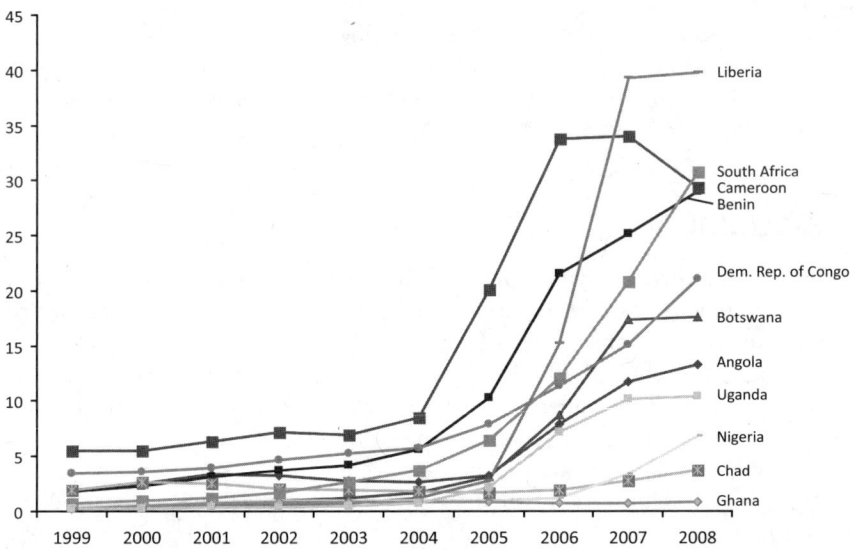

**Figure 9.6** Use of Insecticide-Treated Bed Nets, 1999–2008
Source: IHME (2008).

as well be used to monitor the progress of health care reform, with appropriate action taken in the event that such rates drop precipitously, perhaps because of bottlenecks in the delivery system. Indeed, for this type of care, countries with low rates of use should be encouraged to expand the program (despite the extra cost—as in the movement from point A to point E in Figure 9.3), with appropriate allowances for future budgetary planning.

There is also increased interest in monitoring regional variations in health care utilization within countries. For example, for China, Liu and others (2008) developed a set of measures for Category I treatments, including access to safe drinking water, sanitary toilets, smoking cessation, antenatal care, hospital maternal delivery, postnatal care, vaccines for children, tuberculosis examinations, and hypertension control and effectiveness. They found dramatic variations across regions in these rates. Although some of the variation was explained simply by per capita income, differences remained even for regions with similar income. In theory, parallel measures by region could also be developed for Category III treatments, such as high rates of patients with end-state cancer dying in the hospital (versus hospice care), high rates of Caesarian section, or very high use of intensive care unit days or home health care.[9]

There are many developing countries with strained budgets that would benefit from focusing on cost-effective treatments. Lu and others (2010) showed that foreign aid to developing countries for health care was sometimes diverted to other uses (that is, money formerly used to provide health care was shifted to other parts of the budget), leading in some cases to less than a 50 cent increase in health care spending per dollar contributed by foreign agencies. Since these countries receiving aid are also the ones with the greatest potential to improve Category I treatments, greater monitoring to ensure that the money contributed translates into improved process measures of health care seems reasonable (Murray and Frenk, 2008).

## DISCUSSION

Nearly every country is confronted with budgetary pressures and difficult decisions regarding its provision of health care. For most countries, publicly provided health care systems are growing at rates that will prove difficult to sustain (Clements and others, 2010). Health care reform is an obvious response to these pressures. Yet given the remarkable differences across medical treatments in their cost-effectiveness, the specific nature of the health care reform—which treatments are scaled back and which are enhanced—is central to understanding the success or failure of any reform. In this chapter, we have suggested a convenient typology of treatments to help in assessing both levels and changes in the productivity of a country-specific health care system. This approach in turn leads naturally to approaches designed to assess how health care reforms affect not just budgets, but

---

[9]See http://www.dartmouthatlas.org/tools/downloads.aspx.

also actual health outcomes. Ideally, one would simply monitor health outcomes, but they often take decades to be realized. For example, diminished rates of childhood rheumatic fever in the early twentieth century resulted in a decline 50 years later as the children, by then grown up, experienced fewer valvular cardiac disorders. Thus, we suggest focusing on monitoring measures of health care process, such as immunization rates, use of aspirin, or beta blockers for heart attacks, and access to primary care health providers.

The impact of health care budgetary cuts or restrictions may be reflected in quality measures as well as utilization of Category I treatments such as immunization. For example, during the early 1990s, New Jersey (but not New York) cut its hospital subsidies for uninsured care by half. During this period, mortality following heart attacks for uninsured patients dropped substantially in New York but rose for corresponding patients in New Jersey (Volpp and others, 2003). Other measures of quality may be affected by financial reforms, such as physician rates of absenteeism (Chaudhury and others, 2006), loss of access for low-income households (Birdsall and Hecht, 2011), and higher mortality rates because of restrictive wage policies for nursing staff (Propper and Van Reenan, 2010).

Many efforts to reduce health care costs take the form of across-the-board cuts in reimbursements or wages or increases in patient cost sharing. It is understandable why; it is easy to do and appears to spread the pain uniformly through the health care system. But the arguments here suggest a different approach. Certainly the idea of encouraging Category I treatments is not new; the idea of "value-based" insurance design suggests that for some patients, subsidizing efficient treatments may reduce costs to society downstream (Chandra, Gruber, and McKnight, 2010). Less commonly used is the idea of charging more for the less effective Category II or Category III treatments that are often covered by the same copayments as the more effective treatments. Even small proportional copayments for stent use or full payment for prostate-specific antigen testing for men (something that the United States Preventive Task Force recommends *against*) could serve as the "nudge" that causes patients to make better-informed choices. Similarly, paying providers less for procedures that are not clearly indicated by clinical evidence (and shielding them from malpractice suits if they follow best-practice guidelines) would help to ensure that marginal dollars spent yield positive benefits.

Another approach to reducing costs is through quantity regulation rather than price regulation. While each hospital in a major city may want to have a cardiac catheterization lab with backup facilities to help attract market share, there is also potential for consolidation, which can save money and potentially improve outcomes by raising facility-level volume.

In the future, all countries must seek to restrain growing health care costs, and all countries will seek to improve the efficiency of their own health care systems. Better measurement and monitoring of health outcomes—and preferably those available in real time rather than those that require waiting several years for information—is a necessary though not a sufficient step to ensure that scaled-back spending does not result in serious detriments to health care outcomes. At the same time, developing new approaches for improving the supply side of health care is critical. These include ensuring that providers are paid enough to show up at their offices and that the organization of health care services is not compromised, as was done, for example, in South Africa where the diffusion of local clinics allowed much more effective treatments for AIDS patients (IRIN, 2008). At the same time, countries have often been loath to use higher copayments (or lower provider reimbursements) for specific Category III treatments, most likely because of a concern about the inequity arising from the poor being excluded from such treatments or the difficulty of drawing clinical "lines in the sand." Looking forward to the future, as technological innovations continue to be developed, straining budgets further, it seems likely that new models of pricing and regulation will be developed that are designed to ensure the widespread use of effective treatments and discourage the use of those treatments with little or no incremental health benefit.

## REFERENCES

Baicker, K., and A. Chandra, 2004, "Medicare Spending, The Physician Workforce, and the Quality of Health Care Received by Medicare Beneficiaries," *Health Affairs*, Web Exclusive, April.

Birdsall, N., and R. Hecht, 2011, "Swimming Against the Tide: Strategies for Improving Equity in Health," Working Paper No. 249 (Washington, Inter-American Development Bank).

Boden, W., and the COURAGE Trial Group, 2007, "Optimal Medical Therapy With or Without PCI for Stable Coronary Disease," *New England Journal of Medicine*, Vol. 356, No. 15, pp. 1503–16.

Bynum, J., Y. Song, and E. Fisher, 2010, "Variation in Prostate-Specific Antigen Screening in Men Aged 80 and Older in Fee-for-Service Medicare," *Journal of the American Geriatrics Society*, Vol. 58, No. 4, pp. 674–80.

Chandra, A., and J. Skinner, forthcoming, "Technology Growth and Expenditure Growth in Health Care," *Journal of Economic Literature*.

Chandra, A., J. Gruber, and R. McKnight, 2010, "Patient Cost-Sharing and Hospitalization Offsets in the Elderly," *American Economic Review*, Vol. 100, No. 1, pp. 193–213.

Chandra, A., A. Jena, and J. Skinner, 2011, "A Pragmatist's Guide to Comparative Effectiveness Research," *Journal of Economic Perspectives*, Vol. 25, No. 2: 27–46.

Chaudhury, N., J. Hammer, M. Kremer, K. Muralidharan, and F. Halsey Rogers, 2006. "Missing in Action: Teacher and Health Worker Absence in Developing Countries," *Journal of Economic Perspectives*, Vol. 20, No. 1 (Winter), pp. 91–116.

Clements, B., D. Coady, E. Jenkner, I. Karpowicz, K. Kashiwase, B. Shang, M. Soto, and J. Tyson., 2010, "Macro-Fiscal Implications of Health Care Reform in Advanced and Emerging Economies" (Washington: International Monetary Fund).

Doyle, J. Jr., 2011, "Returns to Local-Area Health Care Spending: Using Health Shocks to Patients Far From Home," *American Economic Journal: Applied Economics*, Vol. 3, No. 3, pp. 221–43.

Fisher, E.S., D.E. Wennberg, T.A. Stukel, D.J. Gottlieb, F.L. Lucas, and E.L. Pinder, 2003a, "The Implications of Regional Variations in Medicare Spending—Part 1: The Content, Quality, and Accessibility of Care," *Annals of Internal Medicine*, Vol. 138, No. 4: pp. 273–87.

———, 2003b. "The Implications of Regional Variations in Medicare Spending—Part 2: Health Outcomes and Satisfaction with Care," *Annals of Internal Medicine*, Vol. 138, No. 4: pp. 288–98.

Ford, E.S., U.A. Ajani., J.B. Croft, J. Critchley, D. Labarthe, T. Kottke, W. Giles, and S. Capewell, 2007, "Explaining the Decrease in U.S. Deaths From Coronary Disease, 1980–2000," *New England Journal of Medicine*, Vol. 356, No. 23, pp. 2388–98.

Garber, A., and J. Skinner, 2008, "Is American Health Care Uniquely Inefficient?" *Journal of Economic Perspectives*, Vol. 22, No. 4, pp. 27–50.

Hall, R., and C.I. Jones, 2007, "The Value of Life and the Rise in Health Spending," *Quarterly Journal of Economics*, Vol. 122, No. 1, pp. 39–72.

Hartwell, D., J. Colquitt, E. Loveman, A. Clegg, H. Brodin, N. Waugh, P. Royle, P. Davidson, L. Vale, and L. MacKenzie, 2005. "Clinical Effectiveness and Cost-Effectiveness of Immediate Angioplasty for Acute Myocardial Infarction: Systematic Review and Economic Evaluation," *Health Technology Assessment*, Vol. 9, No. 17, pp. 1–114.

Institute for Health Metrics and Evaluation (IHME), 2008, *DTP3 Immunization Coverage by Country, 1986–2006* (Seattle). Available at http://www.healthmetricsandevaluation.org/record/dtp3-immunization-coverage-country-1986-2006.

———, 2010, *Sub-Saharan Africa Insecticide-Treated Bed Nets 1999–2008* (Seattle). Available at http://www.healthmetricsandevaluation.org/record/sub-saharan-africa-insecticide-treated-bed-nets-1999-2008.

IRIN, 2008, "South Africa: Solving Treatment Bottlenecks," IRIN: PlusNews. Available at http://www.plusnews.org/Report.aspx?ReportId=76096.

Koechlin, F., L. Lorenzoni, and P. Schreyer, 2010, "Comparing Price Levels of Hospital Services across Countries: Results of Pilot Study," OECD Health Working Paper No. 53 (Paris: OECD). Available at http://dx.doi.org/10.1787/5km91p4f3rzw-en.

Leibenstein, H., 1966, "Allocative Efficiency vs. 'X-efficiency,'" *American Economic Review*, Vol. 56, No. 3, pp. 392–415.

Lim, S.S., D.B. Stein, A. Charrow, and C.J.L. Murray, 2008, "Tracking Progress towards Universal Childhood Immunisation and the Impact of Global Initiatives: A Systematic Analysis of Three-Dose Diphtheria, Tetanus, and Pertussis Immunisation Coverage," *The Lancet*, Vol. 372, No. 9655, pp. 2031–46.

Liu, Y., K. Rao, J. Wu, and E. Gakidou, 2008, "China's Health Care Performance," *The Lancet*, Vol. 372, No. 9653, pp. 1914–23.

Lu, C., M.T. Schneider, P. Gubbins, K. Leach-Kemon, D. Jamison, and C. Murray, 2010, "Public Financing of Health in Developing Countries: A Cross-National Systematic Analysis," *The Lancet*, Vol. 375, No. 9723, pp. 1375–87.

McGlynn, E., S.M. Asch, J. Adams, J. Keesey, J. Hicks, A. DeCristofaro, and E. Kerr, 2003, "The Quality of Health Care Delivered to Adults in the U.S." *New England Journal of Medicine*, Vol. 348, No. 26: 2635–45.

Moseley, J. Bruce, K. O'Malley, N. Petersen, T. Menke, B. Brody, D. Kuykendall, J. Hollingsworth, C. Ashton, and N. Wray, 2002, "A Controlled Trial of Arthroscopic Surgery for Osteoarthritis of the Knee," *New England Journal of Medicine*, Vol. 347, No. 2, pp. 81–88.

Murray, C.J.L., and J. Frenk, 2008, "Health Metrics and Evaluation: Strengthening the Science," *The Lancet*, Vol. 371, No. 9619, pp. 1191–99.

Organization for Economic Cooperation and Development (OECD), 2009a, *Health Indicators at a Glance* (Paris).

———, 2009b, *OECD Health Data 2009—Comparing Health Statistics across Countries* (Paris).

———, 2010, *OECD Health Data 2010* (Paris).

Propper, C., and J. Van Reenan, 2010, "Can Pay Regulation Kill? Panel Data Evidence on the Effect of Labor Markets on Hospital Performance," *Journal of Political Economy*, Vol. 118, No. 2, pp. 222–73.

Silber, J., H. Robert Kaestner, O. Even-Shoshan, Y. Wang, and L.J. Bressler, 2010, "Aggressive Treatment Style and Surgical Outcomes," *Health Services Research*, Vol. 45, No. 6 (Part 2), pp. 1872–92.

Skinner, J., and D. Staiger, 2009, "Technology Diffusion and Productivity Growth in Health Care," Working Paper No. 14865 (Cambridge, MA: National Bureau of Economic Research).

Temel, J., J. Greer, A. Muzikansky, E. Gallagher, S. Admane, V. Jackson, C. Dahlin, C. Blinderman, J. Jacobsen, W. Pirl, J. Billings, and T. Lynch, 2010, "Early Palliative Care for Patients with Metastatic Non-Small-Cell Lung Cancer," *New England Journal of Medicine*, Vol. 363, No. 8, pp. 733–42.

Volpp, K., S. Williams, J. Waldfogel, J. Silber, J. Schwartz, and M. Pauly, 2003. "Market Reform in New Jersey and the Effect on Mortality from Acute Myocardial Infarction," *Health Services Research* Vol. 38, No. 2, pp. 515–33.

Weintraub, W., and the COURAGE Trial Group, 2008, "Effect of PCI on Quality of Life in Patients with Stable Coronary Disease," *New England Journal of Medicine*, Vol. 359, No. 7, pp. 677–87.

Wennberg, J.E., E.S. Fisher, and J. Skinner, 2002, "Geography and the Debate over Medicare Reform," *Health Affairs*, Vol. 21, No. 2, pp. w96–w144.

Wiseman, V., W.A. Hawley, F.O. ter Kuile, P.A. Phillips-Howard, J.M. Vulule, B. Nahlen, and J. Mills, 2003, "The Cost-Effectiveness of Permethrin-Treated Bed Nets in an Area of Intense Malaria Transmission in Western Kenya," *American Journal of Tropical Medical Hygiene*, Vol. 68, No. 4 (Suppl.), pp. 161–67.

# PART IV

# Country Case Studies: Advanced Economies

# CHAPTER 10

# Public Health Expenditure Reforms in Canada, Finland, Italy, the Netherlands, Sweden, the United Kingdom, and the United States

JUSTIN TYSON AND IZABELA KARPOWICZ

This chapter presents country case studies on the public health care expenditures and reform experiences of seven advanced economies. The case studies were designed to highlight specific episodes of success in containing public health spending during the past 30 years.

In each of these episodes, the country reduced the ratio of public health spending to GDP, sustaining that lower ratio for a period of time, and also moderated its real spending growth rates.[1] The advanced countries and time periods covered are Canada (late 1970s and 1990s), Finland (1990s), Italy (1990s), the Netherlands (early 1980s and 1990s), Sweden (1980s and early 1990s), the United Kingdom (1980s), and the United States (1990s). Each country discussion in this chapter begins with an overview of the health care system and comparative data on key health indicators and spending relative to the Organization for Economic Cooperation and Development (OECD) average. It then describes the health reforms made and assesses their impact on spending trends before, during, and afterward, assesses the durability of the reforms, and sums up the lessons learned. (More-detailed case studies provided in separate chapters cover the experiences of Germany, Japan, and the Republic of Korea and focus on health care reforms and long-term public health spending growth.)

Box 10.1 provides a typology of the reforms adopted by advanced economies. It offers a source of reference for comparing the reforms described in the case studies with the variety of reforms undertaken in other economies. The reforms are grouped into three categories: (1) macro-level controls, which constrain inputs, outputs, and prices; (2) micro-level reforms, which improve public management and coordination, contracting methods, and competition and choice; and (3) demand-side reforms.

---

[1]For all of the countries, the five-year moving average of public health spending to GDP declined.

**BOX 10.1**

### *Typology of Reforms in Advanced Economies*

Reforms implemented in advanced countries over the past three decades can be grouped into three categories (Oxley and MacFarlan, 1995):

#### Macro-Level Controls

- *Budget caps:* These are the bluntest instruments for restraining resources allocated to the public health sector. They can be expressed as limits on overall health care spending or on subsectors, such as hospitals or pharmaceuticals. Examples include global budgets for hospitals and expenditure ceilings for general practitioners.

- *Supply constraints:* Here the focus is on regulating the volume of either inputs into or outputs from the health care system. Input controls include limits on admission to physician training colleges, defining positive lists for drugs, and rationing of high-tech capital equipment. Output controls include delisting of certain treatments, such as eye tests and dental treatment.

- *Price controls:* Price controls regulate prices of inputs or outputs. They include wage controls for health care professionals, reference pricing for pharmaceutical products, price controls on specific treatments, and set case-based payments such as capitation or diagnosis-related groups.

#### Micro-Level Reforms

- *Public management and coordination:* These reforms seek to alter the organizational arrangements between different parts of the health care system in order to reduce costs through improved coordination, alignment of responsibility and accountability, better incentive structures, and/or reduction in overlap or redundancy. Examples of such changes include abolition of managerial levels, decentralization of health care functions, and introduction of gatekeeping arrangements (i.e., a physician who manages a patient's health care services, coordinates referrals to secondary and tertiary levels, and helps control health care costs by screening out unnecessary services).

- *Contracting:* How providers are reimbursed is one of the most important factors affecting the micro-level efficiency of health spending. There are many different ways to pay physicians, hospitals, and other providers, but three of the most general methods are (1) salaries or budgets, (2) case-based payment like capitation or diagnosis-related groups, and (3) fee for service.

- *Market Mechanisms:* These reforms seek to improve micro-level efficiency and/or control costs by introducing varying degrees of market mechanisms into the health sector. These reforms operate not so much on the supply side as on the nexus between supply and demand. Examples include creating internal markets (e.g., in which primary care physicians purchase services from hospitals), separating the purchase of health services from provision (thus allowing competition among providers), and promoting patient choice (e.g., in which patients can choose among primary care providers and hospitals).

#### Demand-Side Reforms

- These reforms include policies intended to increase the share of health care costs borne by patients, often with the objective of avoiding excessive consumption of specific health services. The two important issues on the demand side are the level of patient cost sharing (this can take the form of lump sum or percentage copayments) and the tax treatment of private health insurance.

**TABLE 10.1**

Canada: Key Health Indicators, 1970–2008[a]

|  | 1970 | 1980 | 1990 | 2000 | 2008 | OECD 2008[b] |
|---|---|---|---|---|---|---|
| GDP per capita ($US, purchasing power parity) | 4,272 | 11,066 | 19,565 | 28,482 | 39,288 | 35,617 |
| Primary balance (percent of GDP) | — | 1.4 | 3.6 | 10.1 | 4.0 | 1.5 |
| General government primary expenditure (percent of GDP) | — | 36.6 | 36.5 | 34.9 | 34.9 | 40.4 |
| Total health spending (percent of GDP)[c] | 6.9 | 7.0 | 8.9 | 8.8 | 10.4 | 9.3 |
| Public (percent of GDP) | 4.9 | 5.1 | 6.3 | 6.2 | 7.3 | 6.8 |
| Private (percent of GDP) | 2.1 | 1.7 | 2.3 | 2.6 | 3.1 | 2.5 |
| Public health spending per capita ($US) | 190 | 582 | 1,387 | 1,465 | 3,293 | 2,028 |
| Out-of-pocket spending (share of total health spending) | — | — | 14.4 | 15.9 | 14.7 | 16.8 |
| Formal health care coverage (share of population) | 100.0 | 100.0 | 100.0 | 100.0 | 100.0 | 99.0 |
| Life expectancy (years at birth) | 72.9 | 75.3 | 77.6 | 79.0 | 80.7 | 79.9 |
| Measles immunization (share of children 12–23 months) | — | — | 85.0 | 96.2 | 92.7 | 89.6 |
| Physicians (per 1,000 population) | — | — | — | — | — | 3.1 |
| Hospital beds (per 1,000 population) | — | 6.8 | 6.0 | 3.8 | 3.5 | 5.6 |

Sources: Organization for Economic Cooperation and Development; World Health Organization; World Bank, *World Development Indicators*; and IMF staff estimates.

[a]Years as indicated or latest available.

[b]OECD advanced economy unweighted average.

[c]Health spending components may not add up to the total. Public health spending data (as a share of GDP) have been adjusted to account for structural breaks.

# CANADA

## Overview of Health Care System

The health care system in Canada, known as Medicare, is a public contract model: publicly financed with private provision. Canada has maintained a predominantly tax-financed public system since the 1960s, and gatekeeping by primary care physicians is a central element.[2] The health care system is decentralized to the provinces and provides universal coverage.[3] In 2008, the ratio of total health spending to GDP was 10.4 percent, compared with the OECD advanced economies average of 9.3 percent, while public health spending was 7.3 percent of GDP, compared with the OECD average of 6.8 percent (Table 10.1). Private spending (in percent of GDP) has roughly doubled since 1980 and made up 30 percent of total health expenditures in 2008.

---

[2]Gatekeeping is a system in which a primary physician manages a patient's health care services, coordinates referrals, and helps control health care costs by screening out unnecessary services.

[3]Universal health coverage has a long history in Canada. Universal hospital coverage and universal access to essential medical services were introduced in all provinces by 1958 and 1971, respectively.

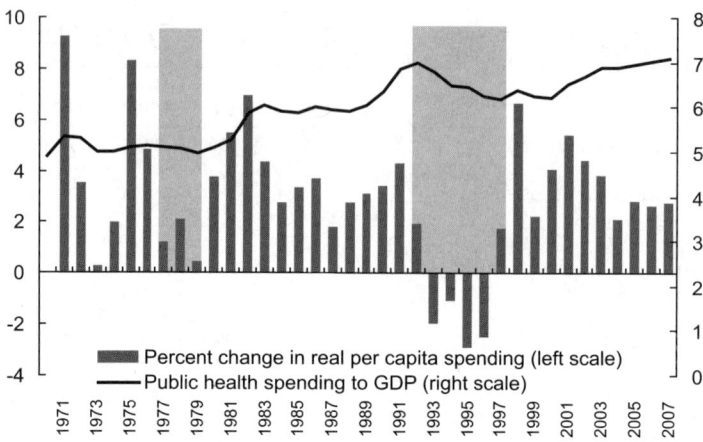

**Figure 10.1** Canada: Public Health Spending, 1970–2007 (Percent)
Sources: Organization for Economic Cooperation and Development, OECD Health Data; and IMF staff estimates.

## Experience with Health Reforms: Late 1970s and 1990s

### Spending Trends

Canada experienced a significant increase in public health expenditure between 1970 and 1992, despite a brief period of stabilization in the late 1970s, and recessions in the early 1980s and early 1990s led to jumps in health spending as a share of GDP. Over this 22-year period, real per capita public health care expenditure in Canada increased at an average annual rate of 3–4 percent, and spending rose to 6.9 percent of GDP from 4.8 percent (in 1970). From 1992 onward, the government applied a strong cost containment policy, and the ratio of public health expenditure to GDP declined to 6.2 percent by 1999. Between 1993 and 1998, the real growth rate of per capita public health spending averaged −1.2 percent. In the 2000s, public health expenditure increased by 3.5 percent per year. In sum, public health expenditure in Canada grew rapidly as a share of GDP during recessions and was generally followed by periods of cost containment (Figure 10.1).

### Cost Containment Reforms

The most successful cost containment reforms in Canada took place during the late 1970s and the 1990s, focused on the introduction of budget caps, supply constraints, and price controls. The budget caps and price controls, which were part of a broader fiscal consolidation effort that took place during the mid-1990s, delivered fiscal surpluses for over a decade.

*Budget caps and supply constraints.* A 1977 federal-provincial fiscal program[4] reformed funding arrangements for health care, including hospitalization, medical care, and extended health care. Under the new system, the federal government

---

[4]The legislative act that incorporates these reforms was the Established Program Financing Act of 1977.

adjusted funding to each province according to an "escalator" that took into consideration per capita growth and inflation—federal transfers were established prospectively and were no longer based on actual provincial expenditures. Initially, each province received an equal per capita transfer for health insurance. The provincial and territorial governments had flexibility to spend the transfer based on their needs and priorities.[5] Per capita transfers were frozen in the early 1990s before resuming in the late 1990s at a rate below GDP growth.

In 1992, budgets for hospitals and physicians were capped in one of the most important cost containment policies of the 1990s. Since nearly all hospitals and physicians in the Canadian health system are financed by federal funds, implementing a budget cap was relatively simple. Canadian physicians are mostly funded based on fee for service, reimbursed by the public system. The fee-for-service rates were also controlled by the federal government in the 1990s and were set to decline once a certain level of service was reached.[6] In addition, the federal government limited enrollment in medical schools starting in 1991, effectively imposing supply constraints—albeit with a significant time lag.

*Price controls.* Pharmaceutical policies differ substantially among the provinces. Since 1994, reimbursement price freezes have been used in at least two provinces (Ontario and Quebec). British Columbia was the first province to use internal or therapeutic price referencing.[7]

## Impact and Durability of Reforms

The annual growth rate of health care expenditure per capita declined from 15.7 percent in 1975 to 1.2 percent in 1977. The impact of spending can also be examined by looking at excess cost growth—that is, real growth of per capita public health spending minus real per capita GDP growth (Figure 10.2). The average excess cost growth in the five years following the 1977 reform was 2.9 percent compared with 0.6 percent in the five preceding years.[8] The cost containment effects of the federal-provincial funding arrangement of 1977 were thus short lived, and excess cost growth increased after two years.

The cost containment reforms in the 1990s considerably reduced public expenditure and were more durable than the 1970s reform. Per capita public spending on health stood at $1,299 in 1996 compared with $1,516 in 1991.[9] Excess cost growth was high during the deep recession in the early 1990s—although real

---

[5]Federal funding for provinces had two components: a tax transfer and a cash transfer. Since 1977, the cash component was derived by linking the growth rate of the transfer to the growth rate in per capita output—in effect, a budget cap. This "escalator" factor was extended to all transfers in 1982. Since then, the government has regularly adjusted the escalator to contain costs: the escalator was reduced twice, in 1986 and 1989, to increase by 2 percentage points and 3 percentage points below the growth rate of GNP, respectively.

[6]In some Canadian provinces where individual physicians are reimbursed according to a fee-for-service schedule, once a certain billing threshold is reached, a declining fraction of the negotiated fee is reimbursed.

[7]Therapeutic price referencing relates the value of an innovative patented product to the price of the established treatments on the market, including off-patent products deemed therapeutically equivalent.

[8]Excess cost growth is defined as the difference between real public health spending growth and real GDP growth.

[9]Throughout this chapter all dollar amounts are in U.S. (not Canadian) dollars.

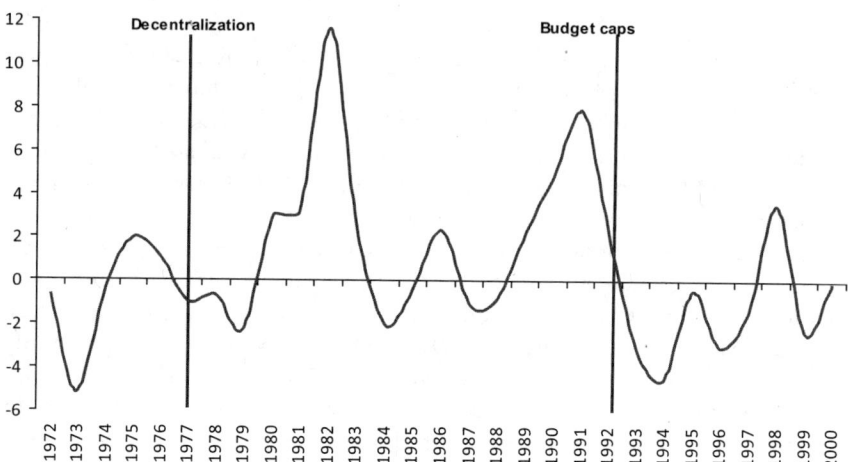

**Figure 10.2**  Canada: Excess Cost Growth and Key Reform Episodes, 1972–2000 (Percent)
Source: Organization for Economic Cooperation and Development, OECD Health Data; and IMF staff estimates.

growth in total public expenditure was relatively strong as well. However, annual excess cost growth averaged −2.3 percent over the rest of the 1990s following the cost containment efforts. Public expenditure on inpatient care declined sharply, from $743 in 1991 to $563 in 1995. As a result of the budget squeeze, hospitals that reduced the number of beds were closed or merged. This led to a decline in the number of both hospitals and beds over the 1990s (Rapoport, Jacobs, and Jonsson, 2009). Reductions in spending during the 1990s may also have resulted in longer waiting times for treatment of breast cancer (Mayo and others, 2001).

The structure of health financing has been affected by reform. As a share of total health spending, public spending declined from 74 percent in 1990 to 70 percent in 2008. Nonetheless, per capita spending in Canada has been higher than the average among OECD countries for the last four decades. As an example, Australia, which has similar health outcomes, managed to spend on average less on health care services.

## Lessons

The Canadian experience shows that budget caps and supply constraints can be successful in limiting growth in health care spending. A single-payer system can facilitate the implementation of cost-cutting reforms and help control administrative costs. Although health indicators remain strong in Canada, this strength is achieved with a lower level of health sector inputs (e.g., hospital beds per thousand). For public contract systems such as Canada's, an important issue is the role of private insurance in the provision of health services. At present, this is allowed in Canada only for services not covered by the public sector (pharmaceuticals and dental services).[10] Expanding the role of private insurance in Canada could potentially reduce waiting lists for services, but would likely increase total health spending.

---

[10]In the United Kingdom, in contrast, private insurance is allowed for a large number of services and generally used as a top-up to the National Health Service, although many treatments are not covered or are restricted.

**TABLE 10.2**

Finland: Key Health Indicators, 1970–2008[a]

| | 1970 | 1980 | 1990 | 2000 | 2008 | OECD 2008[b] |
|---|---|---|---|---|---|---|
| GDP per capita ($US, purchasing power parity) | 3,328 | 9,033 | 17,608 | 25,653 | 35,853 | 35,617 |
| Primary balance (percent of GDP) | — | 3.1 | 7.0 | 9.6 | 5.6 | 1.5 |
| General government primary expenditure (percent of GDP) | — | 39.6 | 42.2 | 40.8 | 40.8 | 40.4 |
| Total health spending (percent of GDP)[c] | 5.5 | 6.3 | 7.7 | 7.2 | 8.4 | 9.3 |
| Public (percent of GDP) | 3.3 | 4.1 | 5.1 | 5.1 | 6.1 | 6.8 |
| Private (percent of GDP) | 1.5 | 1.3 | 1.5 | 2.1 | 2.2 | 2.5 |
| Public health spending per capita ($US) | 99 | 549 | 1,752 | 1,203 | 3,179 | 2,028 |
| Out-of-pocket spending (share of total health spending) | 23.8 | 18.4 | 15.5 | 22.3 | 19.4 | 16.8 |
| Formal health care coverage (share of population) | 100.0 | 100.0 | 100.0 | 100.0 | 100.0 | 99.0 |
| Life expectancy (years at birth) | 70.8 | 73.6 | 75.0 | 77.7 | 79.5 | 79.9 |
| Measles immunization (share of children 12–23 months) | — | 70.0 | 87.0 | 96.0 | 98.7 | 89.6 |
| Physicians (per 1,000 population) | — | — | 2.2 | 2.5 | 2.7 | 3.1 |
| Hospital beds (per 1,000 population) | — | — | 8.3 | 7.5 | 6.5 | 5.6 |

Sources: Organization for Economic Cooperation and Development; World Health Organization; World Bank, *World Development Indicators*; and IMF staff estimates.
[a]Years as indicated or latest available.
[b]OECD advanced economy unweighted average.
[c]Health spending components (as a share of GDP) may not add up to the total. Public health spending data have been adjusted to account for structural breaks.

# FINLAND

## Overview of the Health Care System

The health care system in Finland is based on both public insurance and public provision and offers universal coverage. There is a public spending target for health care, although it is not binding. Patients have limited choice, and gatekeeping is strictly applied. The system is decentralized, with municipalities responsible for health care delivery.

Municipal taxes, state subsidies, and user charges are the financing sources for municipal services, including health care. In 2008, the ratio of total health spending to GDP was 8.4 percent, below the OECD advanced economy average of 9.3 percent. Public expenditure on health services was 6.1 percent of GDP (Table 10.2). The role of the private sector is small, although it has grown during the last two decades—it peaked at 29 percent of total health expenditure in 2000 and stood at 26 percent in 2008.

## Experience with Health Reforms: 1990s

### Spending Trends

From the mid-1960s through the 1980s, public health care spending in Finland grew substantially, rising from 3.2 percent of GDP in 1965 to 6.3 percent in 1990 and then surging to 7.2 percent by 1992 when Finland suffered from a deep

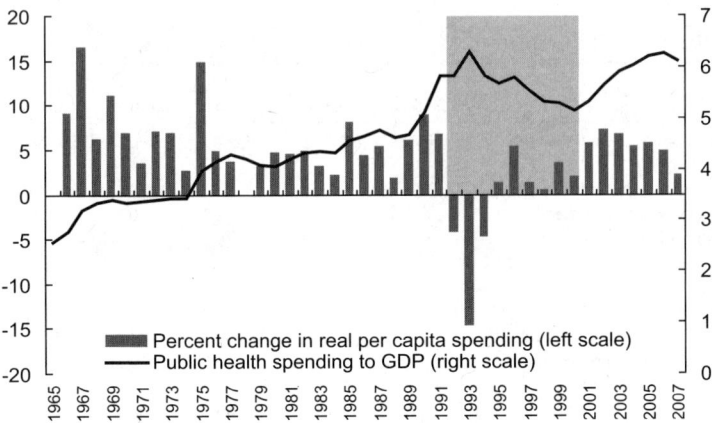

**Figure 10.3** Finland: Public Health Spending, 1965–2007 (Percent)
Sources: Organization for Economic Cooperation and Development, OECD Health Data; and IMF staff estimates.

recession. The central government fiscal balance deteriorated rapidly from the surpluses in the years before the 1991 crisis, reaching a deficit of over 10 percent of GDP by 1994. The ratio of public health expenditure to GDP dropped to 5.1 percent in 2000. However, the decline was partially offset in subsequent years, and in 2008 the ratio remained roughly at the same level as in 1990. Public health spending per capita was $3,179 in 2008, above the OECD advanced economies average (Figure 10.3).

## Cost Containment Reforms

Cost containment in Finland in the 1990s was achieved through a comprehensive set of reforms that took effect at both macro- and micro-levels and included supply constraints, budget caps, price controls, and public management and coordination reforms.

*Public management and coordination.*[11] All municipal hospitals were brought under the ownership and management of 21 health care districts in order to improve coordination within districts and reduce the duplication of services. In 1991, multipurpose hospital districts were created in which each municipality was required to be a member.

*Supply constraints and price controls.* The early 1990s also saw a push to reduce the number of beds in hospitals and the move from an integrated system to a public contract model. In 1997, two hospital districts moved to case-based, diagnosis-related-group (DRG) pricing, and by 2000 most hospital districts followed suit.[12]

---

[11]The Hospital Act of 1990 and the Specialized Medical Care Act of 1991.
[12]DRGs specify treatment protocols and medical conditions and provide an associated price schedule. DRGs can help control spending by reducing incentives for unnecessary treatments to address a given medical condition. Where reimbursement is based on DRGs, health providers are not compensated for costs of treatment that exceed the price schedule associated with a given DRG.

*Budget caps.* Central subsidies to local governments were reduced and greater responsibility devolved to municipalities as the main purchasers of health care services. The financing of operating costs also changed, and hospitals' revenues became dependent on the type and number of services that municipalities purchased from them.[13] Under the new system, subsidies were calculated prospectively according to weighted capitation based on the expected population of patients. This helped address the incentives for overprovision of health care services that exist under a system in which expenditures are reimbursed ex post.[14] Local governments were given more freedom on decisions related to administration, user charges, and arrangement of services. Subsequently, the share of municipal taxes in financing increased. In addition, out-of-pocket payment increased during the 1990s with the abolition of tax deduction for medical expenses and an increase in user charges.

*Pharmaceutical cost sharing.* Early policies focused on increasing cost sharing. Subsequently, controlling the prices of drugs became the key issue at the end of 1990s. The fixed deductible for drugs was raised three times: in 1990, 1992, and 1994. In 1993, regulations were changed to allow pharmacists to substitute cheaper generic options for a prescribed drug.

## Impact and Durability of Reforms

Cost containment reforms had a significant impact on expenditure in the 1990s, and health outcomes remained strong. Per capita public spending on health stood at $1,203 in 2000, compared with $1,752 in 1990. In 2008, life expectancy in Finland stood at 79.5 years, slightly below the OECD advanced economies average of 79.9 years.

Per capita expenditure on inpatient care fell from $743 to $563 between 1991 and 1995. However, by 2008 it rose to $792. As a result of supply-side reforms, hospital beds per 1,000 people decreased from 8.3 in 1990 to 6.5 in 2008. The average excess cost growth in the five years following the state subsidy reforms of 1993 was −3.3 percent, compared with 4.4 percent in the five preceding years (Figure 10.4).

DRG case-based pricing was introduced in hospitals gradually between 1997 and 2000. The average excess cost growth for total public health expenditure during this period was −2.9 percent, although it increased again after 2000. This may have reflected the government's attempt to eliminate waiting times by awarding earmarked funding to municipalities and hospital districts in 2001 (Häkkinen, 2005).

Public expenditure on pharmaceuticals has grown rapidly since 1990, rising from 5.5 percent to 8.4 percent of health expenditure between 1991 and 1995 and to 10 percent by 2000. The substitution of pharmaceutical care for inpatient care may have been one of the reasons behind this increase in pharmaceutical expenditure.

---

[13]Before 1993, hospitals received about half of their revenues from the state and the other half from municipalities.

[14]In the previous system, past expenditures were used as the basis for calculating subsidies.

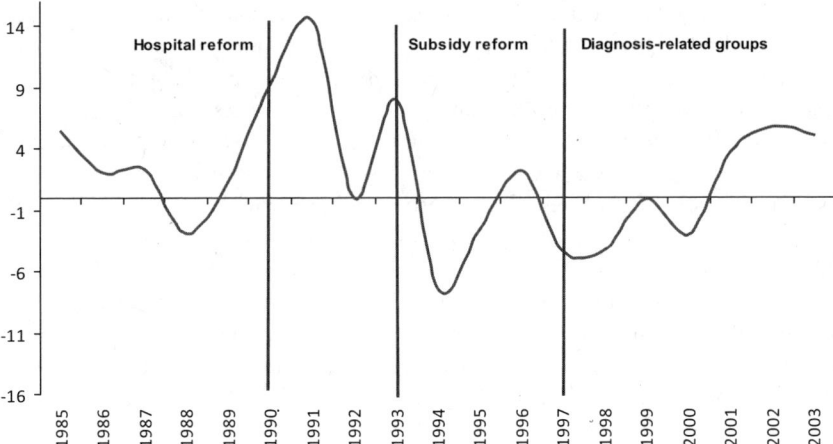

**Figure 10.4** Finland: Excess Cost Growth and Key Reform Episodes, 1985–2003 (Percent)
Sources: Organization for Economic Cooperation and Development, OECD Health Data; and IMF staff estimates.

## Lessons

The 1990s in Finland witnessed a number of reforms in the health sector acting on different fronts. They successfully contained spending. The reform of subsidies in 1993 was implemented during a severe crisis and under a generalized fiscal consolidation effort. The case of Finland is indicative of how costs are better controlled when growth of spending is addressed by a combination of measures acting at various levels—when macro-level reforms are supplemented with micro-level, efficiency-enhancing measures.

The push toward decentralized health provision has had some unintended consequences, however, including inequality between regions. In 2005, the difference in expenditure levels between municipalities was €1,000 per capita (Rapoport, Jacobs, and Jonsson, 2009). Municipalities have different coverage, and hospital districts have different waiting times. Small municipalities cannot benefit from economies of scale to provide specialized health services, and there is no nationally set guideline to determine prices for hospital services. The two-tier financing system (state subsidies and municipal financing) also encourages cost shifting from municipal to nonmunicipal institutions. For example, municipalities and the state cover the drugs used during inpatient care and outpatient care, respectively. This provides an incentive for hospitals to use outpatient drug therapy.

## ITALY

### Overview of Health Care System

Italy's National Health Care System (NHS) coverage is universal, encompassing both citizens and permanent residents. It follows a public integrated model, financed through payroll and general taxation, with both private and public

**TABLE 10.3**

Italy: Key Health Indicators, 1970–2008[a]

| | 1970 | 1980 | 1990 | 2000 | 2008 | OECD 2008[b] |
|---|---|---|---|---|---|---|
| GDP per capita ($US, purchasing power parity) | 3,387 | 9,210 | 17,595 | 25,597 | 31,709 | 35,617 |
| Primary balance (percent of GDP) | — | — | −1.4 | 5.5 | 2.5 | 1.5 |
| General government primary expenditure (percent of GDP) | — | — | 42.4 | 41.7 | 41.7 | 40.4 |
| Total health spending (percent of GDP)[c] | — | — | 7.7 | 8.1 | 9.1 | 9.3 |
| Public (percent of GDP) | — | — | 6.1 | 5.8 | 7.0 | 6.8 |
| Private (percent of GDP) | — | — | 1.6 | 2.2 | 2.1 | 2.5 |
| Public health spending per capita ($US) | — | — | 1,222 | 1,122 | 2,737 | 2,028 |
| Out-of-pocket spending (share of total health spending) | — | — | 17.1 | 24.5 | 19.5 | 16.8 |
| Formal health care coverage (share of population) | 93.0 | 100.0 | 100.0 | 100.0 | 100.0 | 99.0 |
| Life expectancy (years at birth) | 72.0 | 74.0 | 77.1 | 79.8 | 81.5 | 79.9 |
| Measles immunization (share of children 12–23 months) | — | — | 43.0 | 74.1 | 89.5 | 89.6 |
| Physicians (per 1,000 population) | — | — | — | — | — | 3.1 |
| Hospital beds (per 1,000 population) | 10.6 | 9.6 | 7.2 | 4.7 | 3.8 | 5.6 |

Sources: Organization for Economic Cooperation and Development; World Health Organization; World Bank, *World Development Indicators*; and IMF staff estimates.

[a]Years as indicated or latest available.

[b]OECD advanced economy unweighted average.

[c]Health spending components (in percent of GDP) may not add up to the total. Public health spending data have been adjusted to account for structural breaks.

provision of services. Since the reforms initiated in 1992, the system has been highly decentralized, with regions and local health units bearing strong administrative and financial independence. The state sets "essential levels of care," namely, a positive list of services that must be uniformly provided by all regions.[15] Delivery rests with the local public enterprises (Aziende Sanitarie Locali, or ASL), vertically integrated and funded by the region through capitated budgets. In 2008, public expenditure on health services was 7.0 percent of GDP, compared with an OECD advanced economies average of 6.8 percent (Table 10.3). The role of the private sector has remained broadly stable over the last decade at just over 2 percent of GDP, below the OECD average.

## Experience with Health Reforms: 1991–99

### Spending Trends

The 1990s were a period of fiscal consolidation and falling inflation, after an earlier combination of loose fiscal and tight monetary policy. Between 1992 and 1995, the general government primary balance swung into a surplus, exceeding 4 percent of GDP, and the debt ratio recorded its first decline in

---

[15]In practice, essential levels of care are hard to define.

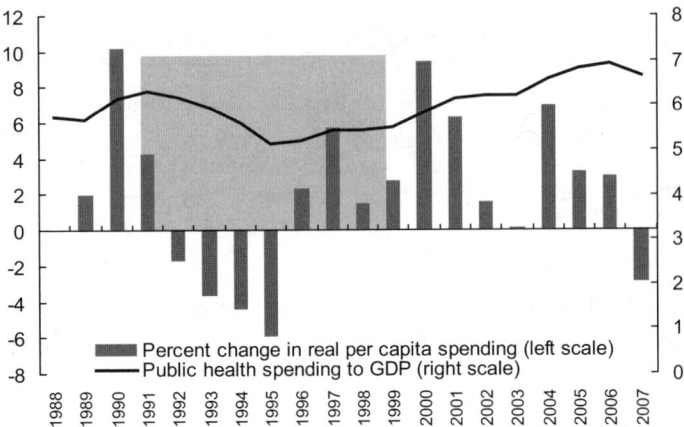

**Figure 10.5**   Italy: Public Health Spending, 1988–2007 (Percent)
Sources: Organization for Economic Cooperation and Development, OECD Health Data; and IMF staff estimates.

many years. The consolidation involved a shift from revenue-based adjustment in the period up to 1993 to expenditure-based adjustment in 1994–95. Public spending on health declined from 6.3 percent of GDP in 1991 to 5.5 percent in 1999. Real per capita growth of public spending was negative, declining by 4.6 percent on average between 1993 and 1995 (Figure 10.5). For most of the period under consideration, real growth of public spending was below the OECD average. Private spending continued to grow, albeit at a slower pace than earlier.

## Cost Containment Reforms

Italy's health care cost containment efforts in the 1990s focused on the control of doctors' salaries and on pharmaceutical expenditure and were part of the wider fiscal consolidation strategy.

*Price controls.* Italy's ratio of doctors to residents is among the highest in the European Union. All doctors employed by the NHS are salaried and have civil servant status. General practitioners (GPs) and pediatricians are paid on the basis of capitation. During 1991–95, control of NHS salaries was achieved in three ways: (1) renewal of national contracts was postponed several times; (2) increases in salaries were less generous than in the past and were kept in line with inflation; and (3) bonuses and compensation for overtime were cut.

The pharmaceutical sector was also targeted for cost control. In 1994, the positive list was redefined and fixed charges were introduced for all prescriptions.[16] Moreover, a ceiling on the pharmaceutical budget for 1994 was set to be 2.4 percent lower than the 1993 budget in nominal terms. Government funding

---

[16]A positive list is a list of drugs that are reimbursable. At times, governments also define negative lists, which include medicine that cannot be reimbursed.

for several hundred active ingredients was suspended. A new system of prices was also defined so that prices could not exceed average European prices. In 1995, a generalized price cut was mandated by the government, and one year later a version of reference pricing was introduced. However, prices were not freed, and this resulted in the delisting of over 400 drugs.[17] Further, in 1997, pharmacists were forced to sell at discount to the NHS with margins that were the smallest for the highest-priced drugs (Fattore, 1999).

*Public management and coordination reforms.* These were implemented in 1992, granting administrative and financial independence to ASLs (and to hospitals) and reducing their number. The reforms also introduced quasi-markets, in which providers competed for contracts. The design of these markets was different from that used in the United Kingdom, but it never materialized fully since the separation between purchasing and provision was left to the regions, which maintained a dominant role in managing the system.

*Supply constraints and contracting methods.* Hospitals were not the direct target of cost containment measures in the early 1990s, mainly because the pressure to contain costs at the regional level was weaker and because the introduction of mixed markets (see below) was in conflict with hospital cost containment. However, in 1996 a national program of bed closures was launched, and in 1994 DRGs were introduced and made operational in 1996 with the aim of introducing market competition, containing costs, and enhancing efficiency. Another cost containment measure was to cut capital expenditure, which in 1995 equaled only 0.3 percent of current expenditure.

## Impact and Durability of Reforms

Italy has been very effective in cutting public expenditure on pharmaceuticals. Between 1991 and 1995, such expenditure declined by 35 percent in nominal terms. However, delisting drugs has in some cases caused a rise in private spending, whose share of total spending on drugs increased from 20 percent in 1990 to over 35 percent in 1995 (Fattore, 1999) (Figure 10.6).

In 2001, drug copayments were abolished and restrictions on prescribing were reduced. As a result, doctors prescribed more expensive and newer drugs, so earlier reductions in expenditure on drugs were reversed. Subsequent measures cut prices on drug industry sales to the NHS, introduced reference prices for drugs no longer covered, reintroduced restrictions on prescribing, and imposed a ceiling on drug spending by the NHS.

The new payment system provided incentives for the regions to cut hospital tariffs or individual DRG tariffs when expenditure exceeded a predetermined level, also discouraging the provision of certain services. Combined with that, tighter limits on the number of beds led to a decline in hospitalization rates and length of stay. The measures aimed at controlling salaries were very effective, curbing their growth to less than an 8 percent increase over the entire 1991–95

---

[17]Delisting implies that a drug will no longer be eligible for reimbursement from the public sector.

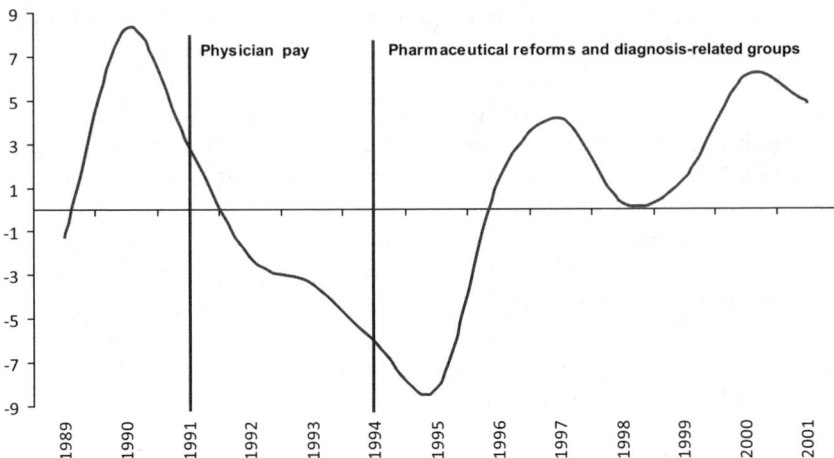

**Figure 10.6** Italy: Excess Cost Growth and Key Reform Episodes, 1989–2001 (Percent)
Source: Organization for Economic Cooperation and Development, OECD Health Data; and IMF staff estimates.

period. The decline in public sector spending on health over the same period was only partly compensated for by a growth in private-sector spending, so that total expenditure on health declined by 7.2 percent. Excess cost growth of public health spending was 3.7 percent between 1992 and 1996.

However, measures aimed at containing growth of NHS salaries were only partly sustainable. First, the postponement of contracts only postponed expenditure but did not cut it, since the new contracts included compensation for the period not covered by the previous contracts (Fattore, 1999). Moreover, control of the variable part of salaries may have weakened incentives and decreased health sector output, leading to a shifting of some services to the private sector.

## Lessons

The Italian experience of the 1990s demonstrates that control of prices and cost sharing can represent very effective cost containment measures that have an immediate effect on public health care spending. However, their durability is questionable. Restraining salaries can provide incentives to reduce output and create pressures to increase salaries in the future. Increases in copayments beyond a certain level may undermine the system's equity objectives and be subsequently reversed.

What appears to have been crucial to the success of Italy's cost containment was the shared recognition that, in contrast with its past behavior, the central government would not bail out regional health systems burdened with large deficits. This belief was made possible by the preceding severe financial crisis and the Maastricht constraints for joining the European Union's Economic and

Monetary Union. Indeed, health spending accelerated again after it was clear that Italy would join the Economic and Monetary Union (Bordignon and Turati, 2009).

# THE NETHERLANDS

## Overview of Health Care System

The Dutch health care system is a public contract model with a social insurance tradition. A single compulsory insurance scheme was introduced in 2006, changing the role of health insurers and patients. There is little reliance on regulation of prices paid by third-party payers to control public spending growth. GPs play the role of gatekeepers; their referral is required for hospital care and specialist care.

The health insurance system has three sectors: (1) compulsory social health insurance for high-risk patients, (2) a sickness fund scheme, and (3) voluntary health insurance. The compulsory social health insurance is financed with contributions linked to the level of income. The basic insurance is financed by a flat-rate premium and an employer contribution. Supervision of the system has been passed on from the government to independent bodies. In 2008, the ratio of total health spending to GDP was 9.9 percent, ½ percentage point higher than the OECD average of 9.3 percent, while public health spending was 7.4 percent of GDP (Table 10.4).

**TABLE 10.4**

| Netherlands: Key Health Indicators, 1970–2008[a] | | | | | | |
|---|---|---|---|---|---|---|
| | **1970** | **1980** | **1990** | **2000** | **2008** | **OECD 2008[b]** |
| GDP per capita ($US, purchasing power parity) | 4,013 | 9,869 | 17,624 | 29,403 | 41,189 | 35,617 |
| Primary balance (percent of GDP) | — | — | — | 5.6 | 2.5 | 1.5 |
| General government primary expenditure (percent of GDP) | — | — | — | 42.2 | 43.0 | 40.4 |
| Total health spending (percent of GDP)[c] | — | 7.4 | 8.0 | 8.0 | 9.9 | 9.3 |
| Public (percent of GDP) | 4.2 | 5.3 | 5.5 | 5.2 | 7.4 | 6.8 |
| Private (percent of GDP) | 2.7 | 2.3 | 2.6 | 2.9 | 2.5 | 2.5 |
| Public health spending per capita ($US) | — | 659 | 1,055 | 1,209 | 3,971 | 2,028 |
| Out-of-pocket spending (share of total health spending) | — | — | — | 9.0 | 5.7 | 16.8 |
| Formal health care coverage (share of population) | 69.0 | 68.3 | 61.4 | 97.6 | 98.8 | 99.0 |
| Life expectancy (years at birth) | 73.7 | 75.9 | 77.0 | 78.0 | 80.2 | 79.9 |
| Measles immunization (share of children 12–23 months) | — | 91.0 | 94.0 | 96.0 | 96.0 | 89.6 |
| Physicians (per 1,000 population) | — | — | — | — | — | 3.1 |
| Hospital beds (per 1,000 population) | — | — | 5.8 | 4.9 | 4.3 | 5.6 |

Sources: Organization for Economic Cooperation and Development; World Health Organization; World Bank, *World Development Indicators*; and IMF staff estimates.

[a]Years as indicated or latest available.

[b]OECD advanced economy unweighted average.

[c]Health spending components (in percent of GDP) may not add up to the total. Public health spending data have been adjusted to account for structural breaks.

## Experience with Health Reforms: Early 1980s and 1990s

### Spending Trends

Per capita public health expenditures grew significantly in the 1970s. Between 1972 and 1982, the real rate of growth averaged 4 percent and the ratio of public health expenditure to GDP also increased, from 4.1 to 5.5 percent. Between 1982 and 1990, the rate of public health expenditure growth declined considerably, averaging less than 2 percent. Health spending picked up again in the early 1990s, reaching 6.2 percent of GDP by 1993. This was followed by a period of negative average annual growth rates (1995 to 2000), and by 2000 the share of public health expenditure declined to 5.0 percent of GDP (Figure 10.7). By 2008, public health spending per capita was $3,971, compared with the OECD average of $2,032.

### Cost Containment Reforms

There were three waves of cost containment reform in the Netherlands in the 1980s and 1990s. They focused first on hospitals' budgets, then on managed competition, and finally, starting in 1994 after a change in government, on greater use of budget caps and pharmaceutical reform.

*Budget caps.* The main focus of policies in the early 1980s was reining in the inpatient sector. The change in the hospital reimbursement system started in 1983 when the government replaced open-ended reimbursement with a global budget system. In 1984, the government expanded the scope of budget controls to include all inpatient care, moving to annual budgets calculated prospectively. In 1985, part of the budget was made variable, which was prospectively determined and depended on the agreement between hospitals and health insurers

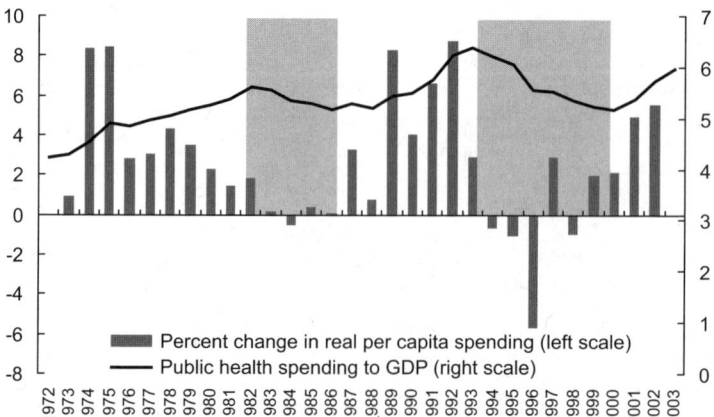

**Figure 10.7**   Netherlands: Public Health Spending, 1972–2003 (Percent)
Sources: Organization for Economic Cooperation and Development, OECD Health Data; and IMF staff estimates.

in four types of inpatient care.[18] Under prospective payment, payment is no longer based on expenditures but is instead based on expected demand and the provision of services at reasonable cost. In 1988, the weight in the budget formula increased for hospitals that provided more-sophisticated medical services. During the reforms beginning in 1994, there was also an expansion of global budgets. In addition, certain services (dental care, nonprescription drugs, and physiotherapy, among others) were delisted from the compulsory social health insurance and sickness funds.

*Public management and coordination.*[19] The original proposals to introduce managed competition in 1987 and 1989 were never fully implemented. The reform attempted to implement a single national insurance provider. The 1994 reforms for managed competition reversed some of the previous elements. For instance, reform of the financing system was suggested to replace provision of basic health insurance for all citizens. The new health insurance scheme addressed this by introducing the following features: (1) setting up a risk equalization scheme between health insurers, with risk adjustments for factors such as age, gender, labor status, and health status;[20] and (2) moving from an overall budget scheme and introducing diagnosis-related-groups reimbursement (Schut, 1996).

*Pharmaceutical supply and price reforms.* In 1996, reference pricing was introduced, and the government set maximum prices on two-thirds of prescription drugs covered by social health insurance. Moreover, between 1993 and 1998, the government limited the inclusion of innovative medicines in the benefit package of social health insurance.

## Impact and Durability of Reforms

Budgetary control on the hospital sector in the mid-1980s seemed to slow growth of public health expenditure (inpatient care has the highest share of public health expenditure). Average excess cost growth in the five years following 1983 was −1.3 percent compared with 2.5 percent in the five preceding years. Public health expenditure declined from 5.5 percent to 5.4 percent of GDP over 1982–88. However, public health spending rose again to 6.7 percent of GDP in 1993 during the unsuccessful attempts to introduce managed competition. This implies that per capita public spending grew at an average of 5 percent a year during 1987–93.

Public health expenditure started to decline again in the early 1990s, despite increasing coverage, although the main cost containment reform started after a change in the government in 1994. The decline in expenditure may be attributed to the introduction in 1991 of the drug reimbursement system, which defined limits for reimbursement of drugs by the sickness fund,

---

[18]Number of expected inpatient days, admissions, day treatments, and visits to the outpatient clinics per hospital per year were considered.
[19]Dekker Plan of 1987 and the Simons Plan of 1989.
[20]Pharmaceutical cost groups and diagnostic cost groups are proxies for health status.

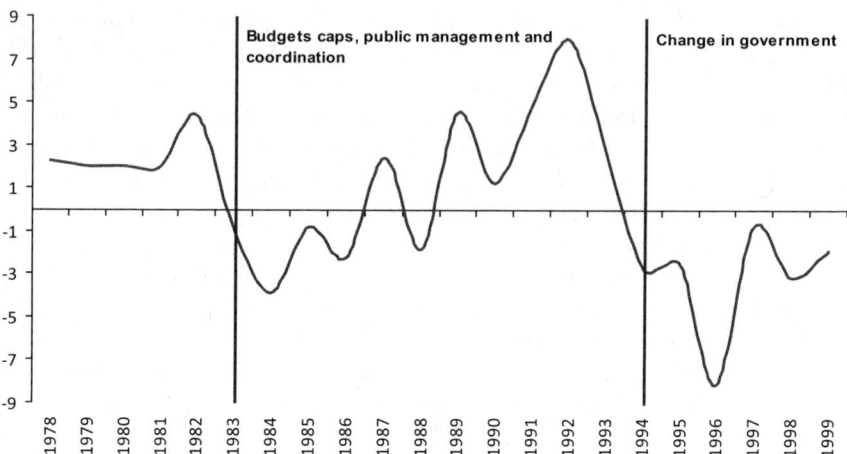

**Figure 10.8** Netherlands: Excess Cost Growth and Key Reform Episodes, 1978–99 (Percent)
Source: Organization for Economic Cooperation and Development, OECD Health Data; and IMF staff estimates.

and to delisting of some health services (e.g., cosmetic surgery in 1991 and eye treatment in 1993).

The mix of different cost containment reforms introduced by the coalition government (1994) reduced public health expenditure substantially. Average excess cost growth in the five years after 1994 was −3.3 percent compared with 4.4 percent in the preceding years (Figure 10.8). Public health expenditure declined from 6.5 percent of GDP in 1994 to 5.2 percent in 2000. Reforms in this period changed the form of financing expenditure. The role of private spending increased (i.e., the share of private spending in total spending increased from 21.6 percent to 32 percent between 1993 and 2000).

### Lessons

The Netherlands succeeded with cost containment despite having multiple public and private insurers. Nonetheless, the history of the managed-competition reform in the Netherlands indicates that implementing radical reform of the system is difficult and takes time.

## SWEDEN

### Overview of the Health Care System

Sweden has a decentralized, public integrated health care system, and delivery of health care is primarily the responsibility of the 18 country councils and two regional bodies.

There is no gatekeeping. Automatic health coverage is provided to the entire population and financed from taxes. In 2008, total health spending to GDP was 9.4 percent, in line with the OECD average for advanced economies, while public health spending was 7.7 percent of GDP, compared with 6.8 percent in advanced OECD countries. Private spending has increased from 0.7 to 1.7 percent of GDP in the last three decades (Table 10.5).

## Experience with Health Reforms: 1980s and Early 1990s

### Spending Trends

Public spending on health as a share of GDP was the highest in the OECD in the 1980s and 1990s. However, since then, near-zero excess cost growth has seen it fall to around seventh. In line with wider public spending, health expenditures expanded considerably in the 1960s and 1970s—growing at an average real rate of about 4.5 percent between 1970 and 1982, and increasing by over 2 percentage points of GDP. Between 1982 and 1994, expenditure growth slowed dramatically, with a mildly negative average annual growth rate over this period—public health spending declined from 8.5 percent of GDP to 7.2 percent. However, these figures include two changes in definition—in 1985, care for the mentally handicapped was excluded from health and classified under education and social services, and in 1992 care for the elderly was transferred to social services. Public health care spending picked up after 1995, but by 2007 was still below the levels seen in 1982 (Figure 10.9).

**TABLE 10.5**

| Sweden: Key Health Indicators, 1970–2008[a] | | | | | | |
|---|---|---|---|---|---|---|
| | **1970** | **1980** | **1990** | **2000** | **2008** | **OECD 2008[b]** |
| GDP per capita ($US, purchasing power parity) | 4,586 | 10,578 | 19,319 | 27,761 | 36,946 | 35,617 |
| Primary balance (percent of GDP) | — | −1.8 | 8.1 | 7.2 | 4.1 | 1.5 |
| General government primary expenditure (percent of GDP) | — | — | — | 50.0 | 48.0 | 40.4 |
| Total health spending (percent of GDP)[c] | 6.8 | 8.9 | 8.2 | 8.2 | 9.4 | 9.3 |
| Public (percent of GDP) | 5.9 | 8.3 | 7.5 | 7.2 | 7.7 | 6.8 |
| Private (percent of GDP) | 0.9 | 0.7 | 0.8 | 1.2 | 1.7 | 2.5 |
| Public health spending per capita ($US) | 257 | 1,310 | 2,116 | 1,936 | 3,994 | 2,028 |
| Out-of-pocket spending (share of total health spending) | — | — | — | — | 15.6 | 16.8 |
| Formal health care coverage (share of population) | 100.0 | 100.0 | 100.0 | 100.0 | 100.0 | 99.0 |
| Life expectancy (years at birth) | 74.7 | 75.8 | 77.6 | 79.7 | 81.0 | 79.9 |
| Measles immunization (share of children 12–23 months) | — | — | 96.0 | 91.0 | 96.0 | 89.6 |
| Physicians (per 1,000 population) | 1.3 | 2.2 | 2.6 | 3.1 | 3.6 | 3.1 |
| Hospital beds (per 1,000 population) | — | — | — | — | — | 5.6 |

Sources: Organization for Economic Cooperation and Development; World Health Organization; World Bank, *World Development Indicators*; and IMF staff estimates.
[a]Years as indicated or latest available.
[b]OECD advanced economy unweighted average.
[c]Health spending components (in percent of GDP) may not add up to the total. Public health spending data have been adjusted to account for structural breaks.

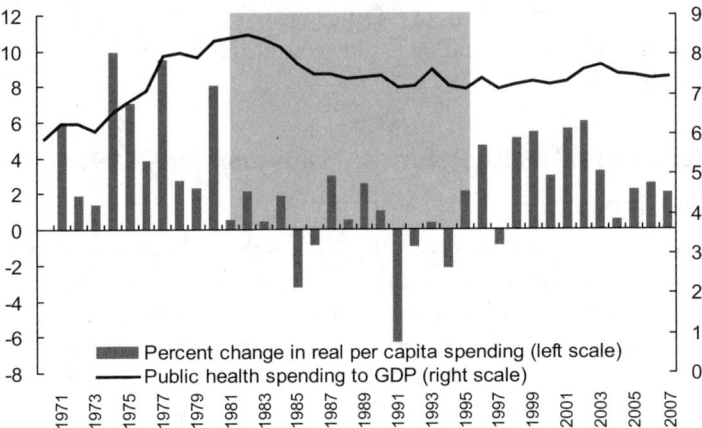

**Figure 10.9** Sweden: Public Health Spending, 1970–2007 (Percent)
Sources: Organization for Economic Cooperation and Development, OECD Health Data; and IMF staff estimates.

## Cost Containment Reforms

*Budget caps, public management and coordination reforms, and increased involvement of local governments.* The reforms of the 1980s focused on budget caps, public management and coordination (including greater decentralization), and price controls. Market mechanisms were introduced in the early 1990s.[21]

In 1982, the power over health care activities of county councils, the second level of government, was consolidated. County councils gradually got more responsibility for planning and resource allocation and started using global budgets for recurrent and capital expenses, connected to both formal and informal rules on how to carry out activities. These reforms were introduced at different times and with different strategies across county councils.

In 1985, the regulatory and planning capacity of county councils was further strengthened by transferring to them the responsibility for costs of both publicly and privately owned ambulatory health care, which previously lay with the Swedish Social Insurance Agency. The main purpose was to cap central government grants allocated to the health sector. Before the reform, outpatient services from both public and private providers were paid for by the Social Insurance Agency according to fee for service. After the reform, grants were disbursed to county councils based on weighted capitation—private practitioners were still paid on a fee-for-service basis, but had to negotiate with the council on volumes. In 1988, the parliament prohibited county councils and municipalities from raising income taxes starting in 1990, owing to concerns about the growth in expenditure. In 1991, decisions on copayment levels for outpatient care were also

---

[21]This section deals with the Health and Medical Care Act of 1982, the Dagmar reform of 1985, and the Ädel reform of 1992.

devolved to county councils, and these payments were increasingly used to steer patients toward primary care.

*Price controls.* In the late 1980s, the payment system changed; health service providers were to be reimbursed through prospective per case payments instead of through activity budgets. Reference prices for generic drugs were introduced in 1993. DRG pricing was also introduced in the 1990s, particularly in Stockholm County.

*Public management and coordination: improving incentives under decentralization.* A more market-oriented approach took over from the earlier focus on planning and cost containment following the election of a new conservative-led government in 1992. The reform involved the transfer of responsibility for providing long-term care to the elderly and disabled from the county councils to local municipalities. The objective was to integrate activities related to the care of the elderly and the mentally handicapped with municipal social services, thereby improving quality and efficiency. Fees were levied on municipalities if they were not ready to receive discharges from hospitals, for example, if no nursing homes were lined up.

*Market mechanisms.* The 1990s also saw greater use of planned markets and purchaser-provider splits: by 1994, 14 out of the then 26 councils had separate purchasing organizations, which varied in form.[22]

## Impact and Durability of Reforms

Global budgets, introduced by county councils, clearly seemed to have slowed the rate of health expenditure expansion—average excess cost growth in the five years following the 1982 reforms was −2.4 percent compared with 3.5 percent in the five preceding years. However, the introduction of global budgeting was not sufficient with regard to efficiency. Although the system performed well with respect to cost containment, productivity was still considered low. In the five years following the 1985 reform to the payment system, excess cost growth was negative (−0.8 percent) (Figure 10.10).

The subsequent fiscal squeeze on county councils triggered by limits to taxation in 1990 led to the accumulation of debt and hospital closures. Long waiting lists arose, especially for elective care. To address this problem, in 1992, a three-month guarantee was issued for 12 selected treatments, with the patient offered treatment at a hospital in another county or at a private facility after three months. Nonetheless, long waiting lists for elective treatment continued to be a challenge for county councils and may have been one of the reasons behind the growing market for voluntary health insurance.

The reforms also led to changes in the level and composition of inputs. Since 1992, the number of hospital beds has decreased substantially, falling by more than 40 percent between 1993 and 2003. This reduction is partly due to a decline

---

[22]Purchaser-provider splits (Italy, Sweden, and the United Kingdom) separate the roles of purchasing and providing health care services within government, allowing for more active contracting for health care services by primary care providers.

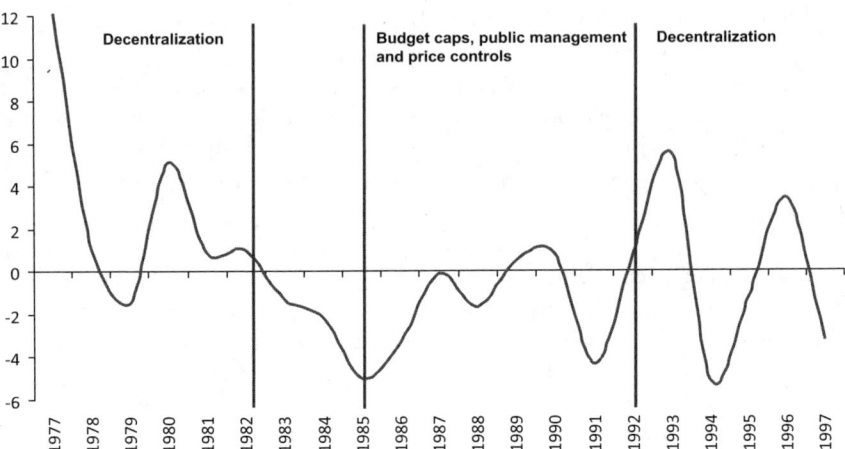

**Figure 10.10** Sweden: Excess Cost Growth and Key Reform Episodes, 1977–97 (Percent)
Source: Organization for Economic Cooperation and Development, OECD Health Data; and IMF staff estimates.

in the number of non-acute-care beds (e.g., for long-term patients, psychiatric patients), resulting from the 1992 reform. The number of health care staff has also decreased since the beginning of the 1990s, with the exception of physicians, nurses, and midwives. The number of staff employed in the health care sector dropped from 46.7 per 1,000 people in 1992 to 31.9 in 2002. The main reason for this reduction in staff was the shift from hospital-based care toward primary care. Overall, health expenditure avoided the wider surge in total public expenditure in 1989–93.

Other reforms not focused solely on cost containment, but also on performance, were pursued throughout the 1990s. While there is some evidence of increases in productivity, it is hard to attribute this entirely to these reforms, which, at least to some degree, might have made achievement of cost containment easier.

## Lessons

Budget caps and public management and coordination reforms, in particular those related to strengthening accountability under decentralization, were successful in reining in spending. However, some negative consequences in regard to supply could not be avoided. To counter this, market mechanisms were introduced to improve efficiency.

# UNITED KINGDOM

## Overview of the Health Care System

The United Kingdom has a public integrated health care system—heavily regulated, with strict gatekeeping, little decentralization, and central government budget financing of health care provision. Hospital providers are part of the government sector. Reforms in the 1990s introduced elements of a public contract model. Health care is universal and free. In 2008, total health spending was 8.7 percent of GDP, compared with the OECD average of 9.3, while public health spending was 7.2 percent of GDP, compared with the OECD advanced economies average of 6.8 percent (Table 10.6). Though small, private spending has more than doubled since 1980 as a percentage of GDP.

## Experience with Health Reforms: Late 1970s and 1980s

### Spending Trends

From the 1960s through the mid-1970s, health care spending in the United Kingdom grew at an average real rate of 4.8 percent per year—episodes of real declines in 1962 and 1969 were quickly reversed—and health expenditure climbed as a percentage of GDP from 3.3 percent to almost 5 percent. Expenditure rose particularly fast as a share of GDP during the recession that followed the 1973 oil shock and the 1973–74 stock market crash. The late 1970s saw a short period of negative or low real growth rates and a three-year period of declining expenditure as a percentage of GDP as first Labor and then the new Conservative governments tried to rein in spending. However, the public-health-spending-to-GDP ratio rose again during the recession of the early 1980s before falling from 4.9 percent in 1981 to 4.5 percent in 1989. Real growth rates of health spending during the first

**TABLE 10.6**

| United Kingdom: Key Health Indicators, 1970–2008[a] | | | | | | |
|---|---|---|---|---|---|---|
| | 1970 | 1980 | 1990 | 2000 | 2008 | OECD 2008[b] |
| GDP per capita ($US, purchasing power parity) | 3,586 | 8,380 | 16,322 | 26,074 | 36,128 | 35,617 |
| Primary balance (percent of GDP) | — | 1.5 | 2.0 | 4.0 | −2.7 | 1.5 |
| General government primary expenditure (percent of GDP) | — | 35.9 | 34.1 | 34.9 | 38.3 | 40.4 |
| Total health spending (percent of GDP)[c] | 4.5 | 5.6 | 5.9 | 7.0 | 8.7 | 9.3 |
| Public (percent of GDP) | 3.6 | 4.6 | 4.6 | 5.6 | 7.2 | 6.8 |
| Private (percent of GDP) | 0.6 | 0.6 | 1.0 | 1.5 | 1.5 | 2.5 |
| Public health spending per capita ($US) | 86 | 480 | 875 | 1,403 | 3,171 | 2,028 |
| Out-of-pocket spending (share of total health spending) | — | 8.6 | 10.6 | 13.4 | 11.1 | 16.8 |
| Formal health care coverage (share of population) | 100.0 | 100.0 | 100.0 | 100.0 | 100.0 | 99.0 |
| Life expectancy (years at birth) | 71.9 | 73.2 | 75.7 | 77.9 | 79.7 | 79.9 |
| Measles immunization (share of children 12–23 months) | — | 53.0 | 87.0 | 88.0 | 85.9 | 89.6 |
| Physicians (per 1,000 population) | 0.9 | 1.3 | 1.6 | 2.0 | 2.6 | 3.1 |
| Hospital beds (per 1,000 population) | — | — | — | 4.1 | 3.4 | 5.6 |

Sources: Organization for Economic Cooperation and Development; World Health Organization; World Bank, *World Development Indicators*; and IMF staff estimates.
[a]Years as indicated or latest available.
[b]OECD advanced economy unweighted average.
[c]Health spending components (in percent of GDP) may not add up to the total. Public health spending data have been adjusted to account for structural breaks.

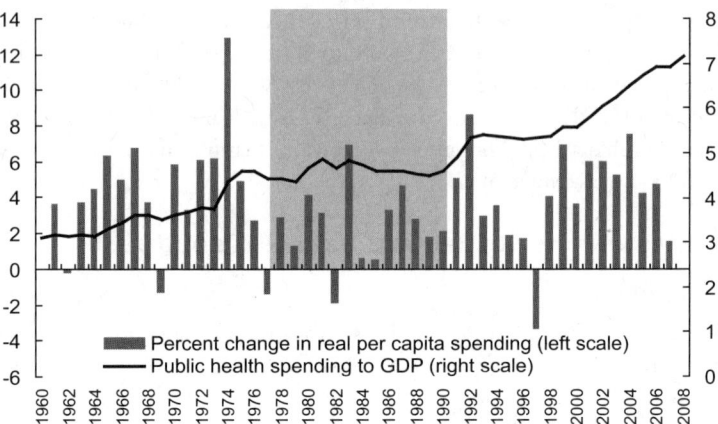

**Figure 10.11** United Kingdom: Public Health Spending, 1960–2008 (Percent)
Sources: Organization for Economic Cooperation and Development, OECD Health Data; and IMF staff estimates.

two Thatcher governments averaged 2.2 percent, compared with 4.2 percent in the preceding decade, which included both a Conservative and Labor government (Figure 10.11).

## Cost Containment Reforms

Budget caps were implemented in the United Kingdom in the early 1970s, while the 1980s saw a number of public management and coordination reforms implemented.

*Budget caps.* Following the rapid growth in public spending on health in the first half of the 1970s, the government revised the budgeting process to strengthen the control function. Cash limits were introduced on departmental budgets, which were not allowed to overshoot. The National Health Service (NHS) budget was set centrally and subject to these cash limits, which were determined by weighted capitation.[23]

*Public management and coordination.* A reform aimed at containing costs and reducing bureaucracy started in 1982, with the abolishment of 90 area health authorities (a level of administration that sat between the budget-holding regional health authority and district management teams). Subsequently, in 1983, the Griffiths Report introduced the concept of "new public management" into the NHS—essentially replacing consensus-style teams with hierarchical general management. Managers were expected to hold health service professionals accountable for levels, types, and quality of services, and also for resource use.

*Introduction of market mechanisms and competition.* Another series of reforms was initiated in 1989, with the objective of introducing competition, to provide

---

[23]Age structure, local inputs costs, and standardized mortality rates were originally used as weighting factors.

incentives for efficiency and responsiveness. The Working for Patients reform proposed introducing an internal market with a split between health care purchasers and health care providers. This created two types of purchasers: the district health authorities and GP groups (fund holders). The fund-holding GP could be described as a "mini-ambulatory" health maintenance organization (HMO), that is, an entity that receives a fixed, prepaid sum of money from which it must deliver or arrange for the delivery of secondary health care to a defined population group. NHS Trusts (hospitals that became semi-independent) were established on the provider side and had to compete for contracts from GP fund holders and district authorities to provide services. Other reforms to restrict the supply of certain outputs emerged in 1989 to reduce costs: access to eye tests and equipment was restricted.

*Pharmaceutical reforms.* Since 1957, the U.K. government has regulated the profitability of pharmaceutical companies instead of product prices. The Pharmaceutical Price Regulation Scheme (1993–98) limited the return on capital deriving from sales to the NHS. Other efforts to control costs have included limiting the supply of pharmaceutical outputs by delisting of products from NHS coverage (1985 and 1993) and attempting to reduce overprescription by GPs. A prescribing scheme in 1992 and 1994 tried to increase awareness of GPs by comparing actual prescription costs with a target.

*Other reforms.* Under a new Labor government, the fund-holding scheme was replaced in 1998 by primary care trusts. Most GPs work in these trusts, which are financed by weighted capitation from the Department of Health budget—pharmaceutical spending is included in the budgets. This reform maintained the earlier focus on primary-care-led health services. While effectively a mechanism to both control resources and coordinate care, the political imperative of the day was to increase health expenditure and close the performance gap with OECD countries.

In the 1990s efforts focused on improving performance in the NHS. The Health of the Nation Green Paper set out a public health strategy based on setting quantified targets and measuring performance against these targets. The Patient's Charter set out for the first time patients' rights and the standards of service they could expect from the NHS, such as reduced waiting times and increased responsiveness.

## Impact and Durability of Reforms

At 1.2 percent, excess cost growth in the five years following the cash limits was one-fourth the growth rate in the five preceding years. Excess cost growth in the five years after the Griffiths Reforms was −1.3 percent, compared with 1.1 percent in the five years before (Figure 10.12). However, the Conservative government held total public spending broadly flat in real terms over most of the 1980s, so it is hard to attribute the cost containment to these specific reforms as opposed to budget limits.

The impact of the internal market and GP fund holding on health expenditure is hard to determine. While Working for Patients was published in 1989,

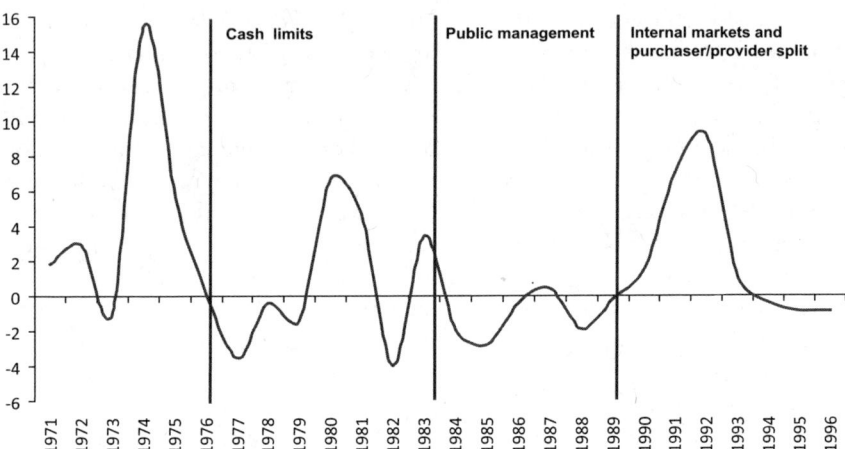

**Figure 10.12** United Kingdom: Excess Cost Growth and Key Reform Episodes, 1971–96 (Percent)
Source: Organization for Economic Cooperation and Development, OECD Health Data; and IMF staff estimates.

the reforms were legislated in 1990, and implementation started the following year. By then, the government had initiated other reforms more focused on improving performance, as opposed to efficiency. Moreover, further reforms followed to develop primary-care-led health services—the Health Authorities Act (1995) led to closer integration of primary and secondary care through the creation of merged district health authorities and family health service authorities, and in 1996, regional health authorities were replaced by offices of the NHS Executive.

## Lessons

The 1976 cash limits imposed on the NHS appear to have temporarily reduced the growth of health expenditure. However, limits could be renegotiated every year, and expenditure began to climb again in subsequent years. The abolishment of area health authorities and introduction of new management practices seems to be associated with more success in controlling expenditure growth, even five years after initial implementation.

Critics of the 1989 reforms point to increased transaction costs associated with the internal market, which may not have been offset by productivity gains, the emphasis on costs over quality, and increasing inequity. Others point to evidence that fund-holding GPs have seen less growth in prescription costs than non–fund holders. A 1996 Audit Commission report on the topic was inconclusive.

Long waiting times for elective inpatient care have been a feature of the NHS since its formation in 1948 and have worsened during the cost containment period. Since 2001 there has been a considerable effort to reduce long waiting times, driven by a strictly enforced system of waiting-time targets for individual hospital trusts (Smith and Goddard, 2009).

# UNITED STATES

## Overview of the Health Care System

The United States has a mainly private insurance and provider health care system. Private insurance is largely tied to employment, but individuals can purchase policies in the nongroup market. There are two large public insurance programs, both incorporated in the Social Security Act of 1965: Medicare for the elderly and Medicaid for the poor; each one covers about 15 percent of the population. There is some gatekeeping through managed care. In 2008, total health spending to GDP was 16 percent, compared with the OECD average for advanced economies of 9.3 percent, while public health spending was 7.4 percent of GDP, compared with the OECD average of 6.8 percent. Private spending has grown rapidly in recent decades, but less than public spending (Table 10.7).

## Experience with Health Reforms: Mid- to Late 1990s

### Spending Trends

The growth in U.S. public health expenditure took off in the mid-1960s with the creation of Medicare and Medicaid. From 1970 through 1990 public health care spending in the United States grew at an average real rate of about 5.3 percent per

**TABLE 10.7**

| United States: Key Health Indicators, 1970–2008[a] | | | | | | |
|---|---|---|---|---|---|---|
| | **1970** | **1980** | **1990** | **2000** | **2008** | **OECD 2008[b]** |
| GDP per capita ($US, purchasing power parity) | 4,998 | 12,180 | 23,054 | 35,078 | 47,193 | 35,617 |
| Primary balance (percent of GDP)[c] | — | — | — | — | −3.9 | 1.5 |
| General government primary expenditure (percent of GDP)[c] | — | — | — | 31.1 | 33.6 | 40.4 |
| Total health spending (percent of GDP)[d] | 7.1 | 9.0 | 12.2 | 13.4 | 16.0 | 9.3 |
| Public (percent of GDP) | 2.6 | 3.7 | 4.8 | 5.8 | 7.4 | 6.8 |
| Private (percent of GDP) | 4.5 | 5.3 | 7.4 | 7.6 | 8.5 | 2.5 |
| Public health spending per capita ($US) | 129 | 445 | 1,102 | 2,032 | 3,507 | 2,028 |
| Out-of-pocket spending (share of total health spending) | 34.2 | 23.4 | 19.4 | 14.5 | 12.1 | 16.8 |
| Formal health care coverage (share of population) | — | — | — | 85.0 | 85.2 | 99.0 |
| Life expectancy (years at birth) | 70.9 | 73.7 | 75.3 | 76.7 | 77.9 | 79.9 |
| Measles immunization (share of children 12–23 months) | — | — | — | 90.5 | 92.1 | 89.6 |
| Physicians (per 1,000 population) | — | — | — | 2.3 | 2.4 | 3.1 |
| Hospital beds (per 1,000 population) | 7.9 | 6.0 | 4.9 | 3.5 | 3.1 | 5.6 |

Sources: Organization for Economic Cooperation and Development; World Health Organization; World Bank, *World Development Indicators*; and IMF staff estimates.
[a]Years as indicated or latest available.
[b]OECD advanced economy unweighted average.
[c]Data prior to 2000 are not available based on the IMF's 2001 *Government Finance Statistics Manual* (GFSM2001) methodology.
[d]Health spending components (in percent of GDP) may not add up to the total. Public health spending data have been adjusted to account for structural breaks.

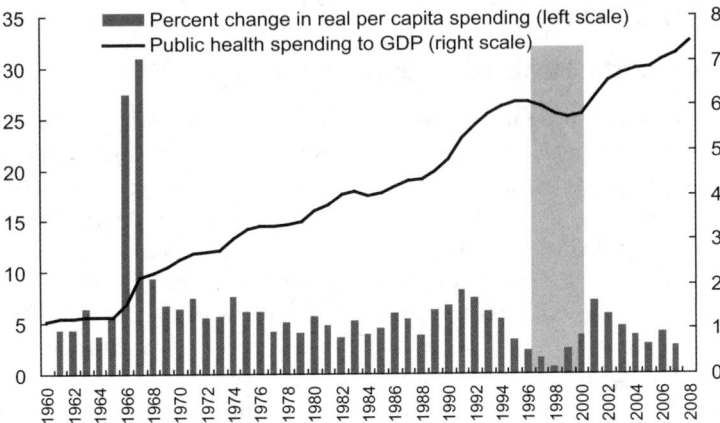

**Figure 10.13** United States: Public Health Spending, 1960–2008 (Percent)
Sources: Organization for Economic Cooperation and Development, OECD Health Data; and IMF staff estimates.

year. Health expenditure climbed from 1.2 percent of GDP in 1960 to 6.1 percent in 1995. The Clinton administration focused on fiscal deficit reduction—over the 1990s the U.S. federal deficit was steadily reduced, becoming a surplus in 1997/98. Growth rates of health expenditure began to moderate in real terms in the first part of the 1990s and dipped below the rate of increase in output in the second part of the decade—by 1999 public health expenditure had dropped to 5.7 percent of GDP. However, expenditure growth resumed strongly in 2001 and public health spending to GDP rose by over 1½ percentage points by 2008 (Figure 10.13).

## Cost Containment Reforms

*Public management and coordination—including the use of managed care.* Developments that also helped control the growth of public health care expenditure in the 1990s could be broadly identified as public management and coordination reforms. In 1992, Medicare established a new fee schedule for physicians receiving payments from Medicare in order to help control costs and provide consistency—the Resource-Based Relative Value Scale assigns procedures performed by a physician or other medical provider a relative value, which is adjusted by geographic region and multiplied by a conversion factor. The conversion factor is adjusted annually. The new fee schedule set prices based on three separate producer factors: physician work, practice expense, and malpractice expense. It is currently used by Medicare and by nearly all HMOs.

The 1990s saw a rapid expansion in managed care and away from the traditional fee-for-service reimbursement from insurance.[24] This was particularly true

---

[24]Managed care is a general term for health plans that are proactive in seeking to affect the type or amount of care their enrollees receive. Unlike traditional insurance-based plans, they tend to have detailed contractual or employment relationships with health care providers. Cost containment approaches used in managed care include requiring preauthorization for services (gatekeeping), selective contracting with providers who are willing to accept the plan's payment arrangements, and utilization reviews.

in the private sector, in which employers embraced it as an opportunity to gain control over sharply increasing costs. However, the popularity of managed care in the private sector encouraged its adoption by the public sector, for example, through the expansion of Medicare managed care—enrollment in Medicare managed care increase from 1 million in 1991 to more than 6 million in 1999 (Lagoe, Aspling, and Westert, 2005). State governments also availed themselves of managed-care plans for Medicaid to constrain the growth of costs.

*Other reforms.* An attempt to reduce Medicare spending by reducing payments to providers such as hospitals and nurse practitioners took place in 1997–98. However, those payments were raised in subsequent legislation a year later. The Medicare+Choice program was established, which pays private health plans a monthly capitation fee based on the amount Medicare spends per beneficiary in that area, leaving the administration of benefits and payment of providers to each health plan. This period witnessed also the introduction of the State Children's Health Insurance Program, which was an effort to expand the coverage of uninsured children. States could obtain matching funding at a higher rate than available under Medicaid for children in poor families.

## Impact and Durability of Reforms

Studies have found evidence that managed-care arrangements—particularly HMOs—can reduce health care costs, at least in the short term, resulting from the transfer of purchasing power toward well-informed and price-sensitive insurers and employers. Also, their presence is associated with reduced cost growth in areas with a higher penetration of managed-care plans (Docteur and Oxley, 2003). Managed care in the United States appears to have been fairly effective in reducing public sector expenditure, with excess cost growth dropping fairly steadily, by −0.7 percent, over the second half of the 1990s as use of this system was expanded (Figure 10.14).

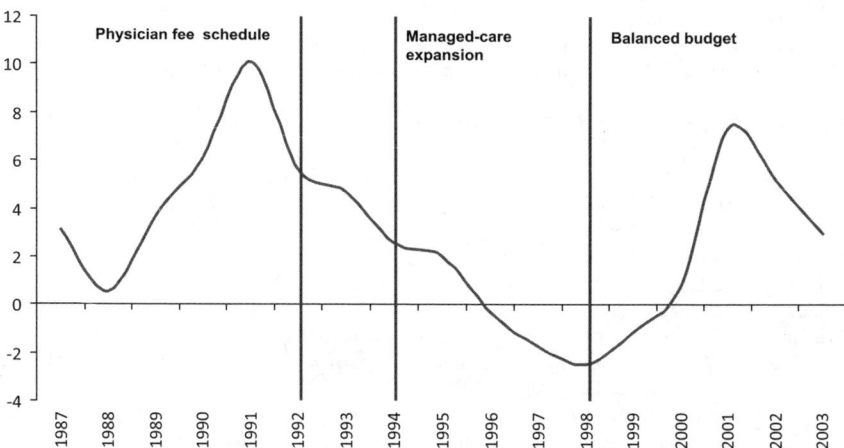

**Figure 10.14**   United States: Excess Cost Growth and Key Reform Episodes, 1987–2003 (Percent)
Sources: Organization for Economic Cooperation and Development, OECD Health Data; and IMF staff estimates.

However, the same strategies (i.e., limits on patient choice of provider and treatment, intervention in physician practice decisions, and selective contracting with alternative providers and suppliers) that helped contain costs fed discontent among both health care providers and patients, resulting in a backlash against managed care's most restrictive characteristics. There followed a move away from such tight plan management and a rise in the concept of patients' rights—this led to Congressional debate on national legislation to establish certain patients' rights; passage of state-level patients' rights laws; and the imposition by many purchasers, including the federal government, of patient rights on the health plans with which they do business.

## Lessons

The major slowdown in health spending in the United States in the 1990s was attributable to the widespread adoption of managed care, which introduced gate-keeping and utilization reviews into the system. Negotiated prices for health services between the managed-care plans and providers also contributed to lower care costs.

## REFERENCES

Bordignon, M., and G. Turati, 2009, "Bailing Out Expectations and Public Health Expenditure," *Journal of Health Economics*, Vol. 28, No. 2, pp. 305–21.

Docteur, E., and H. Oxley, 2003, "Health-Care Systems: Lessons from the Reform Experience," OECD Health Working Paper No. 9 (Paris: Organization for Economic Cooperation and Development).

Fattore, G., 1999, "Cost Containment and Reforms in the Italian National Health Service," in *Health Care and Cost Containment in the European Union,* ed. by E. Mossialos and J. Le Grand, pp. 733–81 (Aldershot: Ashgate).

Häkkinen, U., 2005, "The Impact of Changes in Finland's Health Care System," *Health Economics*, Vol. 14, pp. S101–18.

Lagoe, R., D. Aspling, and G. P. Westert, 2005, "Current and Future Developments in Managed Care in the United States and Implications for Europe," *Health Research Policy and Systems*, Vol. 3, No. 4, pp. 360–73.

Mayo, N., S. Scott, N. Shen, J. Hanley, M. Goldberg, and N. MacDonald, 2001, "Waiting Time for Breast Cancer Surgery in Quebec," *Canadian Medical Association Journal*, Vol. 164, No. 8, pp. 1133–38.

Mossialos, E., and J. Le Grand, 1999, *Health Care and Cost Containment in the European Union* (Aldershot: Ashgate).

Or, Z., C. Cases, M. Lisac, K. Vrangbæk, U. Winblad, and G. Bevan, 2010, "Are Health Problems Systemic? Politics of Access and Choice under Beveridge and Bismarck Systems," *Health Economics, Policy and Law*, Vol. 5, No. 3, pp. 269–93.

Oxley, H., and M. MacFarlan, 1995, "Health Care Reform: Controlling Spending and Increasing Efficiency," OECD Economic Study No. 24 (Paris: Organization for Economic Cooperation and Development).

Rapoport, J., P. Jacobs, and E. Jonsson, 2009, "Canada," Chapter 2 in *Cost Containment and Efficiency in National Health System: A Global Comparison*, ed. by J. Rapoport, P. Jacobs and E. Jonsson (Weinheim: Wiley-Blackwell).

Schut, F.T., 1996, "Health Care System in Transition: The Netherlands Part I—Health Care Reform in the Netherlands: Miracle or Mirage?" *Journal of Public Health Medicine*, Vol. 18, No. 3, pp. 278–84.

Smith, P., and M. Goddard, 2009, "The English National Health Service: An Economic Health Check," OECD Economics Department Working Paper No. 716 (Paris: Organization for Economic Cooperation and Development). Available at http://dx.doi.org/10.1787/222707115448.

Tsai, T.C., and J. Ji, 2009, "Neoliberalism and Its Discontents: Impact of Health Reforms in Chile," *Harvard International Review* (June). Available at http://hir.harvard.edu/agriculture/neoliberalism-and-its-discontents.

Wagstaff, A., W. Yip, M. Lindelow, and W. Hsiao, 2009, "China's Health System and Its Reform: A Review of Recent Studies," *Health Economics*, Vol. 18, pp. S7–23.

# CHAPTER 11

# Challenges in Reforming the Japanese Health Care System

MASAKO II

Countries around the world are anxiously searching for better health care systems. The development of health care systems has followed a different route in each country, influenced by differing cultures, histories, and ideas. One distinction that is particularly vital when developing a health care system is whether health care is considered to be a merit good (a good that everyone should receive) or a general resource (something that should be allocated depending on the ability of the users to pay for it). Since 1961, Japan's health insurance system has been predicated on the first of these two approaches.

Experience shows that when a health system works well, it produces good results. Japan has achieved some of the world's best scores on health indicators, with low infant mortality rates and very long average life expectancy. Weaknesses in the Japanese health care system include an inefficient primary care system, a lack of differentiation among health care providers, and a lack of standard clinical guidelines.

Currently, Japan's health care system is facing a financial crisis. Health care costs are increasing partly as the result of the aging of Japanese society, the development and utilization of new health care technologies, and patients' increasing demand for quality and safety in health care. Health sector reforms have been discussed for more than a few decades, but they have made slow progress and have not been very effective because of the outdated decision-making process that has been preserved. Meanwhile, the Republic of Korea (in 1989) and Taiwan Province of China (in 1995) have adopted national health insurance, following the Japanese health insurance model, and have been moving ahead of Japan through various reforms, such as integration in the management of health insurance and the introduction of information technology infrastructure.

This chapter first gives an overview of Japan's health care system and then discusses current challenges and lessons that can be drawn from the Japanese experience. A brief history of the country's health care system is included in Appendix 11.1.

The author would like to thank Dr. Etsuji Okamoto, National Institute of Public Health, for his insightful comments.

# OVERVIEW OF THE HEALTH CARE SYSTEM

## Health Care Provision and Financing

One of the characteristics of the Japanese health care system is the high number of hospital beds per capita. As a result, employee-bed or nurse-bed staffing ratios are lower than the Organization for Economic Cooperation and Development (OECD) average, and to maintain the utilization rate of all these beds, hospital stays are also longer than the OECD average (Table 11.1).

During the 1990s, most of the OECD nations greatly reduced the number of acute-care hospital beds, the average length of acute-care hospital stays, and the number of acute-care hospitals per capita. In Japan, those figures are also decreasing, but they are still the highest. A lack of differentiation among types of health care providers and a lack of standard clinical guidelines both contribute to these rather high figures. For example, in Japan a hospital is defined as any medical facility with at least 20 beds, including long-term geriatric care facilities.

Another characteristic is a free-access system that allows people to be examined and treated at the medical institutions of their choice, regardless of their symptoms. This has led to the problem of excessive demand from patients who visit doctors too often. The frequency of doctor visits per patient in Japan far outstrips the OECD average.

Private hospitals dominate the hospital system, accounting for 80 percent of the hospital market and 70 percent of total hospital beds. The government's control over prices for all procedures, drugs, and devices applies uniformly to all physicians and hospitals, both public and private.

Hospitals operate as closed systems, and clinic-based doctors do not have visiting privileges at hospitals. Exclusive specialty board certification is nonexistent, and doctors practice in any specialty they choose. Hospitals and physicians

**TABLE 11.1**

## International Comparison of Health Care Systems

| | Number of hospital beds per 1,000 people | Number of physicians per 1,000 people (% of GP) | Number of nurses per 1,000 people | Average length of stay in hospital: acute care (days) | Number of doctor visits as outpatient (times/year) | CT per 1 million | MRI per 1 million |
|---|---|---|---|---|---|---|---|
| United States | 3.1 | 2.43 (12%) | 10.75[b] | 5.5 | 4.0 | 34.3 | 25.9 |
| Japan | 13.8 | 2.15 (–) | 9.54 | 18.8 | 13.4 | 97.3 | 43.1 |
| Germany | 8.2 | 3.56 (18%) | 10.68 | 7.6 | 7.8 | | |
| United Kingdom | 3.4 | 2.61 (29%) | 9.52 | 7.1 | 5.9 | 7.4 | 5.6 |
| France | 6.9 | 3.34[a] (49%) | 7.93[b] | 5.2 | 6.9 | | |
| Canada | 3.5 | 2.27[a] (48%) | 9.20 | 7.5 | 5.7 | 13.9 | 8.0 |
| Republic of Korea | 7.8 | 1.86 (37%) | 4.36 | 10.6[c] | 13.0 | 37.1 | 19.0 |
| The Netherlands | 4.3 | 2.88 (24.9%) | 11.24 | 5.9 | 5.9 | 10.3 | 10.4 |
| Australia | 3.9 | 2.97 (51%) | 10.08 | 5.9 | 6.4 | 38.8 | 5.9 |

Source: Organization for Economic Cooperation and Development, OECD Health Data 2010.
[a]Professionally active physicians.
[b]Professionally active nurses.
[c]Data are for 2003.

freely choose their practice mode and are paid on a fee-for-service basis. Referrals and an organized distribution of functions between facilities have been sorely lacking. Clinics frequently provide both primary and more-specialized care. This lack of differentiation of providers and the lack of an efficient primary care system are serious weaknesses in the system. Since the Japanese do not have a sound system of primary care provided by well-trained family doctors (note that the number of general practitioners [GPs] in Table 11.1 is missing for Japan), it is quite common for patients to visit a general hospital or even a university medical center for minor illnesses without referral.

Japan has no postgraduate training system for primary care. Traditionally, Japanese primary care has been managed by specialists who are self-trained to be generalists. The Japan Medical Association, which represents mainly doctors working at clinics, has strong vested political power, and this has delayed various health care reforms, including the establishment of formal training in family practice.

Sophisticated medical technology has spread to small clinics and general hospitals, both of which compete for outpatients. Fee-for-service payment further induced demand for new medical technologies, such as computed tomography (CT) and magnetic resonance imaging (MRI), causing their wide proliferation. Although bureaucratic control helps the Japanese government contain health care expenditure, the high prevalence of CTs and MRIs is extraordinary (Table 11.1).

Remuneration is fundamentally through a fee-for-service system, but a diagnosis-based per diem payment system, called diagnostic procedure combination in Japan, has gradually been introduced in acute-care hospitals. The payments that doctors receive for medical services are the same nationwide, with rates set by the central government. Therefore, there are few incentives for quality improvement and little competition among providers on quality (Tatara and Okamoto, 2009).

A country comparison of health expenditure data (Table 11.2) reveals wide variation in the ratio between public and private expenditure, with Japan at the

**TABLE 11.2**

## Proportion of Health Care Expenditure by Funding Source

| | Japan | Germany | France | Republic of Korea | United Kingdom | United States | Sweden | Canada |
|---|---|---|---|---|---|---|---|---|
| Public spending on health (%) | 81.3 | 76.7 | 78.4 | 54.7 | 81.9 | 45.3 | 81.6 | 69.9 |
| General taxation (%) | 15.4 | 9.2 | 5.1 | 12.9 | 81.9 | 32.6 | 81.6 | 68.5 |
| Social health insurance (%) | 64 | 67.5 | 73.4 | 41.8 | | 12.7 | | 1.4 |
| Private spending on health (%) | 18.7 | 23.3 | 21.6 | 45.3 | 18.1 | 54.7 | 18.4 | 30.1 |
| Out-of-pocket (%) | 15.1 | 13.4 | 7 | 36.5 | 11.4 | 12.3 | 16.2 | 14.9 |
| Private health insurance (%) | 2.6 | 9.2 | 12.9 | 3.8 | 1.4 | 35.1 | 0.1 | 12.3 |
| Expenditure on prescription drug/total health care expenditure | 17.3 | 13.3 | 13.5 | 16.4 | | 10.3 | 9.7 | 14.3 |
| Total health care expenditure/ GDP | 8.3 | 11.3 | 11.7 | 6.5 | 9.3 | 16.2 | 9.9 | 10.9 |

Source: Organization for Economic Cooperation and Development, OECD Health Data 2010.

high end of public expenditure (81.3 percent) and the Republic of Korea less committed to public funding (54.7 percent).

A more-detailed breakdown of the sources of health care financing shows that while public expenditure in Japan is made up of general taxation and social health insurance, private expenditure is a mix of out-of-pocket spending for coinsurance and for services not covered by health insurance, together with the premiums paid by families and individuals for private health insurance. As shown in Table 11.2, the share of total health spending that is privately financed varies considerably across countries. The range is as high as 45.3 percent in the Republic of Korea to as low as around 18 percent in Japan, Sweden, and the United Kingdom.

The aging of Japan's population is causing severe problems for the country's public finances. The elderly often suffer from multiple symptoms, and given the lower copayments required of the elderly, they often visit specialists for each episode of an illness.

The elderly in Japan account for a significant portion of the country's health care expenditures. People age 65 and over make up 22 percent of the total population but account for 54.6 percent of the total expenditure, and in 2008 the per capita health expenditure among the elderly was almost four times higher than the amount spent on the 0–64 age group.[1] As will be discussed in the next sections, financing structures for the elderly do not have incentive mechanisms to contain health expenditure among the elderly.

## Organizational Structure of Health Insurance Programs in Japan

The most important health care policy in postwar Japan was the establishment of equality through guaranteed health care access for all Japanese. Under the universal public insurance system, people can receive universal medical service any time, anywhere throughout the country at a relatively low cost. In addition, in 1997 the coinsurance rate for employees' health insurance and community health insurance was made equal, with the insured paying 30 percent and insurers paying 70 percent of medical costs. Benefits are uniform nationally.

However, there are large regional differences in the actual amount of health care services that people receive, which are reflected in both medical expenses and the amount of public insurance premiums. Unequal contributions are one of the most serious issues in the health care insurance system (Table 11.3).

Japan's universal health insurance system is composed of four main insurance systems, namely, (1) community health insurance for the self-employed and unemployed (National Health Insurance—NHI), (2) society-managed employees' health insurance, (3) public-corporation-run health insurance, and (4) the medical system for the elderly, age 75 and over. Each system comprises multiple insurance plans or subschemes with differing premium rates. Insurance premiums

---

[1]Since 2000, long-term care insurance has been in effect, and benefits offered under this insurance are not included in these statistics.

**TABLE 11.3**

## Japanese Health Care Insurance Schemes

| | National Health Insurance | Society-managed health insurance | Public-corporation-run health insurance | Medical system for the elderly (age 75 and over) |
|---|---|---|---|---|
| Number of insurers (2009) | 1,788 | 1,497 | 1 | 47 |
| Number of members (2009) | 35.97 million | 30.34 million (insured: 15.91 million) (dependent: 14.43 million) | 34.7 million (insured: 19.5 million) (dependent: 15.22 million) | 13.46 million |
| Average age of members (2008) | 49.2 years | 33.8 years | 36.0 years | 81.8 years |
| Average income (total compensation) (2008) | ¥0.79 million per member (former provisory income) | ¥2.93 million per member (total compensation) | ¥2.18 million per member (total compensation) | ¥0.758 million per member (former provisory income) |
| Health care expenses per member (2008) | ¥282,000 | ¥126,000 | ¥145,000 | ¥865,000 |
| Premium per member (2008) | ¥83,000 | ¥91,000 (¥203,000 including the employer's payment) | ¥89,000 (¥177,000 including the employer's payment) | ¥64,000 |
| Proportion of public subsidies | 50% | — | 16.4% | 50% |
| National budget (2010) | ¥3,027.4 billion | ¥2.4 billion | ¥1,044.7 billion | ¥3,734 billion |

Source: Japan, Ministry of Health, Labor and Welfare.

are calculated based on the insured person's income (ability to pay) regardless of his or her risks and the amount of benefits paid out to him or her. The method of calculating the premium rate for each system is different, depending on its insurers. The number of such insurers in Japan now exceeds 3,000 (Table 11.3).

The employees' health insurance programs have relatively high ratios of healthy and wealthy enrollees. The society-managed health insurance is a scheme for employees of large corporations and their dependents (1,497 insurers). Employers deduct the employees' premiums directly from their paychecks and bonuses. Premium contributions are typically borne equally by employers and employees. However, for society-managed health insurance, many companies pay more than half of their employees' premiums. In 2009, premium rates for this form of health insurance ranged from 3.12 percent to 10 percent of an employee's (indexed) monthly earnings, with the average rate at 7.45 percent. Employers that year paid 55 percent of the total premiums. In the same year, the average premium rate for public-corporation-run health insurance, covering employees of small and medium-sized firms and their dependents, was 9.34 percent of an employee's monthly salary, with half the contribution paid by the employer.

NHI covers the self-employed, the unemployed, workers at companies with fewer than five employees and retirees. This insurance is managed by the municipalities and 1,788 insurers all over Japan. NHI has a relatively high ratio of ill and poor enrollees. Most of the self-employed declare their own earnings, and NHI premiums are collected on the basis of household income, fixed assets, and other wealth. Premium rates vary among insurers. On average, NHI enrollees have the lowest incomes, followed by enrollees of public-corporation-run health insurance and society-managed health insurance, respectively. Governments, both central and local, subsidize 16.4 percent of public-corporation-run health insurance benefits and 50 percent of NHI benefits.

The health insurance system is structured such that fiscal resources are transferred from workplace-based employees' insurance (whose members tend to be younger and have higher incomes) to the health insurance systems run by the national government (many of whose members are elderly or unemployed) and the public corporations.

The health care costs of the elderly are shared among insurers by a mutual adjustment scheme based on the proportion of people insured age 75 or over. About 50 percent is financed by government subsidy and about 40 percent by contributions from NHI and employees' health insurance. The large increase in costs for the elderly has been the most serious problem, because insurers pay the cost for adjustment. It is very difficult to devise financing mechanisms for the elderly. To contain health expenditures for the elderly, the most effective method is to promote a policy for cost-effective, efficient, and high-quality primary care systems with a combination of fee for service and capitation fee. Such a policy will prevent the elderly from making unnecessary visits to specialists and still detect diseases at the early stage and enhance the health of the elderly.

## ISSUES FACING THE JAPANESE HEALTH CARE SYSTEM

### Issues Related to Health Care Insurance

Since the national universal insurance system was introduced in 1961, medical expenditure has grown rapidly as the result of increased access to medical care, provision of benefits for high-cost medical care,[2] and free medical care for the elderly (since 1973). This has put increasing pressure on the country's finances. It took almost 30 years to correct the 1973 policy; since 2002 the elderly have been required to pay 10 percent (or 20 percent, based on income) of their medical costs up to a relatively low payment limit.

The National Health Insurance system's coverage has changed dramatically since 1961. NHI was originally targeted at farmers when universal insurance was introduced. In 1965, two-thirds of the workforce was either self-employed or in the agriculture, forestry, or fishery industries. Further, lifetime employment and seniority-based corporate structures were a norm, and within corporations

---

[2]If total copayment to a hospital or clinic exceeds the over-the-payment limit, the excess over the limit will be reimbursed.

employees' health insurance systems were established as a unit. However, in subsequent years the aging of the population and changes in the industrial structure fundamentally altered the situation. Currently, more than half of the people insured by NHI are unemployed, 24 percent are employees of offices with fewer than five employees or are part-time workers, and 19.3 percent are self-employed or farmers (Japan, Ministry of Health, Labor and Welfare, 2009). For NHI, each municipality operates as the insurer. Since 2000, mergers have led to a decrease in the number of municipalities, from more than 3,200 to 1,788 in 2009.

The aging of the population, which started around the time the universal insurance system was established, also placed greater pressure on the finances of the National Health Insurance system. People who were insured under employee health insurance were then turned over to National Health Insurance upon retirement, and this entailed a decrease in these people's income and increase in medical expenses for the retirees. The Japanese government established a new medical system for the elderly (age 75 and older) in April 2008. The insurers in this new system for the elderly are designated as an extended association joined by all municipalities in their prefectural governments. Government subsidy becomes available, but the subsidy cannot cover the medical expenses of everyone.

Every time a financial crisis occurs, new financial support measures are adopted in order for the system to keep up with the changes. The insurance premiums for NHI and health insurance for the elderly combined cover only one-third of the programs' operating cost, and only a small amount of municipal financing is used to cover the revenue shortages created by NHI. This trend is more pronounced in rural compared to urban areas.

Since 1988, the National Health Insurance Law has been amended several times, and various ad hoc financial assistance measures have been introduced. As a result, the mechanism for financing the costs of the National Health Insurance system has become extremely complicated and involves joint subsidies between central and local governments. This system now includes an insurance-based stability system for people with low incomes, a joint project to mitigate the effect of high medical expenses, and financial measures to stabilize municipal finances.

Because of their experience of being provided with additional financial support by the central government, municipalities now expect new support measures to be implemented whenever new crises arise, which creates moral hazard for the National Health Insurance system. Thus, overly supportive financial measures have reduced the incentives for municipalities to ensure the collection of insurance premiums and improve the efficiency of health care services. As a result, municipalities' responsibility as insurers remains ambiguous. Moreover, people have come to accept the system without clearly understanding who actually pays for their medical expenses. As a result, the government's share of medical expenditure has continued to grow over the years.

Many of the problems facing the Japanese health care system today are due to the incapacity of the insurers. Insurers and health care providers should be the main actors in insurance contracts that involve the delivery of health care, in determining the insurance premium and benefit package, in reviewing and approving benefits, and in selecting health care facilities. However, in the current system, the government appoints health-insurance-qualifying hospitals and doctors without adequate evaluations, physician service fees are determined in line with administrative guidance, and the original purpose of the insurance contract is ignored. It should be possible for insurers to exclude inefficient health care providers individually from the list of health insurance service providers. However, the Japanese system makes that impossible, and such a system is rare in the world. It is difficult to encourage competition between health care providers and to evaluate them under a system such as Japan's.

The strong correlation between the number of hospital beds and length of hospital stay has been repeatedly pointed out by researchers and government officials. Lack of standardization has also led to excess investment in expensive medical equipment. It is important that insurers, as a responsible party, should become more than just the payers and become involved in responding to their area's medical needs.

Currently, financial support for NHI and the medical system for the elderly come from both national and local governments, as mentioned earlier. In the current system, it is the insurers that receive reductions or exemptions. However, it is the individuals with low incomes who receive such subsidies. In other words, the government should stop subsidizing the budgets of insurers and instead subsidize and reimburse individuals with low incomes.

## Issues Related to Health Care Statistics

The Japanese health care system is often considered to be efficient since the Japanese enjoy longevity and the country has a relatively low health care expenditure among OECD countries. However, it is important to note that Japan's total health care expenditure is underestimated, since the "national health care expenditure" published by its Ministry of Health, Labor, and Welfare (MHLW) is an estimate only of the expenditure under Japan's public medical insurance system and the scope of the estimate is limited to treatment costs for injuries and diseases. The figure is essentially an estimate only of the health care expenses covered by public insurance. Items normally included in the medical costs of other countries are not included in Japan's figures. Such excluded costs include those associated with normal pregnancies and birth, noninsured dentistry, health checkups, vaccinations, and other procedures aimed at maintaining and promoting health. They also include excess room charges when hospitalized, elective therapy charges, the costs related to nonprescription drugs (over-the-counter medicines), administrative costs for operating medical insurance, capital costs of local-government-run hospitals, and transfers from the general accounts of local governments to local-government-run hospitals.

While the current estimate of national health care expenditure may be adequate as an explanation of the range of activities under the jurisdiction of the MHLW, it is wholly inadequate for gaining a clear understanding of the use of health care services by Japanese citizens. This is particularly important when we compare health sector expenditures internationally. Every year, OECD reports the health expenditure for each member country using its System of Health Accounts. However, because of the unavailability of the data as described above, Japanese health care expenditures are underestimated.

For example, in 2007, the national health expenditure reported by the Ministry of Health, Labor, and Welfare was ¥34.1 trillion, whereas Japan's total health care expenditure as reported by OECD was ¥41.9 trillion.[3] According to the Japanese national accounts, in 2007 economic activities in the health sector amounted to ¥47.1 trillion. This number is the sum within the health sector of the general government's final consumption expenditure (¥35.3 trillion) and households' final consumption expenditure (¥11.9 trillion).[4] With this simple calculation, it is clear that Japan's national health care expenditure is underestimated by approximately one-third.

It is important that health care policy be based on a solid understanding of the current reality. However, it is hard to claim that health care policies to date have been formulated and implemented on the basis of solid, readily acceptable evidence. To get beyond the current situation it is vital for the Japanese government to take responsibility in conducting statistical studies and publicly disclosing the resulting data.

## CONCLUSION

Fifty years have passed since universal insurance was implemented in Japan and, in light of the current institutional fatigue, today's Japanese health insurance system needs drastic reform. Changing and enhancing the role of the insurer would be a core task in such a reform.

One of the major issues that Japan's health care system is facing is how to contain the escalating medical costs for the elderly. Health care for the elderly has received substantial subsidies from both central and local governments and transfers from other insurers. Government subsidies finance about 50 percent, and contributions from NHI and employees' health insurance finance about 40 percent.

In Japan, with the free-access system, many patients with primary care problems tend to rush into secondary/tertiary care hospitals. This has interfered with the function of these hospitals too much, and it has contributed to the increasing medical costs, particularly for the elderly. What the Japanese health care system needs in this aging era is good collaboration between specialists in the hospitals and community-based primary care physicians. Japan does not have sound systems of primary care provided by well-trained family doctors. Such countries as Canada, Australia, the United Kingdom, the Netherlands, Singapore, and Malaysia have strong systems for training family doctors as key players to

---

[3]Total health expenditure is estimated using OECD's System of Health Accounts by the Institute for Health Economics and Policy.

[4]It does not include the fixed capital formation for the health sector, since figures on this are not available.

provide continuous, comprehensive, person-centered care in the community (WHO, 2008). An efficient primary care system is important for any country in any stage of development, since primary care usually covers more than 80 percent of health and medical problems.

Another critical challenge for Japanese health care is to create a sustainable financing mechanism for the elderly. In 1983, the central government established elderly insurance, a common fund for elderly medical care that transferred the cost burden from poorer community health insurance to corporation-based workers' insurance through pooled contributions from all the insurance schemes and tax revenues. In 2008, the Japanese government introduced the medical system for the elderly age 75 and over. However, the basic financing structure remains the same. The rapid aging of the population is a major challenge in the sustainability of this financing system.

Other challenges for the Japanese health care system include the need to introduce economic incentives to ensure quality and to improve efficiencies, particularly in primary care systems, based on a solid database and with an adequate payment system. Japanese health care relies too heavily on hospital care. Health care reforms have been focusing on hospital reforms with the aim of controlling hospital costs, but without introducing an efficient primary care system, it will not be possible to maintain the country's health care system given its rapidly aging population.

## APPENDIX 11.1. BRIEF HISTORY OF THE JAPANESE HEALTH INSURANCE SYSTEM

The Japanese health insurance system started in the early 1900s when mutual aid associations began to form at both private and government factories and mines. As the first legislation for the protection of workers in Japan, the Factories Act was enacted in 1911. Japan introduced a social insurance type of health insurance in 1922, making reference to the Bismarckian model of German sickness funds. However, this insurance was applicable only to workers in the manufacturing and mining industry at factories or mines with 15 or more employees. Workers at small-scale factories, government officials, bank employees, and some others were not covered.

In rural villages in Japan, organizations resembling health insurance cooperatives had existed as mutual-aid organizations since the Meiji era. The government introduced the National Health Insurance Law[5] in 1938 to expand it into a national system to cover several tens of millions, mostly farmers, who

---

[5]The municipalities formed the National Health Insurance Associations and became the insurers, or in other words, the chief operator of the system. One of the reasons why a municipality-based association was adopted was that many people in rural areas already had a sense of community through irrigation and rice farming activities in each village, and therefore strong social bonds and mutual assistance already existed. Many rural areas traditionally had mutual financing associations as well, and the National Health Insurance system reflected these social realities (Shimazaki, 2005).

were then about 60 percent of the total population. The National Health Insurance Law was developed and implemented without difficulty because of the enactment of the National Mobilization Law in the same year and the wartime "Healthy Soldier Healthy People" provision. The National Mobilization Law allowed the government to direct orders for the mobilization of labor power, determine wages and other working conditions, and give directives on the production and distribution of goods. Under this law, all resources and materials came under government control (Nakamura, 1995).

In 1939, employees' health insurance was inaugurated, covering salaried workers in the cities. By the end of 1943, the National Health Insurance system already covered 95 percent of the municipalities throughout Japan. This period was considered to be the first universal health insurance era. Although some of the municipal associations were created for number-crunching purposes and the reality was far from universal coverage, a basic framework for the current health insurance system in Japan—such as the fee-for-service system without a ceiling on the maximum total service fee and the medical fee under a national uniform schedule—was established during the Second World War, a period when the government was given a great amount of power over the operation of the system.

With the exception of pension schemes for the farming sector population and the self-employed, a social insurance system that covered almost all citizens was completed during this war period. Although most of the social insurance systems were on the verge of breaking down toward the end of the war, these systems survived and were reconstructed even while many of the prewar institutions and laws were being abolished. In sum, Japan's social insurance systems were a legacy created and fostered by recessions and wars during the early twentieth century.

One of the major changes that took place immediately after the war was that the National Health Insurance Law was amended to ensure that municipalities took responsibility for administering NHI, with the aim of promoting NHI programs across the country. Since the work required to implement this law was similar to the municipalities' routine tasks, municipalities took over the administration of NHI, in principle.

Because there were individuals with low incomes who could not pay the premiums, to make insurance universal the government has subsidized insurers. In this scheme, insurers receive reductions or exemptions.[6] An amendment to the Local Tax Law in 1951 created the National Health Insurance Tax, and the method of collecting NHI premiums then became the same as that of municipal taxes. The purpose was to increase the collection rate, and as about 90 percent of the municipalities still choose the National Health Insurance Tax as the method of collection, people tend not to think of NHI as an insurance system.

In the mid-1950s, about one-third of the Japanese population that engaged in agriculture and other self-owned businesses was not covered by health insurance.

---

[6]As discussed in this chapter, instead of having insurers receive reductions or exemptions, the government should subsidize those individuals with low incomes directly, allowing them to pay lower insurance premiums or nothing at all.

Uninsured people then numbered approximately 30 million, of which 10 million were low-income earners who had no choice but to go on social welfare once they became ill.

In 1953, the government finally introduced subsidies equivalent to 20 percent of medical care benefits. This established the financial base of health insurance and laid the foundation for universal insurance. A new National Health Insurance Law was enacted in December 1958, going into effect in 1959, and was enforced all over the country in 1961. The National Pension Law was also enacted in 1959. Universal health insurance and pension schemes were thus achieved in April 1961.

## REFERENCES

Campbell, J.C., and N. Ikegami, 1998, *The Art of Balance in Health Policy: Maintaining Japan's Low-Cost, Egalitarian System* (Cambridge: Cambridge University Press).

Flath, D., 2000, *The Japanese Economy* (Oxford: Oxford University Press).

Ii, M., 2009a, "Development of Social Health Insurance Systems: Retracing Japan's Experience," in *Making Health Services More Accessible in Developing Countries,* ed. by H. Uchimura (Basingstoke: Palgrave Macmillan).

———, 2009b, "Japan: Development of Social Insurance Systems in Japan," in *Health Systems in Asia,* ed. by M. Ii (Tokyo: Tokyo University Press) (in Japanese).

Ikegami, N., 2007, "The Japanese Health Care System: Achieving Equity and Containing Costs through a Single Payment System," *American Heart Hospital Journal,* Vol. 5, pp. 516–31.

Ikegami, N., and J.C. Campbell, 2004, "Japan's Health Care System: Containing Costs and Attempting Reform," *Health Affairs,* Vol. 23, pp. 326–36.

International Monetary Fund, 2010, *Macro-Fiscal Implications of Health Care Reform in Advanced and Emerging Economies* (Washington).

Japan, Ministry of Health, Labor and Welfare, 2009, "Kokumin Kenko Hoken Jittai Chosa [Survey on National Health Insurance]" (Tokyo).

Japan International Cooperation Agency (JICA), 2004, "Development of Japan's Social Security System—An Evaluation and Implications for Developing Countries" (Tokyo: Institute for International Cooperation, Japan International Cooperation Agency).

———, 2005, "Japan's Experiences in Public Health and Medical Systems" (Tokyo: Institute for International Cooperation, Japan International Cooperation Agency).

Nakamura, T., 1995, *The Postwar Japanese Economy: Its Development and Structure,* 2nd edition (Tokyo: Tokyo University Press).

Organization for Economic Cooperation and Development (OECD), 2004, "The OECD Health Project: Towards High-Performing Health Systems" (Paris).

———, 2010. OECD Health Data 2010. Available at http://www.oecd.org/els/health/data.

Shimazaki, K., 2005, "Japanese Health Insurance and Its Development," in *Iryo Hoken Shinryo Hosho Seido* [Health Insurance and the System of Fee Schedules], ed. by H. Endo and N. Ikegami (in Japanese).

Tatara, K., and E. Okamoto, 2009, "Japan: Health System Review," *Health System in Transition,* Vol. 11, No. 5, pp. 1–164.

World Health Organization (WHO), 2008, *The World Health Report 2008—Primary Health Care (Now More Than Ever)* (Geneva).

# CHAPTER 12

# Coverage Expansion and Cost Containment in the Republic of Korea

SOONMAN KWON

## THE HEALTH CARE SYSTEM IN KOREA

Health insurance was introduced for employees in large corporations in the Republic of Korea in 1977 and incrementally extended to employees in small businesses and the self-employed. Since 1989, the country's national health insurance (NHI) has covered the entire population. NHI experienced a major change in 2000 when it became a single payer by merging firm-based insurance societies for employees and region-based societies for the self-employed. The insurance contribution is proportional to income and shared equally by the employer and the employee. Government provides a partial subsidy for the self-employed and fully subsidizes the premium for the poor. Poor people in the Medical Aid program are exempted from copayments, and the elderly and patients with chronic and catastrophic conditions qualify for discounted copayments for outpatient care.[1]

More than 90 percent of acute-care hospitals and 85 percent of acute-care beds are private. There is service overlap and competition between physician clinics and hospitals, because physician clinics include small inpatient facilities, mostly in surgery and obstetrics. Clinics of specialists compete with hospitals, which have inpatient facilities and large outpatient clinics. The gatekeeping role of primary care physicians is very limited. Inefficiency in the health care system is also closely related to the perverse financial incentive under the provider payment system, which reimburses health care providers on a fee-for-service basis with a fee schedule regulated by the government. In addition to the incentive to increase volume and intensity under the fee-for-service system, health care providers also have a perverse incentive to adopt new services and high-technology care that are not covered by NHI and are outside the regulated fee schedule.

Korea spends 6.5 percent of GDP on health care (Table 12.1). Compared with other OECD countries, this level of expenditure is rather low, but its rate of increase

---

[1] See Kwon (2009a) for detailed descriptions of health care financing in Korea. See Appendix Table 12.1 for the change in aggregate indicators of economic and health outcomes in Korea.

**TABLE 12.1**

| Health Expenditure in Korea, 2002–08 | | | | | | | |
|---|---|---|---|---|---|---|---|
| | 2002 | 2003 | 2004 | 2005 | 2006 | 2007 | 2008 |
| Total health expenditure (THE) as a percentage of GDP | 5.1 | 5.4 | 5.4 | 5.7 | 6.1 | 6.3 | 6.5 |
| Public expenditure on health as a percentage of THE | 51.3 | 50.4 | 51.1 | 52.1 | 54.7 | 55.2 | 55.3 |

Source: Organization for Economic Cooperation and Development, OECD Health Data 2010.

is high. Expenditure in this area was 5.1 percent of GDP in 2001, 6.1 percent in 2006, and 6.5 percent in 2008. The contribution rate levied on wage income has risen from 4.2 percent in 2004 to 5.3 percent in 2010. Despite NHI's universal coverage of the population, the role of social insurance in health care financing is still not extensive in Korea. The role of public expenditure in health care—financed by both taxation and social insurance—has steadily increased in the last 30 years, although in 2008 it accounted for only about 55 percent of the country's total health expenditure. Private expenditure consists of copayment for insured services and full payment for services not covered by insurance.

In July 2008, Korea introduced social insurance for long-term care (LTC). LTC insurance was deemed necessary because of several important social and demographic changes, including the rapid aging of the population as a result of an increased life expectancy and a sharp decline in fertility. The total fertility rate (births per woman) dropped below 1.2 in recent years, from 2.8 in 1980. At the same time, the proportion of the elderly (persons over 65) in Korea is forecast to rise at an unprecedented rate, from only 9 percent of the population in 2005 to 20 percent by 2026 and 38 percent by 2050, when the old-age dependency ratio (persons over 65 divided by those ages 15 to 64) will be 70 percent (Korea, NSO, 2007).

Pharmaceutical expenditure has been rapidly increasing, with the annual rate greater than 10 percent. In 2008, the proportion of pharmaceutical expenditure in total health expenditure was 23.1 percent in Korea, higher than in most Organization of Economic Coooperation and Development (OECD) member countries (OECD, 2010). At the same time, there are too many drugs on the health insurance reimbursement list, although a mechanism to evaluate the cost-effectiveness of medicines was introduced for insurance coverage a few years ago. Aging also contributes to pharmaceutical expenditure: 34.9 percent of total pharmaceutical expenditure is accounted for by the elderly.

# HEALTH CARE REFORMS IN THE EARLY 2000s

## Merger of Health Insurance Societies into a Single Payer System

Before the health care financing reform of 2000, Korea's national health insurance system covered the entire population through more than 350 quasi-public insurance societies. There were three types of health insurance societies, which were subject to strict regulation by the Ministry of Health and Welfare: (1) more than 100 health insurance societies for industrial workers and their dependents; (2) a single health insurance society for government employees, teachers, and their dependents; and (3) more than 200 health insurance societies for the self-employed, referred to as "regional health insurance." Beneficiaries were assigned to insurance societies based on type of employment (workplaces where industrial workers worked) and residential area (for the self-employed), and health insurance societies did not compete to attract the insured.

Korea's health care financing reform in 2000 was intended to solve problems associated with the health insurance system's fragmentation by merging all health insurance societies into a single payer. The merger was also expected to increase the efficiency of risk pooling and minimize administrative costs (Kwon, 2003a). Before the merger, health insurance societies used different methods to set contribution amounts. In self-employed groups, the contribution depended on income, property, and the number of dependents, while in employee groups, income was the only basis for determining the contribution. Differences in the method for setting contributions and in the contribution rates across insurance societies, in spite of identical statutory benefits, raised concerns about equity in contributions. Members of insurance societies in poor or rural areas had to pay a greater proportion of their income for the contribution compared to those in wealthy areas. Before the merger, risk-sharing mechanisms among insurance societies, based on old population and catastrophic expenses, did not address the fiscal insolvency of many regional insurance societies in poor or rural areas.

## Separation of Drug Prescribing and Dispensing

Under the previous policy, physicians and pharmacists in Korea both prescribed and dispensed medicines. This system created financial incentives for physicians and pharmacists to dispense more drugs and to select those with greater profit margins. Because the government strictly regulated the fees for medical services, dispensing drugs was more profitable for physicians than providing medical services. Physicians purchased drugs at prices that were much lower than the cost reimbursed by the health insurance. Perverse financial incentives for physicians and pharmacists and the easy consumer access to drugs contributed to the high proportion of total health expenditure spent on pharmaceuticals in Korea. In addition, under the system of combined prescribing and dispensing, patients had limited information about the medication they received.

Physicians wanted to retain the dispensing of drugs because it was a major source of their income, and pharmacists favored the combined system because they wanted to keep the right to prescribe. Physician and pharmacist lobbies had been influential in health policy and effectively blocked change for a long time. Pharmaceutical reform to separate the prescribing and dispensing roles was finally adopted, but policy implementation in 2000 faced a series of nationwide strikes by physicians and some elements of the reform package were distorted (Kwon, 2003b). For example, brand name prescription was implemented as the result of physicians' opposition to generic prescription.

## Pilot of the Diagnosis-Related Group Prospective Payment System

In 1997, the government began a pilot program involving a prospective payment system based on diagnosis-related groups (DRGs) for five disease categories among voluntarily participating providers (Kwon, 2003c). The government planned to extend the DRG payment system and apply it to all health care providers in 2000. After strikes against the pharmaceutical reform, physicians forced the government to give up the nationwide implementation of the DRG payment system. Physicians further succeeded in pushing the government to increase their fees to compensate for their foregone drug-related revenues as a result of pharmaceutical reform. The huge increase in physician fees contributed to a fiscal crisis in the NHI system when its financial reserve was depleted in 2001 (Kwon, 2007). Increases in the contribution and in the government subsidy have since improved the fiscal status of NHI.

## Introduction of Long-Term Care Insurance for the Elderly

### Background

In July 2008, Korea introduced long-term care social insurance.[2] Along with an increased life expectancy and a rapid decline in fertility, the family structure in Korea has also changed. The proportion of the elderly living with their adult children has been decreasing, and with an increase in labor participation, women have been less able and willing to assume their traditional role of providing informal care to the elderly (Kwon, 2008).

The government's reluctance to extend the (tax-based) public assistance program for LTC to the poor elderly contributed to the rather early adoption (when the proportion of the elderly was still less than 10 percent of population) of a universal financing scheme based on contribution premiums. LTC insurance, separate from health insurance funding, has a potential benefit in "demedicalizing" LTC—that is, in reducing the role of medical care in LTC— because when health insurance provides coverage for LTC, physicians may play a dominating role. Nevertheless, to save administrative costs, Korea's LTC insurance is administered by the National Health Insurance Corporation (NHIC).

LTC insurance has multiple and sometimes unclear goals. From a social welfare perspective, it aims to ease the financial burden borne by the elderly who pay for LTC, by its universal appeal. It can decrease the financial burden on health insurance as well by reducing social admissions in acute-care hospitals. The Ministry of Health and Welfare has tried to persuade the Ministry of Finance and Economy of the potential that LTC insurance has to create jobs by extending social services.

---

[2]See Kwon (2010) for a description of key institutional features of LTC insurance in Korea.

## Population Coverage

Mandatory LTC insurance covers LTC for the elderly aged 65 or above, but it is limited to age-related LTC in case of those under 65 (e.g., dementia or cerebro-vascular disease for the young). As a result, the probability of younger people's receiving benefits is low, as the benefits are limited to age-related LTC. This is a political compromise, because the government wants to make the younger pay contributions by making them at least eligible for the benefits. In contrast, German LTC insurance covers all types of long-term care, while in Japan those under 40 are not covered and those ages 40 to 64 are eligible for age-related LTC only (Campbell, Ikegami, and Kwon, 2009).

A visiting team from the branch offices of the NHIC assesses each patient's functional status for eligibility, using 56 evaluation items based on, for example, "activities of daily living." There are three levels of functional status/limitations with corresponding benefit levels. The assessment process is crucial to determining the size of the population covered. Before the introduction of LTC insurance, it was forecast to cover about 3 to 4 percent of the total elderly population, a proportion that might fall short of demand. In fact, in May 2010, more than 4.5 percent of the elderly were enjoying the benefits of LTC insurance (Table 12.2). Although the Ministry of Health and Welfare wants to increase the population coverage gradually, the speed of extension will affect the financial sustainability of LTC insurance. If government extends the target of population coverage, the contribution of LTC insurance should also increase.

## Level and Type of Benefits of LTC Insurance

The contribution to LTC insurance is determined as a fixed percentage of the health insurance contribution, which was 4.1 percent in 2008, 4.8 percent in 2009, and 6.6 percent in 2010. Overall financing consists of a government sub-sidy of 20 percent, a copayment of 20 percent for institutional care or 15 percent for home-based care, and a contribution of 60 to 65 percent. The poor are exempted from copayment. Meals and private rooms are not covered by LTC insurance.

In principle LTC insurance provides service benefits, while cash benefits are provided only in exceptional cases. Benefits depend on the level of functional limitations (labeled levels 1, 2, and 3, with level 1 applied to those with the

**TABLE 12.2**

| Population Coverage of Long-Term Care Insurance in Korea, 2008–10 | | | |
|---|---|---|---|
| | **July 2008** | **July 2009** | **May 2010** |
| Number that applied (percentage of the elderly) | 295,715 (5.9%) | 513,749 (9.8%) | 676,966 (12.6%) |
| Number certified as eligible (percentage of the elderly) | 146,643 (2.9%) | 268,071 (5.2%) | 308,126 (5.7%) |
| Number that used services (percentage of those eligible) | 78,370 (53.4%) | 184,434 (68.9%) | 244,669 (79.4%) |

Source: NHIC (2010).

greatest limitations) determined in the assessment process. There are ceilings on the benefits for noninstitutional care, ranging from W 1,097,000 (about $1,000) per month for level 1 to W 760,000 per month for level 3. The type of payment to providers varies: pay is administered on a per hour basis for part-time home care, a per visit basis for visiting nursing services or help with bathing, and a per day basis for institutional care and full-time home care.

The limited role of cash benefits in Korea needs to be reconsidered. Korean policymakers are worried about the potential for abusing cash benefits and the potentially low quality of care provided by informal caregivers. However, cash benefits can have positive effects on consumer choice and competition among formal and informal caregivers. Setting the cash benefit level lower than the comparable service (in-kind) benefits can also result in savings, as is the case in Germany. The potential negative impact of cash benefits on women's labor participation depends on labor market conditions and the availability of social security programs such as paid family leave.

### Challenges

Financial sustainability of LTC insurance is a concern, as the number of the elderly who were certified to be eligible and utilized services has increased more than 50 percent in just two years. There is an excess supply of LTC providers albeit with a variation across localities (e.g., shortage in rural areas), which results in supplier-induced demand and wasteful competition. The size of most LTC residential facilities is too small and these facilities fail to reap economies of scale. The government should monitor and evaluate the quality of care at LTC institutions and then disseminate the results so that consumers can make an informed choice of providers. Accreditation of LTC providers/institutions and training programs would also be important for improving LTC quality.

Coordination between health insurance and LTC insurance will be a key to the continuum of care and to reducing the need for LTC. Increased access to medical care and health promotion among the elderly can lessen the need for LTC. Benefit coverage of LTC insurance needs to be coordinated with that of health insurance. The relative generosity of payments to LTC hospitals (paid by health insurance) compared with payments to LTC institutions (paid by LTC insurance) will also affect the incentives and behavior of consumers and providers. If the benefit coverage of LTC insurance is too stringent, the elderly will prefer acute care hospitals, and the problems of social admissions in those hospitals will remain.

## Expansion of Health Insurance Benefit Coverage

In spite of the universal coverage of the population, high out-of-pocket (OOP) payment has been a concern for the health insurance system in Korea. Following President Kim Dae-joong, who actively expanded various programs of the welfare state, President Roh Moo-hyun (2003–08), also from a progressive political party, implemented a series of policies to expand benefit coverage.

The ceiling on cumulative OOP, set at about $3,000 per person for a six-month period, was implemented in 2004. It was reduced to about $2,000 in 2007. For the financial protection of the poor, the ceiling needs to be adjusted to patients' ability to pay. In 2009, differential ceilings were introduced based on (relative) income: $4,000 for those in the top 20 percent of the income range, $3,000 for those between the 20th and 50th percentile, and $2,000 for those below the 50th percentile. The ceiling on cumulative OOP has been effective in reducing the financial burden on patients, but its impact is still limited because it is applied only to copayment for insured (covered) services, and not to OOP payment for uninsured (out-of-coverage) services.

The coinsurance rate for patients with catastrophic diseases, mainly cancer patients, was reduced from 20 percent to 10 percent in 2005, and was reduced further to 5 percent in 2009. Exemption from copayment for inpatient care used by children age six or younger was implemented in 2006, although in 2008 the coinsurance rate was readjusted to 10 percent. Health insurance began to provide coverage for meals with a 20 percent coinsurance rate in 2006, but the coinsurance rate was raised to 50 percent in 2008. Although coinsurance rates for meals and children's inpatient care increased slightly from 2006 to 2008, the current coinsurance rates are still lower than those in the pre-2006 era, which were 20 percent for inpatient care and 100 percent for meals.

As a result of the expansion of health insurance benefit coverage, the share of public sector spending in total health expenditure increased from 50.4 percent in 2003 to 55.3 percent in 2008 (Table 12.1). Health insurance expenditure also started to increase more rapidly in 2004 (Figure 12.1). However, the expansion

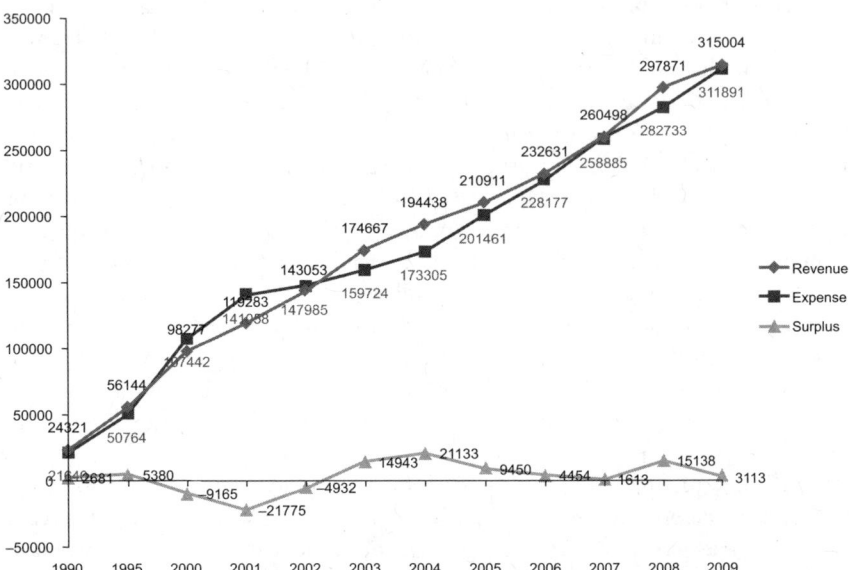

**Figure 12.1**  Fiscal Status of National Health Insurance in Korea, 1990–2009 (Hundreds of millions of Korean won)
Source: NHIC (2010).

of benefit coverage has not reduced the share of private expenditure in total health expenditure as rapidly as expected. Health care is provided predominantly by the private sector in Korea. As government regulates the price of insured (covered) services, private providers tend to increase the provision of noncovered services, for which they can set the price. Demand inducement and the rapid increase in the provision of noncovered services have contributed to the slow increase in the public share in Korea's total health care expenditure.

## Pharmaceutical Cost Containment

The government introduced two major policy measures to contain pharmaceutical expenditures in May 2006: price negotiation and positive listing.

### Pharmaceutical Pricing

Previously, the reimbursement price of a new drug was set as the average price across drugs in seven reference countries (the United States, the United Kingdom, Germany, France, Italy, Switzerland, and Japan). More specifically, the price of innovative new drugs was set as the average of manufacturing prices (65 percent of the list price) plus a value-added tax and the distributors' margin. This pricing mechanism was criticized because it tended to result in high prices that depended on the listed price—rather than the real (transaction) price—in high-income countries. Moreover, information on the real transaction price in other countries is very difficult to obtain. Considering that Korea is a rather early adopter of new drugs, it was often the case that the same or similar medicines were available in only a limited number of countries, where the price was very high. The NHIC was also criticized for not playing an active purchaser role in pharmaceuticals.

Facing rapidly increasing pharmaceutical expenditure, the Korean government decided to change the pricing rules (Kwon, 2009b). Instead of formula-based pricing, the NHIC as a purchaser now bargains with pharmaceutical manufacturers over prices. In the price negotiation, the NHIC considers the size of the market, the substitutability of drugs, the budget impact on health insurance, and other factors. Furthermore, the NHIC takes into account the quantity of drugs to be consumed (that is, volume). At the time of listing, the pharmaceutical manufacturer submits the estimated volume. If the actual sales volume is greater than the expected one, the drug's price will be cut. Linkage of price and volume in price setting makes the manufacturer share the financial consequences of potential overutilization of medicines, but there is still no risk for physicians, who actually play a key role in pharmaceutical expenditure. As price negotiation is adopted, the NHIC is hoping to use its bargaining power as a single payer to reduce the price of pharmaceuticals.

In the new pricing scheme, when a patent expires and a generic medicine enters the market, the price of the originator brand name drug is reduced to 80 percent of the previous price. The price of the first generic medicine is set at 85 percent of the price of the original brand (or 68 percent of the price of the original before the entrance of a generic). The price of the second to fifth generics is set at 85 percent of the price of the first generic medicines. The government is reluctant to reduce

**TABLE 12.3**

International Price Comparisons (Relative to Korea) of Generic Medicines (Price Index)

| | Number of M/P/S | U.S. dollar exchange rate | | U.S. dollars at purchasing power parity | |
|---|---|---|---|---|---|
| | | Laspeyres | Paasche | Laspeyres | Paasche |
| United States | 62 | 0.539 | 0.418 | 0.381 | 0.295 |
| Norway | 46 | 0.540 | 0.304 | 0.233 | 0.131 |
| Sweden | 47 | 0.628 | 0.275 | 0.312 | 0.136 |
| United Kingdom | 62 | 0.760 | 0.301 | 0.437 | 0.173 |
| Spain | 65 | 0.768 | 0.435 | 0.486 | 0.275 |
| Germany | 67 | 0.784 | 0.496 | 0.439 | 0.277 |
| Belgium | 53 | 0.895 | 0.638 | 0.471 | 0.336 |
| Italy | 57 | 0.901 | 0.628 | 0.515 | 0.359 |
| Netherlands | 59 | 0.919 | 0.490 | 0.500 | 0.267 |
| Australia | 50 | 0.993 | 0.845 | 0.555 | 0.472 |
| Austria | 59 | 1.130 | 0.726 | 0.607 | 0.390 |
| France | 54 | 1.131 | 0.881 | 0.590 | 0.460 |
| Switzerland | 44 | 1.205 | 1.098 | 0.559 | 0.509 |
| Japan | 33 | 1.477 | 1.086 | 0.924 | 0.679 |

Source: Kim and others (2010).

Note: Laspeyres index is calculated using the quantity of consumption in Korea. Paasche index is calculated using the quantity of consumption in the country being compared. M/P/S = molecules/presentation/strength.

the price of generic medicines partly because the majority of generic medicines are produced by domestic manufacturers.

A recent study based on IMS Health data by Kim and others (2010) shows that the price of generic medicines in Korea is one of the highest among OECD countries, which implies that the Korean government should be more aggressive in setting the price of generic medicines (Table 12.3). When the price index is smaller than 1, the price in Korea is higher than that in the country being compared. Considering that a high price of originator medicines compensates for research and development, the 15 percent price difference between the originator and the first generic seems too small. A larger price difference between the originator and generics, that is, lowering the price of generic medicines, would contribute to increased market share for generics in Korea.

### Positive Listing and Economic Evaluation

In the past, health insurance reimbursement for pharmaceuticals was based on negative listing, which resulted in too many drugs being listed for reimbursement. As of January 2006, 21,740 drugs (5,411 molecules) were listed for reimbursement. To contain pharmaceutical expenditure, the government decided to introduce the positive listing of drugs for health insurance coverage. Now the listing criteria include economic evaluations, mainly through cost-effectiveness analysis, submitted by pharmaceutical manufacturers to NHI. The positive listing based on economic evaluations will initially be used for new drugs, but the government plans to evaluate and reassess drugs already listed.

The pharmaceutical industry has argued that positive listing can lead to the abuse of market power by a single purchaser (NHIC) covering the entire population. Pharmaceutical manufacturers are worried that as drugs not in the reimbursement list may not survive, the threat of delisting would force them to cut prices. Multinational pharmaceutical manufacturers maintain that positive listing based on economic evaluations will have a serious negative effect on the development and introduction of new innovative drugs, because the policy will favor drugs that are less effective but cheaper.

## Challenges

The Health Insurance Review and Assessment, which reviews claims for reimbursement, is responsible for decisions on the listing of medicines based on economic evaluations. The NHIC negotiates the prices with pharmaceutical manufacturers. Economic evaluation data provide crucial information on the potential price range of drugs, and coordination between the NHIC and the Health Insurance Review and Assessment will be important for the success of the new policy. There are also conceptual and practical challenges to the implementation of economic evaluation for the pricing and listing of pharmaceuticals, including issues related to assumptions used in the analysis and the availability and reliability of data.

Pharmaceutical spending is determined not only by prices, but also by the volume of drugs and the mix of originator and generic medicines. Therefore, pricing policy alone has a limited effect on cost containment. The quantity of pharmaceuticals consumed is determined to a great extent by physicians, so without the regulation of physician prescribing behavior or economic incentives to prescribe in a cost-effective way, pharmaceutical cost containment cannot succeed. A provider payment system and financial incentives for physicians to increase the prescription of less costly but equally effective generics are both essential.

## DIRECTIONS FOR FUTURE REFORM

For Korea's health care system to remain financially sustainable, policy measures to increase revenue and contain costs should be considered. Contributions based on wage income are not equitable, because wage income does not fully represent a patient's ability to pay. Wage-based contributions can also distort labor force participation decisions. Therefore, the contribution base for health insurance should be expanded, and health insurance contributions should be collected based not only on wages, but also on other forms of income.

Health care providers play a key role in health care resource allocation. Provider payment and financial incentive systems are crucial for the financial sustainability of health care as well as for the quality of care. Prospective case-based payment, instead of a fee-for-service payment, should be adopted as soon as possible. Case-based payment still has limitations, such as the distortion of diagnosis coding and the substitution of outpatient for inpatient care, and a budget cap should be introduced to control both the prices and the quantity of the health care provided.

The Korean LTC insurance system is in its infancy and still has many challenges ahead, such as finding a balance between institutional care and home-based (community-based) care and ensuring quality of care. LTC insurance could potentially have a big impact on the health care system, and coordination between LTC insurance and health insurance in terms of benefit coverage and provider reimbursement will be important.

A budget cap on pharmaceutical expenditure is needed in Korea, and the government should make physicians and the pharmaceutical industry share responsibility when pharmaceutical expenditure exceeds the cap. The government needs to consider mandating generic prescription, using financial incentives for physicians to prescribe less costly medicines, or reducing copayments for consumers who choose generics (e.g., reference pricing). Policymakers also need to increase the price differences between the originator brand name drugs and the generic drugs by reducing the price of generic medicines.

Health care reform in Korea faces opposition by vested interest groups. As in 2000, when physicians went on strike against pharmaceutical reform, interest groups today influence the reform process from policy adoption to implementation, affecting the final reform outcomes (Kwon and Reich, 2005). The government's capacity to manage these vested interests and the political strategy it chooses will be crucial for improving the efficiency and equity of the health care system.

## APPENDIX 12.1.

**APPENDIX TABLE 12.1**

### Economic and Health Indicators in Korea, 1977–2008

|  | 1977 | 1989 | 2000 | 2008 |
|---|---|---|---|---|
| GDP per capita (in USD)[a] | 1,042 | 5,430 | 11,347 | 20,591 (2010) |
| Life expectancy[b] | 64.8 | 71 | 76 | 79.9 |
| Mortality (per 100,000 persons)[c] | 690 | 542.3 |  | 497.3 (2009) |
| Infant mortality (per 1,000 births)[b,c] | 38 (average over 1970–75) | 12 | 5.8 (average over 1999–2002) | 3.5 |
| Number of physicians (per 10,000 persons)[b] | 5 (1981) | 8 | 13 | 19 2009) |
| Number of beds (per 10,000 persons)[b] | 17 (1981) | 23 | 47 | 78 |
| Number of physician visits per capita[b] | 3.7 | 6.2 | 10.6 (2002) | 13 |
| Number of admissions per capita[c] | — | 0.06 (1990) | — | 0.13 |
| Number of hospital days per admission[b,c] | 12 | 13.6 | 13.8 (2002) | 14.6 (2009) |

Note: 1977 marked the introduction of health insurance; 1989 marked the onset of universal coverage.
[a]Source: Bank of Korea (2011).
[b]Source: Organization for Economic Cooperation and Development, OECD Health Data (2010).
[c]Source: Korea, National Statistics Office (2011).

# REFERENCES

Bank of Korea, Economic Statistics, 2011 (in Korean) (Seoul).

Campbell, J., N. Ikegami, and S. Kwon, 2009, "Policy Learning and Cross-National Diffusion in Social Long-Term Care Insurance: Germany, Japan, and the Republic of Korea," *International Social Security Review,* Vol. 62, No. 4, pp. 63–80.

Kim, S., S. Kwon, Y. Jung, and J. Heo, 2010, "International Comparison of Generic Medicine Prices" (in Korean), *Korean Journal of Health Economics and Policy,* Vol. 16, No. 3, pp. 41–62.

Korea, National Statistics Office (NSO), *Population Statistics 2007* (in Korean) (Seoul).

Kwon, S., 2003a, "Health Care Financing Reform and the New Single Payer System in Korea: Social Solidarity or Efficiency?" *International Social Security Review,* Vol. 56, No. 1, pp. 75–94.

———, 2003b, "Pharmaceutical Reform and Physician Strikes: Separation of Drug Prescribing and Dispensing in Korea," *Social Science and Medicine,* Vol. 57, No. 3, pp. 529–38.

———, 2003c, "Payment System Reform for Health Care Providers in Korea," *Health Policy and Planning,* Vol. 18, No. 1, pp. 84–93.

———, 2007, "Fiscal Crisis of the National Health Insurance in Korea: In Search of a New Paradigm," *Social Policy and Administration,* Vol. 41, No. 2, pp. 162–78.

———, 2008, "Future of Long-Term Care Financing for the Elderly in Korea," *Journal of Aging and Social Policy,* Vol. 20, No. 1, pp. 119–36.

———, 2009a, "Thirty Years of National Health Insurance in Korea: Lessons for Universal Health Care Coverage," *Health Policy and Planning,* Vol. 24, No. 1, pp. 63–71.

———, 2009b, "Pharmaceutical Policy in Korea," in *Prescribing Culture and Pharmaceutical Policy in the Asia-Pacific,* ed. by K. Eggleston (Washington: Brookings Institution Press), pp. 31–44.

———, 2010, "Population Aging and the Introduction of Long-Term Care Insurance in South Korea," in *Aging Asia: The Economic and Social Implications of Rapid Demographic Change in China, Japan and South Korea,* ed. by K. Eggleston and S. Tuljapurkar (Washington: Brookings Institution Press), pp. 109–17.

Kwon, S., and M. Reich, 2005, "The Changing Process and Politics of Health Policy in Korea," *Journal of Health Politics, Policy and Law,* Vol. 30, No. 6, pp. 1003–26.

National Health Insurance Corporation (NHIC), 2010, *National Health Insurance Statistical Yearbook* (in Korean) (Seoul).

# CHAPTER 13

# Containing Public Health Spending through Market-Based Health Reform in Germany

## Michael Stolpe

## OVERVIEW

For more than 20 years, the main motivation of government interventions in the German health care system has been to contain the growth of nonwage labor costs. Rising payroll taxes for Germany's statutory sickness funds had become a major policy issue amid the country's rising unemployment until 2005. Although total health care spending was not the direct target, the government's main achievement has been to keep this aggregate at a relatively stable proportion of GDP, except for a one-time upward move after Germany's unification in 1990. This long experience with reform illustrates a variety of policy approaches, as the German government has gradually shifted away from its initial recourse to global budgets and replaced these with market mechanisms and pecuniary incentives designed to steer providers' and payers' behavior within an increasingly competitive environment.

Initially, the government found budget caps appealing, as they seemed to provide quick fixes without the need to fully understand the causes of each attention-grabbing spending spurt. But time revealed that budget caps can be difficult to enforce in sectors with a great deal of technology-driven innovation, such as hospitals and the pharmaceutical sector. Global budgets worked best in the remuneration of ambulatory care physicians, in which a periodic sum paid by the statutory system was linked to the sum of workers' wages. And although global budgets have been abandoned, they continue to serve as implicit benchmarks that inform the fees and prices negotiated between sickness funds and care providers or set directly by the government. Nevertheless, their influence will fade with time.

The system's basic setup has been left largely intact. Statutory sickness funds, financed through payroll taxes at 15.5 percent of gross wages, cover more than 90 percent of the population. Workers with annual incomes above €49,500 can opt into private health insurance, but most of them stay on as voluntary members in the statutory system, also known as statutory health insurance (SHI). Such voluntary enrollees are entitled to the same package of care and also pay payroll taxes at the same rate, but the income base of these taxes is capped at €49,500 so that wage income above this threshold is not taxed. The vast majority of services are mandated by law to ensure that all enrollees have equal access to all the care that is considered medically necessary at any point in time.

Private health insurers charge premiums based on individual risk, assessed before signing up, and regulation ensures that all contracts are for life, are terminable only by the insured, and may neither exclude preexisting conditions nor increase premiums for any other reason than general expenditure increases in the entire pool of insureds for a given class of contracts. For all insureds under financial distress above 55 years of age, each private insurer must offer the option of switching to a "cheap" basic care package (*Standardtarif*) that mimics the conditions of SHI. This shifts part of the remaining premium risk from the insureds to the private insurer and provides some protection against overestimating one's personal earnings capacity at older ages or underestimating the rise in premiums which the generous care package of an insured's original private insurance contract may imply. While the *Standardtarif* does not offer the free choice of hospital doctors and other amenities that private patients may have become used to, it should be medically adequate in most cases, given the tight regulation of SHI care that it mimics. In some cases, however, private patients switching to the *Standardtarif* may no longer receive the generous private health insurance reimbursements for expensive new drugs that are not (or not yet) approved for reimbursement by SHI.

Another option for consumers wishing to enjoy private health insurance benefits without the full premium risk is offered by private *supplementary* health insurance. It is available for all enrollees of sickness funds willing to pay a relatively modest extra premium for the same free choice of physicians in hospital care, hospital amenities such as rooms with only one or two beds, and full coverage of dental care that patients with full private health insurance typically enjoy. Sickness funds increasingly cooperate with private insurers in marketing these supplementary insurance schemes to their own enrollees, as the sickness funds see these as a way of keeping their voluntary insureds enrolled. Voluntary enrollees are attractive, as they tend to be highly educated professionals with healthy lifestyles who visit doctors' offices less frequently than the average person. In 2010, some 22 million Germans had some form of private supplementary health insurance, compared with only 8.86 million in full private health insurance, according to the association of Germany's private health insurers.[1]

In 2008, *public* health care expenditures accounted for approximately three-quarters of all health care spending in Germany, according to both the Organization for Economic Cooperation and Development (OECD)[2] and the Federal Statistics Office of Germany.[3] While the OECD definition of public expenditures comprises all health care paid for by federal, state, and local government bodies as well as all spending by the statutory health insurance

---

[1]See http://www.pkv.de/zahlen/.
[2]See http://www.oecd-ilibrary.org/social-issues-migration-health/public-expenditure-on-health_20758480-table3.
[3]See http://www.destatis.de/jetspeed/portal/cms/Sites/destatis/Internet/DE/Presse/pm/2010/04/PD10__126__23611,templateId=renderPrint.psml.

system, the Federal Statistics Office also includes in its measure the relatively small health care spending by the country's statutory long-term care insurance, pension insurance, and accident insurance schemes.

Since the 1980s, German health policy has established a legacy of successfully containing the growth of expenditures (often confused with "costs") in SHI overall. Nonetheless, contribution rates (the payroll taxes used to finance SHI) have continued to claim an increasing percentage of gross wages—mainly owing to the rise in unemployment from the mid-1970s until the mid-2000s, including the extra boost in unemployment after German unification as the result of the relatively low labor productivity and high unemployment in the East.

Another part of the legacy that has drawn increasing attention in the 2000s is the low intensity of competition among care providers, accentuated by a sharp separation between ambulatory and stationary care that is often combined with low productivity in service provision. For example, de Vries, Goldman, and Joyce (2008) report that in 2002, the average inpatient length of stay for acute myocardial infarction was 5.6 days in the United States and 10.3 days in Germany. And from 2001 to 2004, one-year mean expenditure for inpatient care per patient after an acute myocardial infarction was $39,257 in the United States and $10,608 in Germany (at purchasing power parity). But holding prices and population characteristics constant, the mean cost of treating U.S. patients in Germany would have been $45,599, and the mean cost of treating German patients in the Unites States merely $10,196 (at purchasing power parity). Either way, this direct productivity comparison at the disease level is unfavorable for German health care and clearly suggests that it operates below the production possibility frontier in the treatment of an acute myocardial infarction.

The second section of this chapter reviews trends in public health spending since 1970, and the third section briefly explains how waves of reform in the 1980s and 1990s helped contain expenditures. The fourth section discusses why and how the focus of more recent reforms has shifted toward improving incentives and introducing market mechanisms. The chapter closes with a list of specific lessons that may be relevant for other countries and highlights some of the challenges that remain to be addressed in Germany.

## TRENDS IN PUBLIC HEALTH SPENDING

To highlight the distinctive situation in Germany, Figure 13.1 compares the growth in the country's total health care spending per capita with spending growth in other high-income countries (France, the Netherlands, the United Kingdom, and the United States), using OECD data, given in thousands of dollars at purchasing power parity. Throughout the past 30 years, this growth has been both smooth and relatively modest in Germany. Between 1980 and 2008, German spending merely quadrupled, while U.S. spending increased almost eightfold. Growth in German spending has also been relatively slow compared with that in other European countries, despite the fact that German unification at the end of 1990 unexpectedly made an additional 17 million people—equivalent in size to one-quarter of the former West German population, with less than half the per

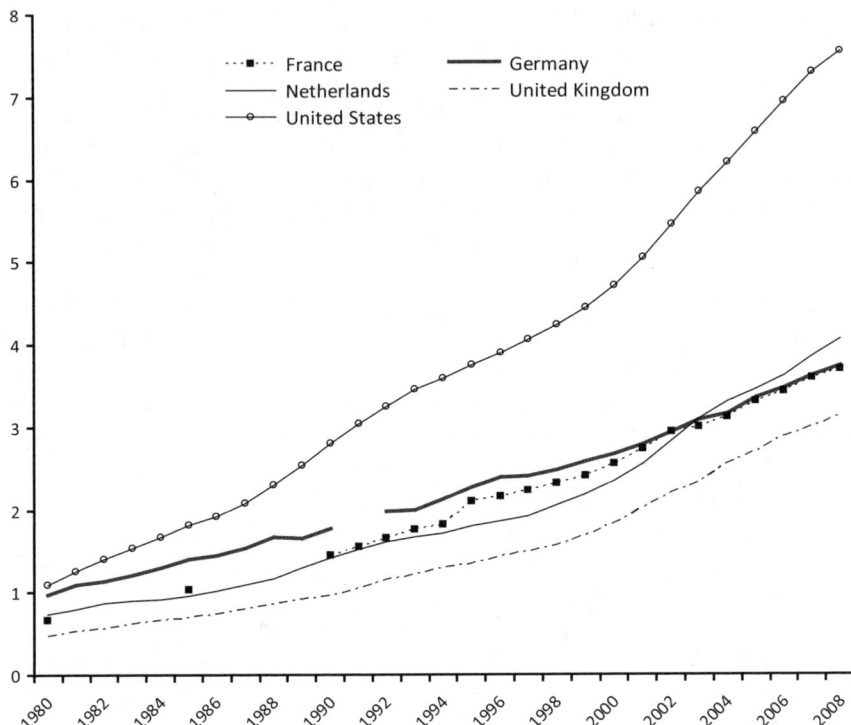

**Figure 13.1** Health Care Spending Growth in Germany and Selected Countries, 1980–2008 (Total health care spending per capita, thousands of U.S. dollars at purchasing power parity)
Source: Organization for Economic Cooperation and Development, OECD Health Data 2010.

capita contributions to health care finance of West Germany—instantly eligible to receive the same level of care. Since international comparative data for the reunified country became available only in 1992 and all data until 1990 refer to West Germany only, there is a gap for 1991 in Figure 13.1. Yet the smooth time series clearly shows that German unification had only a small impact on health care spending per capita, one that seems to have been negligible in the longer term.

As economists have long argued, an important determinant of per capita health spending is people's income. Figure 13.2 therefore shows countries' health care spending as a percentage of GDP. Compared with other leading European countries and the United States, in Germany this share has been remarkably stable—both before and since unification. To be sure, the event of unification marked a structural break, one that increased Germany's share from a narrow range of 8–9 percent of GDP during the 1980s to a new range of 10–11 percent since 1995. The adjustment to the new equilibrium after German unification seems to have lasted several years, during which the people of eastern Germany with their much lower per capita contributions were absorbed and the collapse of the country's unification-induced construction boom as well as the accelerating privatization of East Germany's state-owned firms by the *Treuhandanstalt* led to rapidly rising unemployment.

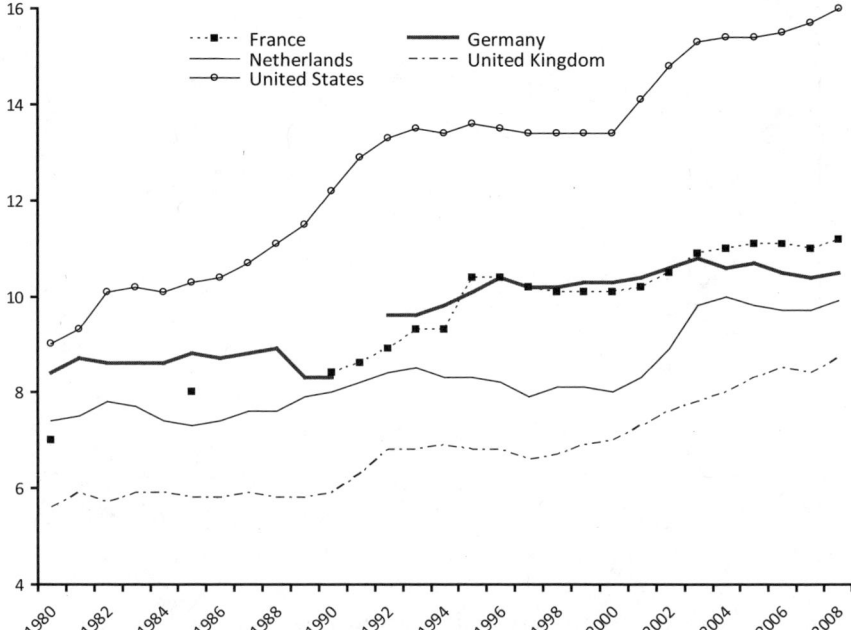

**Figure 13.2**    Share of Health Care in GDP in Germany and Selected Countries, 1980–2008 (Total health care spending in percent of GDP)
Source: Organization for Economic Cooperation and Development, OECD Health Data 2010.

Beyond its negative correlation with GDP, rising unemployment directly undermines the payroll tax base on which the financial viability of Germany's SHI system depends. Amid only nominal contributions paid by or on behalf of the unemployed, the workers remaining in employment must contribute a higher share of their gross wages unless other sources of health care finance can be mobilized. Rising contribution rates in turn may raise the unit costs of labor to firms and may thus trigger further increases in unemployment. Amid high unemployment, stable SHI contribution rates have become a top priority in all health care reform since unification—with considerable success.

As Figure 13.3 shows, the annual average SHI contribution rates of West Germany had increased from 10 percent in 1975 to 13 percent in 1990, but their growth has slowed since the early 1990s. Since 2011, the contribution rate has been permanently fixed for all at 15.5 percent (after rising to 14.9 percent in 2010). As Figure 13.3 further shows, the sharp rise in West German unemployment between the mid-1970s and the mid-1980s was accompanied by a substantial decline in the share of gross wages in GDP (shown *per ten* instead of in *percent*), and thus helped push SHI contribution rates up. After unification, unemployment again rose sharply until 1997 and reached a second peak in 2005, again being accompanied by a declining share of gross wages in GDP, before a reversal of these trends finally set in.

Upward pressure on SHI contribution rates was also due to a rising share of pensioners among SHI enrollees, as shown in the lower part of Figure 13.3. The

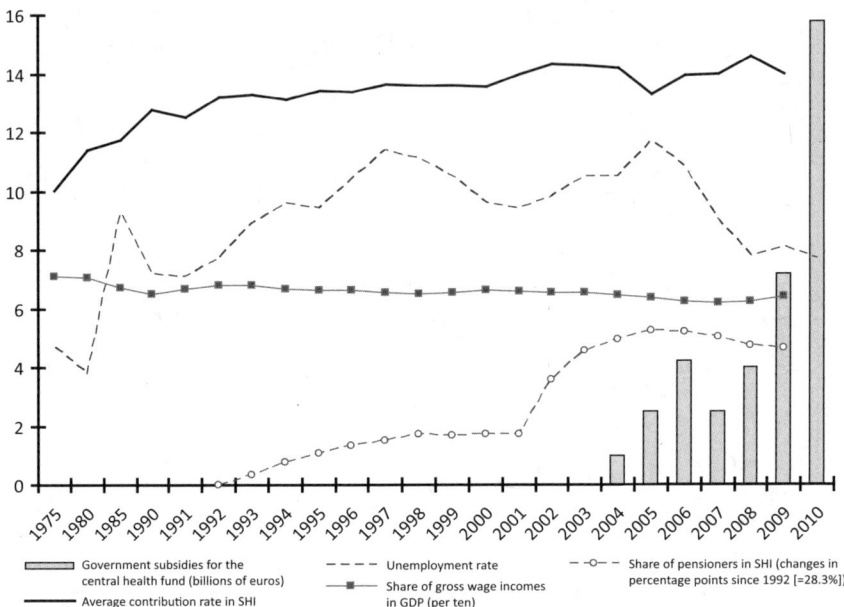

**Figure 13.3** Growth in Contribution Rates in Germany, 1980–2010
Source: BMG (Arbeits- und Sozialstatistik, Bundesarbeitsblatt, KJ 1, KM 1, KV 45), Destatis.

share of pensioners, who generally make relatively low per capita contributions (since the average replacement rate of pensions is well below 50 percent of gross wages), had grown by almost 5 percentage points as of 2009, from 28.3 percent in 1992. An important part of the government's efforts to stabilize SHI contribution rates amid all this change in the payroll tax base has been direct infusions of federal subsidies, which began to be paid on a substantial scale in 2004 and have become fully institutionalized through the central health fund since 2009.

Another important part in stabilizing German health care finance has been played by rising out-of-pocket payments, whose percentage share in total health spending is shown in Figure 13.4. After having been relatively stable in West Germany during the 1980s, this share began to rise soon after German unification, from a low of 9 percent in 1996 to 13 percent in 2008. By contrast, France, the Netherlands, and the United States have all seen substantial declines in the share of out-of-pocket payments since the early 1990s.

## PAST REFORMS TO CONTAIN EXPENDITURES

Taking a detailed look at the evolution of expenditures and revenues in SHI since 1991, Figure 13.5 shows that past reforms had merely temporary effects. The graph uses solid lines to plot real expenditures and revenues in 2005 prices and dashed lines to plot nominal expenditures and revenues. Beginning with the introduction of global budgets in 1993, all the major reforms of the past 20 years achieved immediate reductions in real *expenditures* but had only limited effects on

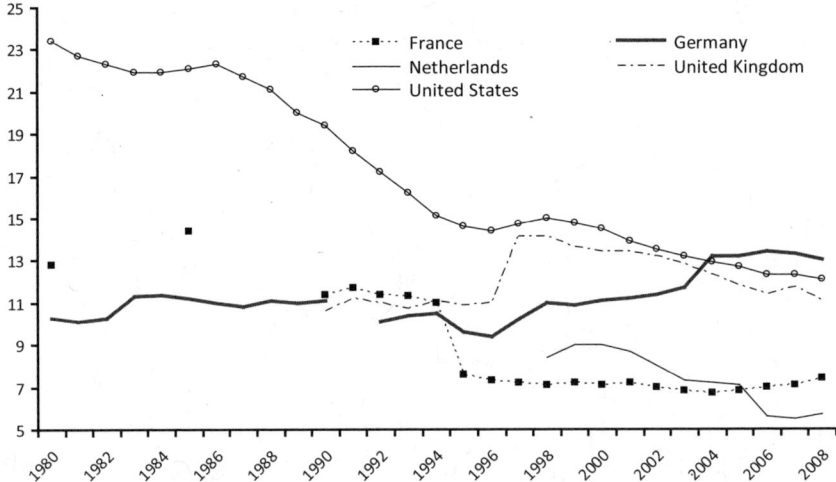

**Figure 13.4** Out-of-Pocket Payments in Germany and Selected Countries, 1980–2008 (Percent of total health spending)
Source: Organization for Economic Cooperation and Development, OECD Health Data 2010.

sickness funds' surpluses, as they also had an impact on real *revenues,* either reducing them or preventing them from growing at the pace at which real expenditures returned to their upward trend. At the time of writing, it is too early to say whether the introduction of a central health fund as part of the 2009 reform will turn out to be the exception to this rule.

An important reason for the limited effectiveness of *past* reforms has been the behavioral response of voluntary enrollees in SHI who have tended to migrate into private health insurance in significant numbers whenever the generosity of services in SHI has been reduced, as evidenced by the fluctuations in SHI membership shown by the bars in Figure 13.5.

Another reason for the limited effectiveness of past reforms has been their emphasis on rigid budget caps, often adopted without proper consideration of their allocative consequences when doctors' and hospitals' incentives remained basically unchanged. Since 1993, global budgets have been used not only to set upper limits on doctors' remuneration for their treatment of SHI patients (in proportion to the aggregate wage income of all SHI enrollees), but also to limit medical practitioners' prescription of pharmaceuticals.

When competition between sickness funds was first introduced in 1997, it did not immediately trigger the productivity gains in the provision of care that policymakers had hoped for. Instead, it led to substantial risk selection. Not only was the list of sickness funds' services almost entirely predetermined by law, but virtually all their contracting with care providers was negotiated and implemented by centralized cartels, including the regional doctors' associations (known as *Kassenärztliche Vereinigungen*), the German Hospital Federation, and the umbrella organization of the sickness funds themselves. The only parameters individual sickness funds could use to compete were the costs of their own administration

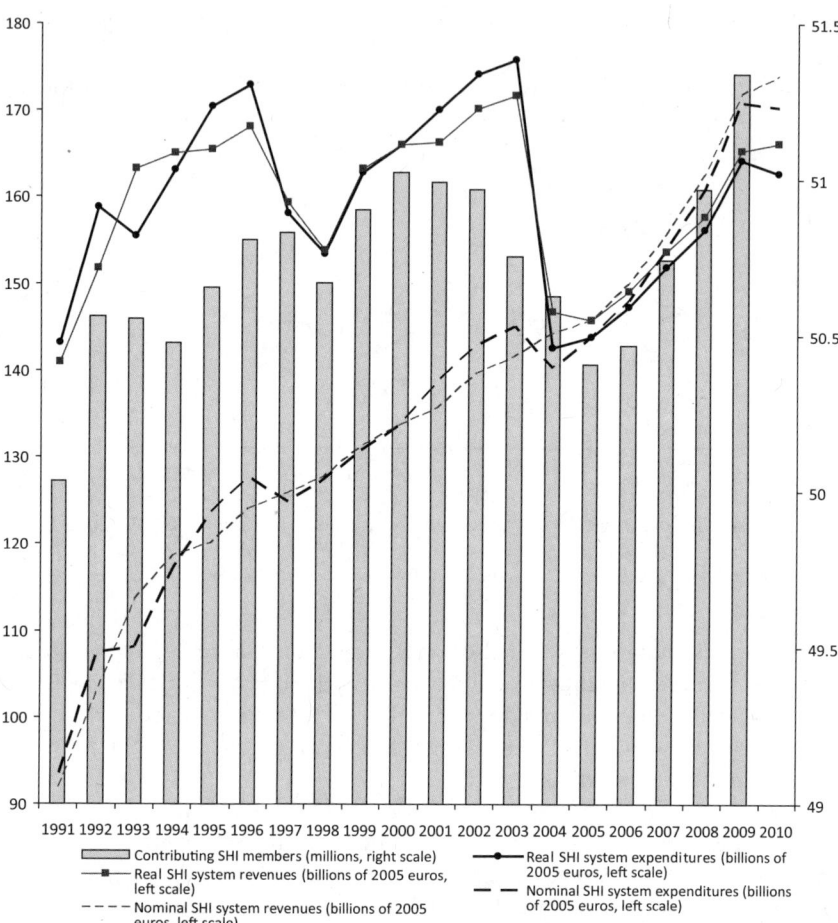

**Figure 13.5**   Past Reforms with Merely Temporary Effects
Source: BMG (Arbeits- und Sozialstatistik, Bundesarbeitsblatt, KJ 1, KM 1, KV 45), using the consumer price index for health care.

and strategies for risk selection. When it became apparent that this very limited mode of competition had failed to stabilize SHI, the government resorted to yet another round of six reforms, implemented between 1999 and 2004, which relied on global budget caps for specific types of expenditure and on other demand-side measures, such as private copayments.

## RECENT REFORMS TO IMPROVE INCENTIVES AND INTRODUCE MARKET MECHANISMS

The centerpiece of recent reforms in SHI has been the introduction of a central health fund, designed to administer a comprehensive risk adjustment scheme as part of a series of reforms to improve incentives and competition between sickness funds as well as among the providers of care. These reforms have not been entirely confined to SHI, because the government recognized that the problem of risk selection within SHI was complicated by an additional problem of risk selection by private insurers at the expense of SHI, as both systems compete for voluntary enrollees. In theory, private health insurance is meant to offer actuarially fair lifetime coverage to those with the right of opting out of SHI, but in practice there were also between 100,000 and 200,000 socially undesirable migrations from private insurance into SHI every year, enabling private insurers to dump a substantial part of the privately insureds' aging-related risks and costs onto SHI. Many of these migrants had joined private health insurance when young, healthy, and single and then discovered upon starting a family that the extra premiums charged by private insurers for each dependent child and spouse could be avoided by switching back to SHI. To achieve a clearer separation between the two systems, force private health insurance into bearing the full lifetime risks for all new privately insureds, and increase the intensity of competition among private insurers, the government coupled the introduction of the central fund in SHI with the introduction of partial portability of aging provisions in private health insurance and put an end to migrations back into SHI.

## Partial Portability of Aging Provisions in Private Health Insurance

Because until 2008 insureds could not transfer aging provisions accumulated on their behalf from their old insurer to a new insurer, competition between private health insurers was quite limited and excessively focused on the acquisition of "good" risks, such as young and healthy university graduates. Private health insurance accumulates aging provisions automatically, since the law rules out raising premiums for any other reason than general expenditure increases in the provision of care. By implication, premiums are higher than the average costs of care for the young and lower than the average costs of care for the old, and the aging provisions serve to balance these differences out over the course of each individual's lifetime. Without the portability of aging provisions, private insurers found it profitable to offer contracts to the young that were priced below the rates that would have been actuarially fair if every insured had stayed in the contract until his or her death. To redress the situation at least partially, the *Gesetz zur Stärkung des Wettbewerbs in der gesetzlichen Krankenversicherung* of 2007 allows all new privately insureds from 2009 on to later transfer to any other private insurer the aging provisions corresponding to the "cheap" standard contract. Although full portability in cases other than the standard contract has not been achieved, the reform has made switching to another private insurer much more affordable, even under nonstandard contracts, and has thus made it politically acceptable that privately insured workers are no longer eligible to switch back to SHI.

Since a clearer separation of private health insurance from SHI should help make reforms *within* SHI more effective, there is likely to be a positive fiscal impact. To be sure, lobbying on behalf of the private health insurance industry has played a role in preventing the introduction of portability for the *full* aging provisions in cases other than the standard contract, yet the intellectual challenge of creating such a scheme also remains an obstacle.

## Central Health Fund

Historically, the central health fund represents a compromise between the social democrats' concept of *Bürgerversicherung* (collecting contributions from all citizens in proportion to their total personal income) and the conservatives' proposal of *Kopfpauschale* (flat-rate premiums). Beginning in 2009, the central fund has been collecting insureds' contributions, fixed at 15.5 percent of gross wages, as well as federal government infusions, and distributing the money among roughly 150 autonomous sickness funds. Sickness funds receive a fixed payment for each of their enrollees, about 50 percent of which is determined by a prospective risk adjustment scheme (known as the Morbi-RSA) and thus depends on the insured's gender, age, and ability to work as well as a number of prespecified morbidity parameters.

The reform was meant to promote consumer choice and competition using market mechanisms. Since each sickness fund's total revenue from the central fund is largely beyond its control, any financial difficulty must be acted upon unilaterally by requesting supplementary flat-rate payments from insureds. Since insureds in turn are free to switch to another sickness fund, this rule is thought to impose competitive pressure on sickness funds' management ex ante to improve efficiency—for example, by generating savings in administration or in contractual relationships with medical care providers.

To accommodate future increases in aggregate expenditures, the rules of the central fund will gradually change the structure of SHI finance. Sickness funds are expected to collect an increasing share of their total revenue through flat-rate premiums directly from enrollees when medical care becomes more expensive— for example, through the proliferation of costly new medical technologies. The Federal Insurance Office has forecast a doubling of the average supplementary premium from €8 per month in 2012 to €16 in 2014. Means-tested federal subsidies will kick in to offset the average flat-rate premium expected across all sickness funds at the beginning of a new year once the premium exceeds 2 percent of a worker's gross wage income. These subsidies will reduce the income-related contributions of eligible enrollees to the central fund. With the size of these subsidies linked to the average expected flat-rate premiums, insureds still have incentives to search for "efficient" sickness funds. However, critics argue that these incentives would be much stronger if the subsidies were linked to the lowest supplementary premiums that any sickness fund charges at a given point in time.

The rules of the central fund also have implications for the industry's evolution. For the first time, sickness funds can go bankrupt (as City BKK did in 2011), in which case the enrollees are seamlessly covered by another sickness fund of their choice. Should adverse selection trigger further bankruptcies or preemptive mergers, this might lead to an ever-increasing concentration of the sickness funds industry. Indeed, that process is well under way. Between 2008 and the beginning of 2011, mergers reduced the number of sickness funds from

221 to 154, according to the German Association of Statutory Sickness Funds.[4] The rules of the central fund are in effect protecting insureds, but not the management of sickness funds, from the gales of market competition.

## Morbidity-Based Risk Adjustment Scheme in SHI

The Morbi-RSA was introduced with the central fund in 2009. It replaces a rudimentary risk adjustment scheme from 1993 that operated merely on the basis of gender and age (as well as a measure of employment limitations due to disability) and left sickness funds with strong incentives for cream skimming, that is, to get rid of the chronically ill and attract young and healthy individuals into their pool of enrollees. To eliminate these incentives for risk selection, the Morbi-RSA categorizes insureds into 152 risk groups, including 40 age and gender categories, 6 earnings capacity categories, and 106 morbidity categories, which in turn are based on 80 well-defined chronic conditions, such as HIV/AIDS, diabetes, and schizophrenia, and in some cases differentiate the severity of the condition. Based on diagnoses made by hospitals or by general practitioners, sickness funds report the relevant diagnoses of their enrollees annually to the Federal Insurance Office. Hospital diagnoses are considered immediately reliable, whereas general practitioners are required to provide a second diagnostic confirmation of the relevant chronic condition within six months, and some of these diagnoses must be further validated by evidence of appropriate drug treatment.

An example from the introduction of the Morbi-RSA in 2009 shows the principle on which risk adjustment payments from the central health fund are based: in addition to a flat monthly base payment of €185.64 per enrollee, sickness funds received an additional €1.28 in adjustments for an insured male between the ages of 85 and 89, an additional €86.87 for dementia, and an additional €38.48 for hypertension, so that the total adjustment for an enrollee meeting all three conditions amounted to an additional €312.27. For younger people, the age adjustments were negative. For example, a female between the ages 13 and 17 and free from chronic conditions triggered an adjustment of minus €117.45. In another example, a regional sickness fund (BKK Bayern) reports the adjustments for a 53-year-old woman as follows: minus €100.21 for age and gender and plus €116.67 for her employment status as a partial-disability pensioner. With further adjustments for hypertension (plus €38.48), diabetes mellitus (plus €66.18), and osteoarthritis of the hip (plus €166.15), the total payment received by the sickness fund was €472.91.

Only time will tell whether the Morbi-RSA will provide an equitable and efficient allocation of funds, immune to abuse by the parties involved. Some observers worry that the Morbi-RSA may introduce incentives to manipulate the coding of medical diagnoses (up-coding) with the aim of obtaining more money from the central health fund. Some sickness funds have reportedly paid doctors to provide "more-detailed" diagnoses—hoping these could justify claiming a

---

[4]See http://www.gkv-spitzenverband.de/ITSGKrankenkassenListe.gkvnet.

chronic condition or a higher level of severity and thus trigger greater Morbi-RSA payments to the sickness fund. Critics say that diagnoses follow the money and could trigger a hunt for the sickest. Doctors would have an incentive to collude in this, since treating more severe conditions is often more generously remunerated under the new SHI payment scheme for physicians' services. Another concern is that the Morbi-RSA may weaken sickness funds' incentives to invest in preventive care.

## Prospective Payment for Hospital Care

The adoption of market mechanisms to rein in rising expenditures in German hospitals preceded the central fund by six years. Since 1970, the cumulative growth in hospital spending has exceeded the growth in pharmaceutical spending, although in the 1990s pharmaceutical spending began to narrow the gap. Over the 40-year period from 1970 to 2009, hospitals' share of all SHI spending rose from 25 to 35 percent, compared with a rise from 21 to 26 percent for pharmaceuticals. Beginning in 2003, Australian-inspired diagnosis-related groups and uniform state-level base rates (i.e., prices for units of service) were implemented gradually in the remuneration of German hospitals and by 2009 covered all stationary care, with the notable exception of psychiatric care. Additional regulation and competitive pressure under diagnosis-related groups have since forced hospitals into increasing specialization to meet quality standards and increase productivity, requiring and inducing substantial new investments in medical technology as well as physical and human capital.

The most immediate fiscal impact of these changes has been on municipalities and states that have traditionally owned the vast majority of hospitals in Germany. The need to raise financial capital for investments has led to a wave of privatizations, especially among municipal hospitals in rural areas and eastern Germany (and one university hospital in Hessen), often through acquisition by large publicly listed hospital chains. In some cases, antitrust issues have prompted the Federal Cartel Office to intervene. With more than 85 percent of German hospital beds still publicly owned in 2009, some observers see potential for further privatizations, yet compared with other countries, there still seems to be a massive oversupply of beds per capita of the population. This has encouraged the export of stationary care to foreign patients from countries with waiting lists for certain procedures, such as Scandinavia and the United Kingdom.

## Diagnosis-Related Payment of Physicians in Ambulatory Care

In contrast to the continued increases in SHI spending on hospital care and pharmaceuticals, nominal SHI spending on physician services in dental and other ambulatory care has been almost flat since the early 1990s, and its percentage share in all SHI spending has been declining since the 1970s. Against this background, the government's priority in adopting market mechanisms for ambulatory care has not been to contain the growth of spending overall, but to improve incentives for physicians to move into underserved areas of care, including underserved geographic regions.

Until 2008, a periodic fixed payment (based on capitation) limited the growth of physicians' aggregate pay to the growth of workers' aggregate gross wage incomes. Remuneration for the treatment of SHI enrollees was paid through doctors' regional associations, the *Kassenärztliche Vereinigungen*, in proportion to the volume of services provided in the preceding three-month period. The remuneration per unit of service fluctuated over time and varied between regions, which contributed to substantial interregional variation in physician density, with unmet medical needs in some and supplier-induced demand for excessive care in others. Rich metropolitan regions were also able to attract more physicians per capita because they offered doctors better prospects of supplementing their incomes from the regional associations by serving private patients, who are charged between 2.3 and 3.5 times as much as SHI patients for a given service.

The SHI reforms of 2009 introduced a new system that uses some principles of prospective payment and combines fee for service with morbidity-related payments and euro prices—listed in the Federal Health Minister's list—with the aim of encouraging investments in doctors' offices and realigning their incentives, for example, to move into underserved fields of care or neglected regions. To prevent supplier-induced demand, the full price is paid only for services within preannounced volume limits (*Regelleistungsvolumina*) that are specific to each doctor or group practice and depend on the type of medical specialization, regional physician density, and morbidity of patients, approximated by age and gender. Additional selective contracting between individual doctors or groups of doctors and sickness funds is possible, but the bulk of services is still subject to collective contracts negotiated and administered by the regional doctors' associations. These associations allocate the bulk of payments to individual practitioners according to the official euro prices listed in the Federal Health Minister's list.

The reforms also introduced elements of managed care. For example, general practitioners have benefited from a requirement since 2007 that all sickness funds offer their enrollees at least two different elective contracts, one of which (*Hausarztvertrag*) must offer reduced patient copayments in exchange for a binding commitment to see a registered primary physician, who will act as a gatekeeper, before consulting any specialist or a hospital. Yet how much extra pay this justifies is still controversial. The government said extra pay was justified only by increases in efficiency and a reduction of costs elsewhere, not by the greater bargaining power that registered primary care physicians have won, since the 2007 law requires sickness funds to negotiate all such contracts (*Hausarztverträge*) with organizations representing at least 50 percent of general practitioners. This has encouraged primary care physicians to break away from the regional cartels of the doctors' associations and form their own unions.

## Quality Control

As the economics of information asymmetry suggests, provider competition without stringent external quality controls could deteriorate into a race to the bottom or trigger systematic discrimination against costly-to-treat patients. Policymakers in Germany seem to have understood early on the need for quality standards and specific incentives for continuing improvements as provider competition is unleashed. Since 2005, hospitals have had to publish structured quality reports on a regular basis, every two years, with information that can be used by all stakeholders, in particular by insureds, patients, general practitioners, and sickness funds. Oversight is provided by the Federal Joint Committee (*Gemeinsamer Bundesausschuss,* or G-BA), the key decision-making body at the interface of sickness funds, doctors' associations, and the hospital sector. The G-BA has developed standards for the quality of structures, processes, and outcomes in the hospital sector and has been given the mandate to do so for ambulatory care as well.

Quality control for general practitioners in private offices is still partly overseen by the chambers of regional physicians (*Ärztekammern*), with particular emphasis on continuing training and its certification and financial penalties in the remuneration of patient care in case of doctors' noncompliance. New schemes to control the quality of longer episodes of care, involving both hospital and outpatient care, are under development and in some cases are already implemented in pilot schemes.

## Pharmaceutical Markets

### Background

Sickness funds are generally required to reimburse retailers for part of the cost of any prescription drug with the chemical entity ordered by a medical practitioner for the insured and pharmacists obliged to sell the cheapest drugs in each therapeutic class. Patient copayment is at 10 percent of the drug's price, up to €10 per refill and up to 2 percent of the insured's income annually. Past reforms mainly aimed at expanding the use of generics. Since 1989, reference prices for generics have limited the level of reimbursement by sickness funds. In addition, global budgets for all pharmaceutical spending in SHI were used during the 1990s and early 2000s. In 2002, the global budgets were replaced by prescription target volumes for individual physicians, who were made financially liable for the costs of prescribing more than 25 percent above target. In 2007, bonus payments were introduced to reward physicians who prescribed low-priced drugs and thus stayed below the prescription target volumes for specific areas of disease, calculated on the basis of the average costs of prescribing the defined daily dosages in those areas. Since 2008, however, physician-specific bonus payments and payment reductions have no longer been applied, as the increased use of volume rebates made it difficult to determine the relevant average costs of prescription drugs.

Sickness funds have been free to directly negotiate volume and other rebates for both generics and branded prescription drugs with suppliers since 2003, and since 2006 they have been able to restrict reimbursement to one brand in each therapeutic category coupled with lower patient copayments or a waiver to make this option an attractive choice for enrollees. But until 2010, there was no regulation to limit the prices of new prescription drugs.

A recent study of international pharmaceutical price differences by Drummond and others (2011) reports that the 2009 off-pharmacy prices of select new drugs in Germany were significantly higher than those in comparable European countries. For example, a typical schizophrenia drug, Risperidone, was priced more than twice as high as in the Netherlands, Sweden, and the United Kingdom, and the insulin analogue Glulisine, priced at €13.82 in Germany, cost only between €7.17 and €8.42 in those other two countries. However, the relatively high German prices were confined to newly introduced drugs still under patent. The overall price index of pharmaceuticals reimbursed by Germany's SHI was stable between 1991 and 2003, and then declined by more than 10 percent until 2009 as sickness funds began to take advantage of the new law allowing them to negotiate volume rebates with suppliers. The decline in pharmaceutical prices, especially since 2003, contrasts sharply with Germany's overall consumer price index for health care, which rose by 60 percent between 1991 and 2009.

To bring down the high average prices of new prescription drugs, the law regulating the reimbursement of drugs, *Arzneimittelmarktneuordnungsgesetz* (AMNOG),[5] which came into effect in January 2011, mobilizes sickness funds' collective monopsony power for negotiations with producers over maximum reimbursement levels, based on proven incremental therapeutic benefits. Although AMNOG's main aim is to limit SHI's spending on new drugs with only marginal improvements on the benefit side—that is, "fake" innovations—the law clearly extends the use of price regulations and has wider implications for the economic evaluation of pharmaceuticals.

Figure 13.6 provides a flow diagram of the process of initial benefit assessment, pricing, and cost-effectiveness analysis for new drugs in SHI. When a producer introduces a new drug into the German market, the producer is initially free to

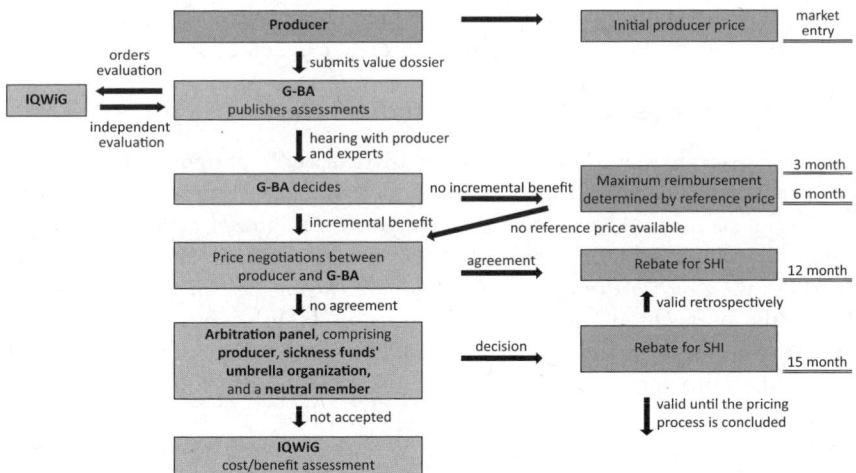

**Figure 13.6** Cost-Benefit Assessment and Pricing of Drugs in SHI
Source: BMG (2010), Die Spreu vom Weizen trennen: Das Arzneimittelmarktneuordnungsgesetz (AMNOG).
Note: G-BA = *Gemeinsamer Bundesausschuss* (Federal Joint Committee); IQWiG = *Institut für Qualität und Wirtschaftlichkeit im Gesundheitswesen* (German Institute for Quality and Efficiency in Health Care); SHI = social health insurance.

---

[5] The law's name could be literally translated as "the law for the reorganization of pharmaceutical markets."

set the price but must at the same time submit a value dossier to the G-BA, the key decision-making body within SHI—made up of voting delegates from the Association of Statutory Sickness Funds, the Associations of Statutory Sickness Funds Physicians and Dentists, and the German Hospital Federation. The G-BA then asks the German Institute for Quality and Efficiency in Health Care (*Institut für Qualität und Wirtschaftlichkeit im Gesundheitswesen* or IQWiG), for an independent evaluation of the dossier, which has to be published within three months. Next, the G-BA organizes a hearing with the producer and outside experts before it decides (within six months) whether the new drug has incremental benefits, relative to existing therapies. If the G-BA sees an incremental benefit, a price for the new drug that takes the benefit into account is negotiated between the producer and the G-BA. If no such incremental benefit is found, the maximum reimbursement is determined by the reference price for existing drugs within the therapeutic class to which the new drug belongs. If no such reference price is available, the producer and G-BA have to negotiate the price for the new drug bilaterally even in the absence of incremental benefits.

Price negotiations are generally expected to reach an agreement within six months, and the agreed price is then implemented as a rebate for all sickness funds on the initial producer price. If no agreement is reached, an arbitration panel, comprising the producer, the Association of Statutory Sickness Funds, and a neutral member, is given another three months to agree on the size of the rebate. If this also fails, the G-BA has to order IQWiG to perform a full analysis of costs and benefits in the spirit of comparative cost-effectiveness research; the drug's price will then be decreed on that basis. In an extension of the original scope of AMNOG, Germany's private health insurers have successfully lobbied the government to enforce the same rebates for private patients.

## Comparative Cost-Effectiveness Studies

Public management and coordination are particularly important with respect to the evaluation and management of medical technology. Efficient filtering and utilization of medical technology has long been recognized as key to creating value for money in health care. Yet Germany is relatively late in the game. In 2000, the *Deutsches Institut für Medizinische Dokumentation und Information,* under the oversight of the Federal Minister of Health, created the *Deutsche Agentur für Health Technology Assessment* and has since produced a large number of health technology assessment reports, apparently with limited impact on medical practice. In 2005, a new and independent agency for comparative cost-effectiveness research was created, the previously mentioned IQWiG, with a legal mandate to assess the medical benefits of new and established technologies and procedures and help create treatment guidelines for specific diseases, using evidence-based medicine.

### Methods Controversy

IQWiG was also mandated to develop methods for its economic evaluations based on established international standards. Yet its 2008 methods paper provoked controversy, with leading European health economists, such as Jönsson (2008), arguing that it neglected important economic aspects and wasted a "historic" opportunity for moving toward European coordination in regulation and reimbursement. IQWiG's methods paper, meant to develop the official guidelines for cost-effectiveness analyses informing regulatory and reimbursement decisions in Germany, invoked the concept of an efficiency frontier from portfolio theory to motivate an empirical production or cost function that can be used to identify and eliminate inefficient technologies, such as expensive new drugs. But the paper created the erroneous impression that the comparative valuation of incremental benefits could be restricted to any given disease under focus, implicitly allowing inefficiencies that may exist in the allocation of resources across diseases to persist or even to grow. The paper has also been criticized for failing to make clear that a societal perspective on benefits and costs should be adopted and how indirect costs ought to be measured. These deficiencies are significant not only because they leave the suppliers of cost-effectiveness research, such as international pharmaceutical firms, in unnecessary uncertainty about the required content and methods of studies that would be most useful in regulatory and reimbursement decisions within SHI, but also because the decision makers themselves may find it difficult to interpret the evidence from studies of a given technology when these are based on inconsistent methods.

## LESSONS AND REMAINING CHALLENGES

Some of the policy lessons that may be of interest to other countries can be summarized briefly as follows. Sickness funds' collective monopoly power vis-à-vis Germany's regional physicians' associations has long been effective in containing the cost of ambulatory physician services in SHI. More recently, diagnosis-related groups have helped to contain the cost of hospital care and triggered important changes in hospitals' competitive behavior and management strategies. In the pharmaceutical sector, reference prices for generics alone have had ambiguous effects. Average prices of pharmaceuticals used in SHI began to decline substantially only after sickness funds were given the freedom to negotiate volume rebates.

Finally, the rudimentary risk adjustment scheme that preceded the Morbi-RSA and was based mainly on age and gender did not work well. It led to an increasing segregation of sickness funds' enrollees by type and size of risk, and it threatened to destabilize the entire SHI system. The Morbi-RSA has substantially reduced sickness funds' incentives for risk selection and even made some types of chronic diseases a financially attractive asset in their pool of enrollees. Whether the Morbi-RSA will provide sufficient flexibility to adjust its own payment schedule in response to future changes in medical technology that change the relative costs and benefits of treating specific diseases remains to be seen.

### The Challenge of Demographic Change

As population aging accelerates and enrollees' average SHI contribution payments begin to decline, the role of Germany's central government in financing health care is certain to increase. However, recent evidence in support of the compression-of-morbidity-before-death hypothesis suggests that population aging per se is not likely to become a major exogenous driver of health care costs. Instead, population aging may provide countries such as Germany with an unprecedented opportunity to make public and private health investments with particularly high social rates of return in the long term. If much of population aging is ultimately driven by an income elasticity of individual demand for health above one, policymakers should allow health care's share in GDP to rise even in the absence of increasing costs per unit of care. The present rules of SHI imply that future increases in costs will be largely borne by individuals via the supplementary flat-rate payments that sickness funds must charge to cover expenditures exceeding their risk-adjusted revenue from the central fund.

Moreover, as population aging is likely to be accompanied by an increasing prevalence of chronic diseases, it may open up new opportunities for innovative pharmaceutical products and treatment strategies in the context of targeted disease management programs (DMPs) that are designed to coordinate elements of the treatment process across time, stages, and providers on the basis of evidence-based medical guidelines. Germany has developed two types of DMPs, one of which became a mandatory service—in 2002—for all sickness funds participating in the risk adjustment scheme preceding the Morbi-RSA. Since 2005, these tightly regulated DMPs, individually approved and supervised by Germany's Federal Insurance Office, have been available for six chronic conditions, including type 1 and type 2 diabetes mellitus, breast cancer, coronary heart disease, asthma, and chronic obstructive pulmonary disease. Around 50 percent of all DMP patients have been enrolled for type 2 diabetes mellitus. In 2011, a total of almost 6 million enrollees of sickness funds (about 8 percent of all SHI enrollees) participated in one or several of about 11,000 programs, according to the Federal Insurance Office.[6] Since DMP patients are generally costly to treat and account for a large share of sickness funds' expenditures subject to risk adjustment payments, their percentage weight in SHI's total annual budget has been two to three times greater than their percentage share of all insured person-years in SHI.

The second type of DMP is neither mandated nor supervised by the Federal Insurance Office, and hence is often called a "free" DMP. Although it too tends to be patient-centered and mainly concerned with tertiary prevention and quality of care, it is also used as a cost-controlling strategy by private health insurers and has become increasingly popular among statutory sickness funds as well.

The greater freedom that sickness funds have been given to negotiate selective DMP contracts with care providers offers a variety of novel opportunities for networks of providers, including general practitioners and specialists within and outside hospitals as well as specialized pharmaceutical firms. Innovative research-based pharmaceutical firms often develop their product portfolios around specific classes of disease, such as HIV/AIDS or cancer. These firms thus tend to acquire a great deal of specialized knowledge and experience that makes them uniquely equipped to help manage or even take a leading role in DMPs. In this

---

[6]See http://www.bundesversicherungsamt.de/cln_115/nn_1046154/DE/DMP/dmp__inhalt.html.

way, they could help overcome the traditional lack of cooperation between hospitals and general practitioners in ambulatory care that may have held back the development and diffusion of DMPs in the past. Competition between provider networks offering DMPs for the same chronic condition could in turn help create financial incentives for pharmaceutical firms to enter this market with more cost-effective drugs, that is, by providing a given level of health outcomes at lower overall costs—for example, by helping to shorten or avoid hospital stays of the chronically diseased. A competitive market for DMPs can thus help to clarify the conditions under which savings in the treatment process as a whole can offset the sometimes-high prices of specific new drugs. Through all this, innovative pharmaceutical firms may find a new business opportunity in a growing segment of the health care market.

## The Opportunity for Greater European Integration

It has been mentioned that the regulation of pricing and reimbursement for new drugs has an important European dimension: many countries within the European Union are simply too small to justify the high fixed costs of building sophisticated systems for health technology assessment on their own. A more-integrated European health care market would enable all countries to better exploit economies of scale in the evaluation, adoption, and diffusion of new medical technologies and services. Because of the large size of its home market, Germany would be well placed to take on a leading role in the creation of such an integrated market, beginning with an increasing harmonization of health technology assessment and the regulation of medical technology.

# REFERENCES

De Vries, H., D. Goldman, and G. Joyce, 2008, *Comparing Medical Productivity Between Germany and the U.S.—An Assessment of Differences and Trends in Costs, Treatments and Outcomes for Acute Myocardial Infarction and Colorectal Cancer* (Baden-Baden: Nomos).

Drummond, M., B. Jönsson, F. Rutten, and T. Stargardt, 2011, "Reimbursement of Pharmaceuticals: Reference Pricing versus Health Technology Assessment," *European Journal of Health Economics,* Vol. 12, pp. 263–71.

Jönsson, B., 2008, "IQWiG: An Opportunity Lost?" *European Journal of Health Economics,* Vol. 9, pp. 205–7.

# CHAPTER 14

# Taiwan Province of China's Experience with Universal Health Care Coverage

## TSUNG-MEI CHENG

Health reform on the ground usually is a far cry from the neat policy designs taught in the classroom. On the way to becoming law, the coherent policy blueprints produced by health policy analysts typically must run the gamut of parliamentary log rolling, which, in turn, is so often influenced by powerful economic and professional interest groups that derive income from health care or jealously guard their professional independence. And there are always groups that oppose health reform on purely ideological grounds. These groups have all the more power in shaping health reform if the country's top leadership is either relatively weak or uncommitted to the proposed reform.

The introduction of Taiwan Province of China's National Health Insurance (NHI) system in 1995—a single-payer, government-run health insurance system coupled with a mixed, mainly private health care delivery system—stands as an instructive exception to this pattern. There, careful study by Taiwan Province of China's health policy analysts and top bureaucrats of alternative health systems that were already functioning abroad, coupled with agreement on the ethical principles to be followed by the reformed health system, produced a coherent blueprint that became law with little of the disfigurement so often deplored by the designers of health policy. The NHI unveiled in 1995 is a hybrid system that leaned heavily on the Canadian and German systems, egalitarian systems based on the solidarity principle.

Taiwan Province of China at the time benefited from two fundamental drivers of successful health reform, namely, a strong and rapidly growing economy and a top leadership passionately committed to making universal health insurance coverage a reality, something that has been achieved since 1995.

The purpose of this chapter is to describe Taiwan Province of China's experience with health reform in the hope that other countries may find lessons in that experience for their own reforms. The chapter begins with a brief review of the genesis of the reform, followed by an overview of the current health system. It describes the modus operandi of the NHI and explores some of the major challenges the reform has encountered and continues to encounter along the way. The chapter ends with a review of the lessons other countries may be able to draw from Taiwan Province of China's experience, including the advantages and

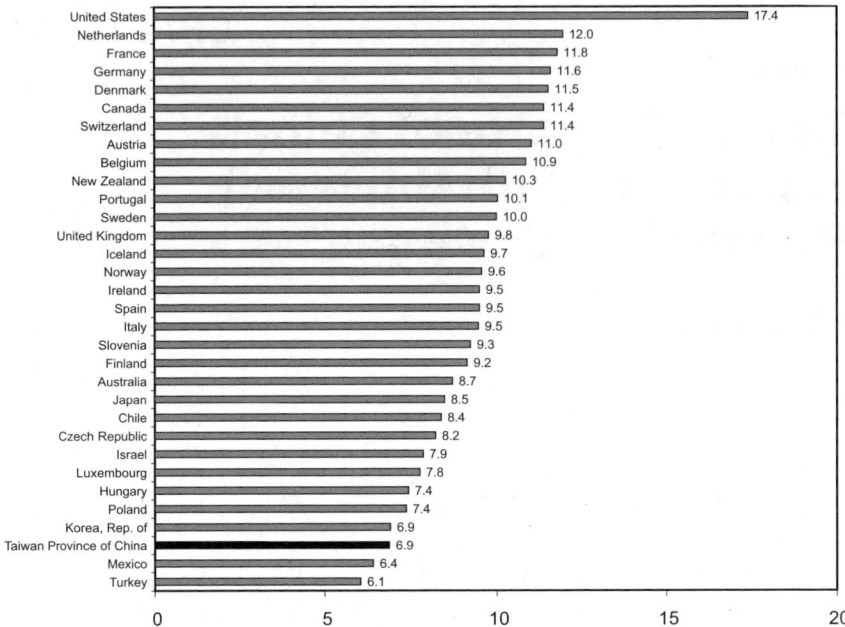

**Figure 14.1** Health Spending as a Percentage of GDP, Selected OECD Countries and Taiwan Province of China, 2008–09
Source: For selected OECD countries, Organization for Economic Cooperation and Development 2011 Database; for Taiwan Province of China, data are based on Taiwan Province of China, DOH (2009).

shortcomings of a single-payer health insurance system, and looks at the agenda for future health reform in Taiwan Province of China.

## OVERVIEW

### Financing Health Care

*Total National Health Spending*

Taiwan Province of China is a highly developed Asian economy. GDP per capita in 2010 was $18,558 at current exchange rates or, in purchasing power parity dollars, $35,604.[1]

Figure 14.1 presents data on total national health spending as a percentage of GDP for 2008–09 in selected Organization for Economic Cooperation and Development (OECD) countries as well as in Taiwan Province of China. One can see that Taiwan Province of China, at 6.9 percent of GDP, ranks at the low-cost end of this array of nations, although its health spending is comparable to the Republic of Korea's (also 6.9 percent). Japan is at the high end of the Asian range, and there is evidence that Japan's actual health spending is considerably higher

---

[1] Based on IMF, World Economic Outlook database, September 2011.

than the 8.5 percent of GDP officially reported by the OECD. In purchasing power parity dollars, Taiwan Province of China spent $2,186 per capita in 2009.[2] The comparable U.S. figure was $7,960.

Regarding the shared concern among the world's advanced economies for the fiscal sustainability of publicly financed health care in future decades, the outlook in Taiwan Province of China may be more optimistic than it is in many other countries. Public debt in Taiwan Province of China is low compared to most OECD countries. For each year from 2007 through 2011, government gross debt as a percent of GDP was, sequentially, 33.4 percent, 35.8 percent, 39.9 percent, 39.7 percent, and finally 37.9 percent. Real GDP growth in Taiwan Province of China was 10.8 percent in 2010, reflecting a strong recovery after the 2008 financial crisis, and growth is estimated to be 5.4 percent in 2011. Inflation has been low: 3.5 percent in 2008, −0.9 percent in 2009, 1 percent in 2010, and an estimated 2 percent in 2011. Unemployment, at 4.6 percent in 2011, is significantly lower than in most OECD countries.

Overall, Taiwan Province of China's economy is strong and its future prospects are good. In addition, the savings rate is high, and Taiwan Province of China has no foreign debt, unlike the United States and many European countries. Experts in Taiwan Province of China believe that the probability of a financial bankruptcy in its government, such as those experienced by Iceland and Greece, is extremely low.

## Sources of Financing

Cross-national comparisons of health care financing can be confusing, because the *sources* of the financing break down differently from the *spending* on health care, that is, the making of payments to providers (Reinhardt, 2011). Although this is not widely recognized, all health spending in a nation ultimately originates in that nation's households, unless additional funds come in from other countries in the form of international aid. But only households' out-of-pocket (OOP) spending when accessing care flows directly from households to the providers of health care. The rest flows from households through government in the form of taxes or, in Taiwan Province of China, premiums paid to the government-run NHI. Economists argue that when private employers contribute to health insurance premiums on behalf of employees, the employers actually reduce the take-home pay of workers to recover that outlay. So households ultimately pay for these employer contributions as well. In other words, governments and employers are only intermediaries in the money flow for health care. So one must be careful to define exactly what is meant by "public sector health spending." Are we talking

---

[2]Officially, Taiwan Province of China's government reports per capita health spending as $1,126 for 2009. But that figure is calculated at the current exchange rate for 2009. The higher figure of $2,186 was given to the author at a meeting on October 6, 2011, with Cheng-Hua Lee, Deputy Director of the Bureau of National Health Insurance in the Department of Health, in Taipei, Taiwan Province of China. It appears to have been calculated at the purchasing power parity exchange rate for 2009.

about sources of financing national health expenditures or are we talking about uses of national health expenditure funds—spending?

## Sources of National Health Expenditure

According to government documents, the sources of financing for health care in Taiwan Province of China in 2009 break down as follows: from government, 27.9 percent; business, 12.6 percent; households, 52.3 percent; nonprofit entities, 6.4 percent; and commercial insurance administrative costs, 0.7 percent (Taiwan Province of China, DOH, 2009).

The bulk of the 27.9 percent attributed to government in the official Taiwan Province of China documents refers to government subsidies toward the NHI budget (revenue). The remainder represents other government outlays for public health, and such things as capital expenditures and personnel salaries for public and military hospitals.

## Uses of National Health Expenditure Funds (Spending)

If we measure the role of government in financing health care by who writes the final check to pay for health care, then government's share is about 57.8 percent, of which the NHI represents the bulk of spending (51.3 percent). The premium-based budget for the NHI, however, draws on three sources of financing: premiums paid in by households, premium contributions made by employers on behalf of employees, and tax-financed government premium contributions for particular population categories. This breakdown is discussed in more detail later in the chapter.

Private sector spending (42.2 percent of NHI) consists of OOP spending by patients for health care (35.1 percent) and spending by private, nonprofit health care organizations (Taiwan Province of China, DOH, 2009).

At 57.8 percent, the government's share of total national health spending is at the low end of the range for most OECD countries. It is comparable, however, to that of the Republic of Korea and Switzerland, where the government shares of total national health spending are 59.5 percent and 59.7 percent, respectively, and it is higher than the 49 percent government share in the United States. Government's share in other OECD member states ranged between 69.6 and 84.5 percent of total national health spending in 2009.[3]

# THE NATIONAL HEALTH INSURANCE

## The Big Bang

On March 1, 1995, Taiwan Province of China implemented the NHI by order of the top political leadership, fully five years ahead of the originally announced 2000 date of implementation. The social policy goals pursued by Taiwan Province of China's policymakers were social solidarity and cost containment.

---

[3]Based on the Organization for Economic Cooperation and Development's OECD Health Data 2011.

Total health spending in Taiwan Province of China had been rising at double digits in the years prior to the establishment of the NHI, and just 59 percent of the population of 22 million then had health insurance. The potential for impoverishment from the medical costs of illness was a serious problem for the 41 percent of the population who had no health insurance at the time. Most of the uninsured were in vulnerable groups, like children under 14, women, the elderly, and the disabled—those who also had the greatest need for health insurance and health care.

Prior to the NHI, Taiwan Province of China had 13 different social insurance schemes. The largest of those was Labor Insurance, established in 1950, which covered 40.1 percent of the population at that time, which was 20 million. Following Labor Insurance were the Government Employees Insurance, begun in 1958, which covered 8.3 percent of the population; Farmers Insurance, begun in 1985, which covered 8.2 percent of the population; and Low-Income Household Insurance, begun in 1990, which covered 0.6 percent of the population. Private health insurance, as it is commonly known in the West, did not exist.

Not all was ready in 1995 for the implementation of the largest social program since Taiwan Province of China's retreat from the Chinese mainland in 1949. The government made the decisive call for full implementation, as it was eager to respond to the public's call for better health care and the economy had sustained robust growth for a number of years, making financing for such a large social program possible. Enrollment in the NHI was mandatory for all citizens and later on for legal residents as well. Overnight, Taiwan Province of China's hitherto uninsured 41 percent of the population became eligible for health insurance coverage.

By the end of its first year, the NHI had enrolled 92 percent of Taiwan Province of China's citizens, and satisfaction levels rose to 70 percent from the low of 20 percent one month after implementation. Since 2002, the NHI has covered 99 percent of the population.

## Who Is Covered—Risk Pooling in the NHI

Because the NHI is a single-payer system, there is but one single risk pool for the entire population. Unlike U.S. private health insurance, in which insurers risk-select ("cherry pick") and can and do exclude from coverage those individuals with poor health status and preexisting conditions, the NHI enrolls all comers. It levies premiums using the uniform national single premium rate (currently at 5.17 percent of salary or wage), thus safeguarding equity in health insurance access.

## Benefit Package

The NHI offers broad benefits in a uniform national benefits package to all insured. Benefits include inpatient and outpatient care, drugs, dental, traditional Chinese medicine, day care for the mentally ill, home nursing care, palliative care, and dialysis, among other things. Former health minister Ching-Chuan Yeh, the founding President and CEO of the Bureau of National Health Insurance (BNHI) and later Minister of Health and a senior statesman in Taiwan Province of China's health policy, described the NHI's benefits as "all you can eat" (Cheng, 2009a).

Taiwan Province of China's NHI currently has no upper limit on spending to save or extend a life. For example, based on ethical and humanitarian considerations, the NHI at present is maintaining the lives of nine pediatric patients (average IQ 60–70) with rare diseases using orphan drugs at an annual cost of $1 million per patient.[4]

## Administration of the NHI

The Bureau of National Health Insurance of the Department of Health administers the NHI. The single risk pool and the uniformity it begets give Taiwan Province of China's single-payer NHI a tremendous advantage in administrative simplicity. Administrative cost was 1.3 percent of total NHI spending in 2011.

## Financing of the NHI

### The NHI as a Premium-Based Pay-as-You-Go System

The NHI is a premium-based single-payer system financed basically by premium contributions plus government subsidies toward these premiums where applicable. For formal sector employees, the premium is collected at the nexus of the payroll, with contributions from both employees and employers.

In theory, premiums can be set as a percentage either of wages or of total income (ability to pay), or on a per capita basis (so that family size matters, as large families will pay more), or actuarially (so that health status matters, as the sick pay higher premiums than the healthy). Taiwan Province of China chose a combination of the first and second approaches in assessing premiums. By contrast, the nongroup U.S. private health insurance system serving individual customers (individual policies) bases premium calculations on the health status of the insured. Individuals in the United States with poor health status can be denied insurance policies by private insurers. The Accountable Care Act of 2010 is designed to change this, but the related provision will not go into effect until 2014 and will most likely cover only half of the currently more than 50 million uninsured (over 15 percent of the U.S. population).

### Premium Contributions

Operationally, the NHI divides Taiwan Province of China's population into six population categories, each receiving varying amounts of government premium subsidies (from 0 to 100 percent). Table 14.1 illustrates these six population

---

[4]Based on author's meeting with Cheng-Hua Lee, Deputy Director-General of the Bureau of National Health Insurance, Department of Health, October 6, 2011, Taipei.

**TABLE 14.1**

## Sources of National Health Insurance Premium Contribution (Percent)

| Population category | Insured[a] | Employer | Government | Percentage of population |
|---|---|---|---|---|
| 1 Employees of publicly or privately owned enterprises or institutions | 30 | 60 | 10 | 51.50 |
| Government employees | 30 | 70 | 0 | |
| Private school teachers | 30 | 35 | 35 | |
| Self-employed, employers | 100 | 0 | 0 | |
| 2 Union members | 60 | 0 | 40 | 17.40 |
| 3 Farmers, fishermen | 30 | 0 | 70 | 13.00 |
| 4 Active military personnel | 0 | 0 | 100 | 0.60 |
| 5 Low-income households | 0 | 0 | 100 | 1.00 |
| 6 Veterans | 0 | 0 | 100 | 16.50 |
| Dependents of veterans | 30 | 0 | 70 | |
| Community population | 60 | 0 | 40 | |

Source: Taiwan Province of China, BNHI, DOH (2010).
[a]"Insured" includes up to three household dependents.

categories and the amount of subsidies each receives from the government. Statutory premium subsidies from government apply to low-income households, the handicapped, the elderly, and the temporarily unemployed.

Like the Swiss health system, Taiwan Province of China's NHI also levies premiums on a per capita basis. But it differs from the Swiss system in that it levies premiums on a "limited" per capita basis.[5] In addition to the insured, each member of an insured's family, up to a maximum of three family members, also pays a premium. Any additional family members beyond three members enjoy NHI benefits at no cost.

Over 98 percent of Taiwanese pay their premiums on time, and more than 98.5 percent of premiums are collected. The premium rate as of 2011 is 5.17 percent of wage or salary. Nonwage or nonsalary incomes are currently not included in the assessment of premiums. This has been judged in Taiwan Province of China to be inequitable, since it means the salaried class and wage earners in Taiwan Province of China are bearing the brunt of the premium load for the NHI.

The BNHI, acting as the government agency that administers the NHI, collects premiums from the insured. Figure 14.2 shows the share of premium contributions made by the government (26 percent), the employer (36 percent), and the insured (38 percent) in Taiwan Province of China's NHI in 2010.

The de facto total government contribution to the total NHI premium revenue in 2010, however, is 34 percent. In addition to contributing 26 percent of the total NHI premium revenue in the form of premium subsidies to the various population categories, the government also contributes an additional

[5]For a more compete discussion of the Swiss health system, see Cheng (2010).

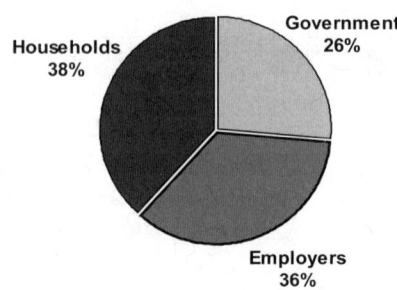

**Figure 14.2** Premium Contribution by Source for National Health Insurance, 2010
Source: Taiwan Province of China, Bureau of National Health Insurance, Department of Health 2010 data.

8 percent to the total NHI premium pool in its role as employer of public sector employees, including employees of public corporations, civil servants, and public school teachers. The two parts together amount to 34 percent of the total NHI premium revenue.[6]

## Copayments in Taiwan Province of China's NHI

Copayments apply for inpatient and outpatient care and drugs in Taiwan Province of China's NHI. Ceilings for and exemptions from copayments apply in order to safeguard patient access to needed care. Table 14.2 illustrates copayments for various types of outpatient care (both with and without referrals), and Table 14.3 illustrates copayments for drugs.

Exemptions from copayment include catastrophic illnesses, which include cancer, end-stage renal disease, and AIDS; psychosis; congenital conditions; prenatal care and delivery; preventive health services; medical services in remote, mountainous, and offshore islands; low-income households; veterans; and children under the age of three. As of 2009, approximately 3.3 percent of the NHI's insured population received catastrophic illness certificates, which entitled them to copayment exemptions; the total cost of their care accounted for 26.2 percent of the total NHI expenditure for the year.

Without a gatekeeper system like that in the United Kingdom's National Health Service, in which the primary care general practitioner acts as the gatekeeper for patients and triages patients to other care institutions as needed, utilization of health care is high under Taiwan Province of China's NHI. The average number of visits per person per year (including visits for dental care [3.1 visits] and traditional Chinese medicine) was 15.2 in 2009. To discourage such high utilization, the BNHI instituted a graduated copayment system whereby patients who access tertiary care Western medicine institutions directly, without referral from primary care physicians, pay a higher copayment, as illustrated in Table 14.2.

---

[6]Based on author's meeting with Cheng-Hua Lee, Deputy Director-General of the Bureau of National Health Insurance, Department of Health, October 6, 2011, Taipei.

**TABLE 14.2**

**National Health Insurance Copayments for Outpatient Visits (New Taiwan dollars)**

| | Western medicine | | | | Traditional Chinese |
| | Referral | No referral | Emergency | Dental | medicine |
|---|---|---|---|---|---|
| Medical centers | 210 | 360 | 450 | 50 | 50 |
| Regional hospitals | 140 | 240 | 300 | 50 | 50 |
| District hospitals | 50 | 80 | 150 | 50 | 50 |
| Clinics | — | 50 | 150 | 50 | 50 |

Source: Taiwan Province of China, BNHI, DOH (2010).

This differential copayment scheme has had a limited effect. Anecdotal observations show that Taiwan Province of China's patients are able and willing to pay much higher copayments than currently are charged by the BNHI. The BNHI does not means-test patients by economic status, because of concerns over creating access problems for the insured.

Total private-household OOP spending in Taiwan Province of China, at 35 percent in 2008 and 2009, appears high compared to that in most OECD countries, except the Republic of Korea, where it was 36.3 percent in 2008 and 34.2 percent in 2009. However, this figure is misleading and inflated, as Taiwan Province of China does not calculate OOP according to the methods of the OECD National Health Accounts but includes such things as diapers, infant formula, and herbal medicines. Official government documents show that OOP in 2009 consisted of the following items: medical equipment and devices, copayments, dentures and orthodontics, expenses associated with child birth, some lab tests, medical supplies, convalescent care for chronic conditions, nursing home care, postdelivery convalescent care (usually up to 30 days at a center),

**TABLE 14.3**

**National Health Insurance Copayments for Drugs (New Taiwan dollars)**

| Cost of drug | Copayment |
|---|---|
| Up to 100 | 0 |
| 101–200 | 20 |
| 201–300 | 40 |
| 301–400 | 60 |
| 401–500 | 80 |
| 501–600 | 100 |
| 601–700 | 120 |
| 701–800 | 140 |
| 801–900 | 160 |
| 901–1,000 | 180 |
| More than 1,000 | 200 |

Source: Taiwan Province of China, BNHI, DOH (2010).

home nursing care, folk therapies and medicines, and supplements. Taiwan Province of China should recalculate its OOP in accordance with OECD methodology to reflect truly medically necessary health spending that is not covered by health insurance, public or private.

That said, OOP spending by patients in Taiwan Province of China has been increasing because of persistent underfunding of the NHI via premiums. Greater revenue for the NHI is necessary in the longer term to fundamentally solve this problem. The NHI Second-Generation Reform, discussed later in the chapter, is designed to address this problem squarely.

## PRIVATE HEALTH INSURANCE IN TAIWAN PROVINCE OF CHINA

In Taiwan Province of China's context, "private health insurance" is a misnomer, since the kinds of "health" insurance offered by private insurers in Taiwan Province of China are often in the form of riders to life or auto insurance policies. This type of insurance is strictly a cash indemnity policy in case of a well-specified contingency, such as cancer. Policyholders may use the cash payment as they see fit, even for items other than health care. Some of these policies are written for single diseases only, such as certain types of cancer. Others cover amenities, such as a semiprivate or private room when hospitalized, or items not covered by the NHI, such as certain types of intraocular lens implants; in the latter example, patients are responsible for paying the cost difference between NHI-paid implants and the particular implants the patients may choose. These policies are also paid out in cash rather than in benefits.

Thus, private insurance in Taiwan Province of China is not defined-benefit insurance. It does not purchase patients' medical services, nor does it contract with providers as is the case with private insurers in the United States, Germany, Switzerland, and the Netherlands. In short, the cash indemnity insurance sold by private insurers in Taiwan Province of China is strictly supplemental to its already quite generous benefit package under the NHI and never functions as a substitute for NHI coverage. It is not necessary for any residents of Taiwan Province of China to procure private health insurance for any of their essential health care needs. Furthermore, the same individual or family can buy multiple private supplementary health insurance indemnity policies and thus collect cash from multiple insurers when the insured contingency occurs. Often such cash payments are used by policyholders as a means to accumulate savings.[7]

In contrast to the finding of an IMF (2010) study that showed that private health insurance decreases utilization, Taiwan Province of China's supplemental "private health insurance" increases utilization, such as length of stay in

---

[7]For a more complete discussion on private health insurance in Taiwan Province of China, see Cheng (2009b), p. 6.

hospitals.[8] This is a long-recognized effect of supplemental insurance in health economics (Sherman and others, 2010, p. 159). Patients can benefit from longer hospital stays, because the longer the stay, the more cash benefits they receive from their private insurer.[9]

## TAIWAN PROVINCE OF CHINA'S HEALTH CARE DELIVERY SYSTEM

The NHI is a largely private delivery system, with 84 percent of hospitals, 70.3 percent of beds, and 98 percent of clinics being private. Ninety-two percent of Taiwan Province of China's providers contract with the BNHI to deliver services, for which they are paid in accordance with a national uniform fee schedule that varies, however, by the type of provider organization (see the next subsection, "Paying the Providers of Health Care").

Patients in Taiwan Province of China have easy access to care. Eighty-five percent of patients reach a hospital or clinic in less than 30 minutes, and 83 percent of patients wait less than 30 minutes before being seen by a doctor. There are no waiting lists for procedures. As noted earlier, utilization of NHI services is high in Taiwan Province of China. Excluding visits to dentists and traditional Chinese medicine doctors, the average number of Western-medicine doctor visits per person per year was approximately 12 in 2009. By contrast, in the United States, physician visits per person per year were 3.8. The average length of stay per hospital episode in Taiwan Province of China is 10 days, compared with 5.5 days in the United States. The number of acute hospital beds per thousand people in Taiwan Province of China is 3.2, compared with only 2.7 in the United States.

Given that fees for health care in Taiwan Province of China are set by the government, as are the global budget caps set by sector in any given year, doctors and hospitals must compete fiercely for patients in perceived quality and patient satisfaction in order to survive and thrive. The beneficiaries of this fierce competition among providers are the patients, who can and do go doctor and hospital shopping freely.

Taiwan Province of China trains 1,300 physicians a year, a quota it has been maintaining for more than 20 years. It had 1.7 physicians and 5.42 nurses per thousand population in 2009, which represents a 34.3 percent increase for physicians and a 71.5 percent increase for nurses from 1999. Overall, the health workforce in Taiwan Province of China grew by 53.3 percent in the 10-year period 1999–2009, although the numbers are still lower than in rich OECD

---

[8]Based on author's meeting with Cheng-Hua Lee, Deputy Director-General of the Bureau of National Health Insurance, Department of Health, October 6, 2011, Taipei.

[9]Based on author's meeting with Cheng-Hua Lee, Deputy Director-General of the Bureau of National Health Insurance, Department of Health, October 6, 2011, Taipei.

countries, which average 2.64 physicians and 9 nurses per thousand population. In Japan and the Republic of Korea, the physician-population ratios are 2.15 for the former (2008) and 1.95 for the latter (2010) per thousand population, and the nurse-population ratios are 9.54 for the former (2008) and 4.51 for the latter (2009). As in most other countries, large cities in Taiwan Province of China have much higher ratios of both physicians and nurses per population than do smaller urban areas or rural areas.

## Paying the Providers of Health Care

Taiwan Province of China's providers receive their revenue from three sources: payment from the NHI for services delivered to patients, which constitutes the largest share of their income; "registration fees" paid by patients directly to providers at the time of a visit or hospitalization, copayments, and coinsurance; and the sale to patients of services and products that are not covered in the NHI benefit package. The NHI uses a mixed payment system. Fee for service is the predominant payment method for outpatient care. For inpatient care, hospitals are paid through a mixture of fee for service and diagnosis-related groups. In addition, there are five single-disease pay-for-performance programs based on quality indicators such as survival (such as for breast cancer).

Within the national uniform fee schedule, there are four levels of fees: the highest fees are paid to tertiary care institutions, such as large hospitals and medical centers, including academic medical centers. The lowest fees are paid to clinics. Such differential fee scales ensure horizontal equity among all care institutions within the same category of provider organization. They also foster equity among patients, who receive the same treatment regardless of their socioeconomic status. Rich or poor patients receive the same care in Taiwan Province of China. By contrast, the U.S. Medicaid program pays providers much lower fees than do private insurers. In effect, Medicaid signals to the providers of care that their work has lower value when applied to poor people, relative to commercially insured patients. This has led providers to refuse to accept patients enrolled in the Medicaid program, creating serious access problems for the poor in the United States.

To forestall rapid and sudden increases in health spending that are hard to manage, Taiwan Province of China's NHI Law had called for the introduction of sectoral global budgets five years after the implementation of NHI. Experience from OECD countries in the 1980s had shown that global budgets can contain costs effectively. Starting with a global budget for the dental care sector in 1998, the BNHI introduced global budgets for traditional Chinese medicine in 2000, for primary care in 2001, for hospitals in 2002, and finally for dialysis in 2003. Taiwan Province of China has a high prevalence of end-stage renal disease.

As of February 2012, Taiwan Province of China was preparing to pilot a project of payment by capitation. Risk-adjusted capitation has the potential to improve care coordination and outcomes and is especially suited for chronic care, an area of growing significance in the majority of industrialized economies, including Taiwan Province of China, as their populations are aging and they are seeing rises in the prevalence of noncommunicable diseases.

Providers in Taiwan Province of China work long hours and must compete for patients to survive. Naturally, many providers resent the strong hand the government has in setting prices, global budgets, and medical reviews. Like providers everywhere, they would prefer to maintain their clinical autonomy and set their own prices according to what the traffic can bear. This would lead, however, to pervasive price discrimination.

The income of providers is one of the most closely guarded secrets in Taiwan Province of China. Although providers are said to be making less income under the NHI than they did before its introduction, their income is still several times higher than that of the average employee in Taiwan Province of China.

## THE INFORMATION TECHNOLOGY SYSTEM IN NHI

Patients who access NHI care use an NHI IC-Card, a credit-card-size card that carries an electronic memory with the patient's personal information, such as name, gender, and date of birth, and insurance data, including medical expenditure, copayments, exemption status, utilization, premium, diagnosis, record of six most recent visits, prescriptions for chronic disease, major examinations, and public health data (childhood vaccination records, organ donation, and do-not-resuscitate order). When a patient registers to be seen at a clinic or hospital, the patient's IC-Card is read by an NHI card reader, which immediately links the patient to the provider, who reads in his or her own provider IC-Card. All information associated with the visit is thus recorded and transmitted to the massive data warehouse of the BNHI. By BNHI regulation, providers must submit electronically all services delivered to each patient within a 24-hour period. However, in reality compliance is less than 100 percent. Still, by international standards—certainly by U.S. standards—this is one of the closest approaches to real-time information on health care utilization and spending.

This timely and efficient reporting system allows the BNHI to monitor not only patients' use of services, but also providers' delivery of services. In addition, the BNHI is enabled to perform continuous real-time surveillance of public health emergencies, such as severe acute respiratory syndrome (SARS) and the influenza A (H1N1) epidemic.

Nearly all providers submit claims electronically to the BNHI by Internet, electronic media, or the virtual private network (which provides a two-way communications channel between the BNHI and provider institutions). The BNHI processes claims and performs electronic profile analyses to identify outliers among patients or providers. Professional peer reviews are conducted for suspect claims. Once a claim is approved, the BNHI makes payment within 15 days by wire transfer to the provider's bank account.

As noted earlier, the administrative cost for the NHI was 1.3 percent of the NHI's budget in 2011. This is made possible largely by the NHI's powerful health information technology.

## NHI PERFORMANCE: HEALTH OUTCOMES

While there is general agreement that the establishment of the NHI has led to excellent access to health care services and therefore greater utilization of services, until recently there has been no consensus on the effect of the NHI on health outcomes in Taiwan Province of China. Life expectancy at birth in Taiwan Province of China, as of 2009, was 76 years for men and 82 years for women. Infant mortality was 4.1 deaths per 1,000 live births and maternal mortality was 8.4 deaths per 1,000 mothers.

According to a 2010 study, the NHI is associated with a reduction in amenable mortality (Lee and others, 2010). The study finds that deaths from amenable causes declined between 1981 and 1993, but the decline slowed between 1993 and 1996. Once the NHI was implemented, the decline accelerated significantly, with deaths from amenable causes falling at 5.83 percent per year between 1996 and 1999. In contrast, there was little change in deaths from nonamenable causes (0.64 percent per year between 1981 and 1999). The effect was highest among the young and old. Coronary heart disease, diabetes, end-stage renal disease, and cancer all show declining mortality and morbidity.[10]

Another recent study on the effect of the NHI on mortality among the elderly in Taiwan Province of China shows that the NHI lowered the mortality hazard ratio of previously uninsured elderly to their continuously insured counterparts by approximately 30 percent (Chang, 2009). In addition, the previously uninsured elderly with chronic conditions also showed a reduced mortality hazard ratio after the introduction of the NHI, suggesting that the NHI has reduced the mortality risk of this vulnerable population by improving their access to care.

Increasingly, patient access to legal recourse in Taiwan Province of China—ability to bring malpractice suits against providers—acts as a safeguard to the quality of care, as providers are under constant threat of being sued by patients who believe themselves to have been harmed by their providers.

The availability of a wide range of public health and medical services, drugs, and devices also continuously improves patient outcomes. For example, a severe complication of liver cirrhosis known as spontaneous bacterial peritonitis, which has a high mortality rate, has a 90 percent cure rate in Taiwan Province of China, whereas in the United States patients with this complication are treated with long-term medication to control the disease.[11]

Satisfaction with the NHI has been in the 70 percent range, and in the 80 percent range since 2008. This may reflect the public's appreciation of having a safety net in economic hard times, as the 2008 global financial crisis affected Taiwan Province of China also. Taiwan Province of China's GDP grew a mere 0.7 percent in that year and contracted by $-1.9$ percent in 2009. Unemployment

---

[10]Based on author's meeting with Cheng-Hua Lee, Deputy Director-General of the Bureau of National Health Insurance, Department of Health, October 6, 2011, Taipei.

[11]Based on author's meeting with Liao Li-Yin, M.D., Chief of Gastroenterology, Taipei Municipal Jen-Ai Hospital, October 6, 2011, Taipei.

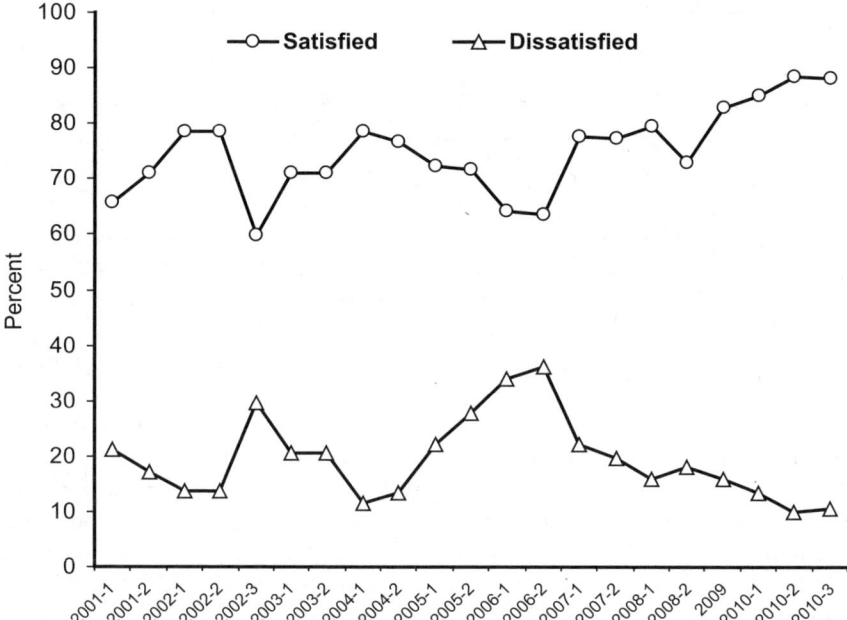

**Figure 14.3**    Public Satisfaction Ratings, 2001–10
Source: Taiwan Province of China, BNHI, DOH (2010).

also grew in that period, from 4.1 percent in 2008 to 5.9 percent in 2009 and then to 5.2 percent in 2010. Figure 14.3 shows the public's satisfaction with the NHI from 2000 to 2010. Convenient accessibility, low premiums, and low copayment rates are some of the main reasons for the high public satisfaction.

## CHALLENGES WITH HEALTH REFORMS

### Financial Stability of the NHI: Financial Crises of 2002, 2006, and 2010

A perennial problem inherent in single-payer health insurance systems is that from time to time they may be underfunded. In the NHI's 17-year history, the government has succeeded in raising premium rates only twice, in 2002 and 2010, even though the NHI Law permits premium rate increases every two years based on actuarial calculations of cost and expenditure. Taiwan Province of China's policymakers have had great difficulties persuading the parliament to pass premium rate increases. The public and parliament have insisted that the NHI be more "efficient" by cutting "waste" before asking for premium rate increases. It is the cry heard around the world, although eliminating "waste" in health care so far has been rather intractable everywhere. Health care that is viewed as wasteful by some experts is viewed as beneficial by others. The problem is a lack of a broad, solid, scientifically tested clinical evidence base for much of applied modern health care.

The financial stability of the NHI was tested time and again in its young history. Each time, the BNHI was able to steer through the storm. Figure 14.4 shows the revenue and expenditure of the NHI from 1995 to 2010. As the figure shows, for the first three years after implementation (1995–98), the NHI ran a surplus, which it banked as a reserve, as called for by the NHI Law. Beginning in 1999, however, the NHI had depleted its reserve and began to run a deficit. By 2002, the BNHI had resorted to borrowing money from banks to pay part of the claims submitted by providers.

The BNHI dealt with this first financial crisis by adopting a range of measures aimed to increase revenue, on the one hand (raising the premium rate from 4.25 percent to 4.55 percent of wage and salary), and containing expenditure on the other hand (cutting pharmaceutical prices, introducing "reasonable patient volume" and diagnosis-related groups, increasing claims reviews, and cutting medical education subsidies). But the most powerful weapon used was the introduction of the global budget for hospitals. Table 14.4 shows the impact of the establishment of the NHI on Taiwan Province of China's total national health spending. It may be seen that spend-

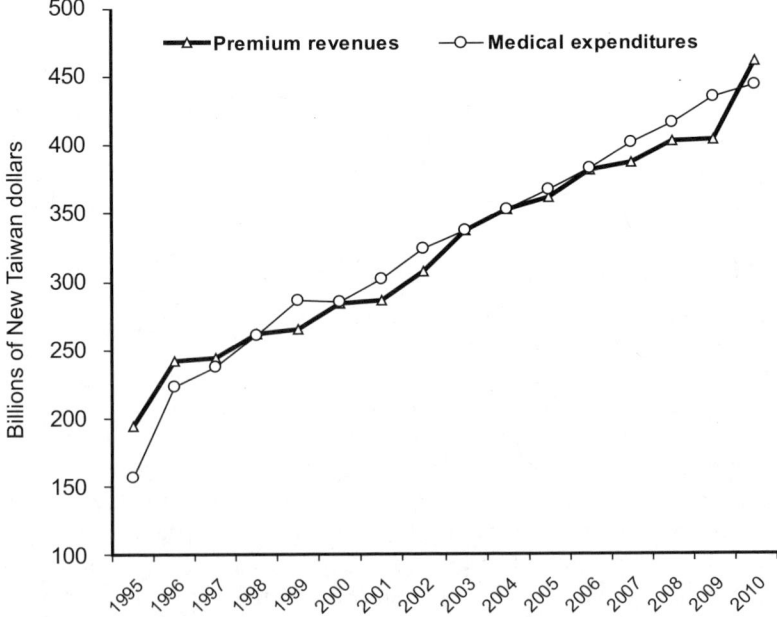

**Figure 14.4** National Health Insurance Financial Status, 1995–2010
(Billions of New Taiwan dollars)
Source: Taiwan Province of China, Bureau of National Health Insurance, Department of Health 2010 data.

**TABLE 14.4**

| Year | National health expenditure/GDP | National health expenditure increase | GDP growth |
|------|------|------|------|
| 1992 | 4.70 | 17.18 | 11.35 |
| 1993 | 4.79 | 12.81 | 10.85 |
| 1994 | 4.87 | 11.31 | 9.21 |
| *1995* | *5.29* | *18.10* | *8.58* |
| 1996 | 5.39 | 11.62 | 9.41 |
| 1997 | 5.40 | 8.52 | 8.47 |
| 1998 | 5.48 | 8.87 | 7.33 |
| 1999 | 5.67 | 8.01 | 3.93 |
| 2000 | 5.67 | 4.10 | 4.02 |
| 2003 | 6.20 | 4.50 | 1.22 |
| 2005 | 6.16 | 3.37 | 3.49 |

Impact of Establishment of National Health Insurance on Total National Health Expenditure

Source: Data based on Department of Health, Taiwan Province of China, Republic of China 2005 Health Statistical Trends, p. V-1.

ing growth started to decline after the introduction of the sectoral global budgets beginning in 1998.

The fiscal reprieve of the NHI was short-lived. By 2004, the NHI was again experiencing financial difficulties because it was unable to persuade the parliament and the public to allow a second premium rate increase, which policymakers had counted on. The government held a civic convention in January 2005 to debate the necessity of a premium rate increase. After three days of deliberations, the civic convention declared the "three nos" as a response: no premium rate increase, no copayment increase, and no reductions in benefits.

With that stubborn response from the public, the government resorted to borrowing from banks once again to pay providers and adopted a policy of "plural fine tuning," which included levying a cigarette surtax, raising revenues from lotteries, stepping up collection of overdue premium payments, and shedding public health costs.

Concerns over the NHI's financial sustainability were widespread. However, the political process in Taiwan Province of China simply did not permit a second premium rate increase until April 2010, when another strong and popular Minister of Health pushed through parliament a premium rate increase, from 4.55 percent to 5.17 percent of wage and salary. President Ma Ying-jeou lent his strong support to the premium rate increase by proclaiming to the public, on March 17, 2010, that the premium rate should be raised as soon as possible to ensure the sustainability of the NHI. It had been expected that the additional premium revenue collected through the higher premium rate would wipe out the NHI's cumulative deficit by the fall of 2012.[12] Surprisingly, BNHI data on

---

[12]Based on author's meeting with Cheng-Hua Lee, Deputy Director-General of the Bureau of National Health Insurance, Department of Health, October 6, 2011, Taipei.

NHI revenues as of mid-February 2012 showed that the cumulative deficit would be eliminated in its entirety by the end of that month, ahead of the expected date.[13]

# LESSONS FROM REFORMS

## Lessons for Taiwan Province of China

A key lesson for Taiwan Province of China's NHI is learning to manage its longer-term financial sustainability. Pressures from both the demand and supply sides require Taiwan Province of China's health policymakers to develop longer-run coping strategies to ensure the financial sustainability of the NHI, the most-cherished social institution in Taiwan Province of China. An encouraging sign in this regard is the passing into law in January 2011 of the Second-Generation NHI Reform Bill, due to be implemented in 2013 at the latest.

The other major lesson for Taiwan Province of China's population and politicians can be found not in Taiwan Province of China's own experience, but by looking abroad, for example, at the financial distress that ill health can visit on families in the absence of comprehensive, universal health insurance. Financial distress due to illness and steep, uncovered medical bills is a reality for many U.S. families and for families in other countries without universal health insurance.

By looking abroad, Taiwan Province of China's people would learn that they are advantaged by a relatively cost-effective health system that produces high value for the money they spend on it. Included in that value is the peace of mind that comes with comprehensive health insurance, which provides both timely access to needed care and financial protection. It is a luxury that 50 million people in the United States do not have. And while Canadians and Europeans do have it, they also spend close to twice as much of their GDP on health care as does Taiwan Province of China.

## Lessons for Other Countries in the Region

### Strengths of the Single-Payer Approach

- Total health spending can easily be controlled through global budgets and the government's ability to set and control prices. In the three-year period before the establishment of the NHI (1992–94), the average annual growth rate of national health spending was 14 to 16 percent, with only 59 percent of Taiwan Province of China's population covered by any kind of health insurance. Since the establishment of the universal NHI, which covers 99 percent of Taiwan Province of China's population, the average annual growth rate of national health spending has been in the 4.5–5 percent range. Had the NHI not been established, total health spending would

---

[13]Personal communication with Cheng-Hua Lee, Deputy Director-General of the Bureau of National Health Insurance, Department of Health, February 13, 2012.

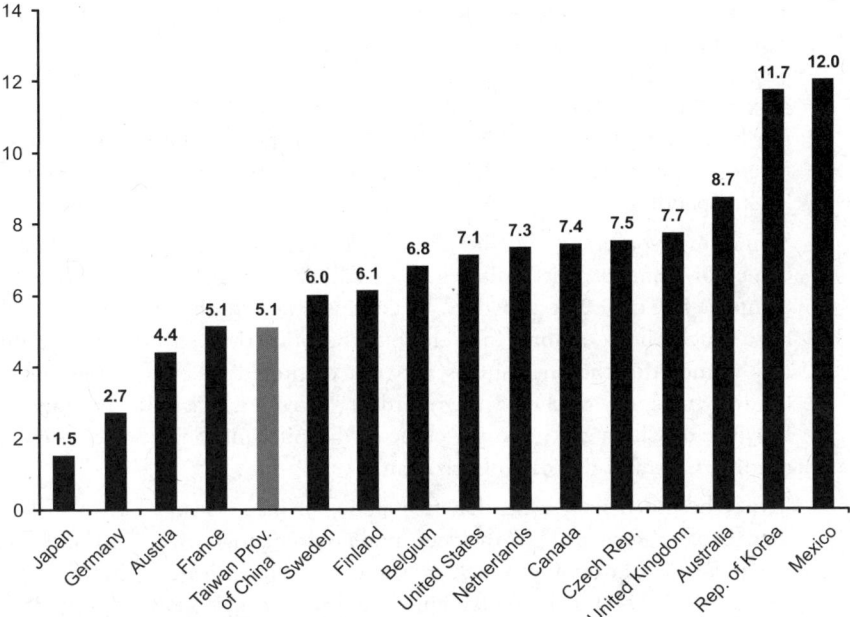

**Figure 14.5** Average Growth Rate of Medical Expenses in Select OECD Countries and Taiwan Province of China, 1999–2008 (Percent)
Sources: Organization for Economic Cooperation and Development, OECD Health Data 2010; Taiwan Province of China, Department of Health.
Note: Data for Japan cover the period 1998–2007, and those for Australia, 1998–2008.

have been much higher than it is now.[14] Effective cost containment is being achieved through both provider fee freezing and sectoral global budgets.[15] As a result, Taiwan Province of China's health care cost is much lower than that of most OECD countries (Cheng, 2009a). Figure 14.5 shows the average growth rate of medical expenses in selected OECD countries and Taiwan Province of China.

- The single-payer system is an ideal platform for an egalitarian health system. The mandate to enroll, government subsidies for the poor, the national uniform benefits package, and the national uniform fee schedule for providers together enable everyone to receive the same health care services regardless of their socioeconomic status.

---

[14]In a meeting with the author on October 6, 2011, in Taipei, Cheng-Hua Lee, Deputy Director-General of the Bureau of National Health Insurance in the Department of Health, indicated that health spending in Taiwan Province of China would easily be 20–40 percent higher had the NHI not been implemented. Price freezing in the fee schedule over the years has forced providers to become ever more efficient. But Dr. Lee also felt that the NHI is approaching the efficiency frontier and that there will be little room for further maneuvering.
[15]Meeting with Cheng-Hua Lee, as cited above.

- The single-payer system is ideal for a uniform information technology platform. Electronic provider billing and claims processing is close to 100 percent in Taiwan Province of China's NHI. This administrative simplicity makes administrative costs to run the NHI extremely low: 1.3 percent of the NHI annual budget. This is in sharp contrast to the United States, where administrative costs absorb a much larger fraction of total national health spending.

- While single-payer systems like Taiwan Province of China's do not offer a choice of insurers, Taiwan Province of China's patients nevertheless have complete free choice of providers. By contrast, those in the United States do have much choice among insurers, but the price they pay for it is to be locked into the chosen insurer's network of providers, that is, they have limited freedom of choice in regard to providers. Patients in Taiwan Province of China can go to the clinics or hospitals of their choice without needing referrals or prior authorization.

  It may be noted in passing that free choice of insurers may be worth less than is often surmised. In the multipayer systems of Switzerland and the Netherlands, for example, which are run by multiple private health insurers, neither the Swiss nor the Dutch appear to exercise their "consumer choice" by switching insurers frequently—choosing insurers that are in theory best suited to their needs—although such switching is what policy planners had intended as a way to increase efficiency through competition among private insurers.

- Solid economic development before, during, and after implementation of universal national health insurance schemes is important to provide the platform (financing) for the establishment and subsequent sustained funding of the universal national health insurance scheme. In Taiwan Province of China's case, there were associated cost increases in the several years prior to the establishment of the NHI, and Taiwan Province of China's economy was able to absorb those increases in costs.

- High productivity of providers is achieved through competition for patients, not prices. The survival of providers depends on whether they can attract patients. Through this competitive process, natural attrition occurs in Taiwan Province of China's health system, as smaller and less efficient providers are weeded out of the system gradually and only bigger and more efficient providers survive.

- Taiwan Province of China's health policymakers believe that moderate budget deficits are "a good thing" because such deficits help to prevent providers from asking the government for higher fees (prices) on the one hand and help prevent unions and the public from asking the government to lower the premium rate on the other hand.[16]

---

[16]Based on author's meeting with Cheng-Hua Lee, Deputy Director-General of the Bureau of National Health Insurance, Department of Health, October 6, 2011, Taipei.

*Weaknesses of the Single-Payer Approach*

- Politicians may underbudget single-payer systems, as has been the case with Taiwan Province of China's NHI, causing severe strains in the system. As shown earlier in this chapter, underfunding has plagued the NHI for most of its 16-year history. As of 2010, its cumulative deficits amounted to 13 percent of its operating budget. Nevertheless, the NHI's financial situation has been improving since 2010 owing to the premium rate increase in April 2010. As noted earlier, the cumulative deficits were expected to be eliminated by the end of February 2012.

- In a single-payer system, mistakes in setting fees or in regulation can have a powerful, unwanted systemwide impact. This could potentially cause access problems. For example, in Taiwan Province of China's NHI, low fees coupled with the more-challenging nature of certain medical specialties, such as obstretrics/gynecology and neurosurgery, have led to a shortage of providers in those specialties.

- When payments are based on fee for service in the absence of global budgets, government can control prices but not volume. This was happening in Taiwan Province of China's NHI until the government introduced sectoral global budgets.

- Global budgets may control costs but offer only a partial long-run solution to the overall disequilibrium in the supply and demand of health care services. Global budgets may create their own problems that could detract from the quality of care in terms of underuse. To prevent underservice by providers, Taiwan Province of China's government has issued a set of patient safety and quality guidelines that accompany the implementation of diagnosis-related groups. To date, there has been no documented evidence of underservice with accompanying patient safety and quality issues.

## General Lessons

- It is important to take advantage of the window of opportunity that opens every so often to build a national universal health insurance system. In Taiwan Province of China's case, a confluence of several factors created this window of opportunity and enabled Taiwan Province of China to build the NHI: decades of robust economic growth, growing popular demand for more and better health care, strong and passionate advocacy by and commitment of the top political leaders, and a parliamentary majority. Other factors that helped to bring about the successful implementation of Taiwan Province of China's NHI included the absence of strong lobbies from the insurance and pharmaceutical industries at the time and growing political competition from the opposition party.

  Finally, Taiwan Province of China's NHI benefited from having a team of competent bureaucrats, whose technical know-how was needed to run the system once it was set up. The BNHI, the government agency that administers the NHI, is staffed with top technocrats who have studied health policy in the United States, Europe, and Japan. They took the international best practices and adapted them to local conditions in Taiwan Province of China.

• A country's political and bureaucratic system needs to be reasonably free from corruption for proper governance of the health system. Corruption can kill the best policy design.

• Most importantly, any health system needs a good health information technology system to provide policymakers and bureaucrats with timely information on the performance of the system and enable them to make needed changes.

# NEXT REFORM STEPS

Taiwan Province of China's health system, which is widely regarded as a high-performing health system, could benefit further from several future reforms to meet the challenges of the coming decades.

## Second-Generation NHI Reform

As underfunding has been a persistent issue for the NHI except for its first three years (1995–98), calls for fundamental reform of the NHI's finances continued and culminated in the passing of the Second-Generation (G2) NHI Reform Act in January 2011. The act broadens the NHI premium base from only wage and salary to include other forms of income on which a 2 percent supplementary premium will be levied: rents from business rentals, interest from bank savings, stock dividends, bonuses (when they exceed the sum of four months of monthly pay), earnings from professional services (e.g., legal and accounting services), and income from part-time employment. In addition, Article 3 of the act stipulates that the government's share of the total NHI premium contribution must not be less than 36 percent, an increase from the current 34 percent.

The G2 NHI reform projects spending out to five years. Once implemented, the reform is expected to bring in an additional 10 to 15 percent of revenue for the NHI. Beyond the first five years, there are plans to further expand the premium base if needed. The government expects that because further expansion of the premium base will include more kinds of income that only the rich in Taiwan Province of China will have, there will be broad public support for the measure.[17]

---

[17]Based on author's meeting with Cheng-Hua Lee, Deputy Director-General of the Bureau of National Health Insurance, Department of Health, October 6, 2011, Taipei.

In the meantime, after the presidential and parliamentary elections in January 2012, tobacco taxes will be further increased. Such taxes are viewed by the public as "sin taxes," and the government expects little public resistance.[18]

Implementation of G2 NHI is scheduled to take place on July 1, 2012. But in view of the elections that took place just months earlier, the more likely date for implementation will be January 1, 2013.

## Comparative Effectiveness Analysis and Health Technology Assessment for the NHI

Comparative effectiveness analysis should be a top policy priority on the agenda of future reforms for the NHI in the next phase. Taiwan Province of China currently performs comparative effectiveness analysis for drugs but does not yet have any formal entity to carry it out, as the United Kingdom does with its National Institute for Health and Clinical Excellence. Establishing an entity based on the U.K. approach would not only help to bring greater cost-effectiveness into NHI care, but also help Taiwan Province of China's health policymakers deal with such challenging issues as the adoption of new, expensive high technology (e.g., new orphan drugs for rare diseases, personalized medicine) that will continue to confront Taiwan Province of China's health policymakers.

The G2 NHI reform calls for voluntary health technology assessment for the time being and plans to introduce formal health technology assessment in 5–10 years' time. In the interim, the government will concentrate on capacity building for comparative effectiveness analysis and social consensus building for such potentially controversial subjects as setting the cost/quality-adjusted life-year ratios.

## Payment Reform

Ideally, payment and coverage decisions in a health system should be based on comparative effectiveness analysis for greater cost-effectiveness, leading to an overall more efficient use of health care resources. The NHI, and for that matter any health system, should no longer pay for care that is not clinically proven and cost-effective. Close to 30 percent of NHI expenditure is for patients in the last three to six months of life, including a significant number of patients in a vegetative state who are kept alive on artificial respiration and cardiac assist devices. There needs to be a public discussion on whether this is a defensible use of resources.

As care coordination is the key to better outcomes, especially in the management of chronic conditions, the NHI should endeavor to move toward greater coordination of care and pay for that generously. Providers must be rewarded with the proper incentives to deliver care that policymakers intend to bring about for desired outcomes.

---

[18]Based on author's meeting with Cheng-Hua Lee, Deputy Director-General of the Bureau of National Health Insurance, Department of Health, October 6, 2011, Taipei.

In the NHI's pay-for-performance program, which targets five chronic conditions (hypertension, diabetes, asthma, tuberculosis, and breast cancer), there is evidence that the fee-for-service payment method significantly increases the costs of care for patients enrolled in these programs as medical resources are "abused." It appears that the NHI's pay-for-performance program built in the wrong incentives for providers by using fee-for-service payment, which does not offer providers an incentive to economize. Risk-adjusted capitation plus fee for service for certain targeted and desired cost-effective interventions should be considered by the BNHI in the management of chronic diseases.

## Noncommunicable Diseases in Taiwan Province of China

According to a World Health Organization report published in September 2011, chronic disease such as cancer, diabetes, cardiovascular disease, and chronic obstructive lung diseases claimed the lives of more than 36 million people globally in 2008. UN Secretary-General Ban Ki-Moon has called noncommunicable disease (NCD) "a public health emergency in slow motion" and convened a high-level global conference on NCDs in September 2011 to highlight the urgency of and need for immediate action on a matter that is affecting all countries around the globe.

According to a 2008 Taiwan Province of China Department of Health survey, 51 percent of the elderly in Taiwan Province of China suffer from at least three NCDs, with hypertension topping the list. In the survey, 90 percent of the elderly reported suffering from at least one NCD and 70 percent from two or more. Other survey findings: cataracts are the second-most-prevalent NCD after hypertension for both men and women; women are more prone to NCDs than men, and many suffer from osteoporosis, arthritis, and rheumatism; and for men, the third- through fifth-most-common NCDs are heart disease, gastric diseases (ulcers), and type II diabetes.

Of all NCDs in Taiwan Province of China, cancer is the leading cause of death. Cancer mortality accounts for 28.1 percent of all deaths annually, and the number of deaths is 2.6 times higher than that from coronary heart disease. Cancer mortality is also the leading cause of deaths for men and women ages 25–44 and 45–64 in Taiwan Province of China, accounting for 24.4 percent of all deaths for the first age group. This has significant socioeconomic implications, as cancer strikes in the most productive years in terms of life cycle stages, resulting in lost productivity to the national economy.

In 2010 the Department of Health in Taiwan Province of China established a national cancer screening program targeting the four leading cancers for early detection and treatment: lung, breast, colon, and oral. Specific funding for this program has been set aside, and the payoff will come in the future, in reduced medical costs associated with late-stage diagnosis and treatment. In the earlier years of the NHI, the BNHI had targeted cervical cancer, as it was the leading cause of cancer mortality among women in Taiwan Province of China. Wide application of Pap smears among women in Taiwan Province of China identified cervical cancers in early stages, saving many lives and much unnecessary medical cost. Community-based coordinated care paid for through risk-adjusted capitation plus fee-for-service for specific desired interventions will go a long way in this area.

Overall, however, addressing the social (nonmedical) determinants of health is perhaps the most important task for Taiwan Province of China's government, or any national government, in the pursuit of improved population health. It is well known that health care access, availability, and affordability account for roughly 10 percent of an individual's health. Other factors, referred to by scholars as "social determinants of health"—such as lifestyle and the environment—matter more to an individual's health.

Improving overall population health goes far beyond mere medical interventions and must involve mobilizing nonmedical sectors in society, such as the food industry, transportation and distribution industries, governments at all levels, and communities to transform the way we eat and live. Taiwan Province of China's government should pursue national policies addressing the social determinants of health to further improve the health of the population.

## Long-Term Care

As of 2011, Taiwan Province of China did not yet have universal long-term care coverage, but is in the process of establishing such a program, targeted to be implemented in 2012. However, in all likelihood implementation will be delayed.

Taiwan Province of China is a rapidly aging society. As of 2009, people over the age of 65 constituted 10.6 percent of the population of 23.12 million. By 2025, 20 percent of the population will be over 65. The population is aging more rapidly than populations in Western countries, and declining fertility is a major contributing factor.

Medical expenses for the care of the elderly accounted for 33.9 percent of the NHI's total expenditure in 2009, the highest among all age groups in the NHI. However, this represents an increase of only 4.5 percentage points from 2001, suggesting stable growth over time. The average number of visits per elderly person in Taiwan Province of China was 27.8 in 2009, almost twice the rate for the general population. Emergency room visits and hospitalizations also are the highest among the elderly in Taiwan Province of China.

Taiwan Province of China should establish long-term care based on international best practices.

## CONCLUSIONS

Taiwan Province of China's single-payer health system has shown that both the public and private sectors play important roles in Taiwan Province of China's health system. Government-financed and -run NHI achieves equity and administrative efficiency, and the private-sector-dominated delivery system performs its function of competition with great productivity and efficiency. Without one or the other, Taiwan Province of China's health system would not be what it is—a system that serves the public's health care needs at a very low cost and to the great satisfaction of the public.

Because income inequality is widening throughout developed countries, it has become more and more difficult to maintain health systems on the principle of social solidarity. So far, Taiwan Province of China's single-payer health system has been able to continue to adhere to that principle, perhaps because it has managed to control the per capita cost of health care.

As countries around the world contemplate health reform to meet current and future fiscal challenges, especially emerging countries that are thinking of establishing universal health care, Taiwan Province of China's NHI provides a useful example of how social justice and fiscal sustainability can be achieved at the same time.

## REFERENCES

Chang, K.H., 2009, "The Effect of Taiwan's National Health Insurance on Mortality of the Elderly: Revised" (Taiwan Province of China: China Center for Human Capital and Labor Market Research, Central University of Finance and Economics).

Chen, H.H., and Y.M. Chang, 2011, "National Health Insurance Enjoys the Highest Public Satisfaction of All Government Programs— Paul Krugman: NHI the World's Best System" (in Chinese), *United Daily News*, September 6.

Cheng, T.M., 2003, "Taiwan's New National Health Insurance Program: Genesis and Experience So Far," *Health Affairs*, Vol. 22, No. 3, pp. 61–76.

———, 2007, "Taiwan's National Health Insurance: 'Sailing into the Perfect Storm?'" Paper presented at the Bertelsmann Foundation Sixth International Symposium on Health Policy, Berlin.

———, 2009a, "Lessons from Taiwan's Universal National Health Insurance: A Conversation with Taiwan's Health Minister Ching-Chuan Yeh," *Health Affairs,* Vol. 28, No. 4, pp. 1035–44.

———, 2009b, "Private Health Insurance in Taiwan: An Author Responds," *Health Affairs*, Vol. 28, No. 6, p. 6.

———, 2010, "Understanding the Swiss Watch Function of Switzerland's Health System," *Health Affairs,* Vol. 29, No. 8, pp. 1442–51.

———, 2011, "How Taiwan Made the Transition to Single Payer," paper presented to the Minnesota Single Payer State Legislators Meeting, Minneapolis/St. Paul, Minnesota, September 25–27, 2011.

Ii, M., 2011, "Health Care Reform in Asia: The Case of Japan," paper presented at the International Monetary Fund (IMF) OAF/FAD conference, Public Health Care Reform in Asia, Tokyo.

International Monetary Fund, 2010, "Macro-fiscal Implications of Health Care Reform in Advanced and Emerging Economies," IMF Policy Paper (Washington).

———, 2011, World Economic Outlook Database, September. Available at www.imf.org/external/pubs/ft/weo/2011/02/weodata/index.aspx.

Lai, C.L., 2009, "Developing a Patient-Centered Care Payment Model," paper presented at the American Public Health Association Annual Meeting and Expo, Philadelphia.

Lee, Y.C., Y.T. Huang, Y.W. Tsai, S.M. Huang, K.N. Kuo, M. McKee, and E. Nolte, 2010, "The Impact of Universal National Health Insurance on Population Health: The Experience of Taiwan Province of China," *BMC Health Services Research*, Vol. 10, p. 225.

Okma, K., T. Marmor, and J. Oberlander, 2011, "Managed Competition for Medicare? Sobering Lessons from the Netherlands," Perspective, *New England Journal of Medicine*, June 15.

Reinhardt, U., 2011, "The Money Flow from Households to the Providers of Health Care," *New York Times* Economix, September 30. Available online at http://economix.blogs.nytimes.com/2011/09/30/the-money-flow-from-households-to-health-care-providers/.

Sherman, F., S. Goodman, C. Allen, and M. Stano, 2010, *The Economics of Health and Health Care* (Upper Saddle River, New Jersey: Prentice Hall).

Taiwan Province of China, Bureau of Health Promotion (BHP), Department of Health (DOH), Executive Yuan, 2011, "Ageing Tsunami Hits Taiwan" (in Chinese), *News*, available online at http://www.bhp.doh.gov.tw/BHPnet/Portal/PressShow.aspx?No=201107110001.

Taiwan Province of China, Bureau of National Health Insurance (BNHI), Department of Health (DOH), Executive Yuan, 2010, "National Health Insurance in Taiwan 2010" (Taipei).

Taiwan Province of China, Department of Health (DOH), 2009, *Health Care Statistical Trends* (in Chinese) (Taipei).

Taiwan Province of China, Information Management Division (IMD), Bureau of National Health Insurance (BNHI), Department of Health (DOH), 2007, "Overview of the Information System in Taiwan's National Health Insurance" (in Chinese) (Taipei).

Taiwan Province of China, Legislative Yuan, 2011, Second-Generation National Health Insurance Reform Act (in Chinese) (Taipei).

"Taiwan Country Report," 2011, *Global Finance*, available online at http://www.gfmag.com/gdp-data-country-reports/166-Taiwan Province of China-gdp-country-report.html#axzz1a9WFcTDG.

Tyson, J., K. Kashiwase, M. Soto, and B. Clements, 2011, "Reforming Health Care Spending: Lessons from Cross-Country Experience in Advanced Economies," paper presented at the International Monetary Fund OAF/FAD conference Public Health Care Reform in Asia, Tokyo, October 3.

Woolhandler, S., T. Campbell, and D. Himmelstein, 2003, "Cost of Health Care Administration in the United States and Canada," *New England Journal of Medicine*, Vol. 349, pp. 768–75.

# PART V

# Country Case Studies: Emerging Economies

# CHAPTER 15

# Health Care Financing Reform in India's Decentralized Health Care System

## M. Govinda Rao and Mita Choudhury

It is very widely acknowledged that health is an important component of human development. The empowerment of people comes from the freedoms they enjoy, and these include, among others, freedom from poverty, hunger, and malnutrition, and freedom to work and lead a healthy life (Sen, 1999). Access to health care is critical to improving health status, and good health is necessary for empowerment. Ensuring access to health care helps to minimize absenteeism, enhance labor productivity, and prevent misery. Government intervention in health is also argued for because of the presence of a high degree of asymmetric information in the health sector. Not surprisingly, throughout the world, governments have had a significant role in providing and regulating health services, and their role is particularly important in developing countries with large concentrations of the poor.

Despite poor health indicators, government spending on health care in most low- and middle-income countries is well below what is needed. A recent analysis suggests that while low-income countries need to spend $54 per capita for a basic package of health services, the average actual per capita health expenditure in these countries is only $27 (Stenberg and others, 2010). Low revenue collections, competing demands for revenues, and relatively low spending priority contribute to this insufficient spending.[1] Consequently, limited access to public health care facilities forces people to go to private providers, resulting in substantial out-of-pocket (OOP) spending, especially for the poor (WHO, 2004).

The Millennium Development Goals have helped to draw attention to the need to ensure universal coverage in many low- and middle-income countries. The 58th session of the World Health Assembly in 2005 defined universal health care as providing "access to key promotive, preventive, curative, and rehabilitative health

The authors without any incrimination thank Dr. Sanjeev Gupta, Dr. Baoping Shang, and Dr. Poonam Gupta for very useful comments on the earlier draft of the chapter. They would also like to thank Mr. Bharatee Bhusana Dash for meticulous research assistance.

[1] Heller (2006) defines fiscal space as "the availability of budgetary room that allows a government to provide resources for a given desired purpose without any prejudice to the sustainability of a government's financial position."

interventions for all at an affordable cost." However, most low- and middle-income countries find this a major challenge, as it would require substantial increases in public spending and productivity increases in an environment of severely strained resources. Of course, there has been considerable success in achieving universal health coverage in some middle-income countries, including Thailand and some Latin American countries, while other countries, such as China, Indonesia, and Vietnam, are focusing their attention on improving access. In Africa, Ghana and Rwanda have recorded remarkable success in expanding coverage, which has inspired other countries on that continent to embark on health sector reforms.

The health sector challenges in India, like those in other low- and middle-income countries, are formidable. Public spending on medical, public health, and family welfare in India is much below what is required. Further, the gap between the actual spending and the required amount is much larger in the low-income states, and this results in marked interstate inequality. The low levels of spending have had an adverse impact on the creation of a preventive health infrastructure. With over 70 percent of the spending on health being OOP, the low level of public spending and its uneven distribution have been a major cause of the immiseration of the poor.

Of course, there have been some recent initiatives to augment public spending on health care, but these have met with only limited success. The National Rural Health Mission (NRHM), established in 2005, and the Rashtriya Swastya Bima Yojana (RSBY), a recently introduced national health insurance scheme for people below the poverty line, are the two most important initiatives by the central government. Several state governments also have come up with their own insurance schemes. Despite these initiatives, actual public spending on health has not shown much increase.

This chapter analyzes public spending on health care in India. The second section presents the salient features of health spending and shows that low levels of public spending have resulted in the population's low health status. The third section examines the impact of low levels of public expenditures on the state of health infrastructure. The fourth section discusses recent reforms for increasing allocation to health and presents estimates of health expenditure needed to provide essential health infrastructure in the states. The fifth section analyzes fiscal space for health care, stimulation, and substitution effects of central transfers for health to states. The final section summarizes the main findings.

## THE PUBLIC HEALTH CARE SYSTEM IN INDIA AND ITS IMPACT ON HEALTH

### Salient Features

The three most important features of the Indian health care system are

1. *Low levels of public spending*: Between 1996–97 and 2005–06, total government spending on health was stagnant at about 1 percent of GDP, and the public expenditure elasticity with respect to GDP was at 0.94, lower than

the average for low-income countries (1.16) for the same period (Tandon and Cashin, 2010). Despite efforts to increase public spending after 2005–06, including the adoption of the NRHM, expenditure increased only marginally to 1.2 percent of GDP in 2009–10.

2. A resulting *poor quality of preventive care and poor health status* of the population.

3. An inadequate level of public health provision, which has forced the population to seek private health providers, resulting in *high OOP spending*— more than four times higher than the public spending on health care.

Thus, reforms in the health sector will have to address the issue of increasing the allocation to health care, focusing on preventive care, ensuring greater access to health care for the poor, and significantly improving the productivity of public spending (Government of India MoHFW, 2005a, 2005b, 2005c).

As India is a federal country, its constitution assigns the states predominant responsibility for the provision of social services and coequal responsibility with the central government for the provision of economic services. However, since all broad-based tax handles except the general sales tax are assigned to the central government, there is a high degree of vertical fiscal imbalance. Further, the wide interstate disparities in revenue capacity make it difficult to ensure comparable levels of public services in different states at comparable tax rates.

The constitution recognizes the need to resolve both vertical and horizontal imbalances and has provided for the sharing of central taxes with the states and for providing grants in aid to the states based on the recommendation of an independent body, the Finance Commission, appointed every five years. Further, the Planning Commission also makes grants for state plan schemes based on a formula (Rao and Singh, 2005; Rao, 2010). In addition to the general-purpose transfers described above, specific-purpose grants are given by the central ministries for various central schemes formulated within each ministry. The Ministry of Health and Family Welfare administers the major transfer scheme under the NRHM, which is discussed in detail later in the chapter. Despite these mechanisms, the transfer system has failed to offset the fiscal disabilities of the poorer states, and states with poor health indicators are left with large unmet expenditure needs (Rao and Singh, 2005).

As mentioned previously, state governments have predominant responsibility for providing health care services. Entry 6 on the "state list" of the Seventh Schedule of the Constitution assigns "public health and sanitation, hospitals and dispensaries" to the state governments. However, "population control and family planning" (entry 20A), "legal, medical and other professions" (entry 26) and "lunacy and mental deficiency, including places for the reception or treatment of lunatics and mental deficiencies" (entry 16) are put in the "concurrent list." Similarly, institutions declared to be of national importance by the parliament and institutions for professional and technical training and research are in the domain of the national government.

Health service delivery in India is characterized by a three-tier system. At the lowest level are the subcenters, each covering a population of about 5,000 in the plains and about 3,000 in hilly and difficult terrain. Only paramedical staff are available in these subcenters. The first points of contact with a doctor are the primary health centers, each covering about 30,000 people in the plains and about 20,000 in hilly and difficult terrain. Community health centers provide secondary care and are organized at the block levels.

Then there are subdivisional hospitals and district-level hospitals. In principle, the subcenters, primary health centers, and community health centers should handle the preventive aspects of health care, institutionalize deliveries, treat minor diseases, and act as referral centers. The subdivision and district-level hospitals would then treat major ailments as referral hospitals. However, in practice this has not been the case, as the subdivision and district-level hospitals deal with all aspects of health care.

## Health Status of the Population

India's health achievements are low in comparison to the country's income level. According to the United Nations Development Program's *Human Development Report* 2010, in a set of 193 countries, while India ranked 119th on the human development index, it ranked 143rd in infant mortality rate, 124th in maternal mortality rate, 132nd in life expectancy at birth, and 145th in under-five mortality rate.[2] Scatter plots across countries between gross national income and each of the four indicators along with their associated trend lines (shown in Figure 15.1) also indicate that India's health indicators are worse than what is expected at India's level of income for three of the four indicators. Summaries of health indicators in various developing regions of the world show that India's performance is better only than that of sub-Saharan Africa (Table 15.1). In fact, among the South Asian countries, the infant mortality rate in India in 2008 was better (lower) only than that of Pakistan and Bhutan (Table 15.2). Furthermore, the rate of improvement in the infant mortality rate over 1990–2008 in India was lower than in most other South Asian countries, including Bangladesh, Nepal, and Bhutan.

An important factor contributing to the slow progress in population health in India is the poor access to primary and preventive health care services.[3] This is evidenced by the fact that India's immunization rates and percentage of births attended by skilled health personnel rank among the worst in the world (Table 15.1). Inadequate preventive health care services results in high incidence of deaths from communicable diseases. According to *Global Burden of Diseases* data published by the World Health Organization (WHO) in 2008, of the total

---

[2]Data are available for 193 countries for infant mortality and under-five mortality rates, for 171 countries for maternal mortality rates, and for 180 countries for life expectancy at birth. Since data for all countries are not available for each of the four indicators, countries for which data on the respective indicators are available have been used to arrive at the ranking.

[3]The *Mid-Term Appraisal of the Tenth Five-Year Plan* (Government of India Planning Commission, 2005), for example, states, "A major concern . . . of the health sector is how best to reach out to the bottom 300–400 million people who perceive health services as unavailable and inaccessible" (p. 74).

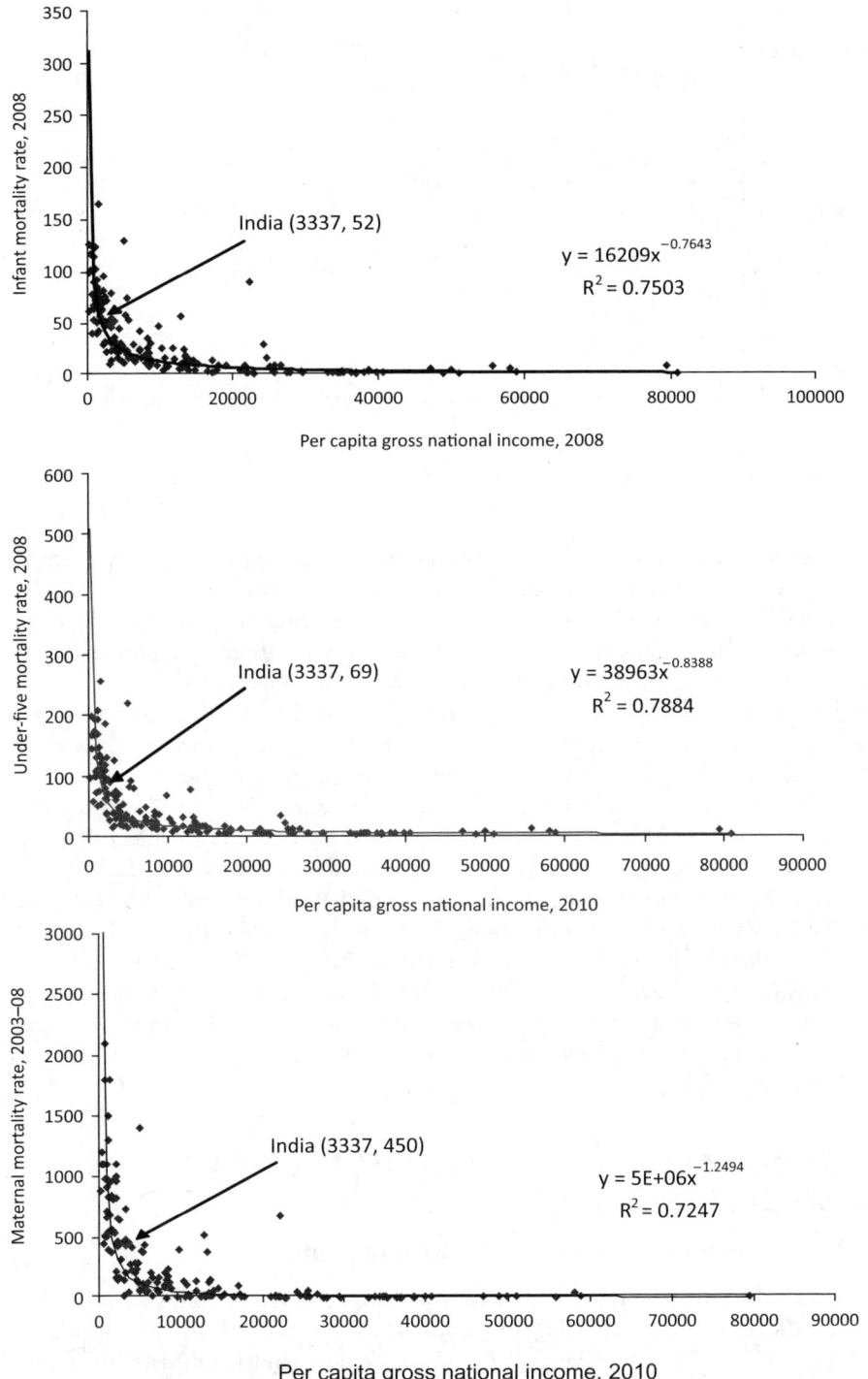

**Figure 15.1** Selected Health Indicators and Per Capita Gross National Income across Countries (2008 U.S. dollars at purchasing power parity) *(continued)*
Source: UNDP (2010).

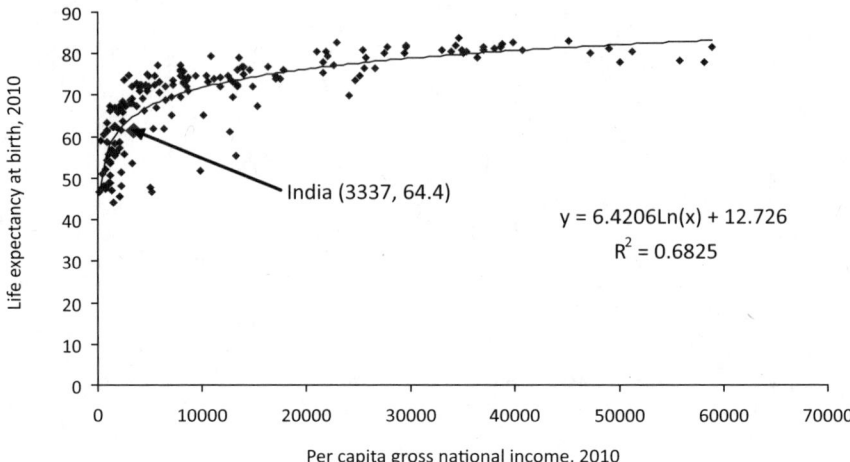

**Figure 15.1** *(Continued)*

number of deaths in a sample of 192 countries across the world, India accounted for nearly one-fourth of the deaths due to diarrhea, more than one-third of the deaths due to childhood cluster diseases (many of which are preventable by basic immunization), more than one-third of the deaths due to leprosy, more than half the deaths due to Japanese encephalitis, and about 30 percent of the deaths due to prenatal conditions (Table 15.3).The overall level of health status masks the large intracountry variations across states. In 2008, the difference in infant mortality rate (IMR) between the best state in India (Kerala) and the worst state (Madhya Pradesh) was nearly sixfold (12 in Kerala and 70 in Madhya Pradesh). In general, the IMR in the four states with the highest rates (Madhya Pradesh, Orissa, Uttar Pradesh, and Rajasthan) was about double the IMR in the best four states in the country (Kerala, Tamil Nadu, West Bengal, and Maharashtra) (Table 15.4). Moreover, the rate of decline in IMR in the four worst states (those with the highest IMR) has been much lower than that in the four best states (those with the lowest IMR). In the 20-year period from 1988 to 2008, the average improvement index (based on Kakwani [1993] and Sen [1981]) in the top four states was markedly higher than the average improvement index in the bottom four states (Table 15.4).

## PUBLIC SPENDING ON HEALTH AND HEALTH INFRASTRUCTURE

### Public Spending on Health: Important Features

It is believed that an important factor contributing to India's poor health status is its low level of public spending on health, which is one of the lowest in the world. In 2007, according to WHO's *World Health Statistics*, India ranked 184th among 191 countries in terms of public expenditure on health as a percentage of GDP.

**TABLE 15.1**

Selected Health Indicators in India and Developing Regions of the World

| | Infant mortality rate (per 1,000 live births), 2008 | 2008 Under-five mortality rate (per 1,000 children under age five), 2008 | Maternal mortality ratio (per 100,000 live births), 2003–08 | Antenatal coverage of at least one visit (percent), 1990–2008 | Births attended by skilled health personnel (percent), 2000–08 | Infants lacking immunization against DTP or measles (percent of one-year-olds) 2008 | |
|---|---|---|---|---|---|---|---|
| | | | | | | DTP | Measles |
| Arab states | 38 | 50 | 238 | 74 | 77 | 15 | 19 |
| East Asia and the Pacific | 23 | 28 | 126 | 91 | 91 | 8 | 9 |
| Europe and Central Asia | 20 | 22 | 41 | 95 | 96 | 5 | 4 |
| Latin America and the Caribbean | 19 | 23 | 122 | 95 | 91 | 10 | 7 |
| South Asia | 56 | 73 | 454 | 70 | 45 | 28 | 25 |
| Sub-Saharan Africa | 86 | 144 | 881 | 73 | 48 | 29 | 28 |
| India | 52 | 69 | 450 | 74 | 47 | 34 | 30 |

Source: UNDP (2010).
Note: DTP = diphtheria, tetanus, and pertussis.

**TABLE 15.2**

### Infant Mortality Rate in Selected South Asian Countries, 1990 and 2008

|  | 1990 | 2008 |
|---|---|---|
| Sri Lanka | 23 | 13 |
| Maldives | 79 | 24 |
| Nepal | 99 | 41 |
| Bangladesh | 103 | 43 |
| India | 83 | 52 |
| Bhutan | 91 | 54 |
| Pakistan | 101 | 72 |

Source: UNDP (2010).
Note: Infant mortality rate refers to the number of deaths of infants under one year old per 1,000 live births.

**TABLE 15.3**

### Estimated Total Deaths by Cause, 2004 (Thousands)

| | Cause of death | | | | | |
|---|---|---|---|---|---|---|
| | Diarrhea | Childhood cluster diseases | Leprosy | Japanese encephalitis | Dengue | Perinatal conditions |
| India | 516 | 295 | 2.1 | 6.1 | 5.2 | 920 |
| World (among 192 World Health Organization member countries) | 2,162 | 847 | 5.4 | 11 | 18.1 | 3,177 |
| Share of deaths in India (percent) | 23.8 | 34.8 | 38.2 | 55.1 | 28.8 | 29 |

Source: WHO (2008).
Note: India's share of population in the sample of 192 countries was about 17.4 percent.

**TABLE 15.4**

### Level and Improvement in Infant Mortality Rate in Selected Indian States, 1988 and 2008

| | Infant mortality rate | | Improvement index, 1988–2008, based on | |
|---|---|---|---|---|
| | 1988 | 2008 | Kakwani (1993) | Sen (1981) |
| **Top four states** | | | | |
| Kerala | 28 | 12 | 0.25 | 0.70 |
| Tamil Nadu | 74 | 31 | 0.20 | 0.62 |
| Maharashtra | 69 | 33 | 0.17 | 0.56 |
| West Bengal | 68 | 35 | 0.16 | 0.53 |
| Average | | | 0.19 | 0.60 |
| **Bottom four states** | | | | |
| Madhya Pradesh | 121 | 70 | 0.12 | 0.44 |
| Orissa | 122 | 69 | 0.13 | 0.45 |
| Uttar Pradesh | 124 | 67 | 0.14 | 0.48 |
| Rajasthan | 103 | 63 | 0.11 | 0.41 |
| Average | | | 0.12 | 0.45 |

Source: Based on figures of the Sample Registration System, reported by the Registrar General, India, in various issues of the *SRS Bulletin* and Government of India, Registrar General (1999).
Note: Kakwani's index and Sen's index have been used to compare improvement in infant mortality rates because these indices take into account the differences in that rate in the base year across states. For calculating the improvement indices, the maximum and minimum values of the infant mortality rate have been assumed to be 130 and 5, respectively.

**TABLE 15.5**

## Expenditure on Health in Selected Countries, 2007

| | Public expenditure | | Total expenditure | |
|---|---|---|---|---|
| | As percentage of GDP | Per capita[a] | As percentage of GDP | Per capita[a] |
| India | 1.1 | 29 | 4.1 | 109 |
| Bangladesh | 1.1 | 14 | 3.4 | 42 |
| Sri Lanka | 2.0 | 85 | 4.2 | 179 |
| China | 1.9 | 104 | 4.3 | 233 |
| Thailand | 2.7 | 209 | 3.7 | 280 |

Source: WHO (2010).
[a]In international purchasing power parity dollars.

In per capita terms, India ranked 164th in the same sample of 191 countries, spending just about $29 (purchasing power parity). This level of per capita public expenditure on health was around a third of Sri Lanka's, less than 30 percent of China's, and 14 percent of Thailand's (WHO, 2010). What is more, public spending on health as a percentage of GDP in India has stagnated in the past two decades, varying between 1990–91 and 2007–08 (most recent year for which data are available) from 0.9 to 1.1 percent of GDP.

While public spending on health care is low, OOP expenditure by households has been large. In 2007, total expenditure on health in India (public and private) was about 4.1 percent of GDP, higher than the level in Thailand and around the levels of Sri Lanka and China (Table 15.5). In 2007, private spending in India constituted nearly 74 percent of the total spending on health (in contrast to 18 percent in the United Kingdom) (Figure 15.2). Nearly 90 percent of this private expenditure in India was in the form of OOP expenditure on health by households (WHO, 2010), one of the highest shares in Asia (Van Doorslaer and others, 2007). The high OOP expenditure has put an increasing financial burden on the poorer sections of the population. Data from the National Sample Survey Organization indicate that between 1986–87 and 2004, the share of ailments not

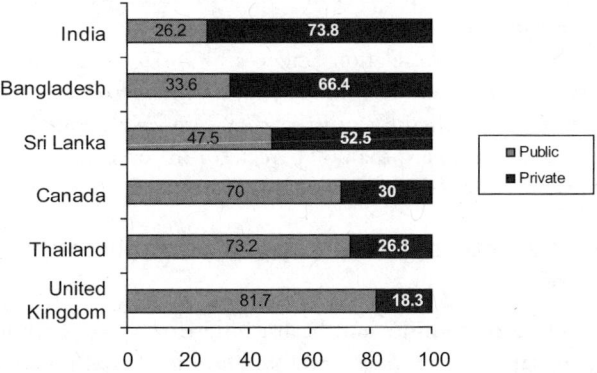

**Figure 15.2** Share of Public and Private Expenditure on Health in Selected Countries, 2007 (Percent)
Source: WHO (2010).

treated due to financial reasons in India increased from about 15 percent to 28 percent in the rural areas. Part of this increased financial burden arises from the fact that the share of visits to private health facilities has increased in recent years. According to the National Sample Survey Organization data, the share of outpatient visits to public facilities has dropped from 25 to 20 percent and for inpatient visits from 60 to 40 percent (Selvaraj and Karan, 2009, cited in Shahrawat and Rao, 2011). Notably, outpatient treatments account for nearly three-fourths of OOP expenditure by households; a large part of this could be reduced through adequate provision of primary and secondary care (NSSO, 2007).

The skewed composition of public spending further reduces its effectiveness. A significant share of that spending is directed toward curative and tertiary health care services as opposed to preventive, primary, and secondary care. According to the latest National Health Accounts data (for 2004–05), about 28 percent of total public expenditure was allocated for tertiary health care services, significantly higher than the target of 10 percent recommended by the National Health Policy of India. Also, an overwhelming portion of the expenditure is for wages and salaries, leaving little for nonsalary (complementary) expenses like drugs and other material supplies. The expenditure is particularly skewed toward salaries in some of the poor-performing states. For example, wages and salaries constituted around 83 and 85 percent, respectively, of total health spending in the states of Madhya Pradesh and Orissa—the two states with the worst health indicators.

The nature of public spending has resulted in a grossly inadequate health infrastructure. The number of allopathic doctors, nurses, and midwives in India (when adjusted for qualification) is less than one-fourth of the WHO benchmark (Rao and others, 2011). This has led to recourse to unqualified medical practitioners in the rural areas (Rao, Bhatnagar, and Berman, 2009). In addition, the ratio of nurses to doctors in India is extremely unfavorable in comparison to those in some of the better-performing countries. When adjusted for qualification, the ratio of nurses to doctors is about 0.6 to 1, that is, less than one nurse per doctor (Rao and others, 2011). In many developed countries, this ratio is about 3:1, three nurses to one doctor. The low share of nonsalary expenditure has also resulted in inadequate essential drugs at subcenters, primary health centers, and community health centers—the first three tiers of primary and secondary health care facilities in the rural areas. According to a facility survey conducted by the International Institute of Population Sciences in 2007–08, about 35 percent of the subcenters and 30 percent of primary health centers had less than 60 percent of the essential drugs required for primary care. Similarly, about one-third of the primary health centers had less than 60 percent of the basic refrigeration facilities required for primary care (IIPS, 2010).

## Interstate Differentials in Public Spending and Health Infrastructure

The level of public expenditure and health infrastructure as a whole is dragged down by that in some of the states. In 2008–09, the level of public spending on

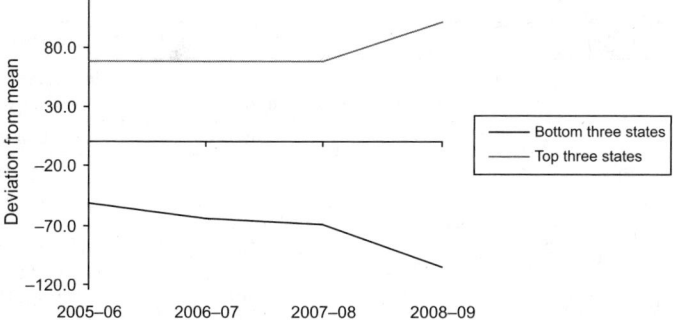

**Figure 15.3** Deviation of Per Capita Public Health Expenditure: Top Three and Bottom Three States, 2005–06 to 2008–09 (Rupees per capita)
Source: Estimates using data from the finance accounts of individual states, compiled by the Comptroller and Auditor General of India.

health in Bihar (the state with the lowest per capita health spending) was less than half that in Kerala and Tamil Nadu (the top two states). Moreover, in recent years, interstate inequalities in health spending have increased. Thus, the difference between per capita public spending in the top three states (Kerala, Tamil Nadu, and Punjab) and that in the bottom three states (Bihar, Madhya Pradesh, and Orissa) has increased, leading to a stronger divergence between the two categories of states (Figure 15.3).

In general, the variation in per capita expenditure across states has increased over the years. Between 1993–94 and 2008–09, the coefficient of variation in per capita public spending across states increased from 0.19 to 0.26 (Table 15.6). It is important to note that public expenditure on health is positively correlated with income levels by states. The correlation coefficients between per capita public spending on health and per capita gross state domestic product (GSDP) were 0.7 and 0.8, respectively, for 1995–96 and 2004–05 (Rao and Choudhury, 2008).

The low-expenditure states are also the states with relatively low per capita GSDP, and they have some of the poorest health indicators and infrastructure in the country. Madhya Pradesh and Orissa, the two states with the worst IMR in the country, have significantly worse access to health infrastructure and professionals than Kerala and Tamil Nadu, the two best states in the country in terms of IMR (Table 15.7). Apart from this low level of access to health facilities, there are large numbers of vacancies for doctors and para-medical staff in these states. Part of the reason for the large numbers of vacancies is the low availability of health workers. The number of health workers per 1,000 people in these states is, on average, half of that in the relatively better-performing states. An important reason is that medical colleges are concentrated in the better-performing and higher-income states (Mahal and Mohanan, 2006).

**TABLE 15.6**

## Per Capita Public Expenditure on Health in 14 Major States (Rupees)

| | Per capita health expenditure | | Per capita net state domestic product |
|---|---|---|---|
| | 1993–94 | 2008–09 | 2008–09 |
| Andhra Pradesh | 75 | 402 | 40,902 |
| Bihar | 53 | 166 | 13,663 |
| Gujrat | 82 | 320 | 49,251 |
| Haryana | 80 | 364 | 68,614 |
| Karnataka | 85 | 405 | 41,513 |
| Kerala | 100 | 507 | 49,316 |
| Madhya Pradesh | 81 | 214 | 21,648 |
| Maharashtra | 86 | 351 | 54,867 |
| Orissa | 58 | 303 | 29,464 |
| Punjub | 110 | 348 | 52,879 |
| Rajasthan | 84 | 405 | 27,001 |
| Tamil Nadu | 98 | 421 | 45,058 |
| Uttar Pradesh | 70 | 269 | 18,710 |
| West Bengal | 73 | 292 | 36,322 |
| | | | |
| Standard deviation | 15.3 | 89.1 | |
| Mean | 81.1 | 340.5 | |
| Coefficient of variation | 0.19 | 0.26 | |

Source: Per capita expenditure has been estimated using data from the finance accounts of individual states, compiled by the Comptroller and Auditor General of India. Per capita net state domestic product has been taken from Government of India, Economic Survey 2010–11.

Note: Data for 2008–09 for Bihar are inclusive of the data for Jharkhand. Similarly, data for Madhya Pradesh are inclusive of data for Chhattisgarh, and those for Uttar Pradesh are inclusive of data for Uttarakhand. Data for 2008–09 include off-budget expenditure under the National Rural Health Mission.

**TABLE 15.7**

## Indicators of Access to Health Care in Selected High- and Low-Expenditure States

| Indicators | High-expenditure states | | Low-expenditure states | |
|---|---|---|---|---|
| | Kerala | Tamil Nadu | Madhya Pradesh | Orissa |
| Average number of villages covered by a primary health center, 2009 | 2 | 13 | 48 | 40 |
| Percentage of primary health centers having at least 60 percent of required cold-chain equipment, 2007–08 | 97.2 | 94.8 | 49.4 | 34.9 |
| Percentage of vacancies for doctors at primary health centers, 2009 | 0 | 0.5 | 53 | 38 |
| Percentage of general-duty medical officers at community health centers, 2009 | 0 | 0 | 56 | n.a. |
| Percentage of primary health centers having regular power supply, 2007–08 | 96.9 | 86.5 | 20.4 | 41.5 |
| Percentage of habitations connected by roads, 2009 | 91.15 | 98.55 | 40.68 | 50.15 |

Source: Data for 2009 have been taken from the *Bulletin on Rural Health Statistics 2009*, compiled by the Ministry of Health and Family Welfare. Data for 2007–08 have been taken from the International Institute of Population Sciences' 2007–08 District-Level Household and Facility Survey (DLHS III).

# RECENT REFORMS TO INCREASE ALLOCATIONS TO HEALTH CARE

## National Rural Health Mission

Low public expenditure allocation and its skewed interstate distribution were the major reasons for the central government's launching in 2005 of a major program, the National Rural Health Mission. The NRHM is a comprehensive program initiated to improve access to effective health care for the poor residing in rural areas. The program covers the entire country but has a greater focus on 18 lagging states. It is to be implemented from 2005 to 2012, and spending on health care is expected to be increased to 2–3 percent of GDP (from about 1 percent of GDP in 2005).

The important components of the NRHM include the initiation of an accredited social health activist program—a voluntary female community health program aimed at improving immunization rates, institutionalized deliveries, reproductive health care, and nutrition. The NHRM also mandates improvements in health infrastructure, human resources for health, and availability of drugs. It is a flexible, decentralized program comprising

1. a mission flexible pool;
2. a reproductive-health flexible pool;
3. pulse polio immunization;
4. infrastructure maintenance; and
5. a national disease control program.

For allocating funds in the first two schemes, the states are divided into focus states (states with poor health status) and nonfocus states. The funds for these schemes are allocated according to population, with focus states getting 30 percent higher weight. The program was supposed to substantially increase the central government allocation for the NRHM (by 30 percent for the first two years and thereafter by 40 percent) until 2012, and the states were required to contribute an additional minimum of 15 percent of the central government's allocations or an increase of 10 percent in their health budgets every year over the period 2007 to 2012. In order to ensure that the funds would be transferred to the implementing agencies without delay, the transfers were made directly to the state-level societies, bypassing the budgets.

There are a number of problems with both the design and implementation of this program. In terms of the design, allocating financial resources on a per capita basis with an additional weight of 30 percent assigned to the focus states does not adequately take account of the requirements. Second, although the program requires the states to make matching contributions, it does not stipulate that the contribution should be additional, so the states can substitute expenditures on health in other areas to fulfill their matching requirements.

The implementation problems have been even more formidable. The expected large increases in central funding simply did not take place, and the actual expenditure incurred by the central government in regard to the program has been only a fraction of what was allocated. In 2009–10, for example, the funding allocated for the program was Rs 115.9 billion, but the actual expenditure was just Rs 46.6 billion or 40 percent of that amount. Second, the pattern of distribution of actual expenditure was vastly different from the original allocation, because when states are unable to make matching contributions or unable to provide utilization certificates to the central government as required under the scheme, the funds are reallocated to the states by the central government, thereby completely altering the original pattern of interstate allocation.

Thus, although the program held much promise, the actual improvement in increasing the health expenditures in poor-performing focus states has been lower than what was expected from the program. Public expenditure could not be increased as proposed, because neither the central government nor the states could find enough fiscal space. Secondly, the involvement of the states in the reform program was much less than desired. As the funds were directly transferred to the implementing societies, the states gave up their own supervisory and management role as well.

## Rashtriya Swasthya Bima Yojana

Another important reform initiative was the introduction of an insurance scheme, not by the Health Ministry, but by the Union Labor Ministry. In an attempt to provide financial protection against high OOP expenditure, in 2007 the Government of India introduced Rashtriya Swasthya Bima Yojana, a health insurance scheme that provides insurance coverage for selected hospitalization expenses and daycare procedures to people below the poverty line.[4] Under this scheme every poor (below the poverty line) family can access free hospitalization care and daycare procedures up to Rs 30,000 per year in selected private and public health facilities. A maximum of five members of a family can be covered under the scheme on a floater basis. A transportation allowance of Rs 1,000 (with a maximum of Rs 100 per visit) is also extended to these families under the scheme.

While the state governments are responsible for identifying the eligible poor families for the scheme, the scheme is actually implemented by insurance companies, which are selected through bids at the state level. Eligible families are provided with a smart card by the insurance company, and treatment can be received at the selected health facilities without cash transactions. The premium for the scheme (estimated to be a maximum of Rs 750 per family per year) is shared between the central government and the state in the ratio of 75:25, subject to a maximum subsidy of Rs 565 per family per year by the central government. For northeastern states, Jammu and Kashmir, the premium burden is shared between the central government and the states in the ratio of 90:10. Additionally, the central government also bears the cost of the smart cards, at Rs 60 per card. The

---

[4]The scheme was initially aimed at providing financial protection to informal workers and was therefore initiated by the Ministry of Labor and Employment. As the bulk of the informal workers were poor, the scheme was designed to cover the entire below-poverty population.

beneficiary family does not contribute to the premium but needs to pay Rs 30 per year as a registration fee.

As of July 2011, the scheme was being operated in 385 (of 640) districts and spanned 26 states. About 27 percent of all poor families in the country were enrolled under the scheme. However, even in the districts where the scheme was being operated, it covered less than 50 percent of the poor population. While some states, like Andhra Pradesh, have chosen not to implement RSBY but implement their own state insurance scheme (like Aarogyasri), others, like Karnataka, have implemented RSBY in selected districts along with state-level health insurance schemes (like Vajpayee Aarogyasri).

## Expenditure Needs of States and the Transfer System

As mentioned earlier, the provision of health care in India is predominantly the responsibility of state governments. However, the ability of these governments to spend on health care, particularly those in the low-income states, is constrained by a number of factors. First, most of the low-expenditure states are also low-income states (as discussed in the previous section) and have limited capacity for generating additional resources. Central transfers to these states have not been able to offset their fiscal imbalances fully, and this is mirrored in the strong correlation between per capita health spending and income levels across states. In addition, most of the existing resources of the states are used up to meet their committed liabilities in regard to wages, salaries, interest payments, and pensions, leaving little room for reprioritizing expenditures toward the health sector. Fiscal responsibility legislation has now been enacted in all states as well, and there is very little room to increase allocations to the health sector. Since they have some of the poorest health infrastructures, improving the level of expenditure and the state of health infrastructure in these states assumes particular importance.

For these reasons, and considering the significant externality associated with the health sector, it is necessary for the central government to introduce specific-purpose transfers to these states to ensure a certain minimum standard of basic health services. At present, transfers from the central government to states (specifically for health) are primarily through the NRHM, and as discussed in the previous section, the grants given under the program do not have any relationship with the requirements. The Twelfth Finance Commission provided grants to states for improving health indicators, but in effect, they recommended that the grants cover only 30 percent of the gap between the state's per capita health expenditure and the expenditure requirements assessed by them for each of the states.

Interestingly, most of the low-income states assign greater priority to spending on the health sector, as evidenced by a relatively higher share of their income GSDP as well as a higher percentage of their total expenditures on health. Despite this, they have some of the lowest per capita expenditure on health in the country. An analysis of health expenditure as a percentage of GSDP across states indicates that the low-income, low-expenditure states spend a relatively higher share of their GSDP on health. In 2008–09, health expenditure as a percentage of GSDP in low-income states like Bihar and Uttar Pradesh was more than double that in high-income states like Punjab, Haryana, Maharashtra, and Gujarat. As a percentage of total budgetary expenditure also, states like Uttar Pradesh and Rajasthan spend a significantly higher share than the high-income states. In fact, the four highest-income states, Punjab, Haryana, Maharashtra, and Gujarat, rank at the bottom in terms of health expenditure as a percentage of budgetary expenditure.

Additional transfers from the central government have to be directed toward primary care and the first level of secondary care by strengthening the related health infrastructure and personnel at the state level. At present, according to the norms set by the central government, a three-tier health care system should be set up, depending upon the population. A subcenter must be provided for every 5,000 people in the plains and for every 3,000 people in hilly or tribal regions, a public health center must be established for every 30,000 people in the plains and every 20,000 people in hilly/tribal regions, and a community health center must be provided for every 120,000 people in the plains and for every 80,000 people in hilly/tribal regions. The requirements for the subcenters, health centers, and community health centers as well as referral hospitals are specified in norms of the Indian Public Health Standards. Strengthening these tiers would be important not only to facilitate basic primary and secondary care, but also to reduce the burden and expenditure share at the tertiary level.

Designing the transfer scheme would require estimating the gaps between the expenditure needs and actual expenditures. A preliminary estimation of expenditure needs of different states based on the norms indicated above suggests that an additional amount of about Rs 3 billion (at 2008–09 prices), or about 0.6 percent of GDP, will be required to be spent across 16 major states in India (Table 15.8).[5] About 65 percent of these additional transfers will be required in just the six states that have the poorest health indicators in the country: Bihar, Uttar Pradesh, Madhya Pradesh, Orissa, Assam, and Rajasthan. If the 16 states are enabled to incur expenditures as required according to the norms, the coefficient of variation of per capita expenditure across the states would decline from about 0.3 in 2008–09 to about 0.15 after such a transfer of resources.

Much of the additional expenditures will have to be generated at the central level for two important reasons. The states do not have broad-based taxes except the sales tax, and considering that they have predominant responsibility for providing social services and coequal responsibility for providing physical infrastructure, resources will have to come by way of transfers from the central government. Second, the significant externalities implicit in health expenditures warrant that the central government should bear a substantial proportion of the cost. Given

---

[5]The norms have been adjusted for the percentage of tribal population in each state. State-level gaps in the number of subcenters, primary health centers, and community health centers have been estimated on the basis of the number of facilities reported in the Ministry of Health and Family Welfare's *Bulletin of Rural Health Statistics 2009*. In existing subcenters, primary health centers, and community health centers, gaps in manpower, drugs, and equipment have been considered for costing. Data on gaps in availability of medicines and equipments in existing facilities have been compiled from the International Institute of Population Sciences' 2007–08 District-Level Household and Family Survey (DLHS III). Data on gaps in availability of manpower have been compiled from both sources. The ratio of salary to nonsalary expenditure in each facility is assumed to be 70:30.

**TABLE 15.8**

Additional Resource Requirement and Per Capita Expenditures in 16 Major States

| | Additional resources required (2008–09 prices) (rupees crore) | Per capita expenditure (2008–09) (current prices) (rupees) | Per capita expenditure (after transfer) (2008–09 prices) (rupees) | Ratio of per capita expenditure (after to before transfer) (rupees) |
|---|---|---|---|---|
| Andhra Pradesh | 2,191 | 353 | 617 | 1.7 |
| Bihar | 4,396 | 137 | 602 | 4.4 |
| Chattishgarh | 701 | 258 | 549 | 2.1 |
| Gujrat | 1,219 | 280 | 494 | 1.8 |
| Haryana | 555 | 315 | 764 | 2.4 |
| Jharkhand | 1,097 | 257 | 440 | 1.7 |
| Karnataka | 1,502 | 358 | 617 | 1.7 |
| Kerala | 764 | 463 | 688 | 1.5 |
| Madhya Pradesh | 2,202 | 198 | 515 | 2.6 |
| Maharashtra | 1,906 | 316 | 491 | 1.6 |
| Orissa | 1,480 | 234 | 604 | 2.6 |
| Punjub | 538 | 305 | 497 | 1.6 |
| Rajasthan | 1,251 | 315 | 506 | 1.6 |
| Tamil Nadu | 1,170 | 374 | 550 | 1.5 |
| Uttar Pradesh | 6,404 | 257 | 589 | 2.3 |
| West Bengal | 2,777 | 248 | 566 | 2.3 |
| India (including special-category states) | 30,152 | 430 | 689 | 1.6 |

the high degree of externality in health spending, it is important for the central government to ensure a certain minimum specified level of spending on health, which is best achieved through specific-purpose matching transfers. However, while designing the specific-purpose transfers, it is important to ensure that the transfer system is incentive-compatible in the sense that it leads to stimulation and not substitution at the state level and also that states with low revenue capacity can utilize the funds by making matching contributions. In other words, matching ratios can be varied among the states depending on their capacity to make matching contributions.[6]

# FISCAL SPACE FOR HEALTH CARE, STIMULATION, AND SUBSTITUTION EFFECTS

The estimated additional expenditure requirements just to provide subcenters, health centers, and community health centers according to the norms is estimated

---

[6]During the Eleventh Plan period, under the NRHM, the states were required to contribute 15 percent of the central government's contribution. However, only a few states could contribute this amount, and the shortfall was particularly glaring in the case of the focus states. In the event, the states could not utilize the funds from the central government. Furthermore, even those states that made the contribution seem to have cut down other aspects of health expenditures.

at 0.6 percent of GDP. There are additional administrative expenditures and requirements for providing health facilities in urban areas, and these could add up to another 0.4 percent. Thus, a minimum of 1 percent of GDP will be required in the medium term to ensure minimum levels of health care as per the norms. The High Level Expert Group on Universal Health Coverage for India actually has recommended that public spending on health should increase to 2.5 to 3 percent in the medium term (Government of India, 2011).

Finding this additional fiscal space will be a formidable challenge. On the one hand, calibrating a sustainable fiscal policy in India requires significant compression of consolidated fiscal deficit (of both the central government and the states) as a ratio of GDP, and the Fiscal Responsibility Act requires the compression of fiscal deficit from 7.6 percent in 2010–11 to 5.4 percent by 2014–15. At the state level, there are competing demands on the resources of the states and additional fiscal space from mobilizing more resources, and reprioritization may not be large. The pattern of unconditional transfers from the Finance and Planning Commissions in the medium term is predictable and is not likely to lead to substantial increases in health care spending. Much of the increase, therefore, will have to come from specific-purpose transfers from the central government to the states.

It is important in this context to determine the impact of the central government transfers—both unconditional and specific-purpose—on states' expenditures on health. In a median-voter model, it is shown that unconditional transfers are a "veil" for tax cuts, and even when there are increases in unconditional transfers, the response to this in regard to health care spending would be similar to the response to general increases in incomes (or own revenues), although in actual empirical studies, there is considerable evidence of a "flypaper effect," that is, of a significantly higher response of expenditures to unconditional transfers.[7]

As far as specific-purpose transfers are concerned, whether the expenditures of the aided sector get stimulated or substituted depends on the way in which the transfer scheme is designed. As mentioned in the previous sections, despite a substantial increase in central government transfers to augment spending on the health sector, aggregate spending has not shown much increase. However, there are no econometric estimates of the extent of stimulation or substitution. A recent cross-country study of international aid to the health sector in developing countries shows a significant substitution of domestic financing of the health sector with international aid (Lu and others, 2010).

Considering the importance of increasing the overall public spending on health and the fact that the central government will have to make substantial additional grants to augment spending on the sector, the fiscal space analysis should incorporate the effect of central grants on actual health expenditures. Measurement of the impact of central grants on states' own spending on health care is important for evaluating the design of the transfer system, which is attempted in the following.

---

[7]For a recent analysis of the "flypaper effect," please see Inman (2008).

In India, given that the states have a predominant role in the provision of health care, the possibility of additional fiscal space at the state level can be due to (1) increase in own revenues of the states; (2) increase in general-purpose transfers from the Finance and Planning Commissions, which include shared taxes and plan and non-plan grants; (3) increase in specific-purpose transfers for the health sector; and (4) changes in prioritization in favor of the health sector. In India, foreign aid is not an important factor in determining the fiscal space, nor are earmarked taxes important.

Thus, increases in per capita expenditure on health in a state excluding the specific-purpose transfers in a year, $[\Delta (PC\_OHE)_{it}]$, depend on increases in own revenues of the state, $[\Delta (PC\_SOR)_{it}]$, increases in unconditional transfers received from the central government, $[\Delta (PC\_GPGC)_{it}]$, increases in specific-purpose transfers, $[\Delta (PC\_CGH)_{it}]$, and changes in priority assigned to health spending in the overall budget allocation, $[\Delta (SPH)_{it}]$. Thus,

$$\Delta (PC\_OHE)_{it} = \alpha + \beta \, \Delta (PC\_CGH)_{it} + \gamma \, \Delta (PC\_SOR)_{it} + \psi \, \Delta (SPH)_{it}$$
$$+ \tau \, \Delta (PC\_GPGC)_{it} + \varphi \, (State\ Dummies)$$
$$+ \sigma \, (Year\ Dummies) + \varepsilon_{it}$$

where

$$\Delta (PC\_OHE)_{it} = [(PC\_OHE)_{it} - (PC\_OHE)_{it-1}]$$

or changes (from the previous year) in per capita own health expenditure of state $i$ in year $t$;

$$\Delta (PC\_CGH)_{it} = [(PC\_CGH)_{it} - (PC\_CGH)_{it-1}]$$

or changes (from the previous year) in the central government's per capita grant for health to state $i$ in year $t$;

$$\Delta (PC\_SOR)_{it} = [(PC\_SOR)_{it} - (PC\_SOR)_{it-1}]$$

or changes (from the previous year) in per capita own revenues of state $i$ in year $t$;

$$\Delta (SPH)_{it} = [(G_{hi}/G_{bi})_t - (G_{hi}/G_{bi})_{t-1}]$$

or changes in the ratio of public expenditure (over the previous year) on health to total budget expenditure of the $i$th state in year $t$; and $\Delta (PC\_GPGC)_{it}$ = changes in the per capita general-purpose grant by the central government to state $i$ in year $t$ = (tax devolution + plan and nonplan grants).

The estimate of $\beta$ in the model measures the impact of a one-unit increase in the per capita health grant on the per capita health expenditures of the state from its resources, including unconditional transfers. A significant negative sign for $\beta$ would indicate that all else being equal, additional central health grants lead to a lowering of states' own health expenditure—an indication that states substitute additional central government health grants for their own health expenditure. A significant positive sign would indicate stimulation of a state's spending when higher central health grants are received. States' own health expenditure may also be affected by changes in other sources of state revenues and by priority accorded to health by the state. We use a set of control variables in the regression specification to account for the effect of these factors.

We have taken the data for 14 major states in India for the period 1991–92 to 2007–08 to estimate the effect, on changes in states' per capita health expenditures (excluding per capita specific purpose transfers), of changes in states' per capita own revenues, unconditional central transfers, specific-purpose central transfers for the health sector, and changes in priorities of the states (Table 15.9). A two-way fixed-effects panel data model has been used to estimate the above specification. All variables (excluding population) have been sourced from the finance accounts of individual states published by the Comptroller and Auditor General of India. Variables expressed in per capita terms have been converted at constant (1999–2000) prices for estimation. Population figures have been sourced from the Central Statistical Organization. Since 2001–02, some of the central government health grants to states have been transferred directly to implementing agencies, bypassing the states' budgets, so the regression has also been estimated separately for two subperiods: 1991–92 to 2000–01 and 2001–02 to 2007–08.

In the two subperiods as well as for the entire period, the coefficient on central government health grants $\beta$ is significantly negative, which implies that increases in the health grants by the central government result in the substitution of those increased resources in place of health expenditure by the states from their own resources. The sign and significance of the coefficient are consistent across all the subperiods. Thus, the results clearly show that increases in the central government grants for the health sector have not led to increases in the states' health expenditure. The states receiving the additional grants have been reducing the

**TABLE 15.9**

## Regression Results

**Dependent Variable: Changes in Per Capita Health Expenditure of Central Health Sector Grants**

| | 1991–2007 (Model I) | 1991–2000 (Model II) | 2001–2007 (Model III) |
|---|---|---|---|
| Center's health grant | −0.952*** | −0.777*** | −1.059*** |
| | (0.074) | (0.114) | (0.109) |
| States' own revenues | 0.012*** | 0.015*** | 0.0001 |
| | (0.003) | (0.004) | (0.006) |
| States' priority to health | 17.649*** | 15.03*** | 19.487*** |
| | (1.828) | (2.038) | (4.231) |
| General (unconditional) transfers by center | 0.019*** | 0.014 | 0.013 |
| | (0.007) | (0.011) | (0.01) |
| Constant | 18.252*** | 17.17*** | 3.552 |
| | (3.561) | (3.885) | (5.035) |
| State-specific fixed effects | Yes | Yes | Yes |
| Time-specific fixed effects | Yes | Yes | Yes |
| Number of observations | 224 | 126 | 84 |
| $R^2$ | 0.69 | 0.62 | 0.77 |

Note: t-statistics are given in parentheses. The standard errors are robust to cross-sectional heteroskedasticity and within-panel serial correlation.
***$p < 0.01$.

expenditures on health from their own resources. Interestingly, the magnitude of the coefficient is significantly larger in the later subperiod than in the earlier period. With most states experiencing relatively higher fiscal stress in the later period than in the earlier period, this possibly indicates that the substitution effect is stronger in the later subperiod, which is a period of fiscal stress.

The regression estimates presented in Table 15.9 also show that the changes in per capita revenues have a significant impact on per capita health expenditures when the whole period (1991–2007) is considered. This is also true of the first subperiod (1991–2000), but the coefficient is not significant in the second sub-period. Perhaps the absence of an increase in health expenditure in response to increased revenues in the post-2000 period may be explained by the focus on fiscal adjustment to adhere to the targets set by fiscal responsibility legislation. It is also seen that the coefficient on unconditional transfers does not show evidence of a significant flypaper effect. The coefficients are broadly similar to those of per capita own revenues. The changes in priority assigned to the health sector clearly show a significant impact on changes in per capita health expenditures.

Also, all the control variables are significant in the entire time period (Model I), which reflects the importance of these variables in determining the level of health expenditure in states (Table 15.9). Besides, in the later subperiod (Model III), the coefficient on states' own revenues is not significant, possibly because in the later period, as the result of the Fiscal Responsibility and Budget Management Act, states were constrained in regard to expanding expenditure from their own revenues, as they were mandated to bring down the fiscal and revenue deficits. On the whole, the preceding analysis points toward the fact that states substitute additional grants received from the central government for the health sector for health expenditures incurred out of untied resources at the state level. This substitution effect appears to be higher in periods of higher fiscal stress.

## CONCLUSION

This chapter analyzes public spending on health care in India. It analyzes public spending in different states in relation to the requirements to provide basic health infrastructure. The chapter also analyzes recent reform attempts to augment spending on health care through specific-purpose transfers to states.

The Indian health care system is characterized by low levels of public spending on health care; poor quality in health care services, with adverse effects on the population's health status; a lack of focus on preventive health care; and dependency of the population, particularly the poor, on private health care providers and consequently high OOP spending and immiseration.

Reforms in the health sector will have to address the need for increasing public spending on health care, focus on preventive health care, ensure greater access to health care by the poor, and significantly improve the productivity of public spending. Not only is public spending on health care in India too low, but its distribution across the country is very uneven. Per capita health care expenditure in the poorest state, Bihar, was Rs 166 in 2008–09, whereas in that same year, it was Rs 421 in Tamil Nadu and Rs 507 in Kerala, relatively more affluent states. This is in spite of the greater emphasis given by the low-income states to health care spending. The coefficient of correlation between per capita expenditures and per capita GSDP was 0.7 and 0.8, respectively, for 1996–97 and 2004–05.

Considering both the existence of a significant vertical imbalance and the fact that health is an important merit good, much of the additional resources for health care will have to come from the central government. Increasing public spending on health care in low-income states will require designing specific-purpose transfers with matching contributions from the states. Such transfers should be equalizing and should not lead to a substitution of states' expenditures on health care from their own resources.

The chapter reviews the introduction of the NRHM, an important specific-purpose transfer program introduced by the government of India in 2005. It shows that the program's objective of increasing expenditures to 2 percent of GDP has not been fulfilled, partly because the low-income states could not avail themselves of the grants by making their own contributions and could not afford to pay for the current component of spending. Furthermore, econometric estimates show significant substitution of central grants for states' spending from their own resources. These findings underline the need to redesign the transfer system. Furthermore, the focus of the NRHM is on rural areas, and there is no program to create health infrastructure in urban areas.

It is imperative for the central government to embark on a major expansion of health infrastructure in both rural and urban areas of the country in its Twelfth Plan (2012–13 to 2016–17). This calls for a significant increase in expenditure. Our estimates show that an additional 1 percent of GDP would be necessary in the medium term to provide basic health care services as per the norms. Finding additional fiscal space will be a major challenge. Calibrating a sustainable fiscal policy will require additional fiscal adjustment of over 2 percentage points of GDP, as set out in the Fiscal Responsibility Act, and with competing demands for additional spending for education and food security, which are supposed to claim an additional 2 percent of GDP, the creation of fiscal space for spending on health care during the Twelfth Plan will be very challenging.

## REFERENCES

Benedict, C., S. Gupta, I. Karpowicz, and S. Tareq, 2010, *Evaluating Government Employment and Compensation*, IMF Technical Notes and Manuals (Washington: International Monetary Fund).

Government of India, 2011, "High Level Expert Group Report on Universal Health Coverage for India," report submitted to the Planning Commission, Government of India, New Delhi; available at http://planningcommission.nic.in/reports/genrep/rep_uhc0812.pdf.

Government of India, Ministry of Finance, *Economic Survey 2010–11* (New Delhi), available at http://indiabudget.nic.in/survey.asp.

Government of India, Ministry of Health and Family Welfare (MHFW), 2005a, *Report of the National Commission on Macroeconomics of Health* (New Delhi).

———, 2005b, *Financing and Delivery of Health Care Services in India*, background papers for the National Commission on Macroeconomics of Health (New Delhi).

———, 2005c, "Burden of Disease in India," background paper prepared for the National Commission on Macroeconomics of Health (New Delhi).

Government of India, Planning Commission, 2005, *Mid-Term Appraisal of the Tenth Five-Year Plan (2002–2007)* (New Delhi).

Government of India, Registrar General, 1999, "Compendium of India's Fertility and Mortality Indicators 1971–1997," Office of the Registrar General and Census Commissioner (New Delhi).

Heller, P., 2006, "The Prospect of Creating Fiscal Space for the Health Sector," *Health Policy and Planning,* Vol. 21, No. 2, pp. 75–79.

Inman, R.P., 2008, "The Flypaper Effect," Working Paper No. 14579 (Cambridge, MA: National Bureau of Economic Research), available at http://www.nber.org/papers/w14579.

International Institute of Population Science (IIPS), 2010, "District-Level Household and Facility Survey (DLHS-3) 2007–08: India" (Mumbai).

Kakwani, N., 1993, "Performance in Living Standards: An International Comparison," *Journal of Development Economics,* Vol. 41, pp. 307–36.

Lu, C., M.T. Schneider, P. Gubbins, K. Leach-Kemon, D. Jamison, and C.J.L. Murray, 2010, "Public Financing of Health in Developing Countries: A Cross-National Systematic Analysis," *Lancet,* Vol. 375, pp. 1375–87.

Mahal, A., and M. Mohanan, 2006, "Growth of Private Medical Education in India," *Medical Education,* Vol. 40, pp. 1009–11.

National Sample Survey Organization (NSSO), 2007, *Household Consumption of Various Goods and Services in India 2004–05. Vol I: Major States and All-India* (New Delhi).

Oates, W.E., 2008, "On the Evolution of Fiscal Federalism: Theory and Institutions," *National Tax Journal,* Vol. 61, No. 2, pp. 313–33.

Rao, K., A. Bhatnagar, and P. Berman, 2009, "India's Health Workforce: Size, Composition and Distribution," in *India Health Beat,* ed. by J. La Forgia and K. Rao (New Delhi: World Bank and Public Health Foundation of India).

Rao, M.G., 2009, "Fiscal Federalism in India: Trends and Reform," in *Decentralization Policies in Asian Development,* ed. by S. Ichimura and R. Bahl (Singapore and London: World Scientific).

———, 2010, "Indian Fiscal Federalism in Globalizing Environment," in *India's Economy and Growth,* ed. by P. Nayak, B. Goldar, and P. Agrawal (New Delhi: Sage), pp. 2761–97.

Rao, M.G., and M. Choudhury, 2008, "Inter-state Equalization of Health Expenditures in Indian Union," Monograph, National Institute of Public Finance and Policy, available at http://www.whoindia.org/LinkFiles/Health_Finance_Inter-State_Equalisation_of_Health_Expenditures_in_Indian_Union.pdf.

Rao M.G., K. D. Rao, A.K. Shiva Kumar, M. Chatterjee, and T. Sundararaman, 2011, "Human Resources for Health in India," *Lancet,* Volume 377, Issue 9765, pp. 587–98.

Rao, M.G., and N. Singh, 2005, *Political Economy of Federalism in India* (New Delhi: Oxford University Press).

Selvaraj, S., and A.K. Karan, 2009, "Deepening Health Insecurity in India: Evidence from National Sample Surveys since the 1980s," *Economic and Political Weekly,* Vol. 44, pp. 55–60.

Sen, A.K., 1981, "Public Action and the Quality of Life in Developing Countries," *Oxford Bulletin of Economics and Statistics,* Vol. 43 (November), pp. 287–319.

———, 1999, *Development as Freedom* (New Delhi: Oxford University Press).

Shahrawat, R., and K.D. Rao, 2011, "Insured Yet Vulnerable: Out-of-pocket Payments and India's Poor," *Health Policy and Planning,* available at http://heapol.oxfordjournals.org/content/early/2011/04/12/heapol.czr029.full.pdf+html.

Stenberg, K., R. Elovainio, D. Chisholm, D. Fuhr, A.-M. Perucic, D. Rekve, and A. Yurekli, 2010, "Responding to the Challenge of Resource Mobilization Mechanisms for Raising Additional Domestic Resources for Health," Background Paper No. 13 (Geneva: World Health Organization).

Tandon, A., and C. Cashin, 2010, "Assessing Public Expenditure on Health from a Fiscal Space Perspective," Health, Nutrition and Population (HNP) Discussion Paper (Washington: World Bank).

United Nations Development Program (UNDP), 2010, *The Real Wealth of Nations:Pathways to Human Development, Human Development Report 2010* (New York), available at http://hdr.undp.org/en/media/HDR_2010_EN_Complete_reprint.pdf.

Van Doorslaer, E., O. O'Donnell, R.P. Rannan-Eliya, A. Somanathan, S.R. Adhikari, C.C. Garg, D. Harbianto, A.N. Herrin, M.N. Huq, S. Ibragimova, A. Karan, T.-J. Lee, G.M. Leung, J.-F.R. Lu, C.W. Ng, B.R. Pande, R. Racelis, S. Tao, K. Tin, K. Tisayaticom, L. Trisnantoro, C. Vasavid, and Y. Zhao, 2007, "Catastrophic Payments for Health Care in Asia," *Health Economics*, Vol. 16, pp. 1159–84.

World Health Assembly, 2005, "Sustainable Health Financing, Universal Coverage and Social Health Insurance," Resolution 58.33 from the Fifty-Eighth World Health Assembly, May 25; available at http://www.who.int/gb/ebwha/pdf_files/WHA58/WHA58_33-en.pdf.

World Health Organization (WHO), 2004, "The Impact of Health Expenditure on Households and Options for Alternative Financing," Technical Paper No. EM/RC51/4 (Regional Committee for the Eastern Mediterranean) (Geneva).

———, 2008, *Global Burden of Diseases* (Geneva); available at http://www.who.int/healthinfo/global_burden_disease/estimates_country/en/index.html.

———, 2010, *World Health Statistics 2010* (Geneva).

# CHAPTER 16

# Evidence-Based Health Financing Reform in Thailand

PONGPISUT JONGUDOMSUK, SUPON LIMWATTANANON, PHUSIT
PRAKONGSAI, SAMRIT SRITHAMRONGSAWAT, KUMAREE
PACHANEE, ADUN MOHARA, WALAIPORN PATCHARANARUMOL,
AND VIROJ TANGCHAROENSATHIEN

## OVERVIEW OF HEALTH CARE SYSTEM AND REFORMS

Thailand is a lower-middle-income country in Southeast Asia with a GDP per capita of $4,720 in 2010. Complete geographical coverage of the health care infrastructure was achieved through an intensive investment in public health care infrastructures by the early 2000s, although an inequitable distribution of health resources remains a problem. Public hospitals, mainly owned by the Ministry of Public Health, accounted for 75.6 percent of total hospitals and 79.8 percent of total hospital beds in 2005 (Wibulpolprasert, 2008).

The health care system is financed through a mix of sources, namely, general taxes, social health insurance contributions, private insurance premiums, and a low level of direct out-of-pocket payments constituting approximately 18 percent of total health expenditure in 2008. The share of public financing increased gradually from 45 percent in 1994 to 56 percent in 2001. After universal coverage was achieved in 2002, the share of public financing increased substantially and had by 2008 reached 75 percent. In addition, average government spending on health had also increased from 18 percent of the total government budget during 1995–2000 to 20.3 percent during 2001–07. In 2008, total health expenditure per capita was $178 or 4 percent of GDP (Tangcharoensathien, Patcharanaruomol, and others, 2010).

A recent study showed that two key strands of reform—investment in primary care services at district and subdistrict levels and expansion of financial risk protection—contributed to the significant improvement in health outcomes, in particular, maternal and child health indicators (Patcharanarumol and others, 2011). Figure 16.1 plots the changes in the under-five mortality rate per 1,000 live births, chronologically by five-year National Economic and Social Development Plans from 1970 to 2007. During the early 1970s, when the under-five mortality rate was high, the rate of annual reduction was higher, 4.2 per 1,000 live births, than when the under-five mortality rate was low. The annual rate of reduction was 0.8 per 1,000 live births in the early 2000s. Various policy interventions noted below the curve in the figure are health infrastructure and human resources developments, whereas those above the curve describe the extensions of financial risk protection to different target populations. Thailand had the highest annual rate of reduction in child mortality among 30 low- and middle-income countries between 1990 and 2006 (Rohde and others, 2008) and the second-lowest level of child mortality in 2006.

Thailand achieved universal coverage in 2002 after a 27-year-long march of expanding financial risk protection for targeted populations—from low-income households in 1975 to the informal sector in 1984 and to private-sector employees in 1990 (Tangcharoensathien, Teokul, and Chanwongpaisarn, 2005; Tangcharoensathien and others, 2009a). Reforms moving toward universal coverage have been incremental, with a range of organizational arrangements and different combinations of sources of financing.

The two parallel financing approaches were payroll taxes for the formal sector employees, the top layer, covered by a social health insurance (SHI) scheme, and a general-tax-financed scheme for the poor, the bottom layer. The coverage of the informal sector, made up of a nonpoor and "not-so-poor" population—the middle layer—has been the most difficult challenge. The two parallel approaches were described at a recent conference as the way to cover the informal sector in the middle layer (Philhealth, 2007). Because Thailand had "squeezed up from the bottom," this meant coverage for the middle layer (the informal sector) was fully financed by general taxation similar to the way the poor were financed. By contrast, the Philippines chose to "squeeze from the top"—the informal sector there is financed by a fixed-rate premium contribution by members (Tangcharoensathien

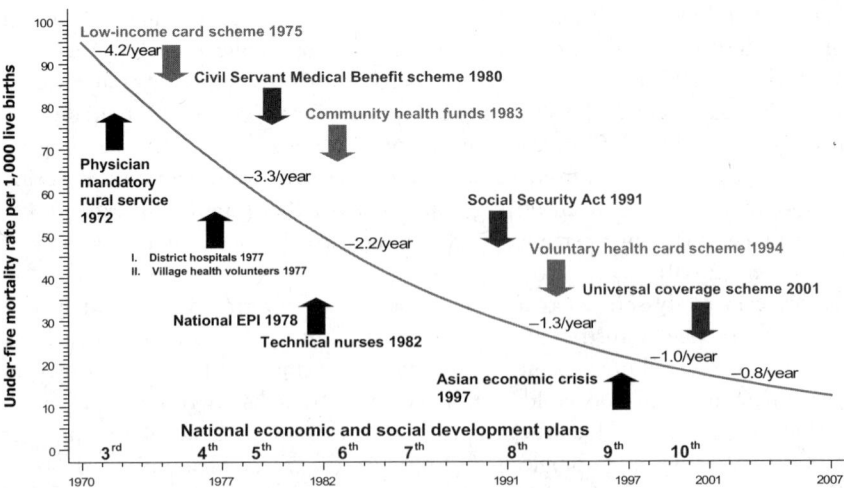

**Figure 16.1** Under-Five Mortality, Development of Human Resources and Infrastructure, and Financial Protection, 1970–2010
Source: Patcharanarumol and others (2011).

**TABLE 16.1**

| Population Coverage by Various Health Insurance Schemes Prior to Universal Coverage Achievement (Percent) | | | |
|---|---|---|---|
| Scheme | 1991 | 1996 | 2001 |
| Social welfare for the poor, the elderly, and socially disadvantaged groups | 12.7 | 12.6 | 32.4 |
| Civil Servant Medical Benefit Scheme | 15.3 | 10.2 | 8.5 |
| Social health insurance | — | 5.6 | 7.2 |
| Voluntary health card | 1.4 | 15.3 | 20.8 |
| Private health insurance | 4.0 | 1.8 | 2.1 |
| Total insured | 33.4 | 45.5 | 71.0 |
| Total uninsured | 66.6 | 54.5 | 29.0 |

Sources: National Statistical Office, Health and Welfare Surveys (various years).

and others, 2011). In 2001, one year prior to 2002's universal coverage achievement, 29 percent of Thailand's total population was still uninsured, while 71 percent were covered by different insurance schemes as a result of the historical application of targeting approaches (Table 16.1).

By 2002, the entire population was covered by one of the three public health insurance schemes: SHI for private sector employees, the Civil Servant Medical Benefit Scheme (CSMBS) for government employees, and the universal coverage scheme for the rest of the population.

Critical enabling factors in achieving universal coverage were the political and financial commitment of successive governments, national income, and the structure of the economy, which determined the size of the formal employment sector and hence the introduction of SHI in 1990. The size of SHI was small—it covered fewer than 2 million people or 4 percent of the country's population of 54.5 million in 1990, and 10 million or 15 percent of the total population of 65 million in 2010. The achievement of universal coverage in Thailand rested on the bold decision in 2002 to cover the informal sector, which would never have been fully covered by SHI because of the sector's sheer size—more than 75 percent of the population—through a tax-financed scheme.

The extensive geographical coverage of primary care services with qualified health workers was part of the foundation for ensuring that services would be available and accessible to the whole population when universal coverage was achieved (Tangcharoensathien, Teokul, and Chanwongpaisarn, 2005). The universal coverage achievement in Thailand helped reach a convincing outcome in terms of improved utilization of health services by the poor and rural population and as measured by benefit incidence analysis (Prakongsai, Limwattananon, and Tangcharoensathien, 2009).

Table 16.2 provides key economic and health financing indicators among seven member countries of the Association of Southeast Asian Nations, excluding those with high incomes (Singapore and Brunei) and Myanmar, for which data are not available. There is a wide variation in economic and poverty indicators among the countries. Fiscal space—the government tax as a percentage of GDP—in 2000 ranged from 8.2 percent in Cambodia to 16.8 percent in

**TABLE 16.2**

Key Background Indicators for Seven Member Countries of the Association of Southeast Asian Nations

| | Malaysia | Thailand | Indonesia | Philippines | Vietnam | Lao PDR | Cambodia |
|---|---|---|---|---|---|---|---|
| Gross national income per capita (dollars at purchasing power parity) (2008) | 13,740 | 5,990 | 3,830 | 3,900 | 2,700 | 2,040 | 1,820 |
| Annual GDP growth (percent) | | | | | | | |
| 2000 | 8.9 | 4.8 | 4.9 | 6.0 | 6.8 | 5.8 | 8.8 |
| 2005 | 5.3 | 4.6 | 5.7 | 5.0 | 8.4 | 7.1 | 13.3 |
| 2008 | 4.6 | 2.6 | 6.1 | 3.8 | 6.1 | 7.5 | 5.2 |
| Fiscal space: government tax (percent of GDP) | 16.6 (2003) | 16.8 (2007) | 12.3 (2004) | 14.3 (2006) | 13.0 (2007) | 10.1 (2007) | 8.2 (2006) |
| Poverty incidence (percent below national poverty line) | 8.7 (2004) | 21.0 (2000) 8.5 (2007) | 20.2 (2009) | 32.9 (2006) | 18.2 (2006) 13.5 (2008) | 32.0 (2002) 27.0 (2008) | 34.7 (2004) |
| Poverty headcount (percent) | n.a. | n.a. | 29.4 (2007) | 22.6 (2006) | 21.5 (2006) | n.a. | 25.8 (2007) |

Source: Tangcharoensathien and others (2011).

Note: n.a. = not available.

Thailand, in contrast to the Organization for Economic Cooperation and Development average of 37.4 percent (World Bank, 2010).

To exemplify and draw lessons on evidence-based health financing reform, this chapter reviews how institutional capacities in health policy and systems research in Thailand were gradually built up, strengthened, and sustained and describes evidence-guided financing reforms using two policy reforms as illustrations: the provider payment reform of CSMBS, and the inclusion of new health interventions in the benefit package of the universal coverage scheme.

# DEVELOPMENT OF INSTITUTIONAL CAPACITY TO GENERATE EVIDENCE

Melgaard (2004) described the strong technical skill and research capacity in Thailand that have backed up reforms and guided sound policy formulation. The effective interfaces between research communities and policymakers made key contributions to evidence-based policy decision making, not only for the universal coverage scheme designs, but for other public health initiatives. These included the establishment of the Thai Health Promotion Foundation, which was financed through an earmarked fund mandated by law, generated from a 2 percent surcharge on tobacco and an alcohol excise tax. This "sin tax"—among the very few in the world specifically earmarked for health—was dedicated to the foundation for its active campaign against the epidemic use of tobacco and alcohol and other health risks (Tangcharoensathien and others, 2009b).

The capacity for health policy and health systems research has been systematically built up through the promulgation of the 1992 Health Systems Research Institute Act and the establishment of the Health Systems Research Institute (HSRI), an autonomous agency with an arm's-length relation to the Ministry of Public Health, also in 1992. HSRI, receiving annual government budget support, is mandated to generate and promulgate knowledge on health systems in support of policy decisions. Over the past decade, HSRI established a number of associated institutions focusing on research in specific areas (Green, 2007). Some of the outstanding associate institutions are the Office for Hospital Quality Improvement and Accreditation, the International Health Policy Program (IHPP), the Central Office for Health Care Information, the Health Insurance System Research Office (HISRO), the National Health System Reform Office, and the Health Intervention and Technology Assessment Program (HITAP), all of which have contributed significantly to informed policy decisions. The evolution of these institutions and their contributions to health system reforms are highlighted below.

## The Introduction of Research Institutes

Hospital accreditation, jointly supported by HSRI and the Thailand Research Fund, was launched in 1997 as pilot research in 35 hospitals. It was well accepted by hospital managers and policymakers and has had a significant impact on quality improvement (Pauls and others, 2002). In 1999, HSRI upgraded the program to the Office for Hospital Quality Improvement and Accreditation. When the universal coverage scheme was launched in 2002, accreditation by the Office for Hospital Quality Improvement and Accreditation gained wide acceptance as a quality standard required by all hospitals in providing services to members participating in the universal coverage. In 2009, the Office for Hospital Quality Improvement and Accreditation gained legal status as an autonomous public agency, established by a royal decree, with reference to the Public Organization Act of 1999 (Thailand, Secretariat of the Cabinet, 2009).

The fee-for-services payment approach resulted in cost escalation within CSMBS. It was not until the 1997 Asian economic crunch that policymakers in the Comptroller General Department of the Finance Ministry, which was responsible for CSMBS, called for cost containment measures. Having worked closely with the Comptroller General Department, HSRI made a number of recommendations that were endorsed by the department in 2000 to apply global budgeting and diagnosis-related group methods for paying for inpatient services, establishing a beneficiaries' database, and direct disbursement to hospitals for chronic outpatient services.

A spinoff of CSMBS reform was the establishment of two agencies: the Central Office for Health Care Information and the Office for Medical Audit (Jongudomsuk, 2010). The Central Office for Health Care Information supported the development of diagnosis-related groups, managing hospital discharges to diagnosis-related groups and advising the Comptroller General Department for payment to hospitals. When diagnosis-related groups were applied widely by two other schemes—SHI and the universal coverage scheme—

the Central Office for Health Care Information extended its service to cover all three public health insurance schemes and became a national data repository for hospital admissions. This national IP data set, covering almost all admissions, is the most valuable one, contributing to knowledge on hospital morbidity and mortality of the Thai population.

Following the introduction of the universal coverage policy in 2002, HSRI launched a research plan on universal coverage monitoring and evaluation. Several studies were undertaken to provide evidence on the impact of universal coverage on both the health system and households (HSRI, 2003; Na Ranong, Na Ranong, and Vongmontha, 2004; Pannarunothai, Patmasiriwat, and Kongsawatt, 2004; Srithamrongsawat and Lapying, 2002; Na Ranong, 2005). In the early 2000s, there were several further reforms, such as

- decentralization;
- increased resources to address determinants of ill health such as tobacco, alcohol and road traffic accidents, as a result of the emergence of Thai Health Promotion Foundation;
- participatory public policy development, enabled by the advent of the National Health Commission Office; and
- downsizing of the public sector.

All these reforms had major effects on health systems.

Recognizing the need for monitoring the impacts of these reforms on health systems, HSRI established HISRO in 2005. HISRO not only mandated the monitoring of the reforms' impacts, but also conducts research on health insurance and contributes to normative work, such as maintaining various national data repositories for monitoring and evaluation.

These institutions have worked closely with national and international partners to generate evidence and translate evidence to reform decisions (Figure 16.2). Multisectoral partnerships with the Ministry of Public Health, the National Statistical Office, and academia have fostered networking at the country level. At the same time, the London School of Hygiene and Tropical Medicine was one of the long-term international partners that contributed substantially to research capacity development in Thailand (Boseley and Mills, 2010).

IHPP was established in 1998 as a semiautonomous body under the Ministry of Public Health, aimed at strengthening health policy and systems research capacity. Almost all IHPP fellows were recruited from among health professionals working in the health system. They underwent a research apprenticeship in IHPP for a few years, under the close mentoring of senior researchers, before placement in a master's or doctoral training program abroad. All fellows returned after graduation, and more than 95 percent have continued their research or academic careers (Bennett and others, 2008).

In the last decade, in conjunction with and with support from partners, IHPP has made noteworthy strides in developing and sustaining individual and institutional capacities in health systems and undertaken important policy research (Pitayarangsarit and Tangcharoensathien, 2009). A number of these

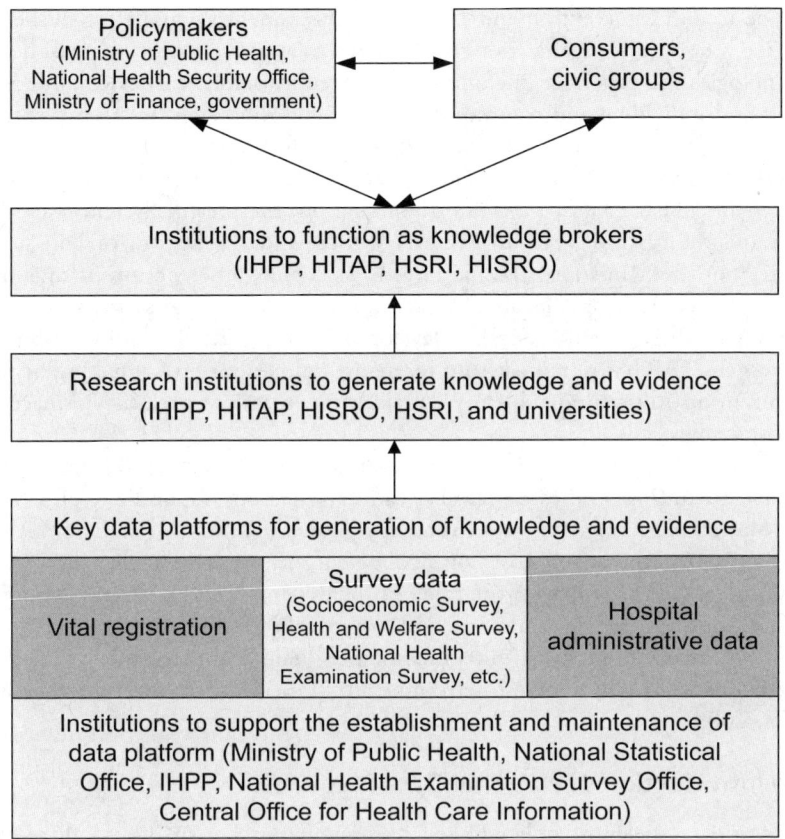

**Figure 16.2** Institutional Arrangements for Generation of Knowledge and Evidence to Support Policy Decision on Health Care Reform
Note: HISRO = Health Insurance System Research Office; HITAP = Health Intervention and Technology Assessment Program; HSRI = Health Systems Research Institute; IHPP = International Health Policy Program.

policy-relevant studies have contributed to policy decisions—for example, work on estimates of the capitation contracting model for the universal coverage scheme (Mills and others, 2000; Tangcharoensathien, Swasdiworn, Jongudomsuk, Srithamrongswat, Patcharanarumol, and Thammatach-Aree, 2010a), development and sustaining the National Health Account since 1994 (Tangcharoensathien and others, 1999), universal renal replacement therapy for universal coverage members (Kasemsup, Prakongsai, and Tangcharoensathien, 2006), assessment of financial sustainability (Tangcharoensathien, Swasdiworn, Jongudomsuk, Srithamrongswat, Patcharanarumol, Prakongsai, and Thammatach-Aree, 2010), and an equity outcome assessment of the universal coverage policy (Limwattananon, Tangcharoensathien, and Prakongsai, 2010; Tangcharoensathien, Swasdiworn, Jongudomsuk, Srithamrongswat, Patcharanarumol, Prakongsai, and Thammatach-Aree, 2010; Limwattananon, Tangcharoensathien, and Prakongsai, 2007).

The Health Intervention and Technology Assessment Program, established in 2007 as a nonprofit organization, is mandated to appraise a wide range of health technologies and programs, including pharmaceuticals, medical devices, interventions, and individual and community health promotion and disease prevention. HITAP is an associate organization under the auspices of IHPP.[1]

HITAP received its main funding support from four public institutions, namely, the Thai Health Promotion Foundation, the Health Systems Research Institute, the National Health Security Office, and the Bureau of Policy and Strategy of the Ministry of Public Health, as well as other nonprofit organizations such as the World Health Organization, the World Bank, the Center for Alcohol Studies, and the Global Development Network. To avoid conflict of interest, HITAP has refrained from receiving grants from profit-making organizations or institutes funded by profit-making organizations such as pharmaceutical companies.

HITAP has contributed to a number of studies having a major policy impact, including studies of cervical cancer screening in the light of a high-cost human papillomavirus vaccine campaign by the industry (Yothasamut and others, 2010); the social costs of alcohol consumption (Thavorncharoensap and others, 2006); policy on the role of provider-initiated HIV/AIDS counseling and testing (Teerawattananon and others, 2009); and the national agreement on the use of gross national income per quality-adjusted life-year gain as a benchmark for public investment in health (Tantivess, Teerawattananon, and Mills, 2009).

## The Introduction of National Data Platforms

In addition to relevant policy-linked research, a number of other studies that helped lay the foundation for regular monitoring of the population's health and the impact of policy on households to guide informed decisions are worth mentioning. Thailand launched its first National Health Examination Survey in 1991–92 through the collective effort of the Ministry of Public Health, the National Epidemiological Board of Thailand, and a number of universities. Though costly, the survey contributed to a deeper understanding of the health status of the Thai population. Subsequent surveys have been conducted every five years, in 1996–97, 2003–04, and 2008–09, with the active leadership of HSRI and the Ministry of Public Health. Recognizing the need to institutionalize this process, since the resulting information is essential for decisions on investing in the health sector and ad hoc surveys are not sustainable, HSRI established the National Health Examination Survey Office, responsible for conducting this survey over the long term.

The National Health Account (NHA) was established in 1994. The most recent data available are for 2010. The NHA provided estimates on how much was spent by different financing agencies, such as the Ministry of Public Health, other

---

[1]See HITAP profiles available at http://www.hitap.net/history_en.php.

ministries, insurance funds, households, and donors; on what types of services the money was spent, such as outpatient and inpatient care, prevention, and public health activities; and where the money was spent on public and private providers. A long series of NHA data from 1994 to 2006 was used as the basis for long-term financial projections that assessed whether health spending would be affordable over the longer term (Tangcharoensathien, Swasdiworn, Jongudomsuk, Srithamrongswat, Patcharanarumol, Prakongsai, and Thammatach-Aree, 2010; Sakunphanit and others, 2009). IHPP is the national focal point and technical secretariat to the Thai working group on the NHA. Capacity to generate and update and technical capacities on methodological advancements were well rooted and became institutionalized by the early 2000s (Tangcharoensathien, Vasavid, and others, 2010).

Since 1999, the capacity to generate evidence on the burden of diseases has been gradually developed and became institutionalized by 2010. IHPP is the national focal point and served as technical secretariat of the Thai working group on the burden of disease. Three versions of burden-of-disease data were produced, for 1999, 2004, and 2009, depicting the decade of changes in the disability-adjusted life-year loss per thousand of population between 1999 and 2009; the top 10 priorities in terms of annual total deaths; years of life loss; years lived in disability; priority risk factors contributing to the disability-adjusted life-year loss; and estimates of healthy adjusted life expectancy for this period (Bundhamcharoen and others, 2011). The burden-of-disease data contributed to priority setting for policy interventions.

In conjunction with its partners, IHPP worked closely with the National Statistical Office on improving national representative household surveys, such as the Socioeconomic Survey and the Health and Welfare Survey, to facilitate routine monitoring of the utilization of health services by wealth quintiles. In the questionnaires for all these household surveys, a standard module of ownership of durables and housing characteristics was introduced as routine for health equity monitoring in terms of wealth (Tangcharoensathien, Limwattananon, and Prakongsai, 2007). This is one of the most important intellectual assets for the Thai health system.

## Lessons: Capacity Building

Key factors behind Thailand's success were its strong ownership and self-initiative in the health reform program, as well as external support from international partners, long-term fellowship programs from various sources, and research networking in the phase of capacity development. The latter positioned the IHPP research portfolio within the current international debates (Bennett and others, 2008).

A number of factors have led to success in building capacity. These included the equitable sharing of benefits, both financial and nonfinancial; the creation of a critical mass of researchers; the production of policy relevant research; political impartiality; programmatic and financial accountability; and a collegial environment that encouraged networking. Scientific linkages with stronger partner institutes played a crucial role in sustaining capacity. Although these lessons are context specific, the principles in sustaining health policy and systems research capacity are applicable to other developing countries (Pitayarangsarit and Tangcharoensathien, 2009).

The development and retention of a critical mass of researchers within institutions with the ability to do high-quality research, attract external research funding, and gain national and international recognition have also been important. The genuine partnership with the National Statistical Office was a real asset in achieving national representative household surveys and in contributing to regular monitoring of the reform's progress and its equity impact on households. Other normative work, although difficult to publish in peer-reviewed journals, contributed to regular monitoring and helped guide reforms.

# TRANSLATING EVIDENCE TO POLICY DECISIONS

Two case studies on the way evidence fed into decision making are highlighted next. The first is the reform of CSMBS, and the second is the determination of the benefit package in view of the advancement of medical technologies, new interventions, and drugs.

## CSMBS: Controlling the Use of Nonessential Drugs

Over the last two decades, CSMBS has been the only public insurance scheme experiencing a continued double-digit cost growth, except for a short period right after the demand-side interventions (for example, copayment for private room and board and limitation of private hospital admission to accidents and emergencies only) following the 1997 Asian financial crisis (Figure 16.3). These interventions had the temporary effect of halting expenditure growth in 1998 and 1999, but growth rebounded in 2000; expenditures started to grow more rapidly between 2001 and 2005, and grew sharply between 2005 and 2009, notably as a result of outpatient expenditure. Demand-side interventions, such as copay, were not effective as long as the scheme applied fee for service for outpatient care.

In light of asymmetric information, the open-ended fee-for-service payment applied by CSMBS sent a perverse signal that encouraged overprescription and excessive use of technologies. Clinical practice variation was reported (Limwattananon and others, 2009) in regard to length of hospital stay, use of drugs, and surgical procedures across the three insurance schemes. CSMBS tended to use more health resources than the other two schemes.

In 2007, reforms were introduced in regard to provider payments: diagnosis-related groups were introduced for paying for inpatient services, as well as direct disbursement to hospitals for outpatient services. Expenditure on outpatient services outpaced inpatient services, which was probably explainable by the effects of direct disbursement, while the diagnosis-related group system contained inpatient expenditure growth. A major (80–85 percent) share of the outpatient expenditure pertained to drugs, especially those administered in large public hospitals, the typical providers for CSMBS beneficiaries.

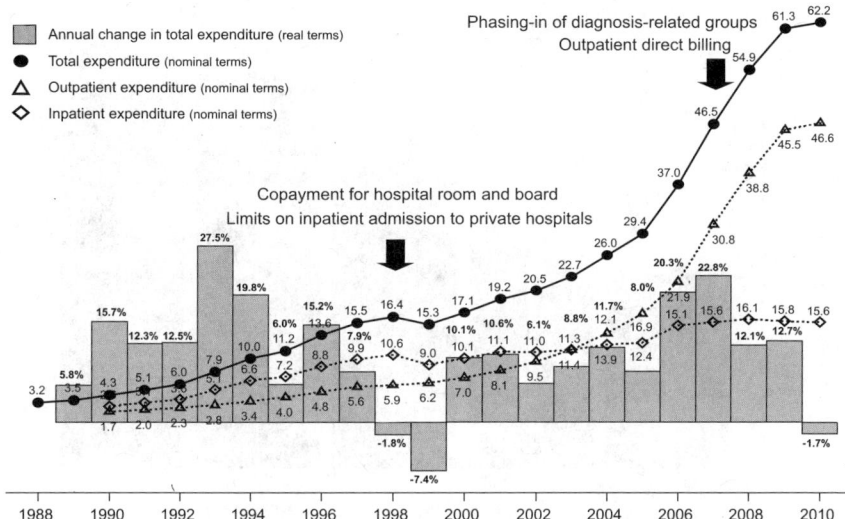

**Figure 16.3** Total, Outpatient, and Inpatient Expenditures and Annual Growth in the Civil Servant Medical Benefit Scheme, 1988–2010 (Thousands of millions of baht)
Source: Ministry of Finance, Comptroller General Department (various years).

Recognizing the high proportion and increasing outpatient expenditure, the Comptroller General Department introduced a negative drug list, as recommended by two HISRO-led studies. There was overuse of nonessential medicines outside the National Lists of Essential Medicines. In the 34 hospitals most visited by CSMBS beneficiaries in 2009 and 2010, use of nonessential items accounted, respectively, for 66 percent and 67 percent of total medicine expenditure, or 34 percent and 41 percent of total prescriptions. For high-cost medicines, non-essential items ranged from 43.9 percent and 47 percent for anticancer medications to 97.2 and 98.0 percent for antiosteoarthritis medications, respectively (HISRO, 2010, 2011); see Figure 16.4.

The 2009 hospital-specific profile of the use of nonessential items was fed back to the management of all 34 hospitals. As a result of such simple interventions, the use of nonessential medicines declined in almost all 23 hospitals for which comparable data before and after are available, while drug expenditure on non-essential items in almost all military hospitals in 2010 dropped from the level in 2009 (see Figure 16.5). Total CSMBS expenditure in 2010 experienced a negative real growth of 1.7 percent (see Figure 16.3).

In December 2010, the Comptroller General Department prohibited reimbursement for four nonessential drugs that were shown to be cost-ineffective for the treatment of osteoarthritis (Thailand, Comptroller General Department, 2010). Glucosamine alone shared 43 percent and 45 percent of the total expenditure on drugs of the same class in 2009 and 2010, respectively (HISRO, 2010, 2011; Tangcharoensathien, Limwattananon, and Prakongsai, 2007). Two months after the imposition of the negative list, consumption dropped, and

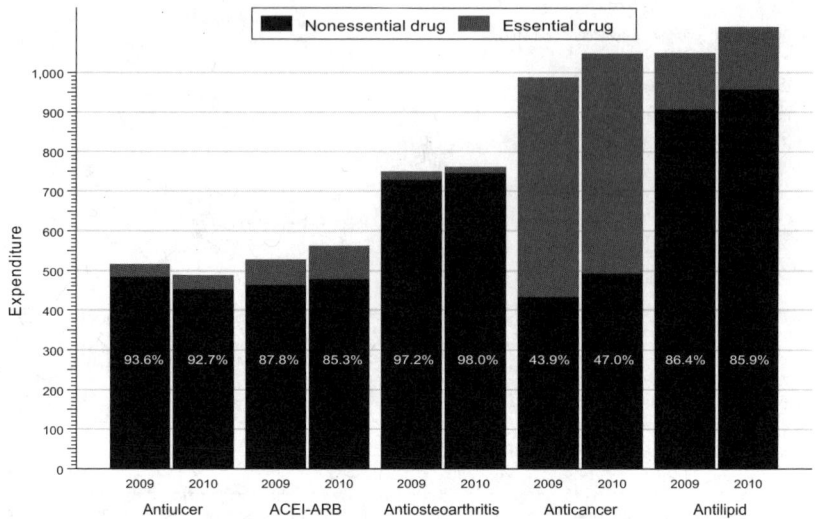

**Figure 16.4** Civil Servant Medical Benefit Scheme Expenditures on Essential and Nonessential Drugs in the Top Five Outpatient Prescriptions, 2009–10 (Millions of baht)

Note: ACEI-ARB = Angiotensin converting enzyme inhibitor and angiotensin-2 receptor blockers (antihypertensive drugs).

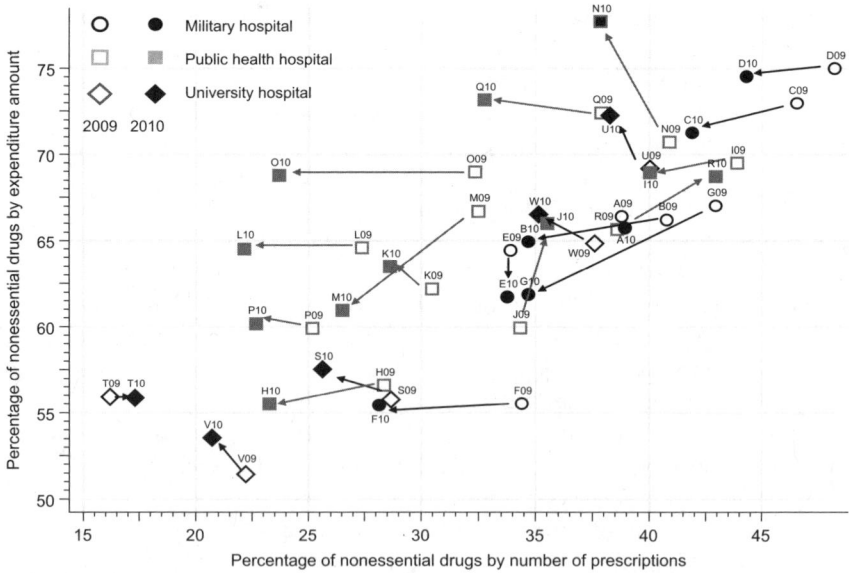

**Figure 16.5** Share of Nonessential Drugs in Expenditures and Prescriptions, 2009 and 2010

Sources: HISRO (2010, 2011).

interest groups such as orthopedic surgeons and government pensioners voiced their opposition through mass media and pressured the Comptroller General Department to withdraw enforcement.

There is ample evidence that pharmaceutical industries have been behind the scenes in the movement against this decision.[2] Debates in a number of newspapers have been heated. For example:

- The Royal College of Orthopedic Surgeons of Thailand (2011) said there are clinical indications for the use of glucosamine.[3]

- The government said that, in light of concerns raised by retirees who are members of CSMBS, it might reconsider the bar on reimbursement.[4]

- The Osteoporosis Foundation expressed its disagreement with the nonreimbursement of glucosamine for CSMBS beneficiaries.[5]

Glucosamine's blacklisted status remained enforced until June 2011, a month before the 2011 general election, when the Comptroller General Department changed its decision as a result of political pressure to allow reimbursement of glucosamine once again, but with strict criteria.

## Fine-Tuning the Benefit Package for the Universal Coverage Scheme

The scope of the benefit package and the level of copayment were two factors contributing to the degree of financial risk protection for beneficiaries against catastrophic health payments by members of the universal coverage scheme. With the application of the negative list approach,[6] the universal coverage scheme package in 2002 was comprehensive, covering diagnostics, treatment, and medicines for outpatient and inpatient services, health promotion and disease prevention, accidents and emergencies, major surgeries, dental services, and a wide range of other high-cost medical services.

However, technological advancement and the proliferation of new medicines, diagnostics, and interventions called for the introduction of systematic and transparent mechanisms for making decisions on which interventions would be covered in the package.

In response to policy demands, in 2009, having reviewed the international experience on the development of benefit packages in seven health technology assessment agencies, a draft guideline was produced and finally adopted after several rounds of stakeholder consultations. IHPP and HITAP, in collaboration with national partners, were involved closely in this process.

---

[2] See "Good Health with PReMA," available at http://www.prema.or.th/patient.php?CId=5&menu=5.
[3] In *The RCOST Newsletter,* Vol. 16, No. 2 (2011).
[4] In *Naew Nar,* March 10, 2011.
[5] In the *Thai Post,* April 11, 2011.
[6] This approach meant that all conditions and interventions were covered except those items on the negative list, which were mostly nonessential services such as cosmetic surgery and interventions that had proven ineffective or were under trial.

The guideline covered (1) selection of topics for appraisal, with full engagement by stakeholders[7] in a transparent manner; (2) economic appraisal of selected interventions using incremental cost-effectiveness ratios; and (3) budget impact analysis. The incremental cost-effectiveness ratio threshold of one gross national income per capita for a quality-adjusted life-year gained has been applied by the Benefit Package Subcommittee of the universal coverage scheme. This subcommittee is a platform for decision making prior to adoption by the National Health Security Board, which is chaired by the Health Minister.

Six criteria for prioritizing topics proposed by stakeholders were adopted by consensus through stakeholder consultations:

1. magnitude of the population affected by disease or health problems;

2. severity of disease or health problems in terms of quality of life;

3. effectiveness of health technology or intervention;

4. variations in clinical practice across three public health insurance schemes;

5. impact on household livelihood; and

6. equity and ethical implications.

In fiscal years 2010 and 2011, this guideline was successfully applied twice a year for topic selection, economic appraisal, and recommendations to the subcommittee and then transmitted to the National Health Security Board for its final decision. Table 16.3 summarizes the outcome.

It is noteworthy that this initiative not only produced and applied evidence-informed decisions in a transparent manner, it also strengthened and sustained institutional capacities in generating evidence on incremental cost-effectiveness ratios, budget impact assessment, and other ethical social considerations. The subcommittee is the platform for interchange between evidence and policies.

## LESSONS: EVIDENCE-INFORMED POLICY

A number of enabling factors were identified. First, a transparent and participatory process in topic submissions by all seven key stakeholders legitimized the process. This is well accepted by Thai society. The process prevents direct submission by any patient or concerned individual or company to the subcommittee that may imply nepotism and favoritism.

Second, the individual and institutional capacity to generate evidence on incremental cost-effectiveness ratios, budget impact assessment, and other considerations was important, contributing to informed policy decision in a deliberate way. This was possible in Thailand, as there is a critical mass of qualified researchers in pharmaco-economics, as well as institutional umbrellas such as HITAP and IHPP

---

[7]Topics of new interventions are proposed by seven groups of stakeholders: (1) policymakers, (2) medical specialists or representatives from royal colleges, (3) public health experts, (4) medical device and pharmaceutical industry representatives, (5) civil society organizations, (6) patient groups, and (7) the general public.

**TABLE 16.3**

## Topic Submission, Selection, and Considerations by the Benefit Package Subcommittee

| Year and round | Topic submissions by seven stakeholder groups | Topics selected for appraisal chaired by Health Systems Research Institute Director | Considerations by the Benefit Package Subcommittee |
|---|---|---|---|
| 2010, round 1 | 18 | 9 | Six rejected. |
| | | | Three deferred: |
| | | | Tobacco cessation services: pending more information on scaling up and financial feasibility |
| | | | Pampers for elderly patients: pending for effectiveness of different brand and long-term financial implications to the National Health Security Office |
| | | | Leukemia in Rayong industrial estate: required evidence from more sites |
| 2010, round 2 | 14 | 5 | Two rejected. |
| | | | Three accepted: |
| | | | Screening for Down Syndrome |
| | | | Treatment for multidrug-resistant tuberculosis |
| | | | Treatment of severe thalassemia by implantation |
| 2011, round 1 | 14 | 5 | In the process of being submitted to the subcommittee for consideration |
| 2011, round 2 | Process commenced 15 July 2011 | 5 | In the process of being submitted to the subcommittee for consideration |

through which they can contribute in a sustainable way. Furthermore, IHPP and HITAP researchers who conducted economic appraisals were free from conflicts of interest in so doing. The funding for economic appraisals is solely supported by the National Health Security Office. Increasingly, a skill mix on health systems research is required for appraisals such as the assessment of supply-side capacities and their resilience in accommodating new interventions and for the assessment of system requirements for new interventions.

Third, a forum that allowed the evidence to be presented to policymakers in a transparent and deliberate manner was essential to Thailand's success. This was provided by the subcommittee on the benefits package. A lesson emerges: there is a need for a national forum in which evidence interacts with policy decisions in a deliberate and transparent manner.

Fourth, in the case of the CSMBS reform, rigorous evidence speaks for itself: the excessive use of nonessential drugs and its huge financial implications called for a total ban on glucosamine reimbursement. Understandably, this was resisted by professionals in the pharmaceutical industry. The negative drug list approach can be ineffective and may face resistance. Policymakers may consider provider payment reforms toward capping spending, such as through capitation.

## Lessons from Health Care Reforms

Many lessons can be drawn from the long experience of health care reform in Thailand.

### Evidence Matters

Evidence marshals the right direction and the right decisions. It should be noted that normative work is equally as important as policy-linked research and that both are key inputs for reform. Additional efforts are needed to improve the quality of routine data as well as establish new data platforms. In the universal coverage scheme analysis of administrative data, generating information for health care purchasers to use in paying health care providers, doing auditing, and providing feedback proved to improve data quality (Pongsanon and others, 2008).

### Evidence-Based Decision Platform Matters

Policymaking is not, in fact, a matter of taking action on the basis of the best available empirical evidence (Sue and Fitzgerald, 2005). Policy cannot be linked to research simply through a presentation of research findings to policymakers (Sudsawad, 2007). The participation of users in the research management process, as well as involvement of civic groups, was a critical success factor for promoting the use of evidence from research.

### Institutionalization of Capacity to Generate Evidence and Translate Evidence to Policy Decisions Matters

This institutionalization aims to sustain evidence-based health care reform, which is context specific and cannot rely only on external technical support. The establishment of HSRI by law in 1992 was a starting point for the process of institutionalization. Subsequently, associated institutions such as IHPP, HISRO, and HITAP played a pivotal role in building up research capacity and translating evidence to policy decisions with the support of international partners.

### Health Systems Capacity and Resilience Matters

Intensive investment in health care infrastructure, as well as human resources for health, were both prerequisites for health financing reform's achieving universal coverage. Many policy measures have been implemented to retain physicians in rural areas, including mandatory rural services, rural recruitment and hometown placement, and additional financial incentives for physicians working in remote areas. In addition, district hospitals worked closely with networks of health centers to form effective district health systems to serve the majority of the rural poor.

# CONCLUSION

This chapter illustrates how capacity was built in Thailand to generate evidence for policy decisions. Undeniably, national ownership, local initiative, and self-reliance in terms of funding for capacity building and policy research are the basis for Thailand's success in this area. In the last two decades, exponential growth of capacity in health systems and policy research has been observed in terms of the number of qualified researchers. This was made possible through national networking, international collaboration, and consistent support by strategic partners such as the London School of Hygiene and Tropical Medicine in capacity building. Also essential for success was the high quality of research, its production in a timely manner, and the fact that it was provided in an environment that was free from conflict of interest.

Translating technical evidence to health systems and policy decisions requires a systematic, transparent, and participatory process to gain full societal support and boost immunity against political manipulation. The official subcommittee provided a strategic forum in which evidence helped shape policy decisions.

The reform of Thailand's health financing system was necessary but not sufficient to ensure universal access to essential and quality health services. Adequate investment in good geographic coverage of health care infrastructure, including human resources for health care with a strong and functioning local health system, is also needed. Without the extensive district health system, the policy of universal coverage would be merely a rhetorical statement: the poor would be unable to access and use health services, and health care would be enjoyed only by the urban elite minority.

Demographic and epidemiological transitions have created another challenge. The increasing number of the elderly in an aging society, as well as the increasing burden of chronic noncommunicable diseases, demands the development of intermediate and long-term care models. The rapid advancement of medical technology also demands an effective assessment of the cost-effectiveness of different health technologies to ensure that the health care system remains fiscally sustainable.

# REFERENCES

Bennett, S., T. Adam, C. Zarowsky, V. Tangcharoensathien, K. Ranson, T. Evans, and A. Mills, 2008, "From Mexico to Mali: Progress in Health Policy and Systems Research," *The Lancet,* Vol. 372, Issue 9649, pp. 1571–78.

Boseley, S., and A. Mills, 2010, "Nurturing a Generation of Health Economists," *The Lancet,* Vol. 375, Issue 9731, p. 2067.

Bundhamcharoen, K., P. Odton, S. Phulkerd, and V. Tangcharoensathien, 2011, "Burden of Disease in Thailand: Changes in Health Gap Between 1999 and 2004," *BMC Public Health,* Vol. 11, No. 53.

Green, A., 2007, *Converting Research on Primary Care into Policy,* Unpublished report submitted to the Health Care Reform Project under the support of the European Union.

Health Insurance System Research Office (HISRO), 2010, "Drug Utilization: Impact on Expenditure and Cost-Containment Measures of 34 Pilot Hospitals under the Civil Servant Medical Benefit Scheme's Ambulatory Direct Disbursement System," final report (Nonthaburi).

————, 2011, "Comparison of the Civil Servant Medical Benefit Scheme's Ambulatory Drug Expenditure under the Direct Disbursement System of 34 Hospitals Between 2009 and 2010," final report (Nonthaburi).

Health Systems Research Institute (HSRI), 2003, *The First Evaluation of the Universal Health Coverage Policy* (Nonthaburi).

Jongudomsuk, P., 2010, "Case Studies and Lessons Learned on Translating Health Systems Knowledge in Thailand," background paper for the WHO Global Symposium on Health Systems Research, Montreux, Switzerland, 16–19 November 2010 (Nonthaburi, Thailand: Health Systems Research Institute).

Kasemsup, V., P. Prakongsai, and V. Tangcharoensathien, 2006, "Budget Impact Analysis of Including Renal Replacement Therapy in the Benefit Package of Universal Coverage in Thailand," *Value in Health,* Vol. 9, p. A385.

Limwattananon, C., S. Limwattananon, S. Pannarunothai, and V. Tangcharoensathien, 2009, *Analysis of Practice Variation Due to Payment Methods across Health Insurance Schemes,* report for the Country Development Partnership in Health Health Financing Project (Nonthaburi: International Health Policy Program and World Bank).

Limwattananon, S., V. Tangcharoensathien, and P. Prakongsai, 2007, "Catastrophic and Poverty Impacts of Health Payments: Results from National Household Surveys in Thailand," *Bulletin of the World Health Organization,* Vol. 85, No. 8, pp. 600–6.

————, 2010, "Equity in Maternal and Child Health in Thailand," *Bulletin of the World Health Organization,* Vol. 88, No. 6, pp. 420–27.

Melgaard, B., 2004, "From Research to Action—A Bridge to Be Crossed," Editorial, *Bulletin of the World Health Organization,* Vol. 82, No. 10, p. 723.

Mills, A., S. Bennett, P. Siriwanarangsun, and V. Tangcharoensathien, 2000, "The Response of Providers to Capitation Payment: A Case-Study from Thailand," *Health Policy,* Vol. 51, pp. 163–80.

Na Ranong, V., 2005, *Monitoring and Evaluation of Universal Health Care Coverage in Thailand,* Phase 2 (B.E. 2546–2547) (Nonthaburi: Development Research Institute Foundation).

Na Ranong, V., U. Na Ranong, and S.Vongmontha, 2004, *Impacts of the Universal Health Coverage and the 30 Baht Health Care Scheme on Household Expenditures and Poverty Reduction in Thailand* (Bangkok: Thailand Development Research Institute Foundation).

Pannarunothai, S., D. Patmasiriwat, and S. Kongsawatt, 2004, *Health Equity at Household Level: The Second Wave of Household Survey and First Health Examination Survey* (Pitsanulok: Center for Health Equity Monitoring, Faculty of Medicine, Naresuan University).

Patcharanarumol, W., V. Tangcharoensathien, S. Limwattananon, W. Panichkriangkrai, K. Pachanee, W. Poungkantha, L. Gilson, and A. Mills, 2011, *Why and How Did Thailand Achieve Good Health at Low Cost? A Cross Country Study on Good Health at Low Cost* (Nonthaburi: Ministry of Public Health, International Health Policy Programme).

Pauls, F., E. Zanon, P. Netwichien, A. Sivayathorn, P. Suchaxaya, and K. Nuntaboot, 2002, *Evaluation Report of Hospital Accreditation in Thailand* (Nonthaburi: Health Systems Research Institute).

Philhealth, 2007, Synthesis Report from the Conference on Extending Social Health Insurance to Informal Economy Workers, October 18–20, 2006 (Manila: Philhealth, GTZ, ILO, WHO, and World Bank).

Pitayarangsarit, S., and V. Tangcharoensathien, 2009, "Sustaining Capacity in Health Policy and Systems Research in Thailand," *Bulletin of the World Health Organization,* Vol. 87, pp. 72–74.

Pongsanon, K., K. Peeyananjarassri, T. Liabsuetrakul, S. Tassee, N. Burapong, C. Getpook, 2008, "Effect of Audit and Feedback on the Accuracy of Diagnosis Summary for Gynecological Conditions in Songklanagarind Hospital, Songkla Province, Thailand," *Journal of the Medical Association of Thailand,* Vol. 91, No. 2, pp. 146–52.

Prakongsai, P., S. Limwattananon, and V. Tangcharoensathien, 2009, "The Equity Impact of the Universal Coverage Policy: Lessons from Thailand," in *Innovations in Health System Finance in Developing and Transitional Economies,* ed. by D. Chernichovsky and K. Hanson (London: Emerald Group Publishing), pp. 57–81.

Rohde, J., S. Cousens, M. Chopra, V. Tangcharoensathien, R. Black, Z. Bhutta, and J.E. Lawn, 2008, "30 Years after Alma-Ata: Has Primary Health Care Worked in Countries?" *Lancet,* Vol. 372, Issue 9642 [Alma-Ata: Rebirth and Revision], pp. 950–61.

Sakunphanit, T., T. Greethong, S. Srithamrongsawat, R. Preechachard, and K. Limpiyakorn. 2009, *Trend of Cost and Service in Thai Health Delivery Systems,* preliminary report.

Srithamrongsawat, S., and P. Lapying, 2002, "Evaluation of the Universal Health Coverage Policy Implementation: A Case Study in Samut Sakorn, Phuket, Sukhothai, and Ubon Ratchathani Province" (Pisanulok: Center for Health Equity Monitoring, Naresuan University).

Sudsawad, P., 2007, *Knowledge Translation: Introduction to Models, Strategies and Measures* (Austin, TX: National Center for the Dissemination of Disability Research).

Sue, D., and L. Fitzgerald, eds., 2005, *Knowledge to Action: Evidence-Based Health Care in Context* (New York: Oxford University Press).

Tangcharoensathien, V., A. Laixuthai, J. Vasavit, N. Tantigate, W. Prajuabmoh-Ruffolo, D. Vimolkit, and J. Lertiendumrong, 1999, "National Health Account Development: Lessons from Thailand," *Health Policy and Planning,* Vol. 14, pp. 342–53.

Tangcharoensathien, V., S. Limwattananon, and P. Prakongsai, 2007, "Improving Health-Related Information Systems to Monitor Equity in Health: Lessons from Thailand," in *The Economics of Health Equity,* ed. by D. Mcintyre and G. Mooney (New York: Cambridge University Press).

Tangcharoensathien, V., W. Patcharanarumol, P. Ir, S.M. Aljunid, A.G. Mukti, K. Akkhavong, E. Banzon, D.B. Huong, H. Thabrany, and A. Mills, 2011, "Health-Financing Reforms in Southeast Asia: Challenges in Achieving Universal Coverage," *Lancet,* Vol. 377, No. 9768, pp. 863–73.

Tangcharoensathien, V., W. Patcharanaruomol, J. Vasavid, P. Prakongsai, P. Jongudomsuk, S. Srithamrongswat, and J. Thammathataree, 2010, *Thailand Health Financing Review 2010* (Delhi: World Health Organization).

Tangcharoensathien V., P. Prakongsai, S. Limwattananon, W. Patcharanarumol, and P. Jongudomsuk, 2009a, "From Targeting to Universality: Lessons from the Health System in Thailand," in *Building Decent Societies: Rethinking the Role of Social Security in Development,* ed. by P. Townsend (Basingstoke, U.K.: Palgrave Macmillan).

Tangcharoensathien, V., P. Prakongsai, W. Patcharanarumol, S. Limwattananon, and S. Buasai, 2009b, "Innovative Financing of Health Promotion," in *Health Systems Policy, Finance, and Organization,* ed. by G. Carrin, K. Buse, K. Heggenhougen, and S.R. Quah (San Diego: Academic Press).

Tangcharoensathien, V., W. Swasdiworn, P. Jongudomsuk, S. Srithamrongswat, W. Patcharanarumol, P. Prakongsai, and J. Thammatach-Aree, 2010, "Universal Coverage Scheme in Thailand: Equity Outcomes and Future Agendas to Meet Challenges," Background Paper No. 43 in *The World Health Report: Health Systems Financing: The Path To Universal Coverage* (Geneva: World Health Organization).

Tangcharoensathien, V., W. Swasdiworn, P. Jongudomsuk, S. Srithamrongswat, W. Patcharanarumol, and J. Thammatach-Aree, 2010a, "How the Contract Model Becomes the Main Mode of Purchasing: A Combination of Evidence and Luck in Thailand," Background Paper No. 44 in *The World Health Report: Health Systems Financing: The Path To Universal Coverage* (Geneva: World Health Organization).

Tangcharoensathien, V., W. Swasdiworn, P. Jongudomsuk, S. Srithamrongswat, W. Patcharanarumol, and J. Thammatach-Aree, 2010b, "Universal Coverage Scheme in Thailand: Equity Outcomes and Future Agendas to Meet Challenges," in *Attaining Universal Health Coverage, A Research Initiative to Support Evidence-Based Advocacy and Policy-Making,* ed. by E. Missoni (Milan: Egea).

Tangcharoensathien, V., W. Teokul, and L. Chanwongpaisarn, 2005, "Challenges of Implementing Universal Health Care in Thailand," in *Transforming the Developmental Welfare State in East Asia,* ed. by H.-J. Kwon (New York: Palgrave Macmillan).

Tangcharoensathien, V., C. Vasavid, W. Patcharanarumol, K. Tisayaticom, and J. Mekkrajang, 2010, *Institutionalizing National Health Accounts in Thailand* (Nonthaburi: International Health Policy Program, Ministry of Public Health).

Tantivess, S., Y. Teerawattananon, and A. Mills, 2009, "Strengthening Cost-Effectiveness Analysis in Thailand Through the Establishment of the Health Intervention and Technology Assessment Program," *Pharmacoeconomics*, Vol. 27, pp. 931–45.

Teerawattananon, Y., Y. Leelukkanaveera, M. Thavorncharoensap, P. Hanvoravongchai, L. Ingsrisawang, S. Tantivess, U. Chaikledkaew, A. Mohara, C. Lertpiriyasuwat, and N. Pimsawan, 2009, "Provider-Initiated HIV/AIDS Counselling and Testing at Health Care Facilities in Thailand: A Cluster-Randomisation Trial," *Journal of Development Effectiveness*, Vol. 1, pp. 450–69.

Thailand, Comptroller General Department, 2010, "Lists of Non-reimbursable Drugs from CSMBS," letter to hospital directors, December 24.

Thailand, Secretariat of the Cabinet, 2009, "Royal Decree on the Establishment of the Health Care Accreditation Institute" (Bangkok).

Thavorncharoensap, M., Y. Teerawattananon, J. Yothasamut, C. Lertpitakpong, K. Thitiboonsuwan, P. Neramitpitagkul, and U. Chaikledkaew, 2006, "The Economic Costs of Alcohol Consumption in Thailand," *BMC Public Health,* Vol. 10, p. 323.

Wibulpolprasert, S., ed., 2008, *Thailand Health Profile 2005–2007* (Nonthaburi: Bureau of Policy and Strategy, Ministry of Public Health).

World Bank, 2010, *World Development Indicators* (Washington), available at http://data.worldbank.org/indicator.

Yothasamut, J., C. Putchong, T. Sirisamutr, Y. Teerawattananon, and S. Tantivess, 2010, "Scaling Up Cervical Cancer Screening in the Midst of Human Papillomavirus Vaccination Advocacy in Thailand," *BMC Health Services Research*, Vol. 10, Suppl. 1: p. S5.

# CHAPTER 17

# The Challenge of Health Care Reform in Estonia, Hungary, China, Chile, and Mexico

BAOPING SHANG AND EVA JENKNER

This chapter provides case studies on Estonia, Hungary, China, Chile, and Mexico. Health care systems and reform experiences vary substantially across emerging economies, and the studies here illuminate both successes and remaining weaknesses in these systems. Each provides an overview of the health care system and comparative data on key health indicators relative to the appropriate comparator group (in terms of level of GDP per capita), a description of the experience with health reforms, the remaining challenges confronting the health care system, and lessons learned.

## EMERGING EUROPE: ESTONIA

### Overview of the Health Care System

The health care system in Estonia is predominately publicly funded through mandatory health insurance contributions, with a mix of public and private provision. The earmarked social payroll tax accounts for almost two-thirds of total health spending, and private spending comprises a quarter of total health spending, mostly in the form of copayments for pharmaceuticals and dental care. Most of the specialists and hospitals are public, with the hospitals owned by local governments. Private provision is largely restricted to primary care, ambulatory services, and pharmacies.

The health status of the population lags behind Organization for Economic Cooperation and Development (OECD) averages. Life expectancy stood at 73.9 years in 2008, 5.9 years below the OECD average of 79.8 years (see Table 17.1). The infant mortality rate was 5.0 deaths per 1,000 live births in 2008, above the OECD average of 3.9.

Public health spending as a share of GDP is moderate compared with that in other OECD countries. In 2008, it was 4.1 percent of GDP, below the OECD average of 6.8 percent. Public health expenditures as a share of GDP decreased during the 1990s (while private out-of-pocket payments as a share of total health spending nearly doubled) and have remained relatively stable since the early

**TABLE 17.1**

**Estonia: Key Indicators, 1995, 2000, 2008**

| | 1995 | 2000 | 2008 | High income: non-OECD average, 2008 | OECD average, 2008 |
|---|---|---|---|---|---|
| GDP per capita (U.S. dollars at purchasing power parity) | 6,318 | 9,876 | 20,640 | 34,549 | 37,899 |
| Total health spending (percent of GDP) | 6.2 | 5.3 | 5.4[a] | 5.1 | 9.2 |
| public (percent of GDP) | 5.6 | 4.1 | 4.1[a] | 3.4 | 6.8 |
| private (percent of GDP) | 0.6 | 1.2 | 1.3[a] | 2.6 | 2.4 |
| Public health spending per capita (U.S. dollars) | 365 | 398 | 836[a] | 1,189 | 2,541 |
| Out-of-pocket spending (share of total health spending) | 10.2 | 19.9 | 22.1[a] | 25.2 | 17.0 |
| Formal health care coverage (share of population) | ... | ... | 100.0 | ... | 97.8 |
| Life expectancy (years at birth) | 67.7 | 70.6 | 73.9 | 75.5 | 79.8 |
| Infant mortality (per 1,000 live births) | 14.9 | 8.4 | 5.0 | 12.2 | 3.9 |
| Measles immunization (share of children 12–23 months) | ... | 93.4 | 95.4 | 90.5 | 93.6 |
| Physicians (per 1,000 population) | 3.2 | 3.3 | 3.4 | 2.3 | 3.2 |
| Hospital beds (per 1,000 population) | 8.3 | 7.2 | 5.7 | 3.8 | 5.7 |

Sources: Organization for Economic Cooperation and Development; World Bank, *World Development Indicators*; and World Health Organization.

Note: Ellipses indicate data are not available.

[a] 2007 data.

2000s. However, in absolute terms, per capita public health expenditures more than doubled between 2000 and 2008, from $398 to $836.

## Experience with Health Reforms

Following the breakup of the Soviet Union, there was a strong desire to move away from the input-based system and embrace market principles, centered on meeting patient needs at an affordable cost. Since the beginning of the 1990s, the health care system has undergone several major reforms:

- *Introduction of a compulsory social health insurance system.* In 1992, an earmarked health insurance fund independent of the state budget was established by the Health Insurance Act. The health insurance fund was financed by a 13 percent payroll tax on salaries, paid fully by employers. Initially, there were 22 noncompeting, district-based funds. As a result, some of the more-deprived districts had lower resources than others. In 2001, the funds were reorganized into a single independent public agency, legally obliged to balance yearly revenues and expenditures, a requirement fulfilled almost every year since its inception.

- *Primary care system reform.* The main tasks of the primary care reform included introducing family medicine as a specialty into health care practice and changing the remuneration system for primary care doctors. The major steps of primary care reform included creating a list system through which the population could register with a primary care doctor, introducing a partial gatekeeping system that controls most access to specialist care, introducing a mixed-payment system for primary care (age-adjusted capitation, fee-for-service payments, and basic allowances complemented by a quality bonus system), and granting doctors the status of independent contractors.

- *Rationalization of the size of the hospital sector.* An important milestone in hospital sector reform was a reduction in the number of acute-care hospital beds by two-thirds and a decrease in the number of acute-care hospitals in 2003.[1] In addition, all public hospitals had to be incorporated under private law as foundations or joint-stock companies.[2] As a result, all public hospitals have full managerial rights over assets and access to financial markets. Diagnosis-related-group-based payment methods were introduced in 2004 and have been used in combination with other payment methods for hospital reimbursement.

- *Other public health system reforms.* The public health reforms included a number of measures, such as the creation of an institutional structure, establishment of a financial mechanism, and definition of the responsibilities of different shareholders.

- *Patient cost sharing.* In 1993, the prescription pharmaceutical reimbursement system was introduced, based on some cost sharing. The cost sharing for dental care is substantial, and about 23 percent of out-of-pocket (OOP) spending goes toward these services. Flat copayments are charged for certain types of health services, such as primary care physician home visits, outpatient visits, and hospital bed-days.

## Main Challenges

### Shrinking Pool of Medical Professionals

The number of doctors and nurses per 1,000 people has been declining. In 2008, the number of doctors per 1,000 people was roughly in line with the European Union average, while there was a shortage of nursing personnel, and an uneven distribution of specialist services across the country. EU accession in 2004 led to a temporary spike in the number of doctors and nurses migrating to neighboring EU countries. In recent years, however, migration has decreased, and the main challenge is to retain qualified professionals in the health care sector.

### Rising Health Care Costs

Wide population coverage has been maintained and a comprehensive range of services are available to the population. Health spending per capita grew, in real

---

[1]The Hospital Master Plan 2015.
[2]The Health Care Services Organization Act, which took effect in 2001.

terms, by an average of 8.8 percent per year between 2000 and 2008, which was more than double the OECD average of 4.2 percent. In addition, demographic factors, technology improvements, and the need to raise the relatively low salaries of medical professionals are all likely to put upward pressure on public health spending.

### High Lifestyle-Related Risks

The main disease burden challenges are premature mortality caused by external causes and lifestyle-related risk factors. The smoking rate remains high; HIV incidence rates are high; and alcohol consumption, at 14 liters per year per adult, is well above the OECD average of 9.3 liters (OECD, 2010a).

## Lessons

Careful planning is crucial for the successful transition from a tax-based health care system to a compulsory social insurance system. Health insurance reforms have included a dedicated 13 percent payroll tax accompanied by carefully phased major changes in the delivery system and regulatory environment. Primary care reform has included thorough changes in the medical educational system together with changes in institutional settings and payment mechanisms. A long-term strategy with explicit objectives and direction was developed to reduce hospital capacity and improve system efficiency.

The development and successful implementation of a long-term strategy was the key to a successful hospital sector reform. The plan to reduce hospital beds included an assessment of future capacity and set targets on the number of hospitals and beds. In 1990, there were about 120 hospitals with 14,000 acute-care beds (Habicht, Aaviksoo, and Koppel, 2006). The number of hospitals and beds has fallen dramatically since then. As a result, inpatient care utilization has decreased while ambulatory care utilization has increased.

Global budgets, if well enforced, can be an effective tool in containing public health spending. The health insurance fund is the main source of health care financing and is independent of the government budget. It is legally obliged to balance yearly revenues and expenditures and has met this requirement almost every year since its inception. Consequently, the share of public health spending in Estonia, as a share of GDP, remains well below the OECD average, although health care spending in Estonia grew more rapidly between 2000 and 2008 than in most OECD countries.

A single health insurance fund allows for more extensive risk pooling and can also help improve efficiency and control costs. Originally there were 22 sickness funds, some of which were small and did not provide sufficient risk pooling. A single fund, on the other hand, can facilitate the redistribution of revenues between regions, have lower administrative costs, and achieve a more economical use of resources. The success of Estonia in using a single insurance fund to control spending echoes the experience of advanced economies (Oxley and MacFarlan, 1995).

# EMERGING EUROPE: HUNGARY

## Overview of the Health Care System

Hungary has a compulsory social insurance system with mostly public provision. Most spending (71 percent in 2008) is financed by compulsory health insurance contributions paid by employees and employers. Municipalities are responsible for primary care, such as doctor services, family physicians services, dental care, and mother and child health nursing services. Provision of secondary care is shared among municipalities, the national government, and private providers. The national government owns hospitals that provide acute and chronic care.

The health status of the Hungarian population has lagged since the 1960s. Life expectancy in Hungary increased by only 1.3 years between 1960 and 1990, a period during which it increased by 8.7 years, on average, in OECD countries (Orosz and Burns, 2000) (see Table 17.2). In 2008, life expectancy in Hungary was 73.8 years, compared with the OECD average of 79.8 years; infant mortality was 5.6 per 1,000 live births, higher than the OECD average of 3.9.

Public health spending as a share of GDP is well below the OECD average. Public health spending as a share of GDP decreased during the 1990s (while the share of OOP payments increased) and has remained relatively stable since the early 2000s. However, in absolute terms, per capita public health spending increased rapidly, from $602 in 2000 to $980 in 2008.

**TABLE 17.2**

### Hungary: Key Indicators, 1995, 2000, 2008

| | 1995 | 2000 | 2008 | High income: OECD average, 2008 | OECD average, 2008 |
|---|---|---|---|---|---|
| GDP per capita (U.S. dollars at purchasing-power parity) | 8,535 | 11,211 | 18,989 | 37,899 | 37,899 |
| Total health spending (percent of GDP) | 7.3 | 6.9 | 7.4[a] | 9.2 | 9.2 |
| public (percent of GDP) | 6.1 | 4.9 | 5.2[a] | 6.8 | 6.8 |
| private (percent of GDP) | 1.2 | 2.0 | 2.2[a] | 2.4 | 2.4 |
| Public health spending per capita (U.S. dollars) | 554 | 602 | 980[a] | 2,541 | 2,541 |
| Out-of-pocket spending (share of total health spending) | 16.0 | 26.3 | 24.9[a] | 17.3 | 17.0 |
| Formal health care coverage (share of population) | ... | 100.0 | ... | ... | 97.8 |
| Life expectancy (years at birth) | 69.9 | 71.7 | 73.8 | 79.8 | 79.8 |
| Infant mortality (per 1,000 live births) | 10.7 | 9.2 | 5.6 | 3.9 | 3.9 |
| Measles immunization (share of children 12–23 months) | 99.8 | 99.8 | 99.9 | 93.6 | 93.6 |
| Physicians (per 1,000 population) | 3.0 | 2.7 | 3.1 | 3.2 | 3.2 |
| Hospital beds (per 1,000 population) | 8.8 | 8.1 | 7.0 | 5.7 | 5.7 |

Sources: Organization for Economic Cooperation and Development; World Bank, *World Development Indicators*; and World Health Organization.

Note: Ellipses indicate data are not available.

[a] 2007 data.

## Experience with Health Reform

Recognizing that the health care system was inefficient and ineffective and that health care costs needed to be reduced, the government has initiated a series of health care reforms since the mid-1980s, which intensified after the transition to a market economy in the 1990s.

- *Compulsory social health insurance system.* The Health Insurance Fund (HIF), established under the compulsory social insurance system, collects premium contributions from formal sector workers and the self-employed. Provisions for noncontributing groups are shared between HIF and the government. HIF is separated from the government budget, and although the government cannot use HIF's surpluses for other purposes, HIF is obligated to cover its own deficit. In addition, HIF is responsible only for recurrent costs, while fixed costs and investments are the responsibilities of the owners of health facilities (local governments and the state). HIF has been effective in imposing discipline on aggregate health spending.

- *Primary care system.* A system of family physicians was established in the early 1990s to deliver continuous, personal, and comprehensive health care, with greater emphasis on prevention, rehabilitation, and home nursing services. Patients are required to seek referral from a general practitioner of their choice to limit access to more expensive specialist services. The payments for general practitioners are based on a capitation fee, and the number of patients is registered.

- *Hospital system.* The hospital system was excessively costly in the pretransition era. The overall number of hospital beds was too high, while the number of hospital beds in intensive care, chronic care, and rehabilitation was too low. Reform efforts have been made to fit the distribution of medical services to the health needs of each specific region. To provide incentives for efficiency, diagnosis-related groups were introduced for inpatient care in 1993. Outpatient specialty services are paid under a fee-for-service system.

- *Patient cost sharing.* Another area of reform focused on individual incentives, such as the introduction of copayments for pharmaceuticals and long-term chronic care. Copayments in primary and outpatient care and a hospital daily fee for inpatient care were introduced during the 2006/07 reform. Demand fell in response. However, these measures were subsequently repealed by a national referendum in 2008. The generosity of the health package has also been reduced through the exclusion of dental coverage from national health insurance, effectively increasing cost sharing.

## Main Challenges

### Rising Pressure on Public Health Spending

The population health status is among the worst in the EU region two decades after health care reform started. In addition, cost pressures on the health care system are likely to increase owing to demographic factors, technology improvements, and the low salaries of medical professionals. The need to achieve fiscal consolidation, however, suggests that financial resources for health care are limited, so improving the efficiency of spending will be essential for improving health outcomes.

### High Lifestyle-Related Risks

Lifestyle-related risks include high alcohol consumption, smoking, an unhealthy diet, and lack of physical activity. For example, alcohol consumption is about one-third higher in Hungary than the OECD average (OECD, 2010b), Hungarian men have one of the highest lung cancer mortality rates in the world, and two-thirds of men and one-half of women are overweight or obese.

### Imbalance of Health Services Professionals

While the overall health care workforce-to-population ratio is comparable to the OECD average, the geographic and interspecialty distribution is unbalanced, and the workforce is biased toward high-skilled specialists. Some geographic areas do not have enough doctors and nurses, and there are shortages in certain specialties such as primary care, public health, and diagnostic specialties.

### Inefficient Use of Health Care Resources

The inefficiency of the health care system is reflected in the excess use of hospital-based care and specialty care. Despite reforms, the rate of hospitalization has increased, and the share of primary care in health care spending has decreased. High utilization of the health care system also suggests inefficiencies and the need for an appropriate regime of copayments to rationalize demand. In 2007, the number of physician-patient contacts per capita was 10.8, about 50 percent higher than the OECD average (Utca, 2009).

## Lessons

Development of a consistent long-term strategy is essential for a successful health system reform. The Hungarian health system was transformed from a centrally controlled, tax-based into a social health insurance system, and different types of reforms have been introduced since the beginning of the 1990s. Nonetheless, reforms that promote cooperation between agencies have received less attention, and reforms have often contradicted one another.

Rectifying the provider payment system and getting the incentive system right are necessary to improve efficiency. The payment system does not provide sufficient incentives for general practitioners to treat patients within primary care because the payments for general practitioners are based on a capitation fee and the number of patients registered. The tendency for hospitals to treat patients on an inpatient basis reflects the higher reimbursements given for inpatient (rather than outpatient) treatment. Furthermore, health institutions have no incentive to use medical equipment in the most economical manner, since provider payments do not cover depreciation costs and the funding for capital costs is the responsibility of the government.

Overextended benefit packages are difficult to roll back. Under the communist regime, health care coverage was comprehensive and was provided free. The benefit package has remained relatively generous. It appears increasingly difficult to roll back health care benefits, as the copayments in primary and outpatient care and the hospital daily fee for inpatient care have been repealed.

Global budgets are an effective way to reduce public health spending, but they should be monitored and refined to improve overall system performance. HIF sets subbudgets for each type of health care services, such as inpatient care, outpatient care, chronic care, and primary care. However, there was no spending cap for pharmaceuticals, which may have contributed to the growth of pharmaceutical spending. In addition, the lack of flexibility in the distribution of the health care budget across different types of health care services provides perverse incentives, since the funding proportions are based on historical spending patterns rather than on medium- to long-term analyses of health care needs.

# EMERGING ASIA: PEOPLE'S REPUBLIC OF CHINA

## Overview of China's Health Care System

The health insurance system in the People's Republic of China is evolving toward a social health insurance system, with dominant public provision. The system consists of the basic insurance scheme for urban formal sector workers, an urban-resident scheme for the rest of the urban population, and a cooperative scheme for all rural residents. All three systems involve a mix of different financing sources, as described later in the section. The medical assistance program provides financial assistance for the poorest and most vulnerable. Only a very small share of the population is under private coverage. Public hospitals provide most of the health care services while private hospitals and clinics play a complementary role (Huang and others, 2009).

The health status of the population has improved dramatically during the last 60 years. Life expectancy has more than doubled (to 74.0 years in 2008), and infant mortality has decreased to 18 deaths per 1,000 live births (see Table 17.3).

Prior to economic reforms in the late 1970s, China had a well-functioning health care system for its level of income. Public health and preventive care were highly developed and prioritized. The health care system dramatically improved the health of the population, as reflected by the remarkable increase in life expectancy and reduction in infant mortality.

In spite of rapid economic growth over the past 30 years, improvements in health care have slowed, and in many respects the health of the population has deteriorated. Although China's economy grew rapidly, with real annual GDP growth averaging 10 percent since 1980, total health spending did not rise in a similar fashion; in 2007, it equaled 4½ percent of GDP (with less than half public), substantially less than that in countries at comparable income levels.[3]

---

[3]Based on CEIC data (which are generally lower than World Health Organization data), public health spending has increased by 0.8 percentage points of GDP since 2007. In 2007, CEIC estimated public health spending at 0.8 percent of GDP, while World Health Organization data indicate spending of 1.9 percent of GDP.

**TABLE 17.3**

| People's Republic of China: Key Indicators, 1995, 2000, 2008 | | | | | |
|---|---|---|---|---|---|
| | 1995 | 2000 | 2008 | Lower-middle-income average, 2008 | OECD average, 2008 |
| GDP per capita (U.S. dollars at purchasing power parity) | 1,351 | 2,163 | 5,389 | 5,894 | 37,899 |
| Total health spending (percent of GDP) | 3.5 | 4.6 | 4.3[a] | 6.0 | 9.2 |
| public (percent of GDP) | 1.8 | 1.8 | 1.9[a] | 3.6 | 6.8 |
| private (percent of GDP) | 1.7 | 2.8 | 2.4[a] | 2.4 | 2.4 |
| Public health spending per capita (U.S. dollars) | 46.0 | 70.0 | 104.4[a] | 177.0 | 2,540.6 |
| Out-of-pocket spending (share of total health spending) | 46.4 | 59.0 | 50.8[a] | 35.4 | 17.0 |
| Formal health care coverage (share of population) | ... | ... | 85.0 | ... | 97.8 |
| Life expectancy (years at birth) | 70.8 | 71.0 | 74.0 | 65.6 | 79.8 |
| Infant mortality (per 1,000 live births) | 37 | 30 | 18 | 39.9 | 3.9 |
| Measles immunization (share of children 12–23 months) | 98 | 85 | 94 | 85.7 | 93.6 |
| Physicians (per 1,000 population) | 1.6 | 1.6 | 1.6 | 1.0 | 31.8 |
| Hospital beds (per 1,000 population) | ... | 2.3 | 2.2 | 2.2 | 57.0 |

Sources: World Bank, *World Development Indicators*; and World Health Organization.
Note: Ellipses indicate data are not available.
[a] 2007 data.

In addition, OOP spending is also high and accounts for more than 50 percent of health care spending (OECD, 2010d).

## Experience with Health Reform

### Coverage Expansion

China has taken a step-by-step approach to expand health care coverage by gradually covering different segments of the population.

- At the end of 1998, a basic insurance scheme for formal sector workers was introduced in urban areas to replace the labor insurance and government insurance schemes. The basic insurance is an employment-based coverage, financed through an employer-funded collective fund (approximately 6 percent of wages) and a beneficiary-funded personal account (about 2 percent of wages). It consists of a pooled fund for inpatient stays and individual medical savings accounts for outpatient visits.
- Introduced in 2003, the rural residents' scheme is financed largely by government premium subsidies and enrollee contributions. The benefit package varies geographically, but a typical package includes a modest household medical savings account for outpatient expenses and a social pooling account for inpatient expenses with high deductibles. Both rates and ceilings for reimbursements have been low. However, as additional funding has gone

into the program, coverage has become more generous (Wagstaff, Lindelow, and others, 2009).

- The medical assistance safety net program was introduced in 2003 to provide financial assistance for the poorest and most vulnerable. This program is jointly funded by central and provincial governments. Early evidence suggests that the program is well targeted (Wagstaff, Yip, and others, 2009).

- The urban-resident scheme, targeting children, the elderly, the disabled, and other nonworking urban residents, was introduced in 2007 and is financed largely by government premium subsidies and enrollee contributions. Enrollment is at the household level, partly to reduce administrative costs and partly to reduce adverse selection.

### Payment Reform

Fee for service remains the most common payment method, with the government setting prices for most services. China attempted to address affordability and access by setting prices below cost for preventive care and basic services and above cost for drugs and high-tech tests. This introduced incentives for providers to shift resources away from low-margin basic health services to high-margin services and has resulted in heavy investment in high-tech equipment, a high share of spending on drugs, and the delivery of medically unnecessary care. In 2000, the government sought to reduce price distortions by increasing the prices of professional services and reducing the prices of high-tech care.[4] Beyond reforms to the price schedule, the government also experimented with other payment methods, including global budgets, capitation payments, and diagnosis-related groups.[5]

## Main Challenges

### High Out-of-Pocket Expenditures

Rapidly rising health care costs and limited insurance coverage has made health care increasingly unaffordable. Even if universal coverage is achieved as planned, because of the limited insurance benefits, many families may still face high OOP expenditures and limited financial protection in case of catastrophic health care events. Addressing these shortcomings will require further government subsidies, especially for rural residents, residents of less-developed regions, and low-income families.[6]

---

[4]Studies suggest that this resulted in a shift from high-tech to basic professional services and a reduction in growth rates of expenditures for secondary and tertiary hospitals, but high-tech services still appear to be very profitable (Eggleston and others, 2008).

[5]Payment reforms have been associated with lower expenditures, compared with fee for service; however, evaluation of the effects on quality of care, risk selection, and cost shifting is not yet available (Eggleston and others, 2008).

[6]Studies show that the New Cooperative Medical Scheme and other insurance have been unable to reduce out-of-pocket spending and improve access to care and health outcomes (Lei and Lin, 2009; Wagstaff, Lindelow, and others, 2009).

## Wide Inequalities

Most health care resources are concentrated in urban areas, and the benefits of urban insurance are much richer than those of the cooperative insurance. Government subsidies to big urban hospitals and insurance coverage for urban residents favor higher-income groups. In addition, there are wide regional disparities in public health spending across local governments at the provincial or county levels, reflecting their differing financing constraints (Wagstaff, Lindelow, and others, 2009).

## Inefficient Use of Resources and Health Care Services

Bed occupancy rates are low at 60 percent, compared with nearly 80 percent in OECD countries. Large hospitals have been expanding rapidly, while beds and health care personnel in small community hospitals and health centers have not been fully utilized. High-tech services and prescription drugs are overused, while preventive care and primary care services are underprovided. In addition, many preventive and primary care services are provided by large hospitals, and some patients who can be effectively treated on an outpatient basis are hospitalized. There is a need to shift from hospital-based care to primary physician services and from large hospitals to small facilities.

## Rapidly Aging Population and Increasing Disease Burden

The share of the population age 60 or above is projected to reach 30 percent by 2050. In addition, the smoking rate remains high, and the obesity rate has been rising rapidly. The incidence of cancer, cerebrovascular disease, and heart disease has increased, and these diseases are now the leading causes of death.

## Lessons

Rapid economic growth is not sufficient to ensure commensurate progress on health indicators. Health spending lagged China's spectacular growth, and flaws in the design of the health system led to slower improvements in health indicators.

An incremental approach can be an effective way to expand insurance coverage and access to adequate health care services. In China, this approach has initially involved limiting the health care packages to basic services and catastrophic events and expanding coverage gradually from formal sector workers in urban areas, then to the rural population, and finally to the rest of the urban population. Increasing both the depth and the breadth of the health care package and ensuring universal coverage will require additional resources.

There is a need to reemphasize preventive care and public health services. The importance of preventive care and public health services has been overlooked during the last few decades. Despite a large increase in public health care spending, progress in public health has slowed as most of the resources have gone to invasive care, high-tech tests, and expensive drugs. Public health and preventive care spending need to be expanded, especially in less-developed regions and rural areas, possibly through more generous earmarked transfers for public health programs (Wagstaff, Lindelow, and others, 2009).

Improving the efficiency of the health care system will require reforming the provider payment system. Over the medium term, China's health care system will need to move toward a more efficient price schedule or payment method beyond fee for service. There have been many payment reform pilots at the provincial and city levels, and the payment method reforms that have been shown to be effective should be implemented at the national level.

# EMERGING LATIN AMERICA: CHILE

## Overview of the Health Care System

Chile has a dual health care system in which citizens can choose public or private insurance coverage. Its mandatory social security system ensures that about 90 percent of the population has formal coverage. Citizens can choose between the public health insurance fund (FONASA) and private health insurance companies (ISAPREs). About 67 percent of the population is covered by FONASA, and 15 percent opts for ISAPREs.[7] A mandatory and universal 7 percent contribution is levied on formal sector workers' or retirees' income, up to a ceiling of 60 UF per month.[8] The poor and the unemployed are entitled to free coverage under FONASA, which relies on contributions (about a third), and receives additional funding through budgetary subsidies (about half) and copayments. ISAPREs are financed through contributions (70 percent) and copayments (30 percent).

The health care delivery system consists of a mix of public and private providers. Municipal governments own primary care facilities and deliver most primary care, including free medical, dental, nursing, and midwifery services at local health centers. Public hospitals are administered and owned by regional health authorities and deliver most secondary and tertiary care for publicly insured patients. The state owns and operates about 200 hospitals, with two-thirds of Chile's total inpatient capacity (Edlin, 2009). Private for-profit and not-for-profit ambulatory centers and hospitals deliver care for patients with private insurance, and physicians in private practice deliver ambulatory specialty care on a fee-for-service basis (Bastias and others, 2008). While patients are free to choose their service provider, copayments are significantly smaller or nonexistent for publicly provided services.

Chile, in terms of health outcomes, is one of the world's strongest performers. The health status of the Chilean population has been improving steadily. Life expectancy had increased from 75.1 years in 1995 to 78.7 years in 2008, which was only slightly below the OECD average of 79.8 years; infant mortality had declined to 7 deaths per 1,000 live births in 2008, from 13 in 1995, but was still

---

[7]The remainder (18 percent) is covered by other not-for-profit agencies or has no coverage (about 10 percent, evenly distributed across income quintiles).

[8]UF is an inflation-indexed unit, worth about $40 in August 2010.

**TABLE 17.4**

Chile: Key Indicators, 1995, 2000, 2008

| | 1995 | 2000 | 2008 | Upper-middle-income average, 2008 | OECD average, 2008 |
|---|---|---|---|---|---|
| GDP per capita (U.S. dollars at purchasing power parity) | 6,828 | 9,018 | 13,926 | 14,150 | 37,899 |
| Total health spending (percent of GDP) | 6.3 | 6.2 | 6.2[a] | 6.3 | 9.2 |
| public (percent of GDP) | 3.3 | 3.0 | 3.7[a] | 4.0 | 6.8 |
| private (percent of GDP) | 3.0 | 3.2 | 2.6[a] | 2.7 | 2.4 |
| Public health spending per capita (U.S. dollars) | 244 | 280 | 507[a] | 518 | 2,541 |
| Out-of-pocket spending (share of total health spending) | 25.1 | 25.0 | 22.0[a] | 27.6 | 17.0 |
| Formal health care coverage (share of population) | 86.6 | 86.6 | 89.5 | … | 97.8 |
| Life expectancy (years at birth) | 75.1 | 76.9 | 78.7 | 71.8 | 79.8 |
| Infant mortality (per 1,000 live births) | 13.0 | 8.9 | 7.0 | 17.4 | 3.9 |
| Measles immunization (share of children 12–23 months) | 97.0 | 97.0 | 96.0 | 90.8 | 93.6 |
| Physicians (per 1,000 population) | 1.1 | 1.1 | … | 2.0 | 3.2 |
| Hospital beds (per 1,000 population) | 3.1 | 2.7 | 2.3 | 3.6 | 5.7 |

Sources: Fondo Nacional de Salud; Organization for Economic Cooperation and Development; World Bank, *World Development Indicators*; and World Health Organization.

Note: Ellipses indicate data are not available.

[a] 2007 data.

higher than the OECD average of 3.9 (see Table 17.4). Compared with those for countries with a similar level of income, health outcomes of the Chilean population are well above the average.

Public health spending has been growing rapidly, although not above economic growth. As of 2008, total health spending in Chile had remained almost constant at 6.2 percent of GDP since 1995. Per capita spending was about $507 a year—well below the OECD average although in line with that in countries with a similar level of income. Public health spending had increased from 3.3 percent of GDP in 1995 to 3.7 percent of GDP in 2008, while private spending as a share of GDP had declined. In terms of composition, the share of out-of-pocket payments in total outlays decreased slightly, likely reflecting the expansion of coverage.

The expansion of the Chilean health care system was made possible by an extended period of economic growth. Chile's economy has performed strongly over the past decades, with GDP growth at above 5 percent annually, on average, between 1990 and 2009, and low and stable inflation. In 2008, the per capita income was $13,926 (purchasing power parity adjusted). Supported by a prudent fiscal framework, public finances have also been remarkably sound, with significant fiscal surpluses, and central government gross debt stood at only 5 percent of GDP in 2009. Poverty declined from 19.9 percent in 1996 to 13.7 percent in 2006, but income inequality has remained stubbornly high, with a Gini coefficient of 0.54 in 2006 (OECD, 2010c).

## Experience with Health Reforms

### Decentralization and Private Sector Participation

The three main changes introduced under the military government in the 1980s included a fundamental restructuring of the system, introduction of private sector participation, and decentralization.

- In 1979/1980, the public sector was reorganized into three distinct branches, including the Ministry of Health (regulation), Health Services (execution), and FONASA (financing), and participants were given free choice between public and private providers.
- In 1981, private health insurance companies (ISAPREs) entered the insurance market, and the responsibility for the provision of primary care was transferred to municipalities.

### Public Management and Coordination

Since the democratic transition in 1990, several reform efforts have been initiated, aimed at addressing inequities and inefficiencies, strengthening the focus on primary care, introducing more competition among ISAPREs, and improving care for the growing elderly population.

- During the 1990s, the main reform steps included increased public investment in the health sector; accelerated decentralization and strengthening of subnational governments; regulation of previously unregulated ISAPREs by a Superintendent of Health; enhanced public sector efficiency, including through separation of functions and new payment mechanisms; and increased coverage for low-income groups and extended benefits (Bitran and Urcullo, 2008).
- In 2000, the Lagos administration defined new goals that ultimately translated into legislative packages separating regulation from provision; improving private sector regulation; securing public resources for the reform; and establishing universal coverage, a minimum benefits package, and a set of explicit guarantees with regard to access, quality, and financial protection.[9]

## Main Challenges

### Cost Containment

Public spending on health care has increased significantly over the past 15 years, as the public sector has sought to extend coverage (especially to high-risk groups) and to improve the quality of care. In addition, new technologies and medicines have increased treatment costs, and higher life expectancy has implied a higher incidence of chronic diseases. The public sector has been forced to purchase services from the private sector in order to meet its service guarantees (Bitran and

---

[9]The Health Authority and Management Law, the Private Health Law, the Financing Government Expenditure Law, and the Regime of Explicit Guarantees in Health Law.

Urcullo, 2008). Public providers' costs are currently controlled by budget ceilings. The elimination of supply-side subsidies has also helped in containing costs, but additional cost containment measures may still be needed.

### Population Aging

Cost pressures on public budgets will be exacerbated as the population ages and the public sector continues to care disproportionately for the elderly.

### Inequities

Reforms were aimed at improving the health status of the poor (Tsai and Ji, 2009), but fundamental socioeconomic inequities remain, with two virtually separate health care systems and continued rationing in the public sector in contrast to superior access and services in the private sector.

## Lessons

Universal coverage requires sufficient resource mobilization. Providing universal coverage in an upper-middle-income country is costly, and public sector health spending has been growing. This could be accommodated in Chile owing to strong public finances as well as a political consensus to subsidize quality care for all through tax revenues. In addition, a high percentage of workers in the formal sector and a relatively high average income enabled significant private funding support through the universal tax deduction of 7 percent.

The delivery of cost-effective high-quality health care depends on efficient institutions. Health care is fraught with market imperfections. Administering a system of public insurance and provision and effectively regulating the private sector require credible and independent institutions. This is a particularly critical factor in providing high quality of care in a cost-effective manner.

Public mandatory insurance is critical to ensure near-universal coverage. In Chile, mandatory insurance ensures the inclusion of low-income and high-risk individuals, reduces adverse selection, and contains public sector costs through some degree of risk pooling. However, cream skimming by the private sector is a concern. As the Chilean population ages and the cost of care increases with technology advancements, FONASA may remain the only affordable option for the elderly and chronically ill.

## EMERGING LATIN AMERICA: MEXICO

### Overview of the Health Care System

Mexico has a segmented social health insurance system. It consists of insurance for private sector, formal salaried workers, government employees, and oil company workers and Popular Health Insurance (PHI) for the rest of the population. Each of the institutions operating in the Mexican health care system owns and runs its own facilities and employs its own staff. While the federal Ministry of Health still finances and controls a series of third-level providers, responsibility for the delivery of most health services has been decentralized to State Health Services.

The private sector is heterogeneous, in terms of both the size of care institutions and the quality of care provided, and is weakly regulated. The health status of the Mexican population has experienced dramatic improvements over the past decades, but Mexico is still behind most OECD countries. In 2008, life expectancy in Mexico was 75.1 years, below the OECD average of 79.8 years but higher than the 71.8 years for countries with a similar income level; infant mortality per 1,000 live births was well above the OECD average of 3.9, but comparable to that in countries with a similar income level (OECD, 2005) (see Table 17.5).

Public health spending in Mexico is low, while OOP spending is high. Mexico spends considerably less on health than other OECD countries but its spending is comparable to that of countries with a similar income level. In 2008, public health spending was only 2.7 percent of GDP, well below both the OECD average of 6.8 percent and the average of 4.0 percent among countries with a similar income level. On the other hand, OOP spending accounted for nearly half of total health spending. The supply of inputs to the health care sector is comparably low by OECD standards, with around 2.0 doctors per 1,000 people, compared with the OECD average of 3.2 doctors.

Mexico has not yet achieved universal insurance coverage for basic health services. It is estimated that the various social security institutes cover about 40 percent of the population, while PHI, administered by the Ministry of Health,

**TABLE 17.5**

## Mexico: Key Indicators, 1995, 2000, 2008

| | 1995 | 2000 | 2008 | Upper-middle-income average, 2008 | OECD average, 2008 |
|---|---|---|---|---|---|
| GDP per capita (U.S. dollars at purchasing power parity) | 7,486 | 10,028 | 14,502 | 14,150 | 37,899 |
| Total health spending (percent of GDP) | 5.6 | 5.6 | 5.9[a] | 6.3 | 9.2 |
| public (percent of GDP) | 2.4 | 2.6 | 2.7[a] | 4.0 | 6.8 |
| private (percent of GDP) | 3.2 | 3.0 | 3.2[a] | 2.7 | 2.4 |
| Public health spending per capita (U.S. dollars) | 166 | 236 | 372[a] | 518 | 2,541 |
| Out-of-pocket spending (share of total health spending) | 56.2 | 50.9 | 50.8[a] | 27.6 | 17.0 |
| Formal health care coverage (share of population) | ... | ... | 65.0 | ... | 97.8 |
| Life expectancy (years at birth) | 72.5 | 73.9 | 75.1 | 71.8 | 79.8 |
| Infant mortality (per 1,000 live births) | 27.7 | 19.4 | 15.2 | 17.4 | 3.9 |
| Measles immunization (share of children 12–23 months) | 89.9 | 95.9 | 91.9 | 90.8 | 93.6 |
| Physicians (per 1,000 population) | 1.7 | 1.6 | 2.0 | 2.0 | 3.2 |
| Hospital beds (per 1,000 population) | 1.9 | 1.8 | 1.7 | 3.6 | 5.7 |

Sources: Organization for Economic Cooperation and Development; World Bank, *World Development Indicators*; and World Health Organization.

Note: Ellipses indicate data are not available.

[a] 2007 data.

accounts for another 25 percent (Schwellnus, 2009). Part of the uninsured population has access to a program providing health care services free of charge in remote areas without access to other health care facilities. Most of the uninsured resort to state health facilities and pay OOP for services and pharmaceuticals in the private sector.

## Experience with Health Reforms

Prior to 2003, the key element of the reforms was decentralization of health care services for the uninsured by transferring responsibilities to states. However, central fund allocations to the states continued to be based on historical budgets and, as a result, funding disparities persisted and even increased as the wealthy states increased their own allocations.

The System of Social Protection in Health aimed to achieve universal coverage by 2011 and reduce system fragmentation. It is part of the continued efforts to move away from a system of vertically integrated insurance/provider institutions toward a more universal system, through contracting State Health Services, the social security institutes, or private providers and encouraging competition among them. Reform of the System of Social Protection in Health was passed in 2003 and went into effect in 2004. Its primary objectives and measures include the following:

- Establishing a system of universal access based on social insurance. A system of family insurance (PHI or Seguro Popular) ensures that all individuals have access to affordable health insurance, particularly the poor. Family contributions to PHI are based on a sliding fee scale and are waived for families meeting the low-income criteria.

- Improving the allocation of resources by defining a package of essential services. The essential package is covered by a fund administered at the state level and includes ambulatory care at the primary level and outpatient consultation and hospitalization for the basic specialties at the secondary level.

- Making the distribution of federal resources to the states more equitable. The federal contributions are based on a per-enrolled family fee plus a solidarity supplement for the poorer states.

- Increasing competition among service providers to raise productivity levels and improving the quality and efficiency of the health sector. The health care services covered by PHI can be provided by accredited public or private clinics and hospitals.

- Protecting the funding of public health interventions. A separate fund is allocated for community health services and can be used only to finance public health programs.

- Protecting families from excessive health expenditures. The package of catastrophic interventions is financed through a fund that aggregates risk at the national level, because the state risk pool may be too small to finance these interventions.

## Main Challenges

### Reducing Fragmentation, Inequality of Access, and Inefficiencies

The public sector is characterized by the presence of several public purchasers that are vertically integrated with providers and serve different parts of the population with little connection between them. In addition, there is a very large and mostly unregulated private sector. Wide inequality exists in terms of access to care, financing, and health status. A recent cross-country study (Schwellnus, 2009) indicates that Mexico has one of the least efficient health care systems in the OECD.

### Achieving Universal Coverage with Voluntary Enrollment

In a voluntary system, such as PHI, healthy individuals may choose not to take up health insurance in order to avoid paying the premiums. Risk selection could eventually undermine the financial sustainability of the system through a deterioration of the risk pool. Mandatory enrollment may be considered to reduce adverse selection and ensure full coverage of the population. Expanding the enrollment in PHI will also depend on improvements in quality of provision and access to care in State Health Services facilities.

### Meeting the Extra Demand for Health Care Services

The increase in insurance coverage would create extra demand for health care services. Given that the number of doctors per 1,000 people in Mexico is considerably lower than the OECD average, coverage expansion could cause the health care system to have difficulties meeting the increasing demand for services, especially in poorer states with weaker capacity and in rural areas.

### Increasing Funding

Additional public funding is required both to reduce OOP spending and to meet the costly demands associated with the treatment of chronic diseases that arise as countries become more developed. Although some resources could be obtained by increasing efficiency, the absolute amount and the share of GDP spent on health from public sources will have to increase for the health care system to respond effectively to the demands of the population, achieve universal coverage, and expand access to new medical interventions.

### Integration of the Insurance System

A major step will have to be taken to break down the institutional barriers at the provider level in order for the states to successfully set up contracts and purchasing arrangements with all types of providers. Further progress toward a system of providers serving all patients on equal terms is likely to require moving toward a unified public health insurance system. The differences in benefit packages between those under social security and those with PHI, as well as differences in the quality of providers in the two systems, may act as a barrier to the integration of the systems.

## Lessons

Fragmentation and lack of competition are major sources of inefficiency. Social security institutes, private insurers, and federal and state health services each have their own vertically integrated service providers with no access to the others' services. This has resulted in a costly duplication of health administration and infrastructure, curtailment of patient choice, and lack of competition between providers.

Separation of financing and provision will be necessary to allow competition and foster efficiency. Insurers should be allowed to contract with any provider. This would reduce the cost of provision because the insurers could choose the providers with the lowest cost, thereby encouraging providers to become more efficient.

Weaknesses in the provider payment system have impeded the best use of health resources. Current methods of payment to providers provide few incentives for improvements in productivity and efficiency. Virtually all of the institutional providers are financed through capped budgets, while workers are paid on a salary basis.

A better balance in the ratio of nurses to doctors could also help reduce costs. Compared with other OECD countries, Mexico has a relatively high ratio of doctors to nurses. As nurses are generally paid less than doctors, increasing the number of nurses per doctor, and increasing their responsibilities, could lead to a more cost-effective mix of inputs.

## REFERENCES

Bastias, G., T. Pantoja, T. Leisewitz, and V. Zárate, 2008, "Health Care Reform in Chile," *Canadian Medical Association Journal*, Vol. 179, No. 12 (December), pp. 1289–92.

Bitran, R.D., and G.C. Urcullo, 2008, "Chile: Good Practice in Expanding Health Care Coverage—Lessons from Reforms," in *Good Practices in Health Financing: Lessons from Reforms in Low- and Middle-Income Countries*, ed. by P. Gottret, G. Schieber, and H. Waters (Washington: World Bank).

Edlin, M., 2009, "Chile's Healthcare Offers Public and Private Plans," *Managed Healthcare Executive*, December 1.

Eggleston, K., L. Ling, Q. Meng, M. Lindelow, and A. Wagstaff, 2008, "Health Service Delivery in China: A Literature Review," *Health Economics*, Vol. 17, pp. 149–65.

Habicht, T., A. Aaviksoo, and A. Koppel, 2006, "Hospital Sector Reform in Estonia," *PRAXIS* (Center for Policy Studies), November.

Huang, C., H. Liang, C. Chu, S. Rutherford, and Q. Geng, 2009, "The Emerging Role of Private Health Care Provision in China: A Critical Analysis of the Current Health System," Asia Health Policy Program Working Paper No. 10 (Stanford, CA: Stanford University Walter H. Shorenstein Asia-Pacific Research Center).

Lei, X., and Lin, W., 2009, "The New Cooperative Medical Scheme in Rural China: Does More Coverage Mean More Service and Better Health?" *Health Economics,* Vol. 18, pp. S25–46.

Organization for Economic Cooperation and Development (OECD), 2005, *OECD Review of Health System: Mexico* (Paris).

———, 2010a, *OECD Health Data 2010: How Does Estonia Compare?* (Paris), available at www.oecd.org/dataoecd/19/58/45554798.pdf.

———, 2010b, *OECD Health Data 2010: How Does Hungary Compare?* (Paris), available at www.oecd.org/dataoecd/43/20/40904982.pdf .

————, 2010c, *Health Data 2010: How Does Chile Compare?* (Paris).

————, 2010d, *Economic Survey of China 2010: Improving the Health Care System* (Paris).

Orosz, E., and A. Burns, 2000, "The Healthcare System in Hungary," Economics Department Working Paper No. 241 (Paris: Organization for Economic Cooperation and Development).

Oxley, H., and M. MacFarlan, 1995, "Health Care Reform: Controlling Spending and Increasing Efficiency," Economic Study No. 24 (Paris: Organization for Economic Cooperation and Development).

Schwellnus, C., 2009, "Achieving Higher Performance: Enhancing Spending Efficiency in Health and Education in Mexico," Economics Department Working Paper No. 732 (Paris: Organization for Economic Cooperation and Development).

Tsai, T.C., and J. Ji, 2009, "Neoliberalism and Its Discontents: Impact of Health Reforms in Chile," *Harvard International Review* (June), available at http://hir.harvard.edu/agriculture/neoliberalism-and-its-discontents.

Utca, A.J., 2009, *Hungarian Health Care System in Brief* (Budapest: Ministry of Health).

Wagstaff, A., M. Lindelow, S. Wang, and S. Zhang, 2009, *Reforming China's Rural Health System* (Washington: World Bank).

Wagstaff, A., W. Yip, M. Lindelow, and W. Hsiao, 2009, "China's Health System and Its Reform: A Review of Recent Studies," *Health Economics*, Vol. 18, pp. S7–23.

Worz, M., and R. Busse, 2005, "Analyzing the Impact of Health-Care System Change in the EU Member States—Germany," *Health Economics*, Vol. 14, pp. 133–49.

# Contributors

**Tsung-Mei Cheng,** Health Policy Research Analyst, Princeton University

**Mita Choudhury,** Associate Professor, National Institute of Public Finance and Policy, India

**Benedict Clements,** Division Chief, Fiscal Affairs Department, International Monetary Fund

**David Coady,** Deputy Division Chief, Fiscal Affairs Department, International Monetary Fund

**Sanjeev Gupta,** Deputy Director, Fiscal Affairs Department, International Monetary Fund

**Masako Ii,** Professor of Economics, Hitotsubashi University

**Eva Jenkner,** Senior Economist, Fiscal Affairs Department, International Monetary Fund

**Pongpisut Jongudomsuk,** Director, Health Systems Research Institute, Thailand

**Ludwig Kanzler,** Principal, McKinsey & Company, Japan

**Izabela Karpowicz,** Economist, Office of Budget and Planning, International Monetary Fund

**Kenichiro Kashiwase,** Economist, Fiscal Affairs Department, International Monetary Fund

**Soonman Kwon,** Professor of Health Policy and Management, Seoul National University

**John C. Langenbrunner,** Lead Economist, World Bank

**Supon Limwattananon,** Associate Professor, Khon Kaen University, Thailand

**Adun Mohara,** Researcher, Health Intervention and Technology Assessment Program, Thailand

**Alexander Ng,** Associate Principal, McKinsey & Company, Hong Kong

**Kumaree Pachanee,** Research Assistant, International Health Policy Program, Thailand

**Walaiporn Patcharanarumol,** Researcher, International Health Policy Program, Thailand

**Phusit Prakongsai,** Director, International Health Policy Program, Thailand

**M. Govinda Rao,** Director, National Institute of Public Finance and Policy, India

**Uwe E. Reinhardt,** James Madison Professor of Political Economy and Professor of Economics and Public Affairs, Princeton University

**Baoping Shang,** Technical Assistance Advisor, Fiscal Affairs Department, International Monetary Fund

**Jonathan Skinner,** Professor of Economics, Dartmouth College

**Mauricio Soto,** Economist, Fiscal Affairs Department, International Monetary Fund

**Samrit Srithamrongsawat,** Director, Health Insurance System Research Office, Thailand

**Michael Stolpe,** Economist, Kiel Institute for the World Economy

**Catherine Suarez,** Investment Management Analyst, Goldman Sachs

**Ajay Tandon,** Senior Economist, World Bank

**Viroj Tangcharoensathien,** Senior Expert, Ministry of Public Health, Thailand

**Justin Tyson,** Senior Economist, European Department, International Monetary Fund

# Index

[Page numbers followed by *f, n,* or *t* refer to figures, footnotes or tables, respectively.]